KU-348-439

THE COUNTY COUNCIL OF STIRLING

John Constable

DRAWN BY C.R. LESLIE R.A.

ON STONE BY R J. LANE A.R.A.

M & N. HANHART, LITH. PRINTERS.

MEMOIRS OF THE LIFE OF

JOHN CONSTABLE, ESQ. R.A.

COMPOSED CHIEFLY OF HIS

LETTERS.

BY C. R. LESLIE, R.A.

"HEAVEN AND EARTH, ADVANTAGES AND OBSTACLES, CONSPIRE TO EDUCATE GENIUS."

FUSELI.

PAUL P. B. MINET
CHICHELEY
1971

This work was originally published by
LONGMAN'S, BROWN, GREEN, AND LONGMAN'S
LONDON · 1845

SBN 7063 1617 7

Reproduced and Printed by
Redwood Press Limited
Trowbridge & London

PREFACE.

N the firſt arrangement of the papers of which theſe Memoirs principally conſiſt, many paſſages were included that, from the fear of making the book too long, were afterwards omitted. The intereſt, however with which the retained portions of Conſtable's correſpondence were read, has encouraged me to reſtore, now, much that had been left out of the firſt edition. To this I have added a few of his early letters, recently placed in my hands, and by a careful examination of ſome of his papers, which I had not before ſeen, I have been enabled to make a few additions to the notes of his Lectures. I have alſo added to the quotations from the letters of Archdeacon Fiſher, ſome paſſages which aſſiſt the narrative, and others which appear to me well worthy of preſervation on their own account.

In changing the form of the volume to one more adapted to general circulation, while I cannot but hope that its additional pages will be found to add to its value, I regret that it muſt appear without the beautiful engravings from Conſtable's works, with which in its firſt ſtate it was adorned.

I muſt again offer my thanks to the members of his family and to others of my friends, for their renewed aſſiſtance in a taſk, to me, far leſs eaſy than intereſting, although, now as before, it has been little elſe than that of an editor.

C. R. LESLIE.

July, 1845.

CONTENTS.

Contents.

CORRIGENDA.

Page 35.—At the conclusion of the first paragraph, for " have contributed," read " must have contributed."

Page 85.—The letter dated March 6th should be placed after the one which follows it.

Page 153.—Line 14th from the top of the page, for " professor," read " possessor."

Page 213.—Line 7th from the top of the page, for " we never see but through a medium," read " we never see her but through a medium."

Page 220.—The enumeration of the contents of Chapter XIII. should end with " *Englefield House.*"

Page 226.—In the note at the foot of the page, for " the following chapter," read " Chapter XV."

DIRECTIONS TO THE BINDER.

Portrait of " JOHN CONSTABLE," to face the Title.
Portrait of " JOHN CONSTABLE, aged 20," to face page 4.
" SPRING," to face page 5.

MEMOIRS OF THE LIFE OF JOHN CONSTABLE.

CHAPTER I.

1776—1810.

Conſtable's Native Scenery. Parentage. Birth. School Days. His Love of Painting. John Dunthorne. Conſtable employed in his Father's Mills. Introduced to Sir George Beaumont. His firſt Sight of a Picture by Claude. Girtin's Drawings. Conſtable's firſt Viſit to London. Farrington. Antiquity Smith. Conſtable engaged in his Father's Counting Houſe. Returns to the Study of Painting. Becomes a Student of the Royal Academy. His Drawings at Helmingham. Viſits Derbyſhire. Anatomical Studies. Exhibits at the Academy. Samuel Strowger. Mr. Weſt. Situation of a Drawing Maſter offered to Conſtable. Diſſuaded by Mr. Weſt from accepting it. Voyage from London to Deal. Altar-Piece for Brantham Church. Viſits Weſtmoreland and Cumberland. Introduced to the Earl and Counteſs of Dyſart. Altar-Piece for Neyland Church. Jackſon. Wilkie.

"EAST BERGHOLT, or as its Saxon derivation implies, Wooded Hill, is thus mentioned in the 'Beauties of England and Wales:'—'South of the church is Old Hall, the manor houſe, the ſeat of Peter Godfrey, Eſq. which, with the reſidences of the Rector the Rev. Dr. Rhudde, Mrs. Roberts, and Golding Conſtable, Eſq. give this place an appearance far ſuperior to that of moſt villages.' It is pleaſantly ſituated in the moſt cultivated part of Suffolk, on a ſpot which overlooks the fertile valley of the Stour, which river ſeparates that county on the ſouth from Eſſex. The beauty of the ſurrounding ſcenery, its gentle declivities, its luxuriant meadow flats ſprinkled with flocks and herds, its well cultivated uplands, its woods and rivers, with numerous ſcattered villages and churches, farms and pictureſque cottages, all impart to this particular ſpot an amenity and elegance hardly any where elſe to be found."

This is Conſtable's deſcription of the "ſcenes of his boyhood," which he was fond of ſaying "made him a painter." From among them moſt of the ſubjects of his pencil were ſelected. The frontiſpiece to the "Engliſh Landſcape," a ſeries of engravings publiſhed by him late in life, is from a ſketch of the houſe in which he was born, and the paſſage I have quoted accompanies the plate. Fearful of having ſaid too much, and yet unwilling to ſay leſs, he adds, "Perhaps, the Author, with an over-weening affection for theſe ſcenes, may eſtimate them too highly, and may have dwelt on them too excluſively."

His anceſtors were from Yorkſhire, where the name is frequent. His great-grandfather, Hugh Conſtable, carried it into Suffolk, and ſettled as a farmer at Bures, on the border which ſeparates that county from Eſſex. Golding Conſtable, the artiſt's father, inherited a conſiderable property from a rich uncle, who was childleſs, including the water-mill at Flatford; he afterwards purchaſed a water-mill at Dedham, and two windmills in the neighbourhood of Eaſt Bergholt; at the latter place he built the houſe which has been mentioned, and to which he removed in the year 1774; having before that period married Miſs Ann Watts, who brought ſome acceſſion to his wealth, but more to his happineſs, for ſhe poſſeſſed in a high degree the virtues beſt ſuited to domeſtic life.

CHAP. I.
1776.

The children of this marriage were three ſons and three daughters. John Conſtable, the ſecond ſon, was born on the 11th of June, 1776, and baptized on the ſame day, not being expected to live. He became, however, a ſtrong and healthy child, and when ſeven years old, was placed at a boarding-ſchool about fifteen miles from Bergholt. He was afterwards removed to a ſchool at Lavenham, the maſter of which, being in love, left the care of his ſcholars to an uſher, who flogged them ſo unmercifully as to incur the hatred of them all; and Conſtable ſecretly reſolved to repay his own ſhare of the caſtigation in kind, if as men, he and the tyrant ſhould ever meet; a reſolution he was well qualified to put in practice, unleſs the uſher had been a man of uncommon perſonal ſtrength. From Lavenham he was removed to the grammar ſchool of the Rev. Dr. Grimwood, at Dedham, where he met with an indulgent maſter, with whom he became a favourite. Dr. Grimwood had penetration enough to diſcover that he was a boy of genius, although he was not remarkable for proficiency in his ſtudies, the only thing he excelled in being penmanſhip. He acquired, however, ſome knowledge of Latin, and ſubſequently took private leſſons in French, in which he made leſs progreſs. He was at this time ſixteen or ſeventeen years of age, and had become devotedly fond of painting. During his French leſſons a long pauſe would frequently occur, which his maſter would be the firſt to break, ſaying, "Go on, I am not aſleep: Oh! now I ſee you are in your painting-room."

But his painting-room was not under his father's roof. He had formed a cloſe alliance with the only perſon in the village who had any love for art, or any pretenſions to the character of an artiſt, John Dunthorne, a plumber and glazier, who lived in a little cottage cloſe to the gate of Golding Conſtable's houſe. Mr. Dunthorne poſſeſſed more intelligence than is often found in the claſs of life to which he be-

CHAP. I.

longed; at that time he devoted all the leiſure his buſineſs allowed him, to painting landſcapes from nature, and Conſtable became the conſtant companion of his ſtudies. Golding Conſtable did not frown on this intimacy, although, he was unwilling that his ſon ſhould become a profeſſional artiſt, and Conſtable's attempts were made either in the open air, in the ſmall houſe of his friend, or in a hired room in the village.

It argued no want of affection or of foreſight in his father that he oppoſed his ſon's choice of a profeſſion in which future excellence cannot with any certainty be predicted from early attempts, and which, even if attained, is leſs ſure than excellence in many other purſuits of ſecuring a competence. He would have educated him for the Church, but finding him diſinclined to the neceſſary ſtudies, he determined to make a miller of him. For about a year, Conſtable was employed in his father's mills, where he performed the duties required of him carefully and well. He was remarkable among the young men of the village for muſcular ſtrength, and being tall and well formed, with good features, a freſh complexion, and fine dark eyes, his white hat and coat were not unbecoming to him, and he was called in the neighbourhood the "handſome miller."

The windmill in an engraving from one of his ſketches entitled "Spring," is one of thoſe in which he worked; and its outline, with the name of "John Conſtable, 1792," very accurately and neatly carved by him with a penknife, ſtill remains on one of its timbers. His acquaintance with the pictureſque machinery both of wind and water-mills, was very uſeful to him in after life. His younger brother, Mr. Abram Conſtable, ſaid to me, "When I look at a mill painted by John, I ſee that it will *go round*, which is not always the caſe with thoſe by other artiſts." By a wind-miller every change of the ſky is watched with peculiar intereſt; and it will appear

1792.

Gardiner pinx^t

T. H. Maguire lithog.

John Constable.

Aged 20

Printed by Messrs M. & N. Hanhart.

John Constable R.A. David Lucas

Spring

London. 1845. Pub.d by Longman & Co. Paternoster Row.

from Conſtable's deſcription of this plate that the time ſpent as one, was not wholly loſt to him as a painter.

"It may perhaps," he ſays, "give ſome idea of one of thoſe bright and ſilvery days in the ſpring, when at noon large gariſh clouds ſurcharged with hail or ſleet ſweep with their broad ſhadows the fields, woods, and hills; and by their depths enhance the value of the vivid greens and yellows ſo peculiar to the ſeaſon. The *natural hiſtory*, if the expreſſion may be uſed, of the ſkies, which are ſo particularly marked in the hail ſqualls at this time of the year, is this:—The clouds accumulate in very large maſſes, and from their loftineſs ſeem to move but ſlowly: immediately upon theſe large clouds appear numerous opaque patches, which are only ſmall clouds paſſing rapidly before them, and conſiſting of iſolated portions detached probably from the larger cloud. Theſe floating much nearer the earth may perhaps fall in with a ſtronger current of wind, which as well as their comparative lightneſs cauſes them to move with greater rapidity; hence they are called by wind-millers and ſailors, *meſſengers*, and always portend bad weather. They float midway in what may be termed the lanes of the clouds; and from being ſo ſituated, are almoſt uniformly in ſhadow, receiving a reflected light only, from the clear blue ſky immediately above them. In paſſing over the bright parts of the large clouds they appear as darks; but in paſſing the ſhadowed parts, they aſſume a grey, a pale, or a lurid hue."

Mrs. Conſtable procured for her ſon an introduction to Sir George Beaumont, who frequently viſited his mother, the Dowager Lady Beaumont, then reſiding at Dedham. Sir George had ſeen and expreſſed himſelf pleaſed with ſome copies made by Conſtable in pen and ink from Dorigny's engravings of the Cartoons of Raphael; and at the houſe of the Dowager Lady Beaumont the young artiſt firſt ſaw a picture by Claude, the " Hagar,"* which Sir George often carried with him when he travelled. Conſtable looked back on the firſt ſight of this exquiſite work as an important epoch in his life. But the taſte of a young artiſt is always the moſt affected by cotemporary art. Sir George Beaumont poſ-ſeſſed about thirty drawings in water colours by Girtin, which he adviſed Conſtable to ſtudy as examples of great breadth and truth; and their influence on him may be traced more or leſs through the whole courſe of his practice. The firſt impreſſions of an artiſt, whether for good or evil, are never wholly effaced; and as Conſtable had till now no opportunity of ſeeing any pictures that he could rely on as guides to the ſtudy of nature, it was fortunate for him that he began with Claude and Girtin.

1795.

In the year 1795, his father conſented to his viſiting London, for the purpoſe of aſcertaining what might be his chance of ſucceſs as a painter; and on this occaſion Priſcilla Wakefield furniſhed him with a letter of introduction to Farrington, of whom, it has been ſaid, he became a pupil. But this was not the caſe, though he, no doubt, received many valuable hints from a landſcape painter, who, though not a man of genius, poſſeſſed a great deal of good ſenſe, and could tell him much of the practice of Wilſon. Farrington predicted Conſtable's future excellence, and ſaid, at an early period of their acquaintance, that his ſtyle of landſcape would one day " form a diſtinct feature in the art."

Soon after his arrival in London, Conſtable became acquainted with John Thomas Smith, known then as a clever draughtſman, engraver, and local antiquary; ſince more gene-

* This little treaſure is now in the National Gallery, where it is called " The Annunciation;" but the ſpring by which the female is ſeated, and the action of the angel who points to the buildings in the diſtance, leave little doubt that Claude's intention was to repreſent the firſt flight of Hagar from the preſence of her miſtreſs.

1795.

rally, I cannot ſay *better*, known as the writer of the "Life of Nollekins." Conſtable's intercourſe with "Antiquity Smith," as he was called, tended, no doubt to ſtrengthen that fondneſs for localities which had ſo much to do with, if indeed it was not the baſis of his art; and it may be inferred that the advice he received from his new friend was generally ſound, from the following ſpecimen. "Do not," ſaid Smith, "ſet about inventing figures for a landſcape taken from nature; for you cannot remain an hour in any ſpot, however ſolitary, without the appearance of ſome living thing that will in all probability accord better with the ſcene and time of day than will any invention of your own." Often has Conſtable, in our walks together, taken occaſion to point out, from what we ſaw, the good ſenſe of Smith's advice.

Conſtable's time was now divided between London and Bergholt; and the following paſſages from the letters he wrote from the country to Smith ſhow what were ſome of his occupations for the next two years. "October 27th, 1796. As the evenings are now long, I find great pleaſure in reading the books I brought home with me, particularly Leonardo da Vinci and Count Algarotti. I ſhould feel obliged to you, when you make up the parcel which I mentioned, if you would encloſe Geſſner's Eſſay on Landſcape. I devote all my evenings to the ſtudy of anatomy." "January 16th, 1797. You flatter me highly reſpecting my 'Cottages,' and I am glad you have found one or two amongſt them worthy of your needle.* I am obliged to you for the directions you ſent me for etching, but they were not exactly what I meant. What I fear I am deficient in is the biting. I have lately copied Tempeſta's large battle, and painted two ſmall pictures in oil, viz. a Chymiſt and an Alchymiſt, for which I am chiefly indebted to our immortal bard. You

1796.

1797.

* Smith was publiſhing a ſeries of etchings of pictureſque cottages, and ſome of Conſtable's letters to him contained ſketches of cottages.

CHAP. I.
1797.

remember Romeo's account of an apothecary's ſhop. I have a great mind to copy one of Ruyſdael's etchings. I have ſeen one at your houſe where there are two trees ſtanding in the water, and there is one your father copied: either of theſe I ſhould like very much, but as they are ſcarce and dear, perhaps you would not like to truſt them; if not, ſend me any others. I want to know if it is poſſible to take the proofs of the plates myſelf."

The little pictures of the Chymiſt and the Alchymiſt, mentioned in this letter have very little merit. Conſtable probably intended a moral by the ragged and poverty-ſtruck appearance of the alchymiſt, while the chymiſt is neat and comfortable; but if he had as yet produced nothing better, it is not ſurpriſing that his own purſuits were regarded by his friends much in the same light with thoſe of his alchymiſt. In a letter to Smith, dated March 2nd, 1797, he ſays, "I muſt now take your advice and attend to my father's buſineſs, as we are likely ſoon to loſe an old ſervant (our clerk), who has been with us eighteen years; and now I ſee plainly it will be my lot to walk through life in a path contrary to that in which my inclination would lead me." The next letter is from Mrs. Conſtable to Smith: "Eaſt Bergholt, October, 1797. Dear Sir, I have great pleaſure in receiving a letter ſo warm in commendation of my ſon John, as yours of the 29th ult. His future conduct I truſt will ever merit the favour of your friendſhip, which I know he highly values. Let me aſſure you, that were you intimately acquainted with his father, you would not wonder at his having ſo worthy a ſon. We are anticipating the ſatisfaction of ſeeing John at home in the courſe of a week or ten days, to which I look forward with the hope that he will attend to buſineſs, by which he will pleaſe his father, and enſure his own reſpectability and comfort."

How long Conſtable was engaged in his father's counting-houſe I know not; but in the year 1799 he had reſumed the pencil, not again to lay it aſide; as I find him thus writing to Dunthorne. "London, February 4th, 1799. I am this morning admitted a ſtudent at the Royal Academy; the figure which I drew for admittance was the Torſo. I am now comfortably ſettled in Cecil Street, Strand, No. 23. I ſhall begin painting as ſoon as I have the loan of a ſweet little picture by Jacob Ruyſdael to copy. Since I have been in town I have ſeen ſome remarkably fine ones by him, indeed I never ſaw him before; yet don't think, by this, I am out of conceit of my own, of which I have ſeen a print, 'tis of the ſame ſize and reverſed. I ſhall not have much to ſhow you on my return, as I find my time will be more taken up in *ſeeing* than in painting. I hope by the time the leaves are on the trees, I ſhall be better qualified to attack them than I was laſt ſummer. All the time that you can conveniently ſpare from your buſineſs may be happily ſpent in this way, perhaps profitably, at any rate innocently. * * * Smith's friend, * * * * * * , has left off painting, at leaſt for the preſent. His whole time and thoughts are occupied in exhibiting an old, ruſty, fuſty head, with a ſpike in it, which he declares to be the real embalmed head of Oliver Cromwell? where he got it I know not; 'tis to be ſeen in Bond Street, at half a crown admittance. How goes on the lay figure?* I hope to ſee it finiſhed when I return, together with ſome drawings of your own from nature."

I have ſeen no ſtudies made by Conſtable at the Academy from the Antique, but many chalk drawings and oil paintings from the living model, all of which have great breadth of light and ſhade, though they are ſometimes defective in outline.

On the 18th of Auguſt he writes to Smith from Ipſwich: "I believe I may be here a fortnight longer. It is a moſt

* Mr. Dunthorne, who was a man of much ingenuity, had undertaken to make a lay figure.

CHAP. I.

1799.

delightful country for a painter. I fancy I ſee Gainſborough in every hedge and hollow tree."*

In a letter to Dunthorne from London, without date, but probably written in the winter of this year, Conſtable ſays: "I paint by all the daylight we have, and that is little enough. I ſometimes ſee the ſky, but imagine to yourſelf how a pearl muſt look through a burnt glaſs. I employ my evenings in making drawings and in reading, and I hope by the former to clear my rent. If I can I ſhall be very happy. Our friend Smith has offered to take any of my pictures into his ſhop for ſale. He is pleaſed to find I am reaſonable in my prices."

In another letter, to the ſame correſpondent, without date, he ſays: "I have copied a ſmall landſcape of A. Caracci, and two Wilſons, and have done ſome little things of my own. I have likewiſe begun to copy a very fine picture by Ruyſdael, which Mr. Reinagle and myſelf have purchaſed in partnerſhip for 70*l*. * * * I hope to ſee you in the ſpring, when the cuckoos have picked up all the dirt. Every fine day makes me long for a walk on the commons. * * * I have finiſhed my copy from Ruyſdael, all but the glazing, which cannot be done till the picture is dry. It has been roaſting in the ſun theſe two or three days. To-morrow I hope to go on with my copy from Sir George Beaumont's little Claude.† I ſhall remain in town the chief of this ſummer. Indeed I find it neceſſary to fag at copying, ſome time yet, to acquire execution. The more facility of practice I get, the more pleaſure I ſhall find in my art; without the power of execution I ſhould be continually embarraſſed, and

* Gainſborough was a native of the ſouthern border of Suffolk. He was born at Sudbury, about fourteen miles from Bergholt; and his earlieſt ſtudies, like thoſe of Conſtable, were from the paſtoral ſcenery of the Stour. Before he ſettled in London he reſided for ſome time at Ipſwich.

† The Hagar.

1799.

it would be a burthen to me. This fine weather almoſt makes me melancholy; it recalls ſo forcibly every ſcene we have viſited and drawn together. I even love every ſtile and ſtump, and every lane in the village, ſo deep rooted are early impreſſions." In a letter, probably ſubſequent to theſe, he ſays, "My viſit to the Whalleys* has done me a world of good. The regularity and good example in all things, which I had an opportunity of ſeeing *practiſed*, (not *talked of* only,) during my ſtay with that dear family, will, I truſt, be of ſervice to me as long as I live. I find my mind much more decided and firm; and ſince I have been this time in town, I have acquired, conſiderably, what I have ſo long and ſo ardently deſired, patience in the purſuit of my profeſſion. I know very little of what is going on in the arts, but I have free admiſſion to Mr. Bryan's picture-room, where are ſome fine works, particularly ſome Landſcapes by Gaſpar; I viſit this once a week at leaſt."

1800.

"(Month illegible), 1800. Dear Dunthorne, Here I am quite alone among the oaks and ſolitudes of Helmingham Park. I have taken quiet poſſeſſion of the parſonage, finding it empty. A woman comes from the farm houſe, where I eat, and makes my bed, and I am left at liberty to wander where I pleaſe during the day. There are abundance of fine trees of all ſorts, and the park on the whole affords good objects rather than fine ſcenery. But I can hardly judge yet what I may have to ſhew you. I have made one or two drawings that may be uſeful."

Two of theſe drawings, dated July 23rd and 24th, are in my poſſeſſion, and though ſlight and merely in black and white, they ſhew that he at that time poſſeſſed a true ſenſe of the beautiful in compoſition. In the year 1801, it appears by one of his ſketch books, he viſited Derbyſhire. The

1801.

* Mrs. Whalley was Conſtable's ſecond ſiſter.

ſketches he made there, like thoſe at Helmingham, are ſlight and general. They are waſhed in one tint only, and with no attempt at the beautiful finiſh or force of chiaroſcuro ſeen in his later ſtudies.

"1801. Dear Dunthorne, * * * I have got three rooms in a very comfortable houſe, No. 50, Rathbone Place. My large room has three windows in front. I ſhall make that my ſhop, having the light from the upper part of the middle window, and by that means I ſhall get my eaſel in a good ſituation. I hope to be able to keep more to myſelf than I did in former times, in London. I have been among my old acquaintances in the art, and am enough diſguſted, (between ourſelves) with their cold trumpery ſtuff. The more canvaſs they cover, the more they diſcover their ignorance and total want of feeling. * * * I have ſeen * * * * * twice. He has painted a Landſcape, Dedham, from the ſketch he took from Mrs. Roberts's. He calls it his beſt picture. It is very well pencilled, and there is plenty of light without *any light at all*."

1802.

"Rathbone Place, January 8th, 1802. Dear Dunthorne, * * * About a fortnight back, I was ſo fully in the hope of making an immediate viſit to Bergholt that I deferred writing. I then knew nothing of the Anatomical Lectures* which I am at preſent attending, and which will be over in about a week or ten days. I am ſo much more intereſted in the ſtudy than I expected, and feel my mind ſo generally enlarged by it, that I congratulate myſelf on being ſo fortunate as to have attended theſe lectures. Excepting Aſtronomy,

* Delivered by Mr. Brookes at his Anatomical Theatre. To theſe lectures, and to his diſſecting room, Mr. Brookes, very liberally, gave the ſtudents of the Royal Academy free admiſſion. Many extremely accurate and beautiful coloured drawings, of a large ſize, made by Conſtable at this time, from diſſections, bear evidence of the intereſt with which he purſued the ſtudy of Anatomy.

and that I know little of, I believe no ſtudy is really ſo ſublime, or goes more to carry the mind to the Divine Architect. Indeed the whole machine which it has pleaſed God to form for the accommodation of the real man, the mind, during its probation in this vale of tears, is as wonderful as the contemplation of it is affecting. I ſee, however, many inſtances of the truth, and a melancholy truth it is, that a knowledge of the things created, does not always lead to a veneration of the Creator. Many of the young men in this theatre are reprobates.

"I have done little in the painting art ſince I have been in town yet. A copy of a portrait and a background to an ox for Miſs Linwood is all. I have not time to ſay half I could wiſh about my Derbyſhire excurſion, therefore, I will ſay nothing."

In 1802, Conſtable's name appeared for the firſt time in the catalogue of the exhibition of the Royal Academy as an exhibitor; the picture being merely called "Landſcape." I think it likely, however, he may have ſent pictures for exhibition in 1800 or 1801, or in both years, which were rejected; as in a letter, apparently written in the winter of 1799, he ſpeaks of preparing ſome little thing for the exhibition.

Thoſe of my brother artiſts who remember the Academy twenty years ago, will not have forgotten Samuel Strowger, the moſt ſymmetrical of models in the Life School, and the beſt of ſervants to the Inſtitution. He was a Suffolk man, and had worked on a farm in Conſtable's neighbourhood, where he was diſtinguiſhed in the country phraſe as "a beautiful ploughman," until he enliſted in the life guards, when his ſtrict attention to his duties ſoon acquired for him the character of the beſt man in his regiment. The models of the Academy are generally ſelected from theſe fine troops; Sam was choſen, and the grace of his attitudes, his intel-

CHAP. I.
1802.

ligence and ſteadineſs, induced the Academy to procure his diſcharge, and to place him in the Inſtitution as head porter and occaſional model. Sam and Conſtable, who had known each other in Suffolk, were thus brought together again in London; and Strowger ſhewed his readineſs to patronize his old acquaintance, as far as lay in his power, by interceding, when he could venture to do ſo, during the arrangements of the exhibitions, in behalf of his works. As they were generally views in Suffolk, they had peculiar charms in Sam's eyes, and he could vouch for the accuracy with which they repreſented all the operations of farming. He was captivated by one of them, a "Corn Field with reapers at work," and pointed out to the arranging committee its correctneſs, "the *lord*," as the leading man among reapers and mowers is called in Suffolk, being in due advance of the reſt. But with all his endeavours to ſerve his friend the picture was either rejected or not ſo well placed as he wiſhed, and he conſoled Conſtable, and at the ſame time apologized for the members of the committee, by ſaying, "Our gentlemen are all great artiſts, ſir, but they none of them know anything about the *lord*."

I cannot take leave of my old friend Strowger without mentioning that towards the cloſe of his life, the ſtudents of the Academy preſented him with a ſilver ſnuff-box of huge dimenſions; and that a very exact portrait of him in his beſt days was painted by Wilkie. It is the head of the intelligent farmer in the "Rent Day," who, ſeated at the table with his finger raiſed, appears to be recalling ſome circumſtance to the recollection of the ſteward.

I have heard Conſtable ſay that under ſome diſappointment, I think it was the rejection, at the Academy, of a view of Flatford Mill, he carried a picture to Mr. Weſt, who ſaid, "Don't be diſheartened, young man, we ſhall hear of you again; you muſt have loved nature very much before you could have painted this." He then took a piece of chalk, and ſhewed Conſtable how he might improve the chiaroſcuro by ſome additional touches of light between the ſtems and branches of the trees, ſaying, "Always remember, ſir, that light and ſhadow *never ſtand ſtill*." Conſtable ſaid it was the beſt lecture, becauſe a practical one, on chiaroſcuro he ever heard. Mr. Weſt, at the ſame time, ſaid to him, "Whatever object you are painting, keep in mind its prevailing character rather than its accidental appearance, (unleſs in the ſubject there is ſome peculiar reaſon for the latter), and never be content until you have transferred that to canvaſs. In your ſkies, for inſtance, always aim at *brightneſs*, although there are ſtates of the atmoſpherein which the ſky itſelf is not bright. I do not mean that you are not to paint ſolemn or lowering ſkies, but even in the darkeſt effects there ſhould be brightneſs. Your darks ſhould look like the darks of ſilver, not of lead or of ſlate." This advice was not addreſſed to an inattentive ear.

Conſtable acknowledged many obligations to the amiable Preſident of the Academy, in whom every young artiſt found a friend; but the greateſt was one which poſſibly affected the whole courſe of his life. In the ſpring of 1802, Dr. Fiſher, Rector of Langham, and afterwards Biſhop of Saliſbury, had procured for him the ſituation of a drawing-maſter in a ſchool; but Mr. Weſt ſtrongly diſſuaded him from accepting it, telling him that if he did ſo he muſt give up all hopes of diſtinction. Such advice, and from ſo high an authority, was very agreeable to Conſtable; the difficulty, however, remained, of declining Dr. Fiſher's well-intentioned offer without giving him offence, which Mr. Weſt undertook and eaſily accompliſhed. To this affair Conſtable alludes in the next letter.

"London, May 29th, 1802. My dear Dunthorne, I hope I have now done with the buſineſs that brought me to town

Chap. I. 1802.

with Dr. Fisher. It is sufficient to say that had I accepted the situation offered, it would have been a death-blow to all my prospects of perfection in the art I love. For these few weeks past, I believe I have thought more seriously of my profession than at any other time of my life; of that which is the surest way to excellence. I am just returned from a visit to Sir George Beaumont's pictures with a deep conviction of the truth of Sir Joshua Reynolds' observation, that 'there is no easy way of becoming a good painter.' For the last two years I have been running after pictures, and seeking the truth at second hand. I have not endeavoured to represent nature with the same elevation of mind with which I set out, but have rather tried to make my performances look like the work of other men. I am come to a determination to make no idle visits this summer, nor to give up my time to common-place people. I shall return to Bergholt, where I shall endeavour to get a pure and unaffected manner of representing the scenes that may employ me. There is little or nothing in the exhibition worth looking up to. *There is room enough for a natural painter.* The great vice of the present day is *bravura*, an attempt to do something beyond the truth. Fashion always had, and will have, its day; but truth in all things only will last, and can only have just claims on posterity. I have reaped considerable benefit from exhibiting; it shews me where I am, and in fact tells me what nothing else could."

1803.

In 1803, Constable exhibited at the Academy two "Landscapes" and two "Studies from nature;" and in April he made a trip from London to Deal, in the Coutts, East Indiaman, with Captain Torin, a friend of his father.

"London, May 23rd, 1803. Dear Dunthorne, I have for some time felt a weight on my mind from having so long neglected writing to you. Indeed there is this strange fatality about me, that I seem to neglect those whose love and friendſhip I moſt value. * * * My voyage I will mention firſt. I was near a month on board, and was much employed in making drawings of ſhips in all ſituations. I ſaw all ſorts of weather. Some the moſt delightful, and ſome as melancholy. But ſuch is the enviable ſtate of a painter that he finds delight in every dreſs nature can poſſibly aſſume. When the ſhip was at Graveſend, I took a walk on ſhore to Rocheſter and Chatham. Their ſituation is beautiful and romantic, being at the bottom of finely formed and high hills, with the river continually ſhowing its turnings to great advantage. Rocheſter Caſtle is one of the moſt romantic I ever ſaw. At Chatham I hired a boat to ſee the men of war, which are there in great numbers. I ſketched the Victory in three views. She was the flower of the flock, a three decker of (ſome ſay) 112 guns. She looked very beautiful, freſh out of Dock and newly painted. When I ſaw her they were bending the ſails; which circumſtance, added to a very fine evening, made a charming effect. On my return to Rocheſter, I made a drawing of the Cathedral, which is in ſome parts very pictureſque, and is of Saxon Architecture. I joined the ſhip again at Graveſend, and we proceeded on our voyage, which was pleaſant enough till we got out to ſea, when we were joined by three more large ſhips. We had almoſt reached the Downs when the weather became ſtormy, and we all put back under the North Foreland, and lay there three days. Here I ſaw ſome very grand effects of ſtormy clouds. I came on ſhore at Deal, walked to Dover, and the next day returned to London. The worſt part of the ſtory is that I have loſt all my drawings. The ſhip was ſuch a ſcene of confuſion, when I left her, that although I had done my drawings up very carefully, I left them behind. When I found, on landing, that I had left them, and ſaw the ſhip out of reach, I was ready to faint. I hope, however, I may ſee them again ſome time or other.

Now I think I muſt have tired you, and I will change the ſubject.

"The exhibition is a very indifferent one on the whole. In the landſcape way moſt miſerable. I ſaw, as I thought, a great many pictures by Sir F. Bourgeois, but it proved that not half of them belonged to him, but to another painter who has imitated his manner exactly. Sir Francis was the hangman, and was ſo flattered by theſe imitations that he has given them as good places as his own. There are, however, ſome good portraits in the exhibition. I have ſeen ſome fine pictures lately, and have made a few little purchaſes; twelve prints by Waterloo, and four fine drawings by him, with ſome other prints. But my beſt purchaſes are two charming little landſcapes by Gaſpar Pouſſin, in his beſt time. * * * I feel now, more than ever, a decided conviction that I ſhall ſometime or other make ſome good pictures. Pictures that ſhall be valuable to poſterity, if I reap not the benefit of them. This hope, added to the great delight I find in the art, itſelf, buoys me up, and makes me purſue it with ardour.

"Panorama painting ſeems all the rage. There are four or five now exhibiting, and Mr. R * * * * * * * is coming out with another, a view of Rome, which I have ſeen. I ſhould think he has taken his view favourably, and it is executed with the greateſt care and fidelity. This ſtyle of painting ſuits his ideas of the art itſelf, and his defects are not ſo apparent in it; that is, great principles are neither expected nor looked for in this mode of deſcribing nature.* He views Nature minutely and *cunningly*, but with no greatneſs or breadth. The defects of the picture at preſent are a

* Sir George Beaumont was of opinion, and, perhaps, with ſome reaſon, that the effect of Panorama painting has been injurious to the taſte, both of the artiſts and the public, in landſcape.

1803.

profuſion of high lights, and too great a number of abrupt patches of ſhadow. But it is not to be conſidered as a whole. * * * I ſhall ſoon be at home again. The weather is not, however, very tempting, and while I find ſo much to intereſt me, at this buſy time of the Arts, in London, I ſhall ſtay a week or two longer."

Conſtable was fortunate enough to recover his marine ſketches, about one hundred and thirty, and the uſe he made of his drawings of the Victory will be ſeen immediately.

Between this period and 1807, no letters either to or from Conſtable have reached my hands. In 1804 he did not exhibit, but he painted an Altar-piece for Brantham Church near Bergholt, the ſubject, " Chriſt bleſſing little Children." The figures are of the ſize of life, and all ſtanding, except a child in the Saviour's arms. The arrangement of the maſſes is good, but it has no other merit; and indeed is no otherwiſe worthy of notice than as a proof that he did wiſely, after one more attempt, in making no farther incurſions into this walk of the art. In 1805 he exhibited a " Landſcape, Moonlight," and in 1806, a drawing of " His Majeſty's Ship Victory in the Battle of Trafalgar, between two French Ships of the Line." This ſubject was ſuggeſted to him by hearing an account of the battle from a Suffolk man, who had been in Nelſon's ſhip.

1804.

1805.

1806.

In this year his maternal uncle, David Pike Watts, recommended to him a tour in Weſtmoreland and Cumberland in ſearch of ſubjects for his pencil, and paid his expenſes. He ſpent about two months among the Engliſh lakes and mountains, where he made a great number of ſketches, of a large ſize, on tinted paper, ſometimes in black and white, but more often coloured. They abound in grand and ſolemn effects of light, ſhade, and colour, but from theſe ſtudies he never painted any conſiderable picture, for his mind was formed for the enjoyment of a different claſs of landſcape.

Chap. I.

1806.

I have heard him ſay the ſolitude of mountains oppreſſed his ſpirits. His nature was peculiarly ſocial and could not feel ſatisfied with ſcenery, however grand in itſelf, that did not abound in human aſſociations. He required villages, churches, farm-houſes, and cottages; and I believe it was as much from natural temperament as from early impreſſions that his

1807.

firſt love, in landſcape, was alſo his lateſt love. In 1807 he exhibited ſome of the reſults of his excurſion; "A View in Weſtmoreland," "Keſwick Lake," and "Bow Fell, Cumberland."

The Earl of Dyſart wiſhing to have ſome family pictures copied, Conſtable was introduced to his lordſhip and the Counteſs as a young artiſt who would be glad to undertake them. The conſequence was, his being employed in making a number of copies, chiefly from Sir Joſhua Reynolds; and although it is to be regretted that much of his time ſhould have been ſpent on any but original works, yet he no doubt derived improvement in his taſte for colour and chiaroſcuro by this intimate communion with ſo great a maſter of both.

About this time his mother, at the concluſion of a letter to him, ſays: "How thankful I am that you ſo much enjoy the invaluable bleſſing of health. It is, I truſt, the kind gift of Providence, rendered the more permanent by your own prudence and good conduct. Long may you enjoy it on ſuch terms!" And his uncle, Mr. Watts, thus ſpeaks of him at the ſame period: "J. C. is induſtrious in his profeſſion, temperate in diet, plain in dreſs, frugal in expenſes, and in his profeſſional character has great merit."

1808.

In 1808 he exhibited at the Royal Academy, three pictures, "Borrowdale," "A Scene in Cumberland," and "Windermere Lake," and at the Britiſh Gallery, "A Scene in Weſtmoreland," probably the one he had exhibited at the Academy the preceding year, and "Moonlight, (a Study.)"

1809.

In 1809 his pictures at the Academy were three, with the

1809.

title merely of "Landſcape;" and at the Britiſh Gallery he had alſo three, "Borrowdale," "A Cottage," and "Keſwick Lake," the latter having been exhibited at the Academy.

In this year he painted his ſecond and laſt attempt in Sacred hiſtory, an altar-piece for Neyland Church, a ſingle half figure of the Saviour bleſſing the bread and wine. Although, from the ſlightneſs of the execution, this picture can only be conſidered as a ſketch of the ſize of life, it is in all reſpects much better than the Brantham altar-piece. There is no originality in the treatment, but a ſubject ſo often painted almoſt precludes originality. The light falls on the face from a lamp, and the colour and effect are very agreeable, broken colours partaking of purple and browniſh yellow, being ſubſtituted in the draperies, for the ordinary blue and red. Still, ſuch are its deficiencies, that it is evident a long courſe of ſtudy and practice would have been required before he could have done juſtice, if ever, to ſubjects of its claſs.

1810.

In 1810 he exhibited at the Academy "A Landſcape" and "A Church Yard."

The following paſſage in a letter from John Jackſon, dated October 23rd, 1810, ſhews that Conſtable's friendſhip with that eminent artiſt had then commenced. They were men who could fully appreciate each other: "I ſpent ten days in Hants, and was delighted beyond meaſure with the New Foreſt. I think it indeſcribably beautiful; but perhaps you may have ſeen it. If not, I wiſh we might find ſome ſequeſtered cottage to put our heads in by night, and in the day explore and ſketch, for a fortnight or three weeks: but more of this when we meet."

Conſtable and Wilkie were alſo much together at that time, and their friendſhip never ſuffered any diminution. Conſtable ſat to Wilkie for the head of the phyſician in his picture of the Sick Lady, and again, in the character of a phyſician, at a late period of their lives; as will be noticed in its proper place.

CHAPTER II.

1811—1812.

Weſt's Picture of Chriſt healing the Sick. Conſtable's Art. Traits of his Character. His health affected. Sir George Beaumont's Preſcription. Another Preſcription. Attachment to Miſs Bicknell. Their Marriage objected to by her Friends. Viſit of Miſs Mary Conſtable to her Brother. Correſpondence with Miſs Bicknell. Exhibition at the Royal Academy, 1812. *Archdeacon Fiſher. Mr. Stothard. Conſtable engaged on Portraits. Fire at his Lodgings.*

1811.

N 1811, an extraordinary event in the hiſtory of Engliſh Art occurred: the Directors of the Britiſh Inſtitution bought Weſt's picture of "Chriſt healing the ſick," for 3000*l.* Conſtable's fond mother, who had ſeen this picture, after ſaying ſhe preferred the principal figure and infant in her ſon's Brantham altar-piece, thus concludes a letter to him: "In truth, my dear John, though in all human probability my head will be laid low long ere it comes to paſs, yet with my preſent light, I can perceive no reaſon why you ſhould not, one day, with diligence and attention be the performer of a picture worth 3000*l.*"

In this year he ſent to the Academy two pictures, "Twilight," and "Dedham Vale," and to the Britiſh Gallery, "A Church Porch," which as well as the "Dedham Vale" remained in his poſſeſſion to the end of his life, and I am therefore well acquainted with them. The "Porch" is that of Bergholt Church, and the ſtillneſs of a ſummer afternoon is broken only by the voice of an old man to whom a woman and girl ſitting on one of the tombs are liſtening. As in many of the fineſt Dutch pictures, the fewneſs of the parts conſtitutes a charm in this little work; ſuch is its extreme ſimplicity, that it has nothing to arreſt attention, but when once noticed, few pictures would longer detain a mind of any ſenſibility. I have heard the word *ſentiment* ridiculed when applied to repreſentations of inanimate objects. But no other word can expreſs that from which the impreſſion of this picture reſults, independently of the figures. In the "Dedham Vale" an extenſive country is ſeen through a ſunny haze, which equalizes the light, without injuring the beauty of the tints. There is a tree of a ſlight form in the foreground, touched with a taſte to which I know nothing equal in any landſcape I ever ſaw. Such pictures were, however, too unobtruſive for the exhibition, and Conſtable's art had made no impreſſion whatever on the public. But when we look back to the fate of Wilſon, and recollect that Gainſborough was only ſaved from poverty by his admirable powers in portraiture, and that the names of Cozens and Girtin are ſcarcely known to their countrymen, we ſhall not haſtily conclude that to fail in attracting general notice is any proof of want of merit in an Engliſh landſcape painter. It may be that the art, ſo ſimple and natural, as it is in the beſt works of theſe extraordinary men, becomes a novelty which people do not know how to eſtimate; Steele, in a paper of the Tatler, ſpeaks of an author "who determined to write in a way perfectly new, and deſcribe things exactly as they happened."

Conſtable's father and mother wiſhed him to apply himſelf to portrait painting, but he had not the happineſs, like Gainſborough, to combine landſcape and portrait in equal

Chap. II.
1811.

perfection. He painted the latter indeed, occasionally, all his life, but with very unequal success; and his best works of this kind, though always agreeable in colour and breadth, were surpassed, in more common qualities, by men far inferior to him in genius. His profession had hitherto been profitless, but it may be doubted whether under any circumstances he would have become a rich man by his own exertions; for although he was an early riser, frugal in his habits of living, and not addicted to any vicious extravagance either of time or money, yet of neither was he an economist. Both were always too readily at the disposal of others; it was as difficult for him to say no to a borrower, as to shut his door against a lounger, still less could he ever resist an appeal to his charity; and if a book or a print he wanted came in his way, the chances were he would buy it, though with the money that should pay for his next day's dinner. He was well aware of this want of resolution, and often formed plans of economy, but failing in a constant and steady adherence to them, they seldom proved of much real advantage to him.

It now became apparent to Constable's friends that his health was declining. It was, I believe, at this time that Sir George Beaumont undertook to be his physician, and prescribed for him that he should copy a picture entirely from memory. He was to walk every day to Sir George's house in Grosvenor Square, look at the picture as long as he pleased, then return home and paint as much of it as he had retained in his recollection, until the copy was finished. The regular exercise and change of scene, combined with an agreeable and not too arduous employment were to work the cure. The picture selected was a landscape by Wilson, and the experiment was tried, but the malady under which Constable laboured was not to be so easily removed.

The following is part of a very long letter from a friend, who often bestowed advice on him less judicious than well intentioned. It is addreſſed to " J. C. aged thirty-five," which marks it as belonging to this period. " Dear John, I am ſorry to ſee too viſible traits in your whole perſon of an inward anxiety which irritates your nervous ſyſtem, deranges the digeſtion, and undermines the health. But health alone, that invaluable poſſeſſion, is not the ſole thing impaired; the mental powers are liable to participate in the depreſſion of the animal ſyſtem. It is not in the power of even your neareſt friend to ſee into the ſecret cauſes of the operations of the mind; but a tolerable opinion may be formed of what paſſes within the thoughts of another perſon by certain external traits. The concluſion to be drawn from theſe is, that your indiſpoſition ariſes from more than one cauſe, though one has of late been predominant, and has become the main trouble which abſorbs the minor ones, and reſolves all the ſubordinate cares into one overwhelming ſolicitude, and this is a deep concern of the heart and affections." I will ſpare the reader any more of this letter, which compriſes four pages of the uſual advice as to the beſt means of combating a hopeleſs paſſion, which is generally thrown away on ſimilar occaſions; one page being a quotation from " an able Divine." Encloſed in the letter I found a printed paper entitled: " A Cure for Love. Take half a grain of ſenſe, half a grain of prudence, &c. &c."

Another long letter, from the ſame kind Mentor, appears to have been written the next day; and however well meant, was certainly not very well timed.

" Dear John, I amuſed myſelf at ſeven o'clock this morning, in tranſcribing the encloſed, which I hope will amuſe you more than my yeſterday's extract. You ſee I copy from the great maſters, whether in Divinity, Morals, or the Arts.*

* I have omitted tranſcribing the encloſure, nor ſhould I have interrupted the narrative with any of the effuſions of this correſpondent, but that the reader may judge, from theſe ſpecimens, of many ſimilar inflictions to which Conſtable

Chap. II.
1811.

I ſometimes wiſh you had copied more; and that at an early age you had put yourſelf under a great maſter. That dread of being a manneriſt, and that deſire of being an original, has not, in my imperfect judgment, produced to you the full advantage you promiſed yourſelf from it. As far as my unqualified, and ſimply native taſte extends, (which I acknowledge to be very inadequate to form a correct judgment), I had rather ſee ſome of the manner of thoſe highly extolled works, which have commanded the applauſe of the public at large, from the perfect connoiſſeur down to the ſimple ſpectator. I have before taken the freedom to offer my ſentiments to you; you have before paid me the compliment to aſk and receive them. I have no motive in my obſervations but your good, or what I conceive to be ſo, joined to a regard to truth, and an averſion to flattery. My opinion is, that cheerfulneſs is wanted in your landſcapes; they are tinctured with a ſombre darkneſs. If I may ſay ſo, the trees are not green, but black; the water is not lucid, but overſhadowed; an air of melancholy is caſt over the ſcene, inſtead of hilarity, &c." How muſt the artiſt have writhed under this friendly advice, ill in body and depreſſed in mind as he then was.

Maria Bicknell, the young lady between whom and Conſtable there now exiſted a mutual attachment, was the daughter of Charles Bicknell, Eſq. of Spring Gardens, Solicitor to the Admiralty, and grandaughter, by her mother's ſide, to the Rev. Dr. Rhudde, Rector of Bergholt, where Conſtable's acquaintance with her had commenced as early as the year 1800, while ſhe was a child. Objections to their union aroſe on the part of Miſs Bicknell's friends, Dr. Rhudde being its chief oppoſer. He was probably unwilling that

was, for ſome years, ſubjected from the ſame quarter. They ſmack of the wiſdom, as well as the ſtyle of Polonius.

his grandaughter ſhould marry a man below herſelf in point of fortune, and whom he might, not unreaſonably, conſider as without a profeſſion, ſince Conſtable could ſcarcely appear in any other light to his beſt friends. A difference had ariſen between Golding Conſtable and the rector, which at that time eſtranged them from each other; and there was a ſtory current in Bergholt of a caricature of the doctor by Conſtable, which, whether true or falſe, was unfortunate. How far any or all of theſe circumſtances operated on Dr. Rhudde's mind, or what other objections he may have had to receive Conſtable as a grandſon-in-law, I know not, but it became afterwards plain that Mr. Bicknell would not long have oppoſed the marriage, had it not been from fear of excluding his daughter's name from the will of her grandfather, who was very rich. As it was, the lovers were doomed for five years to ſuffer all the wearing anxieties of hope deferred, of which their own letters form a deeply intereſting hiſtory.

The firſt I have ſeen of this ſeries is from Miſs Bicknell, who was on a viſit at the houſe of a friend in the country.

"Spring Grove, Nov. 2, 1811. My dear Sir, You have grieved me exceedingly by the melancholy account you give of your health, and I ſhall feel much better ſatisfied when I know you are in Suffolk, where I do not doubt that good air, with the nurſing and attention of your friends, will go a great way towards your recovery. I dare not ſuffer myſelf to think on your laſt letter. I am very impatient, as you may imagine, to hear from Papa, on a ſubject ſo fraught with intereſt to us both; but was unwilling to delay writing to you, as you would be ignorant of the cauſe of ſuch ſeeming inattention. I hope you will not find that your kind partiality to me made you view what paſſed in Spring Gardens too favourably. You know my ſentiments; I ſhall be guided by my father in every reſpect. Should he acquieſce in my wiſhes, I ſhall be happier than I can expreſs. If not, I ſhall have the conſolation of reflecting that I am pleasing him, a charm that will in the end give the greatest satisfaction to my mind. I cannot write any more till the wished, but fearfully dreaded, letter arrives. With the most ardent wishes for your health, believe me, my dear Sir, your obliged friend, Maria E. Bicknell."

Constable's fond mother, who, from the commencement of his attachment to Miss Bicknell, entered warmly into all his feelings on the subject, thus replied to a letter she had received from him :

" East Bergholt, Nov. 3, 1811. Your letter of the 31st ult. pleases me, because it tells me you are 'far better.' But you cannot imagine how you have surprised and filled me with conjecture by saying 'I have been kindly received by the Bicknells this morning, and my mind is in some measure quieted. I have Mr. Bicknell's permission to write to Miss Bicknell, which I have done this afternoon.' Now, my dear son, what may be augured from this? I pray it may prove favourable. They are too good, and too honourable, to trifle with your feelings; therefore I am inclined to hope for the best, and that it will end well."

" To Mr. John Constable, Spring Grove, Nov. 4. I have received my father's letter. It is precisely such a one as I expected, reasonable and kind; his only objection would be on the score of that necessary evil money. What can we do? I wish I had it, but wishes are vain; we must be wise, and leave off a correspondence that is not calculated to make us think less of each other. We have many painful trials required of us in this life, and we must learn to bear them with resignation. You will still be my friend, and I will be yours. Then, as such, let me advise you to go into Suffolk, you cannot fail to be better there. I have written to Papa, though I do not, in conscience, think he can retract anything he has said; if so, I had better not write to you any more, at leaſt till I can coin. We ſhould both of us be bad ſubjects for poverty, ſhould we not? Even painting would go on badly; it could hardly ſurvive in domeſtic worry. I hope you have done a good deal this ſummer; Saliſbury, I ſuppoſe, has furniſhed ſome ſketches. You are particularly fortunate in poſſeſſing the affectionate eſteem of ſo kind and excellent a man as Mr. Watts, whoſe wiſhes you muſt conſult on this moſt important point. Remember, dear Sir, if you wiſh to oblige me and all your friends, it muſt be by taking care of your health. Adieu, and think me always ſincerely yours, M. E. B."

Conſtable, however, abated not "a jot of heart or hope." "Be aſſured," he wrote to her, "we have only to conſider our union as an event that muſt happen, and we ſhall yet be happy." To this ſhe replied, "You grieve and ſurpriſe me by continuing ſo ſanguine on a ſubject altogether hopeleſs. I cannot endure that you ſhould harbour expectations that muſt terminate in diſappointment. I never can conſent to act in oppoſition to the wiſhes of my father; how then can I continue a correſpondence wholly diſapproved of by him? He tells me that I am conſulting your happineſs as well as my own by putting an end to it. Let me then entreat that you will ceaſe to think of me. Forget that you have ever known me, and I will willingly reſign all pretenſions to your regard, or even acquaintance, to facilitate the tranquillity and peace of mind which is ſo eſſential to your ſucceſs in a profeſſion, which will ever be in itſelf a ſource of continued delight. You muſt be certain that you cannot write without increaſing feelings that muſt be entirely ſuppreſſed. You will, therefore, I am ſure, ſee the impropriety of ſending me any more letters. I congratulate you on your change of reſidence. It is, I think, a very deſirable ſituation. Farewell, my dear Sir, and ever believe me your ſincere and conſtant well-wiſher, M. E. B. Spring Grove, Dec. 1811."

Chap. II.
1811.

From his father Conftable received, on the fame fubject, the following letter :

"Eaft Bergholt, Dec. 31, 1811. Dear John, your prefent profpects and fituation are far more critical than at any former period of your life. As a fingle man, I fear your expenfes, on the moft frugal plan, will be found quite equal to the produce of your profeffion. If my opinion were afked, it would be to defer all thoughts of marriage for the prefent. I would farther advife, a clofe application to your profeffion, and to fuch parts as pay beft. At prefent you muft not choofe your fubjects, nor wafte your time by accepting invitations not likely to produce future advantages. When you have hit on a fubject, finifh it in the beft manner you are able, and do not in defpair put it afide, and fo fill your room with lumber. I fear your great anxiety to excel, may have carried you too far above yourfelf, and that you make too ferious a matter of the bufinefs, and thereby render yourfelf lefs capable ; it has impaired your health and fpirits. Think lefs, and finifh as you go, (perhaps that may do). Be of good cheer, John, as in me you will always find a parent and a fincere friend. At your requeft, you may expect to fee your fifter at No. 63, next Thurfday afternoon."

Conftable's youngeft fifter, the lady mentioned in this letter, remained with him in London from the commencement of 1812 to the middle of May; and by the affectionate intereft fhe took in all that agitated his mind, and the truly feminine gentlenefs of her manners contributed much to his comfort.

It was fcarcely to be expected that the injunctions of Mifs Bicknell, to write no more to her, fhould be obeyed by Conftable, now that matters had gone fo far, and a regular interchange of letters foon took place between them.

1812.

"To Mifs Bicknell. 63, Charlotte Street, April, 1812. I have difpatched my pictures to Somerfet Houfe : my friends assure me they are my best; but Leonardo da Vinci tells us to mind what our enemies say of us. It is certainly one of the great ends of a public exhibition, that we hear the truth. I have sent four pictures, the 'View of Salisbury,' 'Flatford Mill,' and two small ones. My good friends the Bishop of Sarum and Mrs. Fisher called to see them. I shall have great pleasure in giving you some account of the exhibition. Lawrence has sent a picture of Kemble in Cato. Mr. Farrington spoke highly of it to me. * * * Let me beg of you to continue to cheer my solitude with your endearing epistles; they are next to seeing you, and hearing you speak. I am now engaged with portraits. Mr. Watts sat to me this morning, and seems pleased with what is going on. I am copying a picture for Lady Heathcote, her own portrait as Hebe. She will not sit to me, though she wants many alterations from the original; but I can have prints, drawings, miniatures, locks of hair, &c. &c. without end. You may be able to tell me, better than I can you, any public matter, as I never have an opportunity of seeing the newspaper."

"63, Charlotte Street, Fitzroy Square, April 24, 1812. * * * * I believe I mentioned to you that I left a card for Dr. Rhudde in Stratton Street. I have had a polite message from him, offering to take any letter, &c. to Bergholt. I called with a letter for my mother, and saw the doctor, who was very courteous. I am glad I have seen him; for though this may not better our cause, it cannot make it worse, and I have not to reflect on myself for any omission or neglect.

"I met Mr. West in the street the other day; he had been much gratified with my picture of the Mill, &c. which passed the Council of the Academy. I wished to know whether he considered that mode of study as proper for laying the foundation of real excellence. 'Sir,' said he, 'I consider that you have attained it.' * * * What happiness it is to me to impart to you any little circumſtances that in any way connect themſelves with our future welfare, when I know how they will be received by you; and though I am denied the pleaſure of communicating them with

'Your arm faſt lock'd in mine.'

yet I have had that pleaſure, and may yet again for many years. Mary Conſtable has left Epſom, and I have detained her here for a few days on her return. She begs her kind remembrance to you."

"63, Charlotte Street, May 6, 1812. My deareſt Maria, I am writing to you on my mother's birth-day and wedding-day. Perhaps you will think me very buſy with my pen; but I am glad to recollect that you may be expecting to hear from me about this time. Your kindneſs will remember that I can ſcarcely gain any intelligence of you but from yourſelf. I have made two haſty viſits to the exhibition. The portraits by Lawrence and Owen are very excellent; and there are ſome beautiful fancy pictures by Thomſon, the Infant Jupiter, and Lavinia reſting her arm on her mother. Mr. Weſt's is truly an heroic landſcape;* and Turner has another, a ſcene among the Alps, with Hannibal and his army. It is ſo ambiguous as to be ſcarcely intelligible in ſome parts, (and thoſe the principal,) yet, as a whole, it is novel and affecting. Mr. Farrington has ſome beautiful landſcapes, but they are heavy and crude. I waited to ſee them by twilight, when they looked much better. My own landſcapes have excellent ſituations. My dear Mary is ſtill with me, but I muſt part with her in a few days."

"To Mr. John Conſtable. Spring Grove, May 14, 1812. I am ſorry, my dear John, that you ſhould have felt any diſappointment by my ſilence. I will not therefore delay

* "Saul before Samuel and the Prophets."

thanking you for your laſt two letters. * * You will, I am ſure, make allowances for me. Think how much of the charm of writing is broken, not having my mother's approbation to add to my joy by ſharing it. But do not let me grieve you by ſorrow, that will intrude its hideous form to me. I am ſure you have ſuffered ſufficiently on my account. What do you think of accompanying Sadak in his ſearch for the waters of oblivion? but were they now within my reach, I could not drink them."

Conſtable's health again ſuffered, and he was adviſed to go into the country. On the 24th of May he wrote to Miſs Bicknell, "I am ſtill looking towards Suffolk, where I hope to paſs the greater part of the ſummer; as much for the ſake of ſtudy as on any other account. You know I have always ſucceeded beſt with my native ſcenes. They have always charmed me, and I hope they always will. I have now a path marked out very diſtinctly for myſelf, and I am deſirous of purſuing it uninterruptedly." This laſt ſentence is worthy of attention, as it ſhews the ſteadineſs of purpoſe which belonged to his character in all matters relating to his art, while to thoſe who knew or obſerved him but ſlightly, there was an appearance of vacillation and indeciſion in his manner entirely at variance with the real ſtability of his mind. It will be ſeen, in the ſequel, how impoſſible it was to drive him out of the path he had choſen, though few indeed were the encouragements he met with to continue in it. In the ſame letter he ſays, "I am getting on with my picture for Lady Heathcote. Lady Louiſa Manners has a wretched copy by Hoppner from Sir J. Reynolds, which ſhe wiſhes me to repaint, ſo that I fear it muſt be, at leaſt, a fortnight or three weeks before I can get into Suffolk. My friend John Fiſher is half angry with me becauſe I will not paſs a little time with him at Saliſbury; but I am determined not to fritter away the ſummer, if I can help it. I will quote part of his letter, (which he has followed to town,) that you may fee what an enthufiaft he is, 'We will try and coax you here, dear Conftable, by an account of the life we will lead. We will rife with the fun, breakfaft, and then fet out for the reft of the day. If we tire of drawing, we can read, or bathe, and then home to a fhort dinner. We will drink tea at the Benfon's, or walk the great aifle of the cathedral, or if the maggot fo bites, puzzle out a paffage or two in Horace. I think this life of Arcadian or Utopian felicity muft tempt you.'

"I believe there are more exhibitions than ufual, open at this time. I have been moft gratified at Wilkie's."

The Rev. John Fifher (afterwards Archdeacon Fifher) was chaplain to his uncle, the Bifhop of Salifbury. He was the eldeft fon of Dr. Fifher, Mafter of the Charter Houfe, and though fixteen years younger than Conftable, they had contracted a friendfhip for each other which never altered excepting by its growth.

"Charlotte Street, June 6th, 1812. Yefterday I took a long walk with Mr. Stothard. I left my door about fix in the morning, we breakfafted at Putney, went over Wimbledon Common, and paffed three hours in Coombe Wood, (Stothard is a butterfly-catcher) where we dined by a fpring, then back to Richmond by the Park, enjoyed the view, and fo home. All this on foot, and I do not feel tired now, though I was a little fo in the morning. I only afferted I was well before, I hope now this is a proof of it."

Conftable had, for fome time, been the chofen companion of Stothard's long walks, the chief relaxation of that admirable artift from the drudgery of working for the publifhers. Thefe walks lengthened with the lengthening days, and I have heard him fpeak of the hilarity with which Stothard would enter his room on a fine afternoon in the fpring and fay, "Come, Sir, put on your hat, my boys tell me the lilacs are out in Kenſington Gardens." I have ſeen a beautiful pencil drawing of a ſhady lane, which Conſtable made during their excurſion to Coombe Wood, while his companion, who was introduced into it, was engaged with his butterfly nets. Stothard was then about fifty years of age; his deafneſs precluded him from the enjoyment of general ſociety, but with a ſingle friend, and, as in this inſtance, a younger man, who looked up to him with great reſpect and admiration, and whoſe mind was in many reſpects a kindred one, he was very communicative. In their walks together, he, no doubt, felt his infirmity as little as poſſible; while the hours paſſed with him have contributed to ſoothe the ſpirits of Conſtable, diſquieted as they then were.

"Charlotte Street, June 10th, 1812. You will ſee by the cover that the good biſhop is as kind to me as ever. He and Mrs. Fiſher were here yeſterday for an hour or two; and I have completed the portrait* quite to their ſatisfaction. I am to make a duplicate of it for the palace at Exeter. During their ſtay, Mrs. Fiſher wrote to the Marchioneſs of Thomond, to introduce me to a ſight of her fine collection of Sir Joſhua Reynolds's pictures. I am going this morning to Pall Mall; (I believe I told you that I had ſomething to do there, with a portrait of Lady Louiſa Manners) from thence to call on Sir George Beaumont; he wiſhes to ſee the Gainſboroughs at Lord Dyſart's, and in return he is to take me to the Marquis of Stafford's Gallery. Theſe things delay my viſit to dear Bergholt, and I am ſighing for the country. I am told the trees never were more beautiful; indeed, I never ſaw them in greater perfection than in my walk with Mr. Stothard to Richmond."

"Charlotte Street, June 15th. I am making ſad ravages of my time with the wretched portraits I mentioned to you.

* Of the Biſhop.

I am ungallant enough to allude entirely to the ladies' portraits.* I ſee no end, if I ſtay, to my labours in Pall Mall. Lady Louiſa was quite diſtreſſed when I told her I muſt order my colours away; but I ſee no alternative, and muſt fly like another Telemachus, though not for the ſame reaſon. I am ſure you will pardon me, when I tell you, that duty and affection to my mother, made it impoſſible for me to withhold ſome of your letters from her. The peruſal of them made her more than ever lament our unhappy ſituation. My father is uncommonly well; on horſeback at ſix o'clock in the morning, purſuing his plans with all the ardour of youth: ſurely this is a delightful proof of the bleſſings of a well ſpent and temperate life. * * * In one of your letters you aſk me, what I have read lately. I have all Cowper's works on my table. I moſtly read his letters. He is an author I prefer to almoſt any other, and when with him I always feel the better for it."

"Eaſt Bergholt, June 22nd. From the window where I am now writing, I ſee all thoſe ſweet fields where we have paſſed ſo many happy hours together. I called at the Rectory on Saturday with my mother. The doctor was unuſually courteous, and ſhook hands with me on taking leave. Am I to argue from this that I am not *entirely* out of the pale of ſalvation? How delighted I am that you are fond of Cowper. But how could it be otherwiſe? for he is the poet of religion and nature. I think the world much indebted to Mr. Hayley. I never ſaw, till now, the ſupplement to the letters; perhaps ſome of his beſt are to be found there, and it contains an intereſting account of the death of poor Roſe, a young friend of the poet's. Nothing can exceed the beautiful appearance of the country; its freſhneſs, its amenity."

* Theſe were copies by Hoppner, with alterations according to the fancies of the ladies.

"July 22nd. I have been living a hermit-like life, though always with my pencil in my hand. Perhaps this has not been much the caſe with hermits, if we except Swaneveldt (the pupil of Claude); who was called the 'Hermit of Italy,' from the romantic ſolitudes he lived in, and which his pictures ſo admirably deſcribe. How much real delight have I had with the ſtudy of landſcape this ſummer! either I am myſelf improved in the art of ſeeing nature, which Sir Joſhua calls painting, or nature has unveiled her beauties to me leſs faſtidiouſly. Perhaps there is ſomething of both, ſo we will divide the compliment. But I am writing this nonſenſe with a ſad heart, when I think what would be my happineſs could I have this enjoyment with you. Then indeed would my mind be calm to contemplate the endleſs beauties of this happy country."

In a letter dated in Auguſt, he ſays, "Many of my friends have urged my leaving a profeſſion ſo unpropitious; but that, you know, is impoſſible."

"Eaſt Bergholt, September 6th, 1812. I am happy to hear of your ſafe arrival at Bognor. * * on the ſame day I found myſelf quietly drinking tea with my father and mother. * * * * I was looking anxiouſly for your letter, and am grieved to find your ſpirits ſo much affected. You have hitherto borne your ſhare of our ſorrows, (and you have had by far the greateſt ſhare) with a fortitude, that has made me aſhamed of myſelf. I can only imagine our feelings to have been very ſimilar; but let me believe that much of our preſent ſuffering may be the effect of parting; and that, with this fine weather, added to the delightful ſcenes you are in, you have recovered your uſual ſerenity * * * I have not reſumed my landſcape ſtudies ſince my return. I have not found myſelf equal to the vivid pencil that landſcape requires. I am going to-morrow to ſtay a few days at General Rebow's, near Colcheſter, to paint his little girl, an only child, ſeven

Chap. II. 1812.

years old; I believe I am to paint the General and his lady at ſome future time: this is in conſequence of my portrait of young Godfrey, which has been much admired." * * *

"To Mr. John Conſtable. Bognor, September 10th. * * * Continue to write to me, my dear John, without the leaſt reſerve; the more I am acquainted with you, the happier I ſhall be. We are both very unfortunately ſituated (but really you muſt think me very ſilly to tell you what is ſo evident). We can, however, make writing alleviate many of our troubles, and be to us one of our higheſt pleaſures. I uſed to diſlike it exceſſively; but now there is no employment I like ſo well * * * Have the goodneſs to remember me kindly to your mother, and tell her how much I am obliged to her for her frequent recollections of me. And you, my deareſt John, accept every affectionate wiſh from M. E. B."

"To Mr. John Conſtable. Bognor, November 6th. It was particularly kind of your mother to call in Spring Gardens. You do not mention anything that paſſed, ſo I ſuppoſe it was merely the common chit-chat of the day. You will believe how earneſtly I hope, my father's viſit to Suffolk will produce ſome change for the better. But I dare not be too ſanguine; for then bitter would be my diſappointment. Grateful for the preſent ſhare of happineſs we enjoy, we muſt not be too anxious for the future. Your letters afford me a continual ſource of pleaſure. * * * Farewell, my deareſt John; may health and ſpirits long attend you, and then I ſhall always ſubſcribe myſelf, your happy and affectionate Maria."

"To Miſs Bicknell. 33, Portland Place, November 10th, 1812. * * * * Should the circumſtance of a fire in Charlotte Street appear in any of the papers, it is poſſible you may meet with it; and I write this haſty line or two, that you may not be uneaſy on my account. The fire did in fact happen on the premiſes I inhabit; but I have loſt nothing.

We ſhall ſuffer a temporary inconvenience; but Mr. Watts has kindly ordered me a bed in his houſe, and a neighbour, Mr. Henderſon, in Charlotte Street, has allowed me a room to paint in while the houſe is under repair. We were put to ſome alarm and buſtle, but no one was hurt; and I hope Mr. Weight's inſurance will cover his loſs. The fire began in a workſhop at the back of the houſe, about four o'clock in the morning, and ſpread ſo very faſt, that at one time we thought of ſaving ourſelves only. I, however, ſecured my moſt valuable letters; and we went to work removing whatever we could into the ſtreet. We were not long without help; but it was an hour before any engine came. It appeared as if nothing could ſave the houſe, and it was very difficult to paſs up and down ſtairs, owing to the great heat of the windows; but we perſevered as long as we could, and while we were getting Lady Heathcote's large picture down, I had a ſhower of glaſs about me from the window on the ſtaircaſe. I ran with it over the way to Mr. Farrington's, and on my return for ſomething elſe, I found the poor woman-ſervant, who had lately nurſed Mrs. Weight, in great diſtreſs, as all her fortune was in the garret, and in her pockets which were under her pillow; there was no time to be loſt, I ran up ſtairs, and ſhe was overjoyed to ſee me return with them, through the ſmoke, quite ſafe. It was now that the engines arrived, and fortunately ſucceeded in putting a ſtop to the flames. Mr. Weight's loſs is greater than he at firſt expected; all the premiſes are burnt at the back of the houſe, the back drawing-room and its contents are deſtroyed, and all the back windows. I cannot bear to leave theſe poor people in their diſtreſs, and we think of taking a temporary place till the houſe is repaired.

"To Mr. John Conſtable. Bognor, Nov. 16. My deareſt John, Had it been merely a letter of form I had to write, you ſhould have received it ſooner; but, as it is, you perfectly know how sincerely and fervently thankful I am that you have sustained no personal harm. You acted considerately and like yourself. I should have been sadly alarmed at any account of the fire previous to yours; but I had not seen it in the papers, though I dare say it has been inserted, as they are always glad of news, and I believe the more melancholy the better."

Constable had presented to his friend Fisher a small landscape, of which that gentleman writes in a letter, dated "Nov. 13, 1812. Your painting has been much criticised; disliked by *bad* judges, gaped at by *no* judges, and admired by good ones. Among these, Coxe the historian, who has seen much, was particularly pleased with it. It put him in mind, he said, 'of the good old Dutch forest painting school.' He looks at it whenever he comes into my room, which is most days. What it wants, he says, is, that 'what is *depth* near, should not be *gloom* at a distance.' By the words far and near, I mean as the spectator recedes from or approaches the picture. This is, I think, a just observation. I am now looking at it. It is most pleasing when you are directed to look at it; but you must be *taken* to it. It does not *solicit attention;* and this I think true of all your pictures, and the real cause of your want of popularity. I have heard it remarked of Rubens, that one of his pictures *illuminates* a room. It gives a cheerfulness to everything about it. It pleases before you examine it, or even know the subject. How he obtained this, or how it is to be obtained—hic labor, hoc opus est. Don't laugh at my feeble criticisms, Constable; I mean your service, and all men are allowed to talk *good-natured* nonsense. You shall have something to put you in mind of the great Escurial* at Lord Radnor's. I have to thank you for the ability to view that work as it ought to

* A Landscape by Rubens.

be viewed. You gave me another ſenſe. * * * * I paſſed three moſt delicious days in this country with Dr. Callcott and his brother the artiſt. * * * * How is your mind? at reſt? Set it ſo, if you can, for your ſucceſs, as you know, depends upon it. I ſhall ſee you ſoon in town, till when

'Adieu—adieu,—remember me!'

though I am no ghoſt. Believe me, my dear fellow, Yours moſt faithfully, John Fiſher."

In a letter, without date, but written about this time Conſtable ſays, "My good friends in Seymour Street continue their great kindneſs to me, I have juſt completed another portrait for them, for the Palace at Exeter. I told Mrs. Fiſher yeſterday, how much I thought his Lordſhip had of the character of the Archbiſhop of Cambray. She was pleaſed to hear me ſay ſo, and ſaid, that although it had not been obſerved to her before, ſhe had always called him her Fenelon. Mr. Watts and I are the beſt friends in the world. Should I not be happy when I conſider all theſe bleſſings, and that you love me?"

The portraits Conſtable had painted, of the Biſhop of Saliſbury and Mr. Watts, had given great ſatisfaction, and on the 30th of November his mother thus wrote to him: "Fortune ſeems now to place the ball at your foot, and I truſt you will not kick it from you. You now ſo greatly excel in portraits that I hope you will purſue a path the moſt likely to bring you fame and wealth, by which you can alone expect to obtain the object of your fondeſt wiſhes."

Portraiture, we are told, originated in love; and Conſtable's friends now hoped that love would make a portrait painter of him. Its immediate effects, however, ſeemed more likely to retard his advance, both in portrait and in landſcape; and Miſs Bicknell, who ſaw this with great grief, thus admoniſhed him. "By a ſedulous attention to your profeſſion, you will very much help to beſtow calm on my mind, which I ſhall look for in vain while I ſee with ſorrow how unſettled you appear, and conſequently, unfitted to attend to a ſtudy that requires the inceſſant application of the heart and head. You will allow others, without half your abilities, to outſtrip you in the race of fame, and then look back with ſorrow on time neglected and opportunities loſt, and perhaps blame me as the cauſe of all this woe. Exert yourſelf while it is yet in your power; the path of duty is alone the path of happineſs. Let us wait with quiet reſignation till a merciful Providence ſhall diſpoſe of us in the way that will be beſt. Believe me, I ſhall feel a more laſting pleaſure in knowing that you are improving your time, and exerting your talents for the enſuing exhibition, than I ſhould do while you were on a ſtolen march with me round the Park. Still I am not heroine enough to ſay, wiſh, or mean, that we ſhould never meet. I know that to be impoſſible. But, then, let us reſolve it ſhall be but ſeldom, not as inclination, but as prudence ſhall dictate. Farewell, deareſt John; may every bleſſing attend you, and in the intereſt I feel in your welfare, forgive the advice I have given you, who, I am ſure, are better qualified to admoniſh me. Reſolution is, I think, what we now ſtand moſt in need of, to refrain for a time, for our mutual good, from the ſociety of each other."

CHAPTER III.

1813—1814.

Conſtable's Pictures in the Exhibitions of 1813. *Exhibition at the Britiſh Gallery of the Works of Reynolds. Turner. J. Dunthorne, Jun. Willy Lott's Houſe. Sale of two of Conſtable's Pictures. His Pictures at the Academy*, 1814. *Excurſion in Eſſex. Picture of Boat-building. Conſtable's Diſpoſition to ſhun Society.*

1813.

TO Miſs Bicknell. 63, Charlotte Street, May 3rd, 1813. Mr. Weſt informs me, it is the opinion of the council, as well as his own, that I have made an advance upon myſelf this year. Since I had laſt the happineſs of ſeeing you, I have had ſo great a ſhare of ill health, that I have not been able to paint; but I hope the ſummer and a look at the country will revive me. I told you I was about to commence a portrait of Lady Lennard. I began it three weeks ago, and it promiſed to be like; but I was obliged to decline it, and this circumſtance has given me real concern, as I am anxious to maintain the friendſhip of this worthy family * * * * Shall I mention my profeſſion again? I am really conſidered to have been more ſucceſsful in it this laſt year; and is it unreaſonable to ſuppoſe, that if, under ſuch untoward circumſtances, I have exerted ſome energy, I might do much more if this load of deſpondency could be removed from me?"

The pictures mentioned in the foregoing letter, were called in the catalogue of the Academy, "Landſcape, Boys Fiſhing," and "Landſcape, Morning." In January he had exhibited at the Britiſh Gallery, one picture, with no title but "Landſcape."

In the ſummer of this year, the Directors of the Britiſh Inſtitution exhibited at their rooms the moſt ſplendid collection of pictures that were ever ſeen together, as the productions of one man; and the reputation of Reynolds, high as it was, was raiſed by this aſſemblage of his works. Through the kindneſs of Mr. Watts, Conſtable received a card for the dinner, given by the Directors, on this memorable occaſion; and the following is the account he gave of the day to Miſs Bicknell: "The company aſſembled at an early hour in the Gallery, from which there was a covered way to Willis's rooms. On the arrival of the Prince Regent, the Marquis of Stafford and the Governors of the Inſtitution haſtened to conduct him up ſtairs. His manner was agreeable, and I ſaw him ſhake hands with many of the company. Dinner was announced at ſeven, the Marquis of Stafford (the Preſident) in the chair, behind which, on a conſiderable elevation, was placed a ſtatue of Sir Joſhua Reynolds, by Flaxman. The Earl of Aberdeen made an excellent ſpeech; he ſaid, that 'although the ſtyle of Sir Joſhua Reynolds might differ in appearance from the ſtyle of thoſe ſpecimens of art, which are conſidered the neareſt to perfection in the ancient Greek ſculpture, and the productions of the great ſchools of Italy; yet his works were to be ranked with them, their aim being eſſentially the ſame—*the attainment of nature with ſimplicity and truth.*' The Regent left the table about ten, and returned to the Gallery, which was now filled with ladies. Among them I ſaw Mrs.

Siddons, whoſe picture is there as the 'Tragic Muſe.' Lord Byron was pointed out to me; his poetry is of the moſt melancholy kind, but he has great ability. Now, let me beg of you, to ſee theſe charming works frequently; and form, in your own mind, the idea of what painting ſhould be from them. It is certainly the fineſt feeling of art that ever exiſted."

"Spring Garden Terrace, June 9th. My dear John. Having only a few minutes to converſe on Friday, you know we did not ſay much. I will, therefore, try what I can do in a letter. Writing I diſlike exceſſively, but ſtill I have no other means of telling you what paſſes here, and I take it for granted you like to know. I think you ſeemed much better than when I ſaw you at the Academy. I was quite hurt then at your appearing ſo very far from well. The portrait you gave me looks pale, as you did then. That is the only fault I find with it. I was enchanted with Sir Joſhua Reynolds's pictures. I think it muſt have been a beautiful ſight to have ſeen them by candle light, and the rooms filled with company elegantly dreſſed. * * * I imagine next month you will like to quit London for Suffolk; as the ſtudy of nature will be more agreeable than the picture galleries. I will not forget to drink your health in a bumper on the 11th. Adieu, dear friend, why are we thus attached when every thing conſpires againſt us!"

"Palace, Sarum, June 14th, 1813. Dear Conſtable, I have heard your great picture ſpoken of here, by no inferior judge, as one of the beſt in the exhibition. It is a great thing for one man to ſay this. It is by units that popularity is gained. I only like one better, and that is a picture of pictures, the Froſt by Turner. But then you need not repine at this deciſion of mine; you are a great man, and like Buonaparte, are only to be beaten by a froſt. I deſpair of ever ſeeing you down here. What a reflection is it in this

Chap. III.
1813.

life, that whenever we have a pleaſant ſcene, there is little hope of repeating the view. How many delightful hours of pleaſantry have I paſſed in a ſociety that will never meet together again, except under the ſod. It is one argument for living while you can live. 'Dum vivimus vivamus.' The ſame argument will, by the bye, hold good of reading. Read a book while it lies before you: ten to one if you read it another time. I only know, the little knowledge I have, has been picked up by odds and ends. In a bookſeller's ſhop, late at night, at breakfaſt, or while waiting for a friend who was late at dinner. Pray, as you regard your intereſt, call on the Biſhop and his lady, as he may attribute your not calling to neglect, and not to humility. Every body does not know, as well as myſelf, that there is an exhibitioner and a painter for fame, who is poſſeſſed of modeſty and merit, and is too honeſt and high-minded to puſh himſelf by other means than his pencil and palette. Believe me, dear Conſtable, Yours very faithfully, John Fiſher."

"63, Charlotte Street, June 30th. When I laſt had the happineſs of ſeeing you, my deareſt Maria, I had fixed a day for going into Suffolk. I was, however, prevented by a call upon me for portraits; for I aſſure you, my reputation in that way is much on the increaſe. One of them, a portrait of the Rev. George Bridgman, a brother of Lord Bradford, far excels any of my former attempts in that way, and is doing me a great deal of ſervice. My price for a head is fifteen guineas; and I am tolerably expeditious when I can have fair play at my ſitter. I have been much engaged for Lady Heathcote, who ſeems bent on ſerving me. My pictures of herſelf and her mother, occupy either end of the large drawing-room in Groſvenor Square; they have magnificent frames, and make a great daſh. She is to bring me a handſome boy at the Chriſtmas holidays. She has a little dance on Friday, when my pictures will be ſeen for the firſt time publicly. I am now leaving London for the only time in my life with my pockets full of money. I am entirely free from debt, (not that my debts ever exceeded my usual annual income) and I have required no assistance from my father. I have arranged matters with Sir Thomas Lennard, and am to pass a month with him very late in the season; which I am delighted to find gives me possession of the three ensuing months to myself, and I hope to do a good deal in that time. I do assure you, my dearest Maria, I am not trying to give you the favourable side, only, of myself; but am merely mentioning facts as they have occurred to me within the last two or three months, during which time, we have unfortunately had so little communication with each other. But I trust the time is at hand, when the ground will be rendered more smooth for us. You may probably know that there has been some correspondence between Mr. Bicknell and myself. when I thought I was leaving town, I wrote to him, to request he would consent to an interview, or some sort of communication between us; he would agree to neither; yet I do not repent of what I have done, as I was happy at least, to have an opportunity of approaching him in a respectful manner. * * * I thank God daily for a thousand blessings which I enjoy; and I can lay my hand on my heart and say, 'I have a conscience void of offence.' I look forward to many happy years with you, but we might have been spared a world of pain. * * * I am quite delighted to find myself so well, although I paint so many hours; but my mind is happy when so engaged. * I dined with the Royal Academy last Monday in the Council room. It was entirely a meeting of artists, (none but the members and exhibitors could be admitted), and the day passed off very well. I sat next to Turner, and opposite Mr. West and Lawrence. I was a good deal entertained with Turner. I always expected to find him what I did. He has a wonderful range of mind.

CHAP. III. 1813.

* * I leave town with a much more comfortable feeling on your account, than I had laſt year. You looked ſo well, and ſeemed ſo happy; and to ſee you comfortable ought to make me happy under any circumſtances."

"Richmond, Auguſt 25th, 1813. Knowing, my deareſt John, that you are expecting a letter from me, I cannot delay any longer thanking you for your laſt letter, which I received the day before I left town; I wiſh I could diveſt myſelf of feeling ſo like a culprit when I write to you. It would be ſo much pleaſanter for you and for me; but I know I am breaking through rules preſcribed to me by thoſe I love, and making you uncomfortable by my ſombre reflections. I think of you equally if I write or do not write; ſo recollect in future, not to expect to hear from me, unleſs I have ſomething very particular to ſay."

1814.

"Spring Garden Terrace, February 18th, 1814. Your wiſh, my dear John, is totally impracticable—of correſponding weekly; but I will write as often as I can. Indeed, I was juſt going to tell you, that your laſt letter had given me much pleaſure; for it ſeemed written in better ſpirits than uſual. * * You have both ſurpriſed, deceived, and pleaſed me. How could you ſay there was no picture of yours at the Britiſh Gallery? I think the cats* exceſſively pretty, comical creatures. I am ſure you muſt have been entertained in painting them. The whole has a richneſs of colour that pleaſes me. You muſt forgive my criticiſing your pictures. * *

In a letter to Miſs Bicknell, dated February, 1814, the firſt mention of young Dunthorne, the ſon of Conſtable's early friend, occurs. Of this young man, to whom he was much attached, and who became an extremely uſeful

* Two martin cats, of which he exhibited a ſmall picture at the Britiſh Gallery.

aſſiſtant to him, he ſays: "I have written to Dunthorne to ſend me Johnny. He is not at all vulgar, and naturally very clever; but were he not, I ſhould love him for his father's ſake." To Dunthorne, Conſtable wrote: "I am rather diſappointed at not ſeeing Johnny here yet; but as the weather is now fine though cold, I wiſh you would let him come. I am deſirous of having him now, for I think he will be uſeful to ſtimulate me to work, by ſetting my palette, &c., which you know is a great help, and keeps me cheerful. I am anxious about the large picture, Willy Lott's Houſe, which looks uncommonly well in the maſſes and tone. I am determined to detail, but not retail it out. Tell Abram, Mr. Coxe* intends having my 'Windmill' engraved, and has put it into the hands of Mr. Landſeer for that purpoſe. It is a pretty ſubject, one of the Stoke Mills. I am determined to finiſh a ſmall picture on the ſpot, for every large one I intend to paint. This I have always talked about, but have never yet done."

The little Farm-houſe, which in the laſt letter is called "Willy Lott's Houſe," is ſituated on the edge of the river, cloſe to Flatford Mill. It is a principal object in many of Conſtable's pictures; but the moſt exact view of it occurs in the one engraved for the "Engliſh Landſcape," with the title of "A Mill Stream," and is taken from the front of the mill, the wheel of which occaſions the ripple ſeen on the ſurface of the water. Willy Lott, its poſſeſſor, was born in it; and it is ſaid, has paſſed more than eighty years without having ſpent four whole days away from it.

So little was Conſtable's art as yet appreciated, that the ſale of two of his pictures, this year, muſt be mentioned as an extraordinary event; a ſmall one exhibited at the Britiſh

* Peter Coxe, the brother of Archdeacon Coxe, and author of a poem called the "Social Day," for which the engraving was made.

CHAP. III.
1814.

Gallery to Mr. Allnutt, and a larger one of a "Lock" to Mr. James Carpenter. The laſt is mentioned in the following note to Mr. Watts:—"63, Charlotte Street, April 12th, 1814. My dear Uncle, I received your kind note this morning. Accept my beſt thanks for the excellent advice it contained, and which, I am well aware, I ſtand much in need of. I am willing to allow that I poſſeſs more than a uſual ſhare of the failings incident to the ſpecies; as an artiſt, I know I have many great deficiencies, and that I have not yet, in a ſingle inſtance, realized my ideas of art. Your kind ſolicitude reſpecting my picture of the Lock is highly gratifying to me; but it may now ceaſe, as the picture has become the property of Mr. Carpenter, who purchaſed it this morning. He is a ſtranger to me, and bought it becauſe he liked it. You ſay, truly, that my mind is not at eaſe. Perhaps there may be ſomething conſtitutional; but it is certainly much increaſed, ſince I have had the misfortune to involve the happineſs of the moſt amiable being on the face of the earth in my own fate. The excellent lady to whom I allude continues faithful to me in my adverſity; and that too amidſt a ſcene of perſecution and unkindneſs, which has continued many years; therefore I may yet be happy; and believe me, my dear uncle, the great kindneſs which you have always ſhewn me at your table, and elſewhere, as a friend and relation, has not a little contributed to ſupport my mind through much trouble, which I believe has been increaſed by an extraordinary ſuſceptibility of feeling."

The picture purchaſed by Mr. Allnutt led to an acquaintance between Conſtable and that gentleman, who has recently favoured me with the following account of its commencement.

"Dear Sir, Many years ago, I purchaſed at the Britiſh Inſtitution a painting by Mr. Conſtable. But as I did not quite like the effect of the ſky, I was fooliſh enough to have that obliterated, and a new one put in by another artiſt; which, though extremely beautiful, did not harmonize with the other parts of the picture. Some years after, I got a friend of Mr. Conſtable to aſk him, if he would be kind enough to reſtore the picture to its original ſtate, to which he readily aſſented. Having a very beautiful painting by Mr. (now Sir Auguſtus) Callcott, which was nearly of the ſame ſize, but not quite ſo high; I ſent it to Mr. Conſtable together with his own, and expreſſed a wiſh, that if he could do it without injury to the picture, he would reduce the ſize of it in height, by lowering the ſky, ſo as to make it nearer the ſize of Mr. Callcott's, to which I wiſhed it to hang as a companion. When I underſtood from him that it was ready for me, I called at his houſe to ſee it; and this was the firſt interview I ever had with him. He aſked me how I liked it; to which I replied, I was perfectly ſatisfied; and wiſhed to know what I was indebted to him for what he had done to it, in order that I might ſettle the account. He then ſaid, he had no charge to make, as he felt himſelf under an obligation to me, which he wiſhed to acknowledge, and was happy he had now an opportunity of doing ſo. I told him I was not aware of any obligation; and, therefore, wiſhed he would name a price. To which he replied, that I had been the means of making a painter of him, by buying the firſt picture he ever ſold to a ſtranger; which gave him ſo much encouragement, that he determined to purſue a profeſſion in which his friends had great doubts of his ſucceſs. He likewiſe added, that wiſhing to make the picture as acceptable to me as poſſible, he had, inſtead of reducing the height of the old picture, painted an entirely new one of the ſame ſubject, exactly of the ſize of the one by Callcott; and that if I was ſatisfied with the exchange (which of courſe I was), it gave him much pleaſure. I remain, dear Sir, yours very faithfully, John Allnutt. Clapham Common, February 2nd, 1843."

Chap. III. 1814.

The pictures Conſtable ſent to the Academy this ſeaſon were, " A Ploughing Scene in Suffolk," and a " Ferry."

From Miſs Bicknell. " Spring Garden Terrace. I deferred writing, my dear John, in hopes of being able to tell you where our ſummer quarters would be fixed; but it ſtill remains undecided. Only think of your not making one among the two hundred thouſand perſons, who I hear are come to town to ſee our illuſtrious viſiters;* I ſuppoſe you intend conſoling yourſelf with a view of their pictures * * * Indeed, my dear John, people cannot live now upon four hundred a year—it is a bad ſubject, therefore, adieu to it. I imagine it will not be very long before you are in town. I wonder if I ſhall ſee you. Alas! that it ſhould be a matter of doubt."

"To Miſs Bicknell. Eaſt Bergholt, July 3rd, 1814. I have been abſent from this place more than a fortnight, on a viſit to the Rev. Mr. Driffield, at Feering, near Kelvedon. He is a very old friend of my father's, and once lived in this pariſh. He has remembered me for a long time; as he ſays he chriſtened me one night, in great haſte, about eleven o'clock. Some time ago, I promiſed him a drawing of his houſe and church at Feering; and, during my viſit, he had occaſion to go to his living at South Church, and I was happy to embrace his propoſal, that I ſhould accompany him; by which I ſaw much more of the county of Eſſex than I had ever ſeen before, and the moſt beautiful part of it; as I was at Malden, Rochford, South End, Hadleigh, Danbury, &c. &c. At Hadleigh there is a ruin of a caſtle, which from its ſituation is vaſtly fine. It commands a view of the Kent hills, the Nore, and the North Foreland, looking many miles to ſea. I have filled, as uſual, a little book of haſty memoranda of the places which I ſaw. My companion,

* The Emperor Alexander, the King of Pruſſia, &c.

though more than ſeventy, is a moſt active, reſtleſs creature, and I never could get him to ſtop long at a place. He could outwalk and outrun me on any occaſion; but he was very kind and good-tempered. Indeed, my dear Maria, this little excurſion was ſo amuſing to me, that although I was never a moment without you in my thoughts, there were times when I was ſo delighted with the ſcenery, as to forget that my mind had been ſo long a ſtranger to happineſs. You tell me that you have an offer of going into Wales. Let me, my beloved child, entreat you to embrace it if you are able to leave your excellent mother, to whom I know you are always ready to devote yourſelf. I am confident that ſuch a tour would be a real bleſſing to you; the change of air, and then the ſublime ſcenery. I did hope that we might have viſited theſe delightful places together for the firſt time; but it will be happineſs enough for me to know that you are happy." * * *

"To Miſs Bicknell. Eaſt Bergholt, Sept. 18th, 1814. This charming ſeaſon, as you will gueſs, occupies me entirely in the fields; and I believe I have made ſome landſcapes that are better than uſual, at leaſt that is the opinion of all here. I do hope that nothing will happen to interrupt my preſent purſuits, but that I ſhall paſs the reſt of the autumn as I have done the ſummer; and I alſo hope on my return to London to have the great happineſs of ſeeing you much oftener than I have hitherto done. I believe we can do nothing worſe than indulge in uſeleſs ſenſibility, but I can hardly tell you what I feel at the ſight, from the window at which I am writing, of the fields in which we have ſo often walked. A calm autumnal ſetting ſun is glowing on the gardens of the rectory and on thoſe fields where ſome of the happieſt hours of my life have been paſſed."

Among the landſcapes mentioned in this letter, was one which I have heard him ſay he painted entirely in the open air. It was exhibited the following year at the Academy, with the title of "Boat-building." In the midſt of a meadow at Flatford, a barge is ſeen on the ſtocks, while juſt beyond it the river Stour glitters in the ſtill ſunſhine of a hot ſummer's day. This picture is a proof, that in landſcape, what painters call warm colours are not neceſſary to produce a warm effect. It has indeed no poſitive colour, and there is much of grey and green in it; but ſuch is its atmoſpheric truth, that the tremulous vibration of the heated air near the ground ſeems viſible. This perfect work remained in his poſſeſſion to the end of his life.

"To Miſs Bicknell. Eaſt Bergholt, Oct. 2nd, 1814. We have had a moſt delightful ſeaſon. It is many years ſince I have purſued my ſtudies ſo uninterruptedly and ſo calmly, or worked with ſo much ſteadineſs or confidence. I hope you will ſee me an artiſt ſome time or other."

Conſtable's cloſe application to his art while at Bergholt, had prevented his paying as much attention to ſome of his friends there, as it would appear he was expected to do, and after his return to town, his mother wrote to him. "I believe it is thought you avoid notice too much: this will damp the ardour of the beſt friendſhips. 'Tis true you have been delightfully buſy this ſummer, and ſo far ſo good."

"To Miſs Bicknell. Oct. 25th, 1814. * * * I am happy to hear of ſome improvement in your mother's health; I hope it may continue to advance. Though any notice or good wiſhes from me I know will be uſeleſs, yet I mention it for your ſake. * * * I have had a diſtreſſing letter from my friend John Fiſher on the death of his uncle, General Fiſher. Poor Fiſher was acting the part of a comforter when no comfort could be imparted. The diſtreſs of the General's daughter, Mrs. Conroy, and of his ſon-in-law, was beyond all belief. A fine manly ſoldier weeping like an infant; and Fiſher was obliged to tear her from the coffin when they were taking it away. He wiſhes me to undertake (as it might prove a means of confolation) a portrait of the General from a drawing. He was extremely like the good bifhop, mild, fenfible, and placid. I could give him little hope of making much of a picture, but fhall willingly try. * * * The ftudies I have made this fummer are better liked than any I have done; but I would rather have your opinion of them than that of all others put together. But fate is ftill favage. I lament every moment the want of your fociety, and feel the lofs of it in my mind and heart. *You* deferved a better fate."

"To Mifs Bicknell. 63, Charlotte-ftreet, Nov. 12th, 1814. You fay you fhall leave Brighton in a fortnight. Let me hope, then, you have received benefit from its good air and general appearance of cheerfulnefs. I never was at a bathing town, but I am told they are amufing. You will judge of my great ignorance of what is going on in the gay world, when I tell you, that till I read your letter yefterday, I did not know that any of the royal family had vifited Brighton this feafon. * * * I never fail to find unceafing delight in the art; but who are feeking for its honours I know not: it is fufficient for me to know that I am not, though I will allow that four or five years ago, when I was more youthful, I was a little on tiptoe for fame. I have hardly yet got reconciled to brick walls, and dirty ftreets, after leaving the endeared fcenes of Suffolk. At the fame moment that I received your letter I had one from my mother fo amufing that I long to fhow it to you. It is quite a journal of the time I was with them, though fhe regrets, at the end, that my natural propenfity to efcape from notice fhould have fo much increafed upon me."

"Brighton, Nov. 15th. 1814. You will be furprifed, my dear John, to hear from me again fo foon. Indeed I fear I fhall ruin you in poftage. But really you have written me fuch a ftrange letter, that I cannot forbear fending you my fentiments upon it, and I am delighted to find that I am

CHAP. III. 1814.

ſupported in them by Mrs. Conſtable. It appears ſtrange to me that a profeſſional man ſhould ſhun ſociety. Surely it cannot be the way to promote his intereſt. Why you ſhould no longer be anxious for fame is what I cannot comprehend. It is paying me a very ill compliment. If you wiſh to remain ſingle, it may do very well. We ſhall return to town next Tueſday. I truſt the following day, if it ſhould be tolerably fine, to have the pleaſure of ſeeing the *recluſe* in St. James's Park about twelve o'clock; if not, the following day at the ſame hour. You can then if you pleaſe make your defence, and promiſe to behave better for the future. I muſt have no more of this propenſity to eſcape from notice: I muſt have you known, and then to be admired will be the natural conſequence. I do not know how you will like my ſtrictures on your conduct, but I cannot help that. It is better you ſhould know my mind now than afterwards. It is not too late to quarrel. It is your turn next to accuſe me, and I am ſure I ſtand convicted of numberleſs errors."

"Dec. 12. When I took leave of you, my deareſt John, laſt Saturday, I fully thought I ſhould ſee you again before you left town; but alas! it is your fate as well as my own to be often diſappointed. It is, I am well convinced, for our mutual benefit that we ſhould not often ſee each other. It is this alone makes me ſupport the privation with tolerable good-humour. But *your* time, ſo infinitely valuable to me, I cannot have it loſt. The genius of painting will ſurely, one day or other, riſe up againſt me for too often keeping one of her favourite ſons from a ſtudy that demands his excluſive attention. * * * Mamma, I am happy to ſay, is much better."

CHAPTER IV.

1815—1816.

Conſtable permitted to viſit Miſs Bicknell. Death of his Mother. Death of Miſs Bicknell's Mother. G. Dawe. Exhibition, 1815. *Delicacy of Miſs Bicknell's Health. Lady Spencer. Conſtable's Studies at Bergholt. Illneſs of his Father. Dr. Rhudde. Exhibition,* 1816. *Death of Conſtable's Father. General and Mrs. Rebow. Pictures painted at Wivenhoe Park. The Rev. J. Fiſher. Conſtable's Marriage. Viſit to Oſmington. Dr. Rhudde's Legacy to Mrs. Conſtable.*

1815.

"EAST BERGHOLT. January 6th, 1815. My dear ſon John. I ſend you a mother's Chriſtmas gift, in the form of ſix new ſhirts. Four of them are hemp, and you ſaid you ſhould like to try them for working ſhirts. The other two are Sunday ones, with the collars cut to the pattern of your couſin * * * * 's. How you will like them I cannot tell. But I hope it will be the only imitation of him you will try; with the exception of the kind intentions of his heart, and his dutiful affection to his mother and ſiſters, which will ſpring up and ſhow themſelves through all the confuſion in his affairs. The magnitude of his debts really terrifies me. O, my dear John, pray keep out of debt, that earthly Tartarus! I return you the pocket book. It is very pretty, and much increafed in value for the donor's fake, who, I hope, will one time or other, be rewarded better than by a *poor* artift. You muft try hard for fame and gain. We have lived to fee the beginning of a new year. Who may be permitted to fee the clofe of it, God only knows. To thofe who do, may it prove a happy one, and to you amongft that number. Ann Conftable."

"Spring Garden Terrace, February 23rd. My deareft John, I have received, from papa, the fweet permiffion to fee you again under this roof, (to ufe his own words) 'as an occafional vifiter.' From being perfectly wretched, I am now comparatively happy. * * * M. E. Bicknell."

Mrs. Conftable, in a letter to her fon, dated, "Eaft Bergholt, March 7th," thus fpeaks of this unexpected gleam of funfhine on the profpect of the lovers. "It gives me pleafure to know you are a vifiter in a friendly way, in Spring Gardens. You muft make every allowance for Mr. Bicknell, who is, moft affuredly, not a free agent in this matter. He is under rigid reftrictions; from which, for the fake of his family, he muft not fwerve. As circumftances ftand, I efteem it a great point gained; and it is a comfort to my mind, which has long been a filent fufferer from the treatment you have met with, fo derogatory to your refpectability and honourable intentions."

Mrs. Conftable was not, however, deftined to fee her fon, and the object of his affections, more happy than they now were. She had lately fuffered much anxiety on account of her hufband's health, which was declining. And this, perhaps, haftened a paralytic attack, with which fhe was feized on the 9th of April, while gardening, a recurrence of which terminated her well-fpent life on the 8th of May. In her laft letter to her fon, fhe earneftly exhorted him to ufe his influence with a friend at Bergholt, whofe conduct had placed him at variance with his wife. "How can he bear," ſhe ſaid, "to worry her, as it were, into her grave. And as to the children, all their budding days of happineſs, their youthful prime, are blighted by their father's imprudence. Do, my dear John, try to perſuade him to the ways that make for peace: 'Bleſſed are the peace-makers; for theirs is the kingdom of God.' May this be your portion in the world to come, and health and happineſs in this. So prays your affectionate mother."

The death of this excellent woman was felt by her ſon as a very heavy blow. She had cheered and encouraged him in his profeſſion, and obtained for him introductions calculated to advance his proſpects, at a time when his other friends conſidered them hopeleſs. She, more than any one elſe, ſhared in all the anxieties ariſing out of his engagement with Miſs Bicknell, which ſhe hoped to ſee happily fulfilled; and ſhe neglected no means, however trifling, to propitiate Dr. Rhudde, as a ſingle inſtance will ſhow. Conſtable had ſent her a preſent of a large drawing in water colours of Bergholt Church,* which, in the letter ſhe wrote to acknowledge its receipt, ſhe deſcribed as "the moſt beautiful drawing ſhe had ever beheld." But it immediately occurred to her to preſent it to the Rector, which ſhe did in the name of her ſon. It was uſeleſs. Dr. Rhudde acknowledged the preſent in a polite letter; but, unwilling to remain the obliged perſon, he encloſed a bank note, requeſting Conſtable to purchaſe with it, ſomething to remember him by, "when he ſhould be no more." The death of Miſs Bicknell's mother, who had long been ill, occurred not many days after that of Mrs. Conſtable.

"To Miſs Bicknell. Eaſt Bergholt, May 21ſt, 1815. My deareſt love, When I left town it was not my intention

* This drawing now belongs to his eldeſt ſiſter, Miſs Ann Conſtable.

Chap. IV. 1815.

to have remained ſo long abſent. I received your kind note, and regretted you were ſo ſituated that you could not ſee me. I called, however, the day before I came here; and, although, your note had ſomewhat prepared me for the afflicting intelligence which I received at your door, I could not but be ſhocked, as I was not aware that your dear mother was ſo near her removal. It is ſingular that we ſhould, both of us, have loſt our neareſt friends, the neareſt we can have in this world, within ſo ſhort a time; and now, more than ever, do I feel the want of your ſociety."

"To Miſs Bicknell. 63, Charlotte Street, June 16th. I have ſeen Spilſbury again; he ſtill urges me to make him a viſit at his cottage, near Tintern Abbey. I ought to ſee another country, and this is a charming one. I am half inclined to go, but I need not decide for a week or ten days. I pine after dear Suffolk; but is not this indolence? My heart, as you know too well, is not there. At leaſt, not all of it. But you ſay, you would not give a farthing for a divided heart; however, make yourſelf eaſy, you have by far the greateſt part; but what vanity is this!"

"June 17th. I have given up all thoughts of Wales, and I now only wonder that I indulged in them. I have ſold myſelf for the work I am engaged in, which is a large landſcape in the background of a picture at Mr. Dawe's.* It occupies me at leaſt twelve, and ſometimes fourteen hours a day. This I do by choice, as well as by agreement, that I may the ſooner get back to dear Bergholt, and find a day to ſee you before I go."

"June 28th. I find there is no end to my labours for Dawe. Therefore, with even a loſs to myſelf, ſhould it be ſo, I am determined to relinquiſh them. He is very anxious

* The portrait of Miſs O'Neil, in the character of Juliet, now in the poſſeſſion of the Garrick Club.

to engage me in other works; and he would even take a promiſe from me for a twelvemonth to come. We are full of anxiety about our relations who were in the late dreadful battle; † we can get no account of them whatever." "June 30th. I have done at Mr. Dawe's, and have given *him* great ſatisfaction; but I have perſiſted in making him no more promiſes; he is an overmatch for me."

Conſtable, this year, exhibited at the Academy eight works, and among them, the exquiſite one I have mentioned, called "Boat building:" the others were, "A View of Dedham," "A Village in Suffolk," "A Landſcape," "A Sketch," and three drawings. At the Britiſh Gallery, he exhibited one picture, called "Landſcape."

"To Miſs Bicknell. Eaſt Bergholt, July 13th. * * * I think I never ſaw dear old Bergholt look half ſo beautiful as now, the weather has been ſo delightful. There is no village news, except that they are all very gay, and the youngeſt man among them is Dr. Rhudde. * * *"

"To Mr. John Conſtable. * * * I was much pleaſed with your letter. You appear calm, reſigned, affectionate, and happy. It communicated the ſame feelings to me. * I am very glad you have had a converſation with papa. In the winter it will be well to renew it. Of the doctor, I can ſay nothing; but, that I believe, it will be wiſeſt to leave him to himſelf. How delightful this ſweet rain will make thoſe dear fields look, that I envy you the view of. I ſhould like to tranſport myſelf there once a week: am I not very moderate? How much you muſt enjoy painting in the open air, after Mr. Dawe's room."

"Eaſt Bergholt, Auguſt 27th. * * * I have, my deareſt

† Of Waterloo; at which were preſent two of Conſtable's couſins, Captain Gubbins, who was killed; and Lieutenant Allen. The mothers of theſe officers and Mrs. Conſtable were ſiſters.

Chap. IV.
1815.

love, little to tell you of what is paſſing here. I live almoſt wholly in the fields, and ſee nobody but the harveſt men. The weather has been uncommonly fine; though we have had ſome very high winds that have diſcompoſed the foliage a great deal. We are all well; my father takes his rides as uſual, and is pretty well, but we think he gradually grows weaker. This, however, we cannot but expect; but his preſent appearance is a ſtriking proof of the bleſſings attending the old age of a virtuous life.† * * * I received a newſpaper containing an account of Mr. Stothard's pictures from Lord Byron's works, &c.—am I not obliged to you for it? It muſt have been directed by your hand."

"Putney Heath, Auguſt 29th. * * * * It *was* I who ſent the newſpaper; juſt to ſhew you that I *ſometimes* think of you, and in expectation of hearing from you, ſo it anſwered my plan exactly."

"Putney Heath, September 9th. I cannot reſiſt, my dear John, taking up my pen again, fearing you ſhould have deemed my laſt letter unworthy of notice; and I may, perhaps, be abſent a week after the 16th; and then, I hope, you would have thought my ſilence long. How charmed you muſt be with this long continuance of fine weather. I ſhould ſuppoſe for many ſeaſons, you have not painted ſo much in the open air. Nature and you muſt be greater friends than ever. I am ſuffering a little, to-day, from being out late yeſterday. Is it not a ſad thing to be ſo delicate? I muſt not be out after ſunſet. It is eaſy enough to avoid it, ſo that trouble is ſoon got over. The moon ſhall tempt me no more. * * * I regret you have not ſeen Mrs. * * * *, ſhe is much intereſted in our future welfare. Fortune, I am ſure, delights to torment us. But hold, my pen! I do not think I am ever long dejected. Tell me what you have been

† Golding Conſtable was then in his 77th year.

reading. But I ſuppoſe you have not found much time for it. I am ſtudying French, quite hard, and I find it very amuſing * * * My dear John, good bye, you will allow this to be, for me, quite a long letter! Will the end of October oblige you to return to London? Though I long to ſee you, I am always ſorry when you leave Suffolk. It muſt be ſo pleaſant for you to be there. I ſhould never like to leave the country while a ſingle leaf remained on the trees."

"Eaſt Bergholt, September 14th. * * * I am concerned to find by your letter that you are ſtill ſo delicate, and that you are ſo liable to be hurt by any little unuſual exertion. Pray take care of yourſelf. I am happy to hear that your father is ſo friendly and kind to you. I ſhall always venerate him for his goodneſs to you, who are all the world to me. I am ſure you will believe me, my dear Maria, when I ſay, that I allow no bad diſpoſition, nor any wrong feeling to remain in my heart, towards any one, for both our ſakes. For ſhould it be, as I truſt it is, God's good pleaſure that we ſhould paſs our lives together; it will be but ſenſible conduct, as well as a religious duty, to have as little to diſturb our peace as poſſible; for, as life advances, our trials will increaſe, and at the end all our ill conduct muſt be accounted for. I have, as you gueſs, been much out of doors."

"To Miſs Bicknell, October 1ſt. I cannot help regretting the departure of our delightful ſummer; but I continue to work as much as poſſible in the fields, as my mind is never ſo calm and comfortable as at thoſe times. * * * This morning we had the ſacrament at our church, and I am happy to ſay my father was able to join us. * * * You do not mention when you leave Putney Heath. Should I be likely to ſtop here a few weeks longer, I ſhall come to town for a day or two, for I am anxious to ſee you. * * * "

CHAP. IV.
1815.

Conſtable remained at Bergholt until the beginning of November. In a letter to Miſs Bicknell, dated the 1ſt of that month, he ſays, "My aunt Allen's ſecond ſon is lately made a poſt-captain; and our couſin, Colonel Gubbins,* is preferred (Mr. Watts writes me word) above fifty other field officers to command the light companies of the army in Paris; and when, added to theſe good things, your papa introduces me to the Prince Regent,†—who cannot do otherwiſe than give me a bit of red or blue riband for my very excellent landſcapes, you may juſtly be proud of the family you are to be connected with."

"Putney Heath, October 2nd. I muſt praiſe you, my dear John, for writing on the day I named. I ſhould have been very ſorry had you not. Is it not delightful that we can depend upon each other? I muſt tell you what a pleaſant ride I had yeſterday, through Wimbledon Park, to ſee Lady Spencer, (very grand, is it not?) who had politely deſired papa to bring his daughter. She appeared to be a very pleaſant woman, but had ſhe not, a title is too apt to make us think ſo. Does it not ſeem ſtrange?—a charming houſe and park, and ſhe ſays, ſhe 'would not give two-pence for it.' Such is the world! what we have we do not value, and what we have not we want. * * * Theſe are charming days for walking, but ſurely too cold and damp for painting."

"Eaſt Bergholt, October 19th. * * * I have been every day intending to write to you, but I have been ſo much out, endeavouring to catch the laſt of this beautiful year, that I have neglected almoſt every other duty. I have put rather a larger landſcape on hand than I ever did before. And this,

* The brother of Captain Gubbins who was killed at Waterloo. Colonel Gubbins had juſt returned from America, where he had been preſent at the attack on New Orleans.

† Mr. Bicknell was Solicitor to the Prince.

it is my wiſh to ſecure in a great meaſure before I leave this place; as I here find many aids, and I am ſure that if I go to London to ſtay, firſt, I ſhall meet with many trifling jobs to interrupt me, which I ſhall do with pleaſure when I have my own pictures under command. You ſhall hear from me again in a day or two."

After a ſhort viſit to London, Conſtable again wrote from Bergholt on the 15th of November. "I have received your kind and affectionate note, and your lovely preſent, which I cannot enough prize. It is the firſt thing of the kind I ever poſſeſſed. It is my intention to continue here till I feel that I have ſecured ſuch a picture as I intend for the exhibition. Here every thing is calm, comfortable, and good; and I am at a diſtance from you, which effectually removes the anxious deſire I always feel, when you are in London, to meet you, perhaps too often for each other's comfort, till we can meet for once, and I truſt, for good. * * * My kindeſt regards to all about you, and, believe me, ever dear Maria, unalterably yours."

"Spring Garden Terrace, December 28th. I dare ſay, my dear John, you are expecting to hear from me, and I am expecting to hear from you; as your laſt letter led me to ſuppoſe, you would write again in a day or two. But it is painting that takes up all your time and attention. How I do diſlike pictures; I cannot bear the ſight of them; but I am very croſs, am I not? You may ſpare yourſelf telling me I am very unreaſonable, for I know it already. But I cannot be reconciled to your ſpending month after month in the country. You ſay you have no expectation of remaining in London for ſome time. At all events it is pleaſant intelligence. But I feel how very often the viſits here are diſtreſſing. I believe you are right to remain where you are; in a comfortable home, and rendering the declining years of your father happy. Whatever attention you can ſhow him, muſt make your hours paſs the more agreeably. Whenever

Chap. IV. 1815.

I wifh you away, I know I do wrong. I wifh we could always like what is right. Henceforth I will endeavour. * * * Accept, my deareft John, the good wifhes of the feafon; not only you, but all your family, and believe me, affectionately yours, M. E. B.—P.S. I am in very good humour now, fo that I fhall be happy to hear your pictures pleafe you. Is Bergholt gay this Chriftmas? Do you not think if I were to write feldom, and fill the paper, it would be better? I certainly will in future."

"Eaft Bergholt, December 31ft. Believe me, my deareft Maria, I have been for fome time paft moft anxious to write to you. I have even written more than one letter, without being able to prevail on myfelf to fend them. This houfe has been the fcene of great anxiety and alarm, owing to the very dangerous ftate of my dear father's health. But, thank God, for the laft two or three days he has revived; and, although in a very weak and low ftate, he feems to be free from immediate danger. As you may fuppofe, I have not been painting much, nor am I likely to return to London for the prefent, at leaft, not to remain. Dr. Rhudde has been very kind in his inquiries after my father, and has fent him word that he will call upon him at the fhorteft notice."

1816.

"Eaft Bergholt, January 7th, 1816. It is impoffible to contemplate, without fatisfaction, the frame of mind my father has been in, all through his illnefs. His pious refignation, in what appeared the hour of death; his calmnefs, and his thankfulnefs for all the bleffings he has enjoyed; will, I hope, be always before me, and prove a guide to my future life. His pillow is light to him, and he is fo kind, as to confider the having all his children about him, as not among the leaft of his bleffings. I have got to work again with alertnefs, and am, I hope, advancing. I have no intention of coming to London to ftay; but I hope, if my father continues as well as he now is, to be there, for a few days, foon.

I have a letter of thanks, from Mr. Watts, for a moſt beautiful brace of pheaſants, which I wiſh it had been in my power to have given to you. But from theſe little courteſies, dear to a heart that is not bad, I am cut off."

"To Mr. John Conſtable. Though I have not written to you, my deareſt John, I have thought continually of you. When you laſt wrote, the idea of danger ſeemed paſt, and, I rejoice that it pleaſes God ſtill to bleſs you with a father. May the impreſſion it has made on you never wear off; it ſhall be a leſſon to me. Of this I am confident, that thoſe who really love and fear God, are the only wiſe people. Remember me kindly to your ſiſters. M. E. Bicknell."

"Eaſt Bergholt, January 14th. * * * My dear father continues charmingly, all things conſidered, and this imparts cheerfulneſs to the whole houſe. * * He will drink your health in a bumper with me to-morrow.† * * * * "

"Miſs Bicknell's next letter alludes to a viſit paid by her father to Dr. Rhudde. "January 18th. * * * I do not think I have been quite ſo comfortable lately, as I ought to be. I had moſt fooliſhly, moſt romantically, I own, flattered myſelf that the late viſit to the Rectory would have produced ſome good for us; but the ſtate of our affairs ſeems as bad as ever; with, to me, the addition of your ſpending the winter in the country. Though, remember, in your father's preſent ſtate of health, I would not for the world, you ſhould be any where elſe. In the ſummer it is a thing of courſe, and we have been uſed to it, and know it muſt be; but in the winter and ſpring months we have always been together. * * * We certainly have not too many enjoyments. * * * I am afraid you will be ſaid to be very unſociable by the Bergholt belles and beaux, if you refuſe being at any of their card parties."

† Her birth-day.

Soon after receiving this letter, Conſtable ſpent a few days in town, and returned to Bergholt, from whence he wrote to Miſs Bicknell on the "25th January * * * On my arrival here, I found my dear father ſadly. There is certainly a great alteration in him ſince I left home. I fear his time is now ſhort indeed. I am glad I went to London; and do let me entreat you to be calm, and let nothing that can be ſaid vex you. * * * I love you entirely, and nothing, ſave death, can prevent our being happy together. We can never be rich; but we can have what riches cannot purchaſe, and what enemies cannot deprive us of. Dr. Rhudde and Mrs. * * * * * * * are entirely inveterate againſt me. But don't let that vex you. The one never ſaw me, and the other has had no opportunity of knowing me. But time will ſet all to rights."

The permiſſion Mr. Bicknell had given Conſtable to pay occaſional viſits at his houſe, had been kept a ſecret from Dr. Rhudde. But an accident now diſcovered it to him; and Miſs Bicknell wrote to Conſtable. "February 7th, * * * The doctor has juſt ſent *ſuch* a letter, that I tremble with having heard only a part of it read. Poor dear papa, to have ſuch a letter written to him! he has a great ſhare of feeling and it has ſadly hurt him. * * * I know not how it will end. Perhaps the ſtorm may blow over; God only knows. We muſt be patient. I am ſure your heart is too good not to feel for my father. He would wiſh to make us all happy if he could. Pray do not come to town juſt yet. I hope by the end of the month peace will be reſtored." Conſtable replied: "I am truly ſorry any thing ſhould have happened to cauſe us any concern from that quarter. But my ſiſters truſt the calm will not long be diſturbed; though I have always feared it was a deceitful one, and that we have been making ourſelves happy over a barrel of gunpowder. But, my love, let me hear from you, and tell me whether I may ſee you when I return to London. All this nonſenſe has been kept from my father, or it muſt have vexed him."

"February 13th. I would rather, my dear John, write too ſoon, than that you ſhould wonder why you do not hear from me; but you have already ſo much to diſtreſs you, that I hardly know if I ſhould tell you, what I fear, will only do ſo more. The kind doctor ſays, he 'conſiders me no longer as his grandaughter,' and from the knowledge I have of his character, I infer he means what he ſays. I have not ſeen his letters. Papa ſays, if we were to marry, and live at Bergholt, he thinks the doctor would leave the place."

"To Miſs Bicknell, February 18th. I truſt, my deareſt love, you have allowed yourſelf to be made as little unhappy as poſſible, by what has been lately paſſing in your houſe. You have always been ſo kind as to believe that my affection for you was never alloyed by worldly motives. I, now, more than ever repeat it: and I aſſure you, that nothing can be done, by any part of your family, that ſhall ever make any alteration in me towards you. I ſhall not concern myſelf with the juſtice or injuſtice of others; that muſt reſt with themſelves; it is ſufficient for us to know that we have done nothing to deſerve the ill opinion of any one. Our buſineſs is now more than ever with ourſelves. I am entirely free from debt, and, I truſt, could I be made happy, to receive a good deal more than I do now by my profeſſion. After this, my deareſt Maria, I have nothing more to ſay, than the ſooner we are married the better; and from this time, I ſhall ceaſe to liſten to any arguments the other way, from any quarter. I wiſh your father to know what I have written if you think with me."

"February 25th. I was expecting to hear from you, my deareſt Maria, all laſt week. I wrote you a long letter laſt Sunday; and I am very anxious to hear from you again, as I fear you are unwell. Do give me a line by return of poſt,

CHAP. IV.
1816.

otherwise it is probable I may come to London on Wednesday. My dear father is no better, but the contrary. His dropsy certainly increases, and Mr. Travis says it is out of his power to help him. Mrs. Whalley is here, who cheers our fireside a good deal. Her mildness and serenity always make her a most welcome guest every where. Do pray write to me. I am restless to see you; yet my poor father is in such a sad state, that every week we look for the change. But tell me that you are well, and I shall be easy."

"Spring Garden Terrace, February 26th. My dearest John, I received your letter at Greenwich. * * * Greenwich, I am told, is a damp, unhealthy place, and I am sorry I went, for it has delayed, a few days, my writing to you. I walked out, foolishly, on a very damp day, and have got a cold. I have had a blister, and shall now be well in a few days; I have only to keep quiet. I will write to you again in a day or two. There is not, my dearest John, the least cause for you to be uneasy. I fully intended writing to-day, and only mention this cold to make my excuse for seeming neglect. We are all perfectly quiet here, and it would be a great pity for you to leave your poor father. Perhaps you might regret it. It must be a pleasure to him to have you with him. Your affection is a source of the greatest happiness to me; but may I entreat that you will not wish to hear very frequently from me. It only makes you uncomfortable if I do not write on the day you imagine I will. Papa says, if we remain as we are, he has no expectation that the doctor will alter his will. Let us then wait any time, rather than you should experience the misery of being much in debt, added to having a very delicate wife. * * * I am glad you have the addition of Mrs. Whalley to your society."

Towards the end of March, Constable arrived in town with two pictures for the Academy, one of which is called in the catalogue, "A Wheat Field," and the other, "A

Wood, Autumn." The latter was purchafed by Mr. Watts.

He was recalled to Bergholt by the death of his father, which in a letter to Mifs Bicknell he thus defcribes: "My dear father died while fitting in his chair as ufual, without a figh or pang, and without the fmalleft alteration of his pofition or features, except a gentle inclination of his head forwards; and my fifter Ann, who was near him, had to put her face clofe to his to affure herfelf that he breathed no more. Thus it has pleafed God to take this good man to Himfelf, the rectitude of whofe life had difarmed the grave of its terrors, and it pleafed God alfo to fpare him the pangs of death. May 19th, 1816."

"Eaft Bergholt, July 17th. My deareft love, You would certainly have heard from me before, had I left London on the day I mentioned, but I could not get away before Tuefday. I found all my friends here quite well, and we make a large family party; nine with Mrs. Whalley's two children, and your portrait (which gives great pleafure here, as an additional proof of your kindnefs to me. * * * We are all very happy among ourfelves; but fo ufed have I been, on entering thefe doors, to be received with the affectionate fhake of the hand of my father, and the endearing falute of my mother, that I often find myfelf overcome by a fadnefs I cannot reftrain. * * * I am fitting before your portrait; which when I look off the paper, is fo extremely like, that I can hardly help going up to it. I never before knew the real pleafure a portrait can afford."

"Putney Heath, Auguft 15th. * * * How well you knew what I fhould like, when you fent me the delightful letters of Geffner. My only regret is, that I have finifhed them fo foon. I fhall fend to the library for the reft of his works. My dear John, you know the moments were too fhort and too precious for me to write a note when you took the box; but I expected you would make a very pretty fpeech

Chap. IV.
1816.

for me when you gave it to your ſiſter. I am very glad ſhe was pleaſed with it. I had great pleaſure in doing it for her. Thank you, my dear John, for ſending me your ſweet picture. Come early this evening."

When Conſtable, on one of his viſits to Spring Garden Terrace, placed himſelf beſide Miſs Bicknell, and took the hand, which was ſoon to be given to him for life, her father ſaid, "Sir, if you were the moſt approved of lovers, you could not take a greater liberty with my daughter."—"And don't you know, Sir," he replied, "that I am the moſt approved of lovers?"—She had been treated, for five years, as if ſhe were a boarding-ſchool girl in danger of falling a prey to a fortune-hunter. But ſhe had now arrived at the age of twenty-nine; a time of life at which, patient as ſhe was, ſhe felt entitled to determine for herſelf, a matter which ſo entirely affected her own happineſs. A journey into Wales, under the care of an uncle, was propoſed to her; and in alluſion to this, ſhe ſays, in a letter to Conſtable, dated July 30th, "I am not to go unleſs I get ſtronger than I am at preſent, and then it will do me much good, the change of air and ſcene. My uncle intends to take plenty of time for the journey, that it may not be fatiguing. I think, therefore, you may ſafely truſt to my diſcretion, and then my dear John ſhall find me ready, if it is his decided wiſh, for another and far pleaſanter journey."

"Putney Heath, Auguſt 20th * * * I do not like, dear John, that you ſhould have to borrow money; and I think you ſaid it would be ſome time before you came into poſſeſſion of your own. I only ſuggeſt this for our conſideration, but, alas! I know too well that you have thought of it with ſorrow. Let me know what you think, for it makes me perfectly uncomfortable. I am glad to be going from home for a ſhort time."

"Eaſt Bergholt, Auguſt 21ſt. My deareſt love, I returned from my very pleaſant viſit at General Rebow's on Monday. * * * The General and Mrs. Rebow are determined to be of ſome ſervice to me. I am going there again, and ſhall ſtay a week, in all probability. Do be ſo kind as to let me hear from you before you go to Mr. Lambert's. I am to paint two ſmall landſcapes for the General; one in the park, of the houſe, and a beautiful wood and piece of water; and another, a wood, with a little fiſhing houſe, where the young lady (who is the heroine of all theſe ſcenes) goes occaſionally to angle. They wiſh me to take my own time about them; but the General will pay me for them when I pleaſe, as he tells me he underſtands, from Mr. Driffield, that *we* may ſoon want a little ready money. They are both well acquainted with our hiſtory, and hope to ſee us there together. I am next year to paint another picture of the little girl with her donkey, for their houſe in town. This, my love, is juſt ſuch a commiſſion as will be of real ſervice to me. I am getting on as well as I can wiſh with my own pictures; but theſe little things will rather interrupt them, and, I am afraid, will detain me here a week or two longer than I could have wiſhed."

"Putney Heath, Auguſt 23rd. I thank you, dear John, for yours, this moment received. How very happy the account of your viſit makes me; you ſeem ſo truly comfortable there. I am delighted that you return on Monday, and that the views you are to paint are ſo pretty. * * * My Uncle ſet off laſt night by the mail. The weather has ſo much improved, that I have been ſilly enough to regret (only for a moment) that I did not go. But then, poor dear papa! I ought *ſometimes* to comply with his wiſhes with pleaſure."

"Wivenhoe Park, Auguſt 30th. My deareſt love, I have been here ſince Monday, and am as happy as I can be, away from you. Nothing can exceed the kindneſs of the General and his lady. They often talk of you, becauſe they know it will pleaſe me, and I am ſure they will ſhow you the ſame attentions they ſhow me. I feel comfortable with them, becauſe I know them to be ſincere people; and though of family, and in the higheſt degree refined, they are not at all people of the world, in the common acceptation of the word. I am going on very well with my pictures for them. The park is the moſt forward. The great difficulty has been to get ſo much in it as they wanted. On my left is a grotto with ſome elms, at the head of a piece of water; in the centre is the houſe over a beautiful wood; and very far to the right is a deer houſe, which it was neceſſary to add; ſo that my view comprehended too large a ſpace. But to-day I have got over the difficulty, and begin to like it myſelf. I think I ſhall make a large picture from what I am now about. When do you return? If I ſhould be delayed longer in the country than I at firſt expected, I ſhall run up for a day, to ſee you. I ſhall write to John Fiſher ſoon."

"Wivenhoe Park, September 7th. My deareſt love, I haſten to ſend you the encloſed letter from our friend Fiſher. I can only ſay, that I am ready to adopt any plan that may meet your feelings on this occaſion, and I repeat Fiſher's words, that, 'I ſhall be happy and ready to marry you,' at the time he mentions. I am adviſed by my good friends here, to try one more effort with the doctor; but I ſhall do entirely in this as you direct."

The following is the letter encloſed. "Oſmington, near Dorcheſter, Auguſt 27th, 1816. My dear Conſtable, I am not a great letter writer, and when I take pen in hand, I generally come to the point at once. I, therefore, write to tell you, that I intend to be in London on Tueſday evening, the 24th, and on Wedneſday, ſhall hold myſelf ready and happy to marry you. There, you ſee, I have uſed no round-about phraſes; but ſaid the thing at once, in good plain Engliſh. So, do you follow my example, and get you to your lady, and inftead of blundering out long fentences about 'the Hymeneal altar,' &c., fay that on Wednefday, September 25th, you are ready to marry her. If fhe replies, like a fenfible woman, as I fufpect fhe is, 'Well, John, here is my hand, I am ready,'—all well and good. If fhe fays, 'Yes, but another day will be more convenient,' let her name it, and I am at her fervice. And now, my dear fellow, I have another point to fettle. And that I may gain it, I fhall put it in the fhape of a requeft. It is, that if you find, upon your marriage, your purfe is ftrong enough to make a bit of a détour, I fhall reckon it a great pleafure, if you and your bride will come and ftay fome time with my wife and me. That lady joins with me in my requeft. The country here is wonderfully wild and fublime, and well worth a painter's vifit. My houfe commands a fingularly beautiful view, and you may ftudy from your very window. You fhall have a plate fet by the fide of your eafel, without your fitting down to dinner. We never fee company, and I have brufhes, paints, and canvafs in abundance. Of an evening, we will fit over our autumnal firefide, read a fenfible book, perhaps a fermon, and after prayers, get us to bed, at peace with ourfelves and all the world. Since I have been quiet down here, out of the way of the turmoil and buftle of * * * * * * * *'s great dinners, I have taken much to my eafel, and have improved much. Your vifit will be of wonderful advantage to me. Tell your lady, that I long to be better acquainted with her, as does Mrs. Fifher; and I beg her to ufe her influence with you to bring you to fee,—yours, with fincerity, John Fifher."

On the 15th September, Conftable wrote to Mifs Bicknell: "What can I do about writing to your father? will it be time enough if I call on him when I come to town? You muft be my adviser." She replied: "Papa is averfe to every thing I propofe. If you pleafe, you may write to

Chap. IV.
1816.

him; it will do neither good nor harm. I hope we are not going to do a very foolish thing. * * * Once more, and for the last time! it is not too late to follow papa's advice and *wait*. * * * Notwithstanding all I have been writing, whatever you deem best, I do. This enchanting weather gives one spirits."

They were married on the 2nd of October, 1816, at St. Martin's Church, by Mr. Fisher, whose invitation to Osmington they accepted. Mr. Fisher had himself been married but three months.

Mr. Bicknell did not long withhold his forgiveness from his daughter, and now that he allowed himself opportunities of knowing Constable, he became extremely fond of him. In one of Miss Bicknell's letters which has not been quoted, she said, "It grieves me that papa and you cannot be better acquainted, but the loss is mutual." Dr. Rhudde was not so soon reconciled to the marriage, but at his death, which occurred in 1819, he left his granddaughter a legacy she probably little expected of 4000*l*.

CHAPTER V.

1817—1821.

Houſekeeping. Birth of a Son. Exhibitions 1817, 18, *and* 19. *Birth of a Daughter. Conſtable elected an Aſſociate of the Royal Academy. Sale of his large pictures "The White Horſe" and "Stratford Mill" to Archdeacon Fiſher. Exhibition* 1820. *Matthews' "Diary of an Invalid." Stothard's Canterbury Pilgrims. White's "Selborne." Exhibition* 1821. *Excurſion in Berkſhire and to Oxford. Studies at Hampſtead. Criticiſms on the "Stratford Mill." Conſtable's remarks on Skies.*

LTHOUGH my acquaintance with Conſtable began about this time, I have little to tell of the next two years of his life but that which the catalogues of the Exhibitions furniſh. I remember him in 1817, living in a ſmall houſe, No. 1, Keppel Street, Ruſſell Square; and that his firſt child, a fine boy, to whom his own name had been given, might be ſeen almoſt as often in his arms as in thoſe of his nurſe, or even his mother. His fondneſs for children exceeded, indeed, that of any man I ever knew.

1817.

In this year he exhibited at the Britiſh Gallery, "A Harveſt-field with Reapers and Gleaners," and at the Academy, "Wivenhoe Park," "A Cottage," a portrait of Mr. Fiſher, and "A Scene on a navigable River;" and in the autumn he paid a viſit to Bergholt, as the dates of ſome of his ſketches ſhow.

In 1818, he ſent to the Academy, "Landſcape, breaking up of a Shower," three other landſcapes, "A Gothic Porch," and "A Group of Elms;" the two laſt being drawings in lead pencil; and to the Britiſh Gallery he ſent, "A Cottage in a Corn-field," probably exhibited at the Academy the year before. The cottage in this little picture is cloſely ſurrounded by the corn, which on the ſide moſt ſhaded from the ſun, remains green, while over the reſt of the field it has ripened; one of many circumſtances that may be diſcovered in Conſtable's landſcapes, which mark them as the productions of an inceſſant obſerver of nature. But theſe and other latent beauties paſſed wholly unnoticed in the Exhibitions; indeed, the pictures that contained them were for the moſt part unheeded, while more ſhowy works by artiſts whoſe very names are now nearly forgotten, were the favourites of the day.

Conſtable's art was never more perfect, perhaps never ſo perfect, as at this period of his life. I remember being greatly ſtruck by a ſmall picture, a view from Hampſtead Heath, which I firſt ſaw at *Ruyſdael Houſe*, as Mr. Fiſher called his reſidence in Keppel Street. I have before noticed that what are commonly called warm colours are not neceſſary to produce the impreſſion of warmth in landſcape; and this picture affords, to me, the ſtrongeſt poſſible proof of the truth of this.* The ſky is of the blue of an Engliſh ſummer day, with large, but not threatening, clouds of a ſilvery

* It is, perhaps, unneceſſary to remark that we aſſociate the idea of warmth with red, orange, and yellow, becauſe they are the colours of fire; and that, in a ſummer landſcape, they can only have place in very ſmall proportions, excepting at the riſing and the ſetting of the ſun, the cooleſt hours of the day.

whitenefs. The diftance is of a deep blue, and the near trees and grafs of the frefheft green; for Conftable could never confent to parch up the verdure of nature to obtain warmth. Thefe tints are balanced by a very little warm colour on a road and gravel pit in the foreground, a fingle houfe in the middle diftance, and the fcarlet jacket of a labourer. Yet I know no picture in which the mid-day heat of Midfummer is fo admirably expreffed; and were not the eye refrefhed by the fhade thrown over a great part of the foreground by fome young trees, that border the road, and the cool blue of water near it, one would wifh, in looking at it, for a parafol, as Fufeli wifhed for an umbrella when ftanding before one of Conftable's fhowers. I am writing of this picture, which appears to have been wholly painted in the open air, after an acquaintance with it of five-and-twenty years; and, on referring to it again and again, I feel my firft impreffions, whether right or wrong, entirely confirmed. At later periods of his life, Conftable aimed, and fuccefsfully, at grander and more evanefcent effects of nature; but in copying her fimpleft afpects, he never furpaffed fuch pictures as this; and which, I cannot but think, will obtain for him, when his merits are fully acknowledged, the praife of having been the moft genuine painter of Englifh landfcape that has yet lived.

1819.

The following beautiful paffage is from a letter written to Mrs. Conftable in May, 1819, while he was on a fhort vifit to Bergholt: "Every thing feems full of bloffom of fome kind, and at every ftep I take, and on whatever object I turn my eyes, that fublime expreffion of the Scriptures, 'I am the refurrection and the life,' feems as if uttered near me."

In 1819, he fent two pictures to the Britifh Gallery, not before exhibited, "Ofmington Shore, near Weymouth," and "A Mill;" and to the Academy he fent the largeft and moft important work he had yet produced, "A Scene on the river

Stour," afterwards called, from a white horſe in a barge near the foreground, "Conſtable's White Horſe." This fine landſcape, which was too large to remain unnoticed, attracted more attention than anything he had before exhibited. It is the one mentioned by him in the following letter to Archdeacon Fiſher,* dated July 17th. I ſhould like of all things to make you a viſit in the autumn, though I cannot allow myſelf to be ſanguine; yet it is cheering to think about it; ſuch a viſit would have many charms for me. Your ſociety, the cathedral, the walks, and thoſe mines of art, Longford and Wilton, to which you could procure me admiſſion to make ſome ſtudies."

"The price I have put on my large landſcape is one hundred guineas, excluſive of the frame; it has ſerved a good apprenticeſhip in the Academy, and I ſhall work a good deal upon it before it goes to the Britiſh Gallery. I ſhould hardly like to part with my copy of Ruyſdael; its being an old ſchool exerciſe, (of which I have too few,) gives it a value to me beyond what I could in conſcience aſk for it. We will talk about the Claude when we meet. I have procured the drawing by Cozens for you, and could pictures chooſe their poſſeſſors, you would have had many like it long ago. I do not wonder at what you tell me of poor * * * * *'s pictures. Such collections and judges always make me melancholy. I neither viſit them nor talk about them if I can help it. But ſuch things are driven down the throats of ignorance, by ignorance ſtill more overbearing, backed, by the bye, with good dinners. * * * I have made a ſketch of the ſcene on the Thames, which is very promiſing."†

"Auguſt 13th. My dear Fiſher. I was happy to re-

* Mr. Fiſher had been inſtalled Archdeacon of Berkſhire, in the latter part of 1817.

† The Opening of Waterloo Bridge.

ceive your friendly letter yesterday. Nothing would give me greater pleasure than to make you a visit, and I hope to be able to accomplish it, ere long. I am under an engagement to paint the portraits of General and Mrs. Rebow, at Wivenhoe Park, about this time. I have written to know if it is still his wish, and when I have his answer you shall hear from me again. My wife thanks you for your kind inquiries after her and her infant. They are both well, and a more lovely little girl, at a month old, was never seen. We are so proud of her, and at the same time so ambitious, as to be induced to ask a great favour: it is our wish to be allowed to name you for her Godfather. We shall take her to church in a few days, and shall be happy to hear from you."

In October, 1819, Constable was called to Bergholt by the division of his father's property, of which his part amounted to 4000*l.*; and in November he was elected an Associate of the Royal Academy, on which occasion he received the following note from Mr. Fisher: "Close, Salisbury, November, 1819. My dear Constable, The Bishop and Mrs. Fisher bid me, with my own, to present their congratulations on your honourable election. Honourable it is, for the Royal Academy is, in the first place, an establishment of this great country, and as such, to be held in great respect; and in the second place, you owe your election to no favour, but solely to your own unsupported, unpatronized merits. I reckon it no small feather in my cap that I have had the sagacity to find them out."

Mr. Fisher did not content himself with praising his friend, but by the purchase of "The White Horse," while he manifested his sincerity, he rendered Constable a service which was, perhaps, of more importance to him at that crisis of his life than it would have been at any later period; and his desire to follow this up, by farther acts of friendship, will be ſeen in a letter dated "April 19th, 1820. My dear Conſtable. I am under obligations to an architect here, who has retired from buſineſs. I want to make him a preſent of ſomething near 20*l.* I would rather give him one of your pictures, if I thought he would appreciate it. See what you can do for me. * * * Do not part with your London and Weſtminſter view without apprizing me; as I rather think I ſhall like to have it, in caſe I am ſtrong enough in purſe. At any rate, *I* can do you no harm by ſaying *no*, if I cannot purchaſe. I am infinitely obliged by your purchaſe of the Claude. You can ſend it me down with the picture. You did right in ſending the ſea-coaſt windmill to the exhibition. Pray come as ſoon as you can, and ſtay as long as you can."

"Saliſbury, April 27th. 'The White Horſe' has arrived ſafe; it is hung on a level with the eye, the frame reſting on the ogee moulding in a weſtern ſide light, right for the light in the picture. It looks magnificently. My wife ſays ſhe carries her eye from the picture to the garden and back again, and obſerves the ſame ſort of look in both. I have ſhewn it to no one, and intend to ſay nothing about it, but leave it to people to find it out, and make their own remarks. I am quite impatient to ſee you here, and wiſh your young family would permit your wife to join the party. J. Fiſher."

The "White Horſe," on many accounts the moſt important picture, to Conſtable, he ever painted, and certainly one of the fineſt, is now in the poſſeſſion of L. Archer Burton, Eſq. of the Woodlands, Hants. In a letter written to Miſs Gubbins, (a lady related to that gentleman and to Conſtable) at a late period of his life, he calls it, "one of my happieſt efforts on a large ſcale, being a placid repreſentation of a ſerene grey morning, ſummer."

"Keppel Street, September 1ſt, 1820. My dear Fiſher, * * * I have ſettled my wife and children comfortably at

Hampſtead. I am glad to get them out of London for every reaſon. Things do not look well, though I fear nothing.* I hear the Duke of Wellington was in the moſt imminent danger yeſterday, and had nearly loſt his life by the hands of an old woman! We had a pleaſant journey to London. In truth, we were all made more fit for ſuch an excurſion by the unbounded kindneſs of yourſelf and Mrs. Fiſher, and our kind friends at the Palace. Indeed, my dear Fiſher, my wife and I feel quite at a loſs how to ſpeak to you of theſe things. My Saliſbury ſketches are much liked; that in the Palace grounds, the bridges and your houſe from the meadows, &c. * * * I have juſt been giving ſome relief to the poor old organiſt you ſaw at my door; he is almoſt in a ſtate of ſtarvation, with a wife and children. He is taken for an Italian, and is, in conſequence, in danger in the ſtreets. I ſhall venture to give him five ſhillings for you, and add it to your running account."

I do not know whether the preſent, mentioned in Mr. Fiſher's letter of the 19th of April, was made; but Mr. Tinney, of Saliſbury, as the Archdeacon's ſolicitor, having rendered him ſome ſervices for which he felt under great obligations, he purchaſed a large picture of Conſtable, which he preſented to that gentleman; but as Mr. Fiſher conſidered the price, one hundred guineas, to be far below its value, he, with much delicacy, in a letter to Conſtable, ſpoke of the tranſaction as "our joint preſent." This noble picture, which I well remember in the exhibition of 1820, and which has ſince been admirably engraved by Mr. Lucas, is about as large as "The White Horſe," and has more ſubject. On the extreme left of the ſpectator, the wheel and part of a water-mill are ſeen. In the foreground are ſome children

* The excitement occaſioned by the trial of Queen Caroline was then at its height.

fiſhing, admirable for the expreſſion of their attitudes, their faces not being ſeen. Sir George Beaumont ſaid of the largeſt boy, that "he was undergoing the agony of a bite." To the right, and in the middle diſtance, a barge lies with extreme elegance of perſpective on the ſmooth river; light clouds throw their ſhadows over a riſing diſtance of great beauty, and a group of tall trees forms the centre of the compoſition. It is a view, and when it was painted, was an exact one of Stratford Mill on the Stour, not far from Bergholt.* Conſtable ſent with it a ſmall picture to the Academy, "A View of Harwich Lighthouſe."

1821.

"Weymouth, February 14th, 1821. My dear Conſtable. I am here paying the laſt duties to my wife's mother. She died ſilently and ſuddenly, on Monday morning at three o'clock. Rather a ſingular accident happened to me in conſequence of her death. I was in the church, at Oſmington, with the old clerk alone, pointing out the ſite of her grave, when the old man ſuddenly exclaimed, 'I cannot ſtand, ſir,' and dropping into my arms, died.

"When you next ſee Stothard tell him the following anecdote. I went to call upon a poor curate, living in one of our mud villages on a lonely part of this coaſt, and was ſhown into a dark low underground parlour. Caſting my eye round the comfortleſs walls, it was refreſhed by ſpying in a corner a moſt charming bit of light and ſhadow; and walking up to ſee what elſe it contained, I found Stothard's Canterbury Pilgrims,† with the morning light breaking over

* Mr. Lucas's engraving of this picture was publiſhed, after the death of Conſtable, with the title of "The Young Waltonians." A title he certainly would not have given to it.

† Conſtable told me he was in Stothard's room when he was finiſhing the picture of the Pilgrims, and that he was then painting the two dogs gambolling at the head of the cavalcade. They were the laſt objects introduced into the compoſition.

the Dulwich Hills. The poor man little lefs than worfhips this print.—Pray get, at your circulating library, the 'Diary of an Invalid.' You will be much amufed with it; for it is written in a lively eafy manner. When you come to his critiques on painting and ftatuary, you will find another corroboration of our often repeated opinion that perfons of the higheft education in the fciences, are often mere children in their knowledge of the art. * * * As foon as the fpring arrives I will make a correct fketch of our ferry houfe at Portland, and fend it to you. I faw it, the other day, ftanding in fea bleached defolation. J. Fifher."

"Clofe, Salifbury, March 6th. My dear Conftable, * * * I am reading, for the third time, 'White's Natural Hiftory of Selborne.' It is a book that would delight you, and be highly inftructive to you in your art, if you are not already acquainted with it. White was the clergyman of the place, and occupied himfelf with narrowly obferving and noting down all the natural occurrences that came within his view: and this for a number of years. It is moft elegantly written. I fear the book is fcarce. But if you can procure it, buy it for me and keep it by you. It is in your own way of clofe obfervation, and has in it that quality that, to me, conftitutes the great pleafure of your fociety. * * * J. Fifher."

Conftable, in his reply to this letter, after condoling with Mr. and Mrs. Fifher on the melancholy news with which it commenced, fays, of another large work he was engaged on, "My picture is getting on, and the frame will be here in three weeks or a fortnight. Believe me, my dear Fifher, I fhould almoft faint by the way when I am ftanding before my large canvaffes, were I not cheered and encouraged by your friendfhip and approbation. I now fear (for my family's fake) I fhall never make a popular artift, *a gentlemen and ladies' painter*. But I am fpared making a fool of myfelf, and your hand ftretched forth, teaches me to value what

I poſſeſs (if I may ſay ſo); and this is of more conſequence than gentlemen and ladies can well imagine. The Biſhop and Mrs. Fiſher attacked me about * * * 's *pantomime*, again, yeſterday; but I ſpoke my mind, as the ſhorteſt way. I could not ſacrifice myſelf to ſuch groſs ignorance."

The "*pantomime*" here alluded to was an extravagant and melo-dramatic conception of hiſtorical art, at that time popular. The Biſhop of Saliſbury, though a man of great refinement of mind, was no judge of painting, and was, therefore, led away, on that ſubject, by the faſhions of the time. His unceaſing kindneſs to Conſtable, whoſe art he did not appreciate, was the reſult of friendſhip alone.

In 1821, Conſtable exhibited four pictures at Somerſet Houſe, "Hampſtead Heath," "A Shower," "Harrow," and "Landſcape, Noon;" the laſt was the third he had painted on a ſix-foot canvaſs, encouraged to proceed with works on ſo large a ſcale by Mr. Fiſher's two purchaſes. This picture is mentioned in the next letter, and will be again ſpoken of as "The Hay Wain."

"To Archdeacon Fiſher. No. 1, Keppel Street, April 1ſt, 1821. * * * My picture goes to the Academy on the 10th; it is not ſo grand as Tinney's. Owing, perhaps, to the maſſes not being ſo impreſſive, the power of the chiaroſcuro is leſſened, but it has a more novel look than I expected. I have yet much to do to it, and calculate on three or four days there. I hear of ſo many clever pictures, particularly by non-members, that it muſt be a capital ſhow. They are chiefly hiſtorical and fancy pictures, and why? the Londoners, with all their ingenuity as artiſts, know nothing of the feelings of a country life, the eſſence of landſcape. * * * How much I am obliged to you for the mention of the books. The 'Diary' is delightful, it has given me new information on ſubjects that I have heard of all my life. No doubt the 'Invalid' is a clever fellow; but theſe touriſts in

Italy think they muſt talk about pictures, and relate anecdotes of painting. I would recommend them to remember the ſtory of Alexander's viſit to the painting room of Apelles. He mentions the landſcapes of Gaſpar Pouſſin, (whoſe works contain the higheſt feeling of landſcape painting,) and imagines defects, that he may afford an opportunity to 'our own Glover' to remedy them. This is too bad; and he here ſhews himſelf to be truly an invalid.* The mind that produced the 'Selborne' is ſuch a one as I have always envied. The ſingle page of the life of Mr. White leaves a more laſting impreſſion on my mind than all that has been written of Charles V. or any other renowned hero. It ſhows what a real love of nature will do. Surely the ſerene and blameleſs life of Mr. White, ſo exempt from the folly and quackery of the world, muſt have fitted him for the clear and intimate view he took of nature. It proves the truth of Sir Joſhua Reynolds's remark, that 'the virtuous man alone has true taſte.' This book is an addition to my eſtate. Stothard was amuſed with your mention of his 'Pilgrims,' but ſaid he believed, 'many of his prints were to be found amongſt the Hottentots.' I dined, laſt week, at Sir George Beaumont's. Met Wilkie, Jackſon, and Collins. It was amuſing to hear them talk of * * * 's picture. Sir George ſaid ſome clever things about it, but he added, 'even allowing the compoſition, its only merit, to be ſomething, ſtill if the fineſt com-

* The following is the paſſage from "Matthews's Diary of an Invalid," which excited his indignation. "Doria Palace. Large collection of pictures; Gaſpar Pouſſin's green landſcapes have no charms for me. The fact ſeems to be, that the delightful green of nature cannot be repreſented in a picture. Our own Glover has perhaps made the greateſt poſſible exertions to ſurmount the difficulty, and give with fidelity the real colours of nature; but I believe the beauty of his pictures is in an inverſe ratio to their fidelity; and that nature muſt be ſtripped of her green livery, and dreſſed in the browns of the painters, or confined to her own autumnal tints in order to be transferred to canvaſs."

poſition of Handel's were played entirely out of tune, what would it be?' "

In June, Conſtable accompanied his friend Fiſher during his viſitation in Berkſhire, and made ſome beautiful pencil and waſhed drawings of the ſcenery in the neighbourhood of Reading, Newbury, and Abingdon. He alſo viſited Oxford, with Fiſher, and made an exquiſite drawing of Blenheim, from the Park.

"Saliſbury, July 19th, 1821. My dear Conſtable, Your picture is hung up in a temporary way at Tinney's, till his new room is finiſhed, and excites great intereſt and attention. How does "The Hay Wain" look now it has got into your own room again? I want to ſee it there, for how can one participate in a ſcene of freſh water and deep noon-day in the crowded copal atmoſphere of the Exhibition? which is always to me like a great pot of boiling varniſh. * * * Yours very ſincerely, John Fiſher."

"No. 2, Lower Terrace, Hampſtead, Auguſt 4th, 1821. My dear Fiſher, * * * I am as much here as poſſible with my family. My placid and contented companion and her three infants are well. I have got a room at a glazier's, where is my large picture, and at this little place I have many ſmall works going on, for which purpoſe I have cleared a ſhed in the garden, which held ſand, coals, mops, and brooms, and have made it a workſhop. I have done a good deal here. I have fitted up my drawing-rooms in Keppel Street, and intend keeping them in order, hanging up only decent works: 'The Hay Wain' looks well in them, but I ſhall do more to it. * * * I am now going to pay my court to the world. I have had experience enough to know that if a man decries himſelf, he will find people ready enough to take him at his word. Sir George Beaumont is going to Italy; he has preſented me with a beautiful little landſcape, a mill, the ſame mill in Tinney's picture, it is quite a Rembrandt, full of tone and chiarofcuro. There is fome hope of the Academy's getting a Claude from Mr. Angerftein's,* the large and magnificent marine picture, one of the moft perfect in the world; fhould that be the cafe, though I can ill afford it, I will make a copy of the fame fize. A ftudy would only be of value to myfelf, the other will be property to my children, and a great delight to me. The very doing it will almoft bring me into communion with Claude himfelf. Lawrence told me that, fhould I really wifh it, it would ftimulate him to farther exertions to get it from Mr. Angerftein. In the room where I am writing, there are hanging up two beautiful fmall drawings by Cozens; one, a wood, clofe, and very folemn; the other, a view from Vefuvius, looking over Portici, very lovely. I borrowed them from my neighbour, Mr. Woodburn. Cozens was all poetry, and your drawing is a lovely fpecimen."

"Salifbury, Auguft 6th, 1821. My dear Conftable, Very few can copy Claude, I exhort you to it by all means. It will fecure two or three hundred pounds to your family, and will furnifh *us* with an inexhauftible ftore of pleafure. I get impatient to know whether your wife will allow you to run down this autumn. Any time from September 1ft to January will be convenient to me, and you need not be at any expenfe at all. One night in the mail and you are here. The affizes are holding, and C * * * * * * * * is here. Your letters lay on the table. He faid, that there were *fome parts* of your laft picture good. I told him if he had faid, *all* the parts were good, it would be no compliment, unlefs he faid the *whole* was good. Is it not ftrange how utterly ignorant the world is of the very firft principles of painting? Here is a man of the greateft abilities, who knows almoft every

* Pictures are lent to the Academy by moft of the poffeffors of collections for the ufe of the painting-fchool.

CHAP. V. 1821.

thing, and yet he is as little a judge of a picture as if he had been without eyes. There's Matthews again with 'his own Glover.'"*

"Hampstead, September 20th, 1821. My dear Fisher, How much I should like to come to you! and I cannot say I will not, but I fear I must go into Suffolk soon, on account of a job.† I have made some studies, carried farther than any I have done before; particularly a highly elegant group of trees (ashes, elms, and oaks), which will be of as much service to me as if I had bought the field and hedge row which contain them; I have likewise made many skies and effects; we have had noble clouds and effects of light and dark and colour, as is always the case in such seasons as the present. The great Claude does not come to the Academy this year (a young lady is copying it), but they expect it next year, and it would have been madness for me to have meddled with it this season, as I am now behindhand with the bridge.‡ The beautiful Ruysdael, 'The Windmill' which we admired, is at the Gallery. I trust I shall be able to procure a memorandum of it; and there is a noble N. Poussin at the Academy, a solemn, deep, still summer's noon, with

* Lord Dudley, in a letter to the Bishop of Llandaff, admirable for its good sense and candour, speaking of the excellencies of the old masters, says, "I believe that merit to be of a sort which requires study, habit, and perhaps, some practical knowledge of the principles of the fine arts, to perceive and relish. You remember that Sir Joshua Reynolds tells us he was at first, incapable of tasting all the excellence of Raphael and Michael Angelo. And if he, already no mean artist, was still uninitiated in some of the higher mysteries of art, and obliged at first to take upon trust, much of that which was afterwards made clear to him by further study and labour, what shall we say about the sincerity of those, who knowing so much less, pretend to feel so much more? For my own part, I think of them, very much as I should think of any body, who, being just able to pick out the meaning of a Latin sentence, should affect to admire the language and versification of the Georgics."

† A portrait.

‡ His fourth large picture.

large umbrageous trees, and a man waſhing his feet at a fountain near them. Through the breaks in the trees are mountains, and the clouds collecting about them with the moſt enchanting effects poſſible. It cannot be too much to ſay that this landſcape is full of religious and moral feeling.* It is not large, about three and a half feet, and I ſhould like to, and will, if poſſible, poſſeſs a fac-ſimile of it. I muſt make time. If I cannot come to you, I will ſend you the reſults of this ſummer's ſtudy. My wife and children are well, we have not had an hour's illneſs all the ſummer."

On the 26th of September, Fiſher wrote to tell Conſtable of objections that were made to the ſky in Mr. Tinney's picture, by a "grand critical party" who had ſat in judgment on it. "After talking in vain for ſome time," he continues, "I brought them out of my portfolio two prints from Wouvermans and a Vander Neer, where the whole ſtreſs was laid on the ſky, and that ſilenced them. While in every other profeſſion the initiated only are judges, in painting, all men, except the blind, think themſelves qualified to give an opinion. The comfort is, that the truth comes out when theſe ſelf-made connoiſſeurs begin to buy and collect for themſelves. At Lord Shafteſbury's, about twelve miles from this place, there is a daylight Vander Neer. When you come we will go and ſee it. I had nearly forgotten to tell you that I was the other day fiſhing in the New Foreſt in a fine deep broad river, with mills, roaring back waters, withy beds, &c. I thought often of you during the day. I caught two pike, was up to the middle in watery meadows, ate my dinner under a willow, and was as happy as when I was 'a careleſs boy.' What have you done with your 'Midſummer Noon,' and what do you intend to do with it?"

"Hampſtead, October 23rd, 1821. My dear Fiſher,

* This picture is in the National Gallery.

CHAP. V.
1821.

* * * I am moſt anxious to get into my London painting-room, for I do not conſider myſelf at work unleſs I am before a ſix-foot canvaſs. I have done a good deal of ſkying, for I am determined to conquer all difficulties, and that among the reſt. And now talking of ſkies, it is amuſing to us to ſee how admirably you fight my battles; you certainly take the beſt poſſible ground for getting your friend out of a ſcrape (the example of the old maſters). That landſcape painter who does not make his ſkies a very material part of his compoſition, neglects to avail himſelf of one of his greateſt aids. Sir Joſhua Reynolds, ſpeaking of the landſcapes of Titian, of Salvator, and of Claude, ſays: 'Even their *ſkies* ſeem to ſympathize with their ſubjects.' I have often been adviſed to conſider my ſky as '*a white ſheet thrown behind the objects*.' Certainly, if the ſky is obtruſive, as mine are, it is bad; but if it is evaded, as mine are not, it is worſe; it muſt and always ſhall with me make an effectual part of the compoſition. It will be difficult to name a claſs of landſcape in which the ſky is not the key note, the ſtandard of ſcale, and the chief organ of ſentiment. You may conceive, then, what a 'white ſheet' would do for me, impreſſed as I am with theſe notions, and they cannot be erroneous. The ſky is the ſource of light in nature, and governs every thing; even our common obſervations on the weather of every day are altogether ſuggeſted by it. The difficulty of ſkies in painting is very great, both as to compoſition and execution; becauſe, with all their brilliancy, they ought not to come forward, or, indeed, be hardly thought of any more than extreme diſtances are; but this does not apply to phenomena or accidental effects of ſky, becauſe they always attract particularly. I may ſay all this to you, though *you* do not want to be told that I know very well what I am about, and that my ſkies have not been neglected, though they have often failed in execution, no doubt, from an over-anxiety about

them, which will alone deſtroy that eaſy appearance which nature always has in all her movements.

"How much I wiſh I had been with you on your fiſhing excurſion in the New Foreſt! What river can it be? But the ſound of water eſcaping from mill-dams, &c. willows, old rotten planks, ſlimy poſts, and brickwork, I love ſuch things. Shakeſpeare could make every thing poetical; he tells us of poor Tom's haunts among 'ſheep cotes and mills.' As long as I do paint, I ſhall never ceaſe to paint ſuch places.* They have always been my delight, and I ſhould indeed have been delighted in ſeeing what you deſcribe, and in your company, 'in the company of a man to whom nature does not ſpread her volume in vain.' Still I ſhould paint my own places beſt; painting is with me but another word for feeling, and I aſſociate 'my careleſs boyhood' with all that lies on the banks of the Stour; thoſe ſcenes made me a painter, and I am grateful; that is, I had often thought of pictures of them before I ever touched a pencil, and your picture is the ſtrongeſt inſtance of it I can recollect; but I will ſay no more, for I am a great egotiſt in whatever relates to painting. Does not the Cathedral look beautiful among the golden foliage? its ſolitary grey muſt ſparkle in it."

"Cloſe, Saliſbury, October 24th. My dear Conſtable, I had a moſt agreeable breakfaſt this morning, your letter ſerving me in lieu of the newſpaper, which is now too dull to read. I was glad to ſee your handwriting ſo clear and ſmooth. A certain proof of a tranquil mind. I ſhall be alone and diſengaged on Saturday the 3rd of November, and continue ſo until the 26th of the ſame month. I think the earlier you come the better. I project, if the weather be fine, to go and ſee Wincheſter Cathedral. The roof has

* The laſt picture he painted, and on which he was engaged on the laſt day of his life, was a mill, with ſuch accompaniments as are deſcribed in this letter.

Chap. V.
1821.

been near falling in, owing to the conſtant cutting away of the great ſupporting pillars to let in monuments (of folly and bad taſte). * * * Our Cathedral looks well this weather, but it is not ſo much relieved by the warm tints as you would imagine. Owing to the moiſture of the ſeaſon, and the great and rapid decompoſition of the vegetation, there is a conſtant humid halo, which makes the ſhadows, at all hours, very blue, and gives the landſcape a cold tone. I am ſorry your children have been unwell. Mine are in high health and good humour. How many dinners a week does your wife get you to eat at a regular hour, and like a Chriſtian?"

In November, Conſtable viſited Saliſbury, where, notwithſtanding the lateneſs of the ſeaſon, he made ſome beautiful ſketches.

CHAPTER VI.

1822.

Mr. Samuel Lane. Farrington. Coxe's Life of Correggio. Gold grounds. Conſtable's fourth large Picture. Stothard's Wellington Shield. Farrington's Houſe. The Biſhop of Saliſbury. Studies of Skies. Illneſs. Syſtem of Copying at the Britiſh Gallery. Picture of Saliſbury Cathedral from the Biſhop's grounds. David's Picture of the Coronation of Joſephine. Conſtable's dread of a National Gallery.

1822.

SOON after his firſt arrival in London, Conſtable had become acquainted with Mr. Samuel Lane, of Greek Street, Soho; and this acquaintance ripened into a friendſhip which continued to the end of his life. The following paſſage is from one of his letters which Mr. Lane has permitted me to make uſe of: " February, 1822. My dear Lane, I have been with my wife to look over Mr. Farrington's houſe, which has left a deep impreſſion on us both. I could ſcarcely believe that I was not to meet the elegant and dignified figure of our departed friend, where I had been ſo long uſed to ſee him, or hear again the wiſdom that always attended his advice, which I do indeed miſs greatly."

" Saliſbury, March 25th, 1822. My dear Conſtable,

Coxe is on the eve of publiſhing 'Correggio;' but he has ſome ſad ſtuff in it about the manner in which he is ſuppoſed to have mixed his colours, and talks about his painting on gold leaf to produce a warm effect. He will ſend you, by my advice, the proof ſheets of that part of his work which treats of Correggio's art, for your correction. * * * The above was written yeſterday. I left off, trying to recollect ſome anecdote I had to tell you. I have juſt recalled it to my memory. It is, as you know, part of the Apocalypſe, that the juſt ſhould reign a thouſand years, and then the conſummation of all things. During the tenth century, in conſequence of this prediction, there was a univerſal expectation that the world was about to end. The agitation of men's minds is deſcribed, by cotemporary writers, as extreme. Among other effects which this expectation produced, was the neglect to repair their houſes and churches. So that when the dreaded period was paſt, their buildings were found to be in a moſt dilapidated condition. The eleventh century, therefore, was much occupied in building, repairing, and beautifying. Hence we know, that few, very few of our buildings can be older than that period. And that the eleventh century and the beginning of the twelfth, are probable periods to which to refer back many of our moſt beautiful ſtructures. It was the ſame cauſe that enriched the church and made it ſo powerful. Men, expecting the day of judgment, were glad to compound for their ſins by granting away their eſtates, (which would not much longer be of uſe to them or their heirs) to religious purpoſes. J. Fiſher."

"Keppel Street, April 13th, 1822. My dear Fiſher, I have not ſeen any of the ſheets of Mr. Coxe's 'Life of Correggio;' but I hear of a letter from him to Jackſon, expreſſing a deſire that they may be ſeen by his friend Conſtable. There is no doubt but it will be intereſting, but as to painting on gold grounds, it is all over with the *alchymy* of the art, I hope never to be revived again. Yet dark ages may return, and there are always dark minds in enlightened ones. In the early German and Italian pictures, gold was used for glories, &c. and made to appear as a thing unconnected with the painting, and so far supernatural; and this has been done as late as Carlo Dolci, and it sometimes appears very beautiful when blended into transparent colour behind the heads of saints, &c. But still it looks like trick, and Correggio was above all trick, nor do I believe he ever resorted to any such nonsense to aid his brightness. I have sent my large picture to the Academy. I never worked so hard before. I do not know that it is better than my others, but perhaps fewer vulgar objections can be made to it." (The writing is here interrupted by a beautiful pen sketch, which has the force of a mezzotinto engraving.) "The composition is almost totally changed from what you saw. I have taken away the sail, and added another barge in the middle of the picture, with a principal figure, altered the group of trees, and made the bridge entire. The picture has now a rich centre, and the right hand side becomes only an accessory. I have endeavoured to paint with more delicacy, but hardly any body has seen it. I hear of some excellent pictures. I am going into Suffolk about an altar-piece, a gift from a gentleman. * * * is annoyed by your designating his old masters trash. He goes by the *rule of name*.

"I have some nibbles at my large picture of the Hay Wain, in the British Gallery. I have an offer of 70*l.* without the frame to form part of an exhibition in Paris. I hardly know what to do. It might promote my fame and procure me commissions, but it is property to my family; though I want money dreadfully; and, on this subject, I must beg a great favour of you, indeed I can do it of no other person. The loan of 20 or 30*l.* would be of the greatest use to me at this

Chap. VI.
1822.

time, as painting these large pictures has much impoverished me. If you can, I know you will oblige me. If not, say so. This summer I shall devote to money getting, as I have several commissions, both landscape and otherwise. But a large picture, and if possible, a good one, was necessary this year. The next must take its chance. I hope, indeed I really believe, I have never yet done any thing so good as the one now sent."

"Stothard has published his beautiful etching of the shield of Wellington, three and a half feet circle. Oblige me and my dear old friend by purchasing one. My conscience acquits me of any neglect of my last picture. I have dismissed it with great calmness and ease of mind."

Of this picture,* another view on the Stour, and very near Flatford Mill; an admirable line engraving, by Mr. W. R. Smith, is published in Messrs. Finden's "Gallery of British Art;" and a first sketch of the subject is engraved in the "English Landscape."

"Keppel Street, April 17th. My dear Fisher, Accept my thanks for your very kind letter. The contents will be highly useful, for, as I told you, I had been so long upon unprofitable canvass that I was getting hard run. But I am now busy on some minor works which will bring things soon about again. My writing requires much apology; but I seldom sit down till I am already fatigued in my painting-room, and near the post hour, and I must say of my letters as Northcote says of his pictures, 'I leave them for the ingenious to find out.' I made two or three fruitless attempts to read the last I sent you, and the postman ringing his bell at the moment, I dismissed it. I must work hard this summer, but I should like much to take the Windsor coach to hear your sermon, though I can ill spare a day, and now that

* At present in the possession of Mr. William Carpenter.

I have an opportunity of earning a little money, I muſt make it a religious duty to do it. I ſhall not let the Frenchman have my picture. It would be too bad to allow myſelf to be knocked down by a Frenchman. In ſhort, it may fetch my family ſomething one time or other, and it would be diſgracing my diploma to take ſo ſmall a ſum, leſs by near one half than the price I aſked.

"Several cheering things have lately happened to me, profeſſionally. I am certain my reputation riſes as a landſcape painter, and that my ſtyle of art, as Farrington always ſaid it would, is faſt becoming a diſtinct feature. I am anxious about this picture. My neighbour * * * * *, who expects to be an Academician before me, called to ſee it. He has always praiſed me; now he ſaid not a word; till, on leaving the room, he looked back and ſaid, he hoped his picture would not hang near it."

"I truſt you will come to London on your viſitation; I ſhall be much diſappointed if you do not. I am about Farrington's houſe; I think this ſtep neceſſary; I ſhall get more by it than my family, in conveniences, though I am loth to leave a place where I have had ſo much happineſs, and where I painted my four landſcapes; but there is no end to giving way to fancies; occupation is my ſheet anchor. My mind would ſoon devour me without it. I felt as if I had loſt my arms after my picture was gone to the Exhibition. I dare not read this letter over, take it as one of my ſketches."

"April. My dear Fiſher, I have been to Farrington's this morning; they are ſharp about the houſe, and wiſhed me to take the fixtures, and ſuch of the furniture as I may like, at a valuation. I have refuſed the latter, ſo ſtands the matter at preſent; they will ſell the Wilſons;* they are well worth ſixty, or eighty, or even a hundred guineas the pair.

* Two beautiful little views in Italy, now in the poſſeſſion of Miſs Rogers.

Chap. VI.
1822.

"Tinney is confined to town by indiſpoſition; I have ſeen him often, and he views me favourably for your ſake, and is determined to love painting as an intellectual purſuit of the moſt delightful kind, in preference to dirt, and old canvaſs, varniſh, &c. He has deſired me to paint him, as a companion to his landſcape, another picture at my leiſure for a hundred guineas.* If, however, I am offered more for it, even five hundred guineas, I may take it, and begin another for him. This is very noble, (when all the nobility let my picture come back to me from the Gallery,) and will enable me to do another large picture, to keep up and add to my reputation. * * * How much I ſhould like to be now at Oſmington; but work I muſt and will. If I recollect, the aſhes have very beautiful moſſes, and their ſtems are particularly rich at Oſmington. I have never thanked you for your account of the middle ages and the expectation of the laſt day. I was not aware that its influence was ſo enormous."

In 1822, Conſtable exhibited at the Academy five pictures, "Hampſtead Heath," "A View on the Stour, near Dedham," "Malvern Hall, Warwickſhire," "A View of the Terrace, Hampſtead," and "A Study of Trees from Nature."

The next letter is from the Biſhop of Saliſbury. "Malmſbury, Auguſt 3rd, 1822. Dear Sir, My daughter Elizabeth is about to change her ſituation, and try whether ſhe cannot perform the duties of a wife as well as ſhe has done thoſe of a daughter. She wiſhes to have in her houſe in London a recollection of Saliſbury; I mean, therefore, to give her a picture, and I muſt beg of you either to finiſh the firſt ſketch of my picture, or to make a copy of the ſmall

* This commiſſion from Mr. Tinney was never executed; why, I know not; but I believe Conſtable afterwards painted for him one or two ſmall pictures.

Painted by John Constable, R.A. Engraved by David Lucas.

HAMPSTEAD HEATH, MIDDLESEX.

"Ut Umbra sic Vita."

ſize. I wiſh to have a more ſerene ſky. I am now on my viſitation, and ſhall not be at Saliſbury till the 20th, but my letters follow me."

"Oſmington, October 1ſt. My dear Conſtable. * * * Captain Forſter, a gentleman of property, near Windſor, is an admirer of your art. He is to meet you at Saliſbury, he was firſt caught by a ſketch-book of yours which I had. Your pencil ſketches always take people, both learned and unlearned. Surely it would anſwer to publiſh a few of them. Get one done on ſtone, as an experiment, unleſs it is derogatory from the ſtation you hold in the art. * * * J. Fiſher."

"To Archdeacon Fiſher. Hampſtead, October 7th, 1822. My dear Fiſher, Several adverſe circumſtances had yielded to my wiſhes, and I had determined on meeting you at Saliſbury on the day appointed; but things have changed again, and I know not how to come ſo far as Weymouth. The loſs of four days on the road is ſerious, and I am now in the midſt of a great ſtruggle, and time is my eſtate. I have got ſeveral of my commiſſions into tolerable forwardneſs, eſpecially two kit-cat landſcapes for Mr. Ripley, and I am determined to overcome all my difficulties while a great deal of health and ſome little youth remains to me. I have got things into a train, by following which they are made comparatively eaſy. Such a journey would turn me inſide out, and a viſit to your coaſt would waſh my brains entirely. I muſt wait, and ſtill hope to meet you when quite convenient to yourſelf, and when you return to the Cloſe. I ſhall ſend you ſome picture to look at. 'Green Highgate' has now changed its frame, and become a very pretty picture, and deſerves a better, or at leaſt, a new name. I have made about fifty careful ſtudies of ſkies, tolerably large to be careful. I do not regret not ſeeing Fonthill; I never had a deſire to ſee ſights, and a gentleman's park is my averſion.

Chap. VI.
1822.

"It is ſingular that I happened to ſpeak of Milman; no doubt he is learned, but it is not fair to encumber literature. The world is full enough of what has been already done, and as in the art there is plenty of fine painting but very few good pictures, ſo in poetry there is plenty of fine writing, and I am told his is ſuch, and as you ſay, 'gorgeous;' but it can be compared; Shakſpeare cannot; nor Burns, nor Claude, nor Ruyſdael, and it has taken me twenty years to find this out. This is, I hope, my laſt week here, at leaſt this ſummer; it is a ruinous place to me; I loſe time here ſadly. One of my motives for taking Charlotte Street was to remain longer in London. In Keppel Street we wanted room, and were 'Like bottled waſps upon a ſouthern wall;' but the five happieſt years of my life were paſſed there."

Twenty of Conſtable's ſtudies of ſkies made during this ſeaſon, are in my poſſeſſion, and there is but one among them in which a veſtige of landſcape is introduced. They are painted in oil, on large ſheets of thick paper, and all dated, with the time of day, the direction of the wind, and other memoranda on their backs. On one, for inſtance, is written, "5th of September, 1822. 10 o'clock, morning, looking ſouth eaſt, briſk wind at weſt. Very bright and freſh grey clouds running faſt over a yellow bed, about half way in the ſky. Very appropriate to the 'coaſt at Oſmington.'"

"35 Charlotte Street, Fitzroy Square, October 31ſt, 1822. My dear Fiſher, We left Hampſtead a fortnight ago laſt Friday, and I have not yet had my pencil in my hand. I got laid up attending bricklayers and carpenters at ſix and ſeven in the morning, leaving a warm bed for cold damp rooms and waſhhouſes, for I have had immenſe trouble to get the houſe habitable; but, though I am now quite well, I am aware that the time is paſt in which it was convenient for you to receive me. It has proved a very great diſappointment to me, and I fear that my not coming has vexed you, eſpecially as I have not heard from you. I have got the large painting-room into excellent order; it is light, airy, ſweet, and warm; I, at one time, deſpaired of attaining either of theſe qualities. I have now two ſix-footers in hand,—one of which I ſhall ſend to the Gallery at 200*l.*

"*The art will go out;* there will be no genuine painting in England in thirty years. This will be owing to pictures driven into the empty heads of the junior artiſts by their owners, the Directors of the Britiſh Inſtitution, &c. In the early ages of the fine arts, the productions were more affecting and ſublime, for the artiſts being without human exemplars, were forced to have recourſe to nature; in the latter ages, of Raphael and Claude, the productions were more perfect, leſs uncouth, becauſe the artiſts could then avail themſelves of the experience of thoſe who were before them, but they did not take them at their word, or as the chief objects of imitation. Could you but ſee the folly and ruin exhibited at the Britiſh Gallery, you would go mad. Vander Velde, and Gaſpar Pouſſin, and Titian, are made to ſpawn multitudes of abortions: and for what are the great maſters brought into this diſgrace? only to ſerve the purpoſe of ſale. Hofland has ſold a ſhadow of Gaſpar Pouſſin for eighty guineas, and it is no more like Gaſpar than the ſhadow of a man on a muddy road is like himſelf."*

A letter from the Biſhop of Saliſbury to Conſtable, dated November 12th, contained a draft with theſe words: "Law-

* The Directors of the Britiſh Inſtitution are aſſuredly not accountable for the abuſe of the privilege they grant annually to artiſts of making copies from the old maſters at their Gallery; a privilege of which ſome of our beſt painters have availed themſelves with advantage to their own practice, and of which Conſtable had himſelf intended to make uſe. He did not ſufficiently conſider that thoſe who are content to ſpend much of their time in copying pictures, are not of that claſs who would advance or even ſupport the art under any circumſtances.

CHAP. VI.
1822.

yers frequently receive retaining fees, why ſhould not painters do the ſame?" The picture he was engaged on for the Biſhop, was finiſhed and exhibited in the following ſpring. It is an extremely beautiful work, and one with which he took great pains, a view of the Cathedral from the Biſhop's Grounds. In the foreground he introduced a circumſtance familiar to all who are in the habit of noticing cattle. With cows there is generally, if not always, one which is called, not very accurately, *the maſter cow*, and there is ſcarcely any thing the reſt of the herd will venture to do until the *maſter* has taken the lead. On the left of the picture this individual is drinking, and turns with ſurpriſe and jealouſy to another cow approaching the canal lower down for the ſame purpoſe; they are of the Suffolk breed, without horns; and it is a curious mark of Conſtable's fondneſs for every thing connected with his native county, that ſcarcely an inſtance can be found of a cow in any of his pictures, be the ſcene where it may, with horns.

"Charlotte Street, December 6th. My dear Fiſher, There is nothing ſo cheering to me as the ſight of your handwriting, yet I am dilatory in anſwering you. I will gladly do all I can for R * * *† and his picture, but you know I can only ſend it, I poſſeſs no favour in that place, I have no patron but yourſelf, and you are not a grandee; you are only a gentleman and a ſcholar, and a real lover of the art. I will mention R * * * 's picture to Young, and this is all that is in my power. Is it not poſſible to diſſuade him from coming to London, where he will be ſure to get rid of what little local reputation he may have? But perhaps he prefers ſtarving in a crowd, and if he is determined to adventure, let him by all means preſerve his flowing locks, they will do

† A young artiſt of Saliſbury who had ſent a picture to town for exhibition at the Britiſh Gallery.

him more ſervice than even the talents of Claude Lorraine, if he poſſeſſed them.

"* * * ſhall have his picture when I can find an opportunity of ſending it. Had I not better grime it down with ſlime and ſoot, as he is a connoiſſeur, and perhaps prefers filth and dirt to freſhneſs and beauty?

"I have been to ſee David's picture of 'The Coronation of the Empreſs Joſephine.' It does not poſſeſs the common language of the art, much leſs anything of the oratory of Rubens or Paul Veroneſe, and in point of execution it is below notice; ſtill I prefer it to the productions of thoſe among our hiſtorical painters who are only holding on to the tail of the ſhirt of Carlo Maratti, ſimply becauſe it does not remind me of the *ſchools*. I could not help feeling as I did when I laſt wrote to you of what I ſaw at the Britiſh Inſtitution. Should there be a National Gallery, (which is talked of) there will be an end of the art in poor old England, and ſhe will become, in all that relates to painting, as much a nonentity as every other country that has one. The reaſon is plain; the manufacturers of pictures are then made the criterions of perfection, inſtead of nature."

Here, as well as in his remarks on the ſyſtem of copying purſued at the Britiſh Gallery, Conſtable's inference ſeems haſty. Neither connoiſſeurs nor legiſlators can promote the riſe or haſten the decline of the arts in any material degree. A multitude of concurring circumſtances, varying in every age and nation, contribute to theſe; meantime, it is ſomething that a collection of fine pictures ſhould be acceſſible to the public; and if the National Gallery ſhould help, only in a ſmall degree, to keep our young artiſts from the diſſipation of their time, and the injury their unformed minds receive while running all over Europe in queſt of the art, which can only be acquired by years of patient and ſettled induſtry, it may effect ſome good.* Conſtable, at this moment, forgot what at other times he fully admitted, that good pictures are the neceſſary interpreters of nature to the ſtudent in art. If the reader will turn to the end of the book, he will find in the remarks on Claude, in the lecture he delivered on the 2nd of June, 1836, at the Royal Inſtitution, and on Rembrandt at the cloſe of the next lecture, his ſettled opinions on this ſubject. But that his dread of picture worſhip ſhould lead him to expreſs himſelf as he did, in the letter laſt quoted, I can well underſtand, knowing as I do the notions prevailing among the artiſts and amateurs with whom he lived. Among the laſt, may be particularly mentioned the amiable and accompliſhed Sir George Beaumont, at that time the leader of taſte in the faſhionable world. Few men better diſcriminated, than did Sir George, the various excellencies of the old maſters; but he never conſidered how many beauties might remain in nature untouched by their pencils, and conſequently he was averſe to any deviation from their manner. It is curious, that throughout the whole of his intercourſe with Conſtable, Sir George aſſumed the character of a teacher.

* Thoſe who are old enough to compare the preſent ſtate of painting, among us, with what it was before the Continent was thrown open to our artiſts, cannot but have miſgivings as to the advantage of foreign travel to Britiſh ſtudents. If, as it may be feared, we are more and more loſing ſight of nature, it may be leſs owing to the influence of the National Gallery, than to the example from abroad of, I will not call it imitation but *mimicry* of early art. This is ſo eaſy a thing to ſucceed in, and is ſo well calculated to impoſe on ourſelves and others a belief that we poſſeſs the ſpirit of the primitive ages of art, that we cannot too carefully guard againſt its ſeduction. The purity of heart belonging to childhood is, no doubt, as deſirable to the painter as to the Chriſtian, but we do not acquire this by merely imitating the *liſp* of infancy.

CHAPTER VII.

1823.

Illneſs. Picture of Saliſbury Cathedral. Sir John Leiceſter's Pictures. Wilſon. Conſtable's Pictures at the Exhibition. Sir Godfrey Kneller's Houſe. Life of Correggio. The Rev. T. J. Judkin. Sir William Curtis. Viſit to Archdeacon Fiſher. Fonthill. The Diorama. Viſit to Cole Orton Hall. Adventure on the Road. Sir George and Lady Beaumont. Pictures at Cole Orton. Manner of paſſing the day there. Scenery of its neighbourhood. Southey. Difference of opinion between Sir George and Conſtable on Art. Studies at Cole Orton. Return to London. Illneſs. Pictures for the Exhibition. Southey and the Church.

1823.

CONSTABLE was prevented by illneſs from finiſhing either of the large pictures he had on hand, in time for the exhibitions of 1823, and even from writing again to Fiſher until the 1ſt of February in that year, when he thus reſumed their correſpondence: "My very dear Fiſher, Ever ſince Chriſtmas my houſe has been a ſad ſcene of ſerious illneſs; all my children,* and two of my ſervants laid up at once. Things are now, thanks to God, looking better, but poor John is ſtill in a fearful ſtate. I am unfortunately taken ill again myſelf, but to-day I am

* He had now two ſons and two daughters.

better, and determined to write to you. What with anxiety, watching, nurſing, and my own indiſpoſition, I have not ſeen the face of my eaſel ſince Chriſtmas, and it is not the leaſt of my troubles that the good Biſhop's picture is not fit to be ſeen; pray, my dear Fiſher, prepare his Lordſhip for this; it has been no fault of my own. Your excellent mother and family, hearing of our diſtreſs, moſt kindly called here. The ſight of Mrs. P. Fiſher always does one good; her looks ſay we ſhould patiently ſubmit to all things, and this is confirmed in her own conduct, for ſhe can."

"Charlotte Street, February 21ſt. My dear Fiſher, I was cheered by your letter and kind inquiries. I am now at work again, and ſome of my children are better, but my poor darling boy John is in a ſad ſtate indeed; God only knows how it will end. Baillie and Gooch ſee him continually, and are not without hope; but I am worn with anxiety. * * * I am weak and much emaciated. They took a great deal of blood from me which I could ill ſpare. I have fretted for the loſs of time, and being away from my eaſel, but moſt of all for my poor dear boy; but I will leave my houſe, and go into my painting-room. I have put a large upright landſcape in hand, and I hope I ſhall hold up to get it ready for the Academy, with the Biſhop's picture."

"I am ſorry to ſee you again haunted by that *phantom*, 'The Church in danger;' it does not ſpeak a juſt ſtate of mind or thinking. That the vultures will attack it, and every thing elſe that is valuable, is likely enough; but you ſay, 'they have failed on the State;' that, therefore, ſtill ſtands between the Church and them, for they can only fall together. The nobility know the value of intellect, and endeavour to arm themſelves from the ſame ſources as you do, the Univerſities; and conſider the ages they have ſtood, and the ſtorms they have weathered. * * * I look forward to coming to you at Gillingham to do ſomething at the mill."

"May 9th. I had many interruptions in my works for the Exhibition, as you know, so that I have no large canvass there. My Cathedral looks uncommonly well; it is much approved of by the Academy, and moreover in Seymour Street. I think you will say when you see it, that I have fought a better battle with the Church than old H * * e, B * * * * * * m, and all their coadjutors put together. It was the most difficult subject in landscape I ever had on my easel. I have not flinched at the windows, buttresses, &c.; but I have still kept to my grand organ colour, and have, as usual, made my escape in the evanescence of the chiaroscuro. I think you will like it, but you could have done me much good. I am vexed to see the good Bishop looking ill; it may be a temporary cold, but he breaks, no doubt. This has been a fearful winter for old and young. Callcott admires my Cathedral; he says I have managed it well. Wilkie's pictures are the finest in the world. Perhaps the out-door scene is too black.* Fuseli came up to him and said, 'Vell, vat dis? is dis de new vay, de Guercino style?' Speaking of me, he says, 'I like de landscapes of Constable; he is always picturesque, of a fine colour, and de lights always in de right places; but he makes me call for my great coat and umbrella.' This may amuse you, when contemplating this busy but distant scene; however, though I am here in the midst of the world, I am out of it, and am happy, and endeavour to keep myself unspotted. I have a kingdom of my own, both fertile and populous,—my landscape and my children. I have work to do, and my finances must be repaired if possible. I have a face now on my easel, and may have more."

Speaking in this letter of Italy, Constable continues, "'Oh

* The "Parish Beadle." The other was the small whole length portrait of the Duke of York, painted for Sir Willoughby Gordon.

CHAP. VII.
1823.

dear, oh dear, I ſhall never let my longing eyes ſee that famous country!' Theſe are the words of old Richardſon, and like him I am doomed never to ſee the living ſcenes that inſpired the landſcape of Wilſon and Claude. No, but I was born to paint a happier land, my own dear old England; and when I ceaſe to love her, may I, as Wordſworth ſays,

'never more hear
Her green leaves ruſtle, or her torrents roar!'*

I went to the Gallery of Sir John Leiceſter, to ſee the Engliſh Artiſts. I recollect nothing ſo much as a large, ſolemn, bright, warm, freſh landſcape by Wilſon, which ſtill ſwims in my brain like a delicious dream. Poor Wilſon! think of his fate, think of his magnificence. But the mind loſes its dignity leſs in adverſity than in proſperity. He is now walking arm in arm with Milton and Linnæus. He was one of thoſe appointed to ſhow the world the hidden ſtores and beauties of nature."

With the picture of Saliſbury Cathedral from the Biſhop's Garden, Conſtable exhibited, at the Academy, "A Study of Trees, a Sketch," and "A Cottage;" and to the Britiſh Gallery he ſent a picture of Yarmouth Jetty.

"Gillingham, Shafteſbury, May 9th. My dear Conſtable, * * * I dined, yeſterday, at the houſe built by Sir Godfrey Kneller, that man of wigs and drapery. On the ſtaircaſe hung a beautiful portrait of Pope, by him. How unlike his uſual efforts! I long to hear how you have ſucceeded in the exhibition. The Courier mentions you with honour. 'Con-

* "O England! dearer far than life is dear,
If I forget thy prioweſs, never more
Be thy ungrateful ſon allowed to hear
Thy green leaves ruſtle, or thy torrents roar!"
Thankſgiving Ode on the General Peace.

ſtable has ſome admirable ſtudies of landſcape ſcenery.' * * * J. Fiſher."

"Gillingham, May 18th. My dear Conſtable, * * * Coxe ſhowed me the proof ſheets of his Life of Correggio. It is really very nicely done. He has got over the critical part better than I expected. But he has, evidently, not quite a clear idea of chiaroſcuro. He has no notion that harmony and brilliancy of effect are connected with light and ſhade; or that Correggio's great originality lay in that department. But ſtill, his book is well done. He proves, I think, very ſatisfactorily, that Correggio did not die in poverty or of the load of copper. He ſhows that he had bought houſes and property in the city of Correggio. And what is more, gold was the currency of the country, and they never paid in copper. It would not have been a legal tender. * * * J. Fiſher."

In a letter to Mr. Fiſher, dated July 3rd, after ſpeaking of ſome purchaſes which he had made for that gentleman, one of which was a Flemiſh picture of fruit, &c. Conſtable ſays, "I have been for a day or two at Southgate, at Judkin's. We dined with Sir William Curtis; he is a fine old fellow, and is now ſitting for his portrait to Lawrence for the King, who deſired it in theſe words, 'D—n you, my old boy, I'll have you in all your canonicals, and then I can look at you every day.' He is a great favourite,—birds of a feather. Let me know your wiſhes about the picture."

"My dear Conſtable, Where real buſineſs is to be done, you are the moſt energetic and punctual of men. In ſmaller matters, ſuch as putting on your breeches, you are apt to loſe time in deciding which leg ſhall go in firſt. I thank you heartily for the ſpeed with which you have executed both my commiſſions. I have never had this picture out of my eye ſince I ſaw it. Still-life is always dull, as there are no aſſociations with it; but this is ſo deliciouſly freſh that I could not reſiſt it. If you have one of your coaſt windmills hanging on your wall framed, I wiſh you would put it up with the fruit-piece. And now with regard to our meeting, I am unwilling to put off your viſit to the old age of ſummer, when all the aſſociations are thoſe of decay; I will therefore work hard at the Infirmary ſermon, which I am to preach at the Cathedral in September, and get it finiſhed by the 20th of Auguſt, about which time I ſhall expect you, and I care not how long you ſtay. I have diſcovered *three mills*, old, ſmall, and pictureſque, on this river. I have a great deſire to poſſeſs your 'Wain;' but I cannot now reach what it is worth, and what you muſt have; but I have this favour to aſk, that you will not part with it without letting me know. It will be of the moſt value to your children by continuing to hang where it does, till you join the ſociety of Ruyſdael, Wilſon, and Claude. As praiſe and money will then be of no value to you, the world will liberally beſtow both. Tinney ſays his picture is inferior to mine. He cannot find out that mine hangs alone, and that his is hurt, as is always the caſe, by villanous company. J. Fiſher."

"July 10th. My dear Fiſher, I am always pleaſed with myſelf when I have pleaſed you. You have made an excellent purchaſe of a moſt delightful work: it is a pearly picture, but its tone is ſo deep and mellow that it plays the very devil with my landſcapes; but I ſhall make my account of it, as I am now working for tone. The painter is C. de Vris, an artiſt cotemporary with Rubens. De Heem painted his excellent fruit and flower pieces at the ſame time, but this painter's works are more ſcarce, and Mr. Bigg thinks, more excellent; I have ſtripped it of its trumpery border which was cemented on the ſurface of the picture, and hid two inches all round, to the great injury of the compoſition. It has coſt me ſome trouble to make good the background, but it was well worth recovering, as the want of an efficient field crowded the compoſition. I count much on our meeting; it will be my only holiday. The time you ſpeak of will do exactly for me. My wife is amuſed with your temptation; you think '*three mills*' irreſiſtible, but it is *you* I want. I have a propoſal to make to Tinney; he muſt let me have his picture and fifty or ſixty guineas, and I will paint him another, more for the ladies and old hums. Sir William Curtis has a hankering after my 'Wain,' but I am not ſanguine, and you I ſhould much prefer; we can talk about it when we meet; it was born a companion to your picture; it muſt be yours. It is no ſmall compliment to the picture, that it haunted the mind of the Alderman from the time he ſaw it at the Inſtitution; but though a man of the world, he is all heart, and really loves nature.* It does me a great deal of good where it now is, therefore let it remain for the preſent. Should Tinney and I agree, it will enable me to paint another large picture for the Exhibition; I am hurt this year for the want of one. * * * ſhowed me a pretty picture he is painting, but it is inſipid, and far too pretty to be natural. Sir George Beaumont has juſt left me; he is pleaſed with a large wood I have toned."†

"Charlotte Street, Auguſt 18th. My dear Fiſher. Aſtley Cooper often arrives an hour ſooner than the time fixed for performing an operation, by which the patient is ſpared the anticipation of the approaching moments; I had fixed Wedneſday, the 20th, to come to you, and I now make it Tueſday, the 19th. Your beautiful fruit-piece has left my houſe, but it will not arrive ſoon enough at Saliſbury to meet us; you will not grudge what it has coſt you; it is

* Conſtable told me of Sir William Curtis, that during an illneſs he had a fine picture by Gainſborough hung in his chamber, that he might ſee it through the opening of his bed curtains.

† A large ſketch of the dell in Helmingham Park.

lovely, and always puts me not only in good humour, but in the humour for painting. I have not the ſea-piece; I gave it to Gooch for his kind attention to my children for which he would receive no fee. Half an hour ago I received a letter from Woodburne to purchaſe it, or one of my ſea-pieces; they are much liked, and you have my ſketch of Oſmington. I have a great deal to ſay which muſt be deferred till to-morrow. I leave my family with great pleaſure becauſe they are all ſo well. My wife laughed much at your ſaying, 'But I don't expect you to come.' I was at the Counteſs of Dyſart's fête champêtre at Ham Houſe. I have pleaſed her by painting two portraits lately, and ſhe has ſent me half a buck."

"To Mrs. Conſtable. Gillingham, Dorſetſhire, 29th Auguſt. My deareſt love. I was at Fonthill yeſterday. It was very good natured of Fiſher to take me to ſee that extraordinary place. The ticket to admit two perſons is a guinea, beſides impoſitions afterwards. Fiſher ſays, there have been great changes in the articles ſince laſt year; ſo that it is quite an auctioneer's job. Many ſuperb things are now not there, and many others added; eſpecially pictures. One of the latter, (or I am greatly miſtaken) a battle by Wovermans, I ſaw at R * * * * * 's juſt before I left town. Yeſterday, being a fine day, a great many people were there. I counted more than thirty carriages, and the ſame number of gigs, and two ſtage coaches; ſo that in ſpite of the guinea tickets there was a great mixture of company, and indeed very few genteel people. There was a large room fitted up with boxes like a coffee-houſe, for dinners, &c. &c. Mr. * * * * * * * * 's name (the auctioneer's) ſeemed here as great as Buonaparte's. Cards of various kinds, and boards were put up, 'Mr. * * * * * * * * deſires this,—Mr. * * * * * * * * takes the liberty of recommending the following inns for beds,' &c. &c. But I obſerved many long faces coming away from the ſaid inns.

"I wandered up to the top of the tower. Saliſbury, at fifteen miles off, darted up into the ſky like a needle, and the woods and lakes were magnificent; and then the wild region of the downs to the north. But the diſtant Dorſetſhire hills made me long much to be at dear old Oſmington, the remembrance of which muſt always be precious to you and me. The entrance to Fonthill and the interior are beautiful. Imagine Saliſbury Cathedral, or indeed, any beautiful Gothic building, magnificently fitted up with crimſon and gold, ancient pictures, and ſtatues in almoſt every niche; large gold boxes for relics, &c. and looking glaſſes, ſome of which ſpoiled the effect. But on the whole it is a ſtrange ideal, romantic place; quite fairy-land. The ſpot is choſen in the midſt of mountains and wilds. We have had ſuch ſad weather that I have been able to do but little, but I have made one or two attacks on the old mill."

"September 30th. My dear Fiſher. I ſhould have thanked you before now for my delightful viſit; but I found on my return ſo much occupation that my writing has been too long delayed. But I truſt forms will weigh as little with you as with me, in a friendſhip which is at once the pride, the honour, and the grand ſtimulus of my life. My Gillingham ſtudies give great ſatisfaction; Mr. Bigg likes them better than any thing I have yet done. I found my wife and children all well; better than I ever had them. I am now pretty full handed, but my difficulty lies in what I am to do for the world next year; I muſt have a large canvaſs. I muſt write to Tinney about his picture, which I wiſh to have up; I ſhall be glad of it, frame and all. * * * aſked me to ſee his picture; it is ſuch art as I cannot talk about; heartleſs, vapid, without intereſt. I was at the private view of the Diorama; it is in part a tranſparency; the ſpectator is in a dark chamber, and it is very pleaſing, and has great illuſion. It is without the pale of the art, becauſe its object is deception. The art pleaſes by *reminding*, not by *deceiving*. The place was filled with foreigners, and I ſeemed to be in a cage of magpies."

"Saliſbury October 2nd. My dear Conſtable, Tinney conſents to let his picture come to London, but he does it, he confeſſes, becauſe he can deny you nothing. He dreads you touching it. L * * * *, the engraver, ſays it, 'has a look of nature which ſeems diffuſed over the canvaſs as if by magic, and this Conſtable may in an unlucky moment deſtroy, and he will never paint another picture like it, for he has taken to repeat himſelf.' I know not whether this remark was his own, or merely the echo of what he had heard ſaid by other artiſts; in either caſe it is right you ſhould be told of it. I muſt repeat to you an opinion I have long held, that no man had ever more than one conception. Milton emptied his mind in his firſt book of Paradiſe Loſt, all the reſt is tranſcript of ſelf. The Odyſſey is a repetition of the Iliad. When you have ſeen one Claude you have ſeen all. I can think of no exception but Shakſpeare; he is always varied, never mannered."

"October 19th. My dear Fiſher, Thank you for your kind, amuſing, and inſtructive letter. I ſhall always be glad to hear any thing that is ſaid of me and my pictures. My object is the improvement of both. L * * * *, like moſt men living on the outſkirts of the art, and like followers and attendants on armies, &c. is a great talker of what *ſhould be*, and this is not always without malignity. Such perſons ſtroll about the foot of Parnaſſus, only to pull down by the legs thoſe who are laboriouſly climbing its ſides. He may be ſincere in what he tells Tinney; he wonders at what is done, and concludes the picture cannot be made better becauſe he knows no better. I ſhall write to Tinney and requeſt the picture, but with a promiſe not to meddle with it, even if I ſee any thing material that would improve it, without firſt informing him of my intention.

"By the time you receive this, I ſhall be at breakfaſt with Sir George and Lady Beaumont, at Cole-Orton Hall, Leiceſterſhire, near Aſhby de la Zouch. I look to this viſit with pleaſure and the hope of improvement. All Sir George's beautiful pictures are there, and if I can find time to copy the little Claude, evidently a ſtudy from nature,* it will much help me. Sir George will not poſſeſs theſe things longer than until a room can be got ready, at the Britiſh Muſeum, to receive them. After my delightful viſit to you, I ſhould have been content. But Sir George ſo much deſired to ſee me, and is ſuch a friend to art, that I thought it a duty to myſelf to go. * * * I want to get back to my eaſel in town, and not to witneſs the rotting, melancholy diſſolution of the trees which two months ago were ſo beautiful. I muſt talk to you about 'Coxe's Life of Correggio;' he has made ſuch confuſion and nonſenſe about art, with the letter of A. Caracci, and the letter itſelf is ſo beautiful."

"To Mrs. Conſtable. Cole-Orton Hall, October 24th. My very dear love. I haſten to fulfil my promiſe of writing to you on my arrival here, though Sir George and Lady Beaumont wiſh me to defer it to another day, as he wants me in his painting room. * * * O dear! this is a lovely place indeed, and I only want you with me to make my happineſs complete. Such grounds, ſuch trees, ſuch diſtances, and all ſeems arranged to be ſeen from the various windows of the houſe. All looks like fairy-land."

"I wiſh you to write to Mrs. Whalley, ſhe will take it ſiſterly and kind. Tell her what an adventure I had at Leiceſter, as I was determined not to go by without ſeeing

* Now in the National Gallery. This picture he mentions again as "The Little Grove."

CHAP. VII. 1823.

Alicia.* I did not chuſe to dine at Northampton, but counted much on tea at Leiceſter. Juſt as it was made, and almoſt poured out, I ran to Miſs Linwood's, and found that ſhe and all her young ladies were at the theatre (about half paſt eight). Thither I haſtened, ſaw Alicia,—ſhook hands, kiſſed her,—ſhe looked delightfully,—her hair curled and beautifully parted on her fair round forehead,—her cheeks roſy, owing to being ſo ſurpriſed,—her chin dimpled, and her teeth beautifully white. Saw three ſtrange figures on the ſtage, who had juſt ended a ſtrange ſong,—the audience were all clapping their hands, and all this took place in half a minute. Haſtened back to the inn to finiſh my tea,—party broken up,—coach driving off,—and myſelf nearly left behind. Will not this amuſe her? Copy it, and your letter will be almoſt formed.

"Only think, I am now writing in a room full of Claudes, (not Glovers, but real Claudes,) Wilſons, and Pouſſins. But I think of you and am ſad in the midſt of all. And my ducks,—my darling Iſabel, my Charley boy, my Minna, and my dear, dear John. J. C."

"Cole-Orton Hall, November 2nd. My very dear Fiſher. Your letter is delightful, and its coming here ſerves to help me in the eſtimation of Sir George and Lady Beaumont. Nothing can be more kind, and in every poſſible way more obliging than they both are to me. I am left entirely to do as I like, with full range over the whole houſe, in which I may *ſaturate* myſelf with art; only on condition of letting them do as they like. I have copied one of the ſmall Claudes; a breezy ſunriſe, a moſt pathetic picture.† Perhaps a ſketch would have ſerved my preſent pur-

* Mrs. Whalley's daughter, who was at ſchool at Leiceſter.

† The "Cephalus and Procris," another of Sir George Beaumont's valuable gifts to the National Gallery.

pose, but I wished for a more lasting remembrance of it; and a sketch of a picture is only like seeing it in one view; it will not serve to drink at again and again. I have likewise begun the little grove by Claude; a noon-day scene 'which warms and cheers, but which does not inflame or irritate.' Through the depths of the trees are seen a waterfall, and a ruined temple, and a solitary shepherd is piping to some goats and sheep.

> 'In closing shades and where the current strays,
> Pipes the lone shepherd to his feeding flocks.'

I draw in the evening, and Lady, or Sir George Beaumont reads aloud. Sir George has known intimately many persons of talent of the last half century, and is full of anecdote. This is a magnificent country, abounding in the picturesque. The bell is now going for church. Sir George and Lady Beaumont never miss, morning and evening every Sunday, and have family prayers. * * * In the breakfast room hang four Claudes, a Cozens, and a Swaneveldt; the sun glows on them as it sets. In the dark recesses of the gardens, and at the end of one of the walks, is a cenotaph erected to the memory of Sir Joshua Reynolds, and on it some beautiful lines by Wordsworth. There is a magnificent view from the terrace over a mountainous region, and there is a winter garden, the thought taken by Sir George from 'The Spectator.'" †

"To Mrs. Constable, November 2nd. The weather has been bad, but I do not at all regret being confined to this house. The mail did not arrive yesterday till many hours

† Wilkie, who, in company with Mr. Haydon, visited Cole-Orton Hall in August 1809, thus describes the house and its situation. "Dance, who designed it, has acquitted himself well. We found it most spacious and magnificent. We entered first through a large portico into the lobby which leads into a

Chap. VII.
1823.

after the time, owing to ſome trees being blown down, and the waters out. * * * I am now going to breakfaſt before the Narciſſus of Claude. How enchanting and lovely it is; far, very far ſurpaſſing any other landſcape I ever beheld. Write to me. Kiſs and love my darlings. I hope my ſtay will not exceed this week."

In one of his letters from Cole-Orton to his wife, Conſtable ſays, "Sir George riſes at ſeven, walks in the garden before breakfaſt, and rides out about two, fair or foul. We have had breakfaſt at half-paſt eight, but to-day we began at the winter hour, nine. We do not quit the breakfaſt-table directly, but chat a little about the pictures in the room. We then go to the painting-room, and Sir George moſt manfully ſets to work, and I by his ſide. At two the horſes are brought to the door. I have had an opportunity of ſeeing the ruins of Aſhby, the mountain ſtream and rocks (ſuch Everdingens) at Grace Dieu, and an old convent there, Lord Ferrars', a grand, but melancholy ſpot. At dinner we do not ſit long; Lady Beaumont reads the newſpaper (The Herald) to us, and then to the drawing-room to tea, and after that comes a great treat; I am furniſhed with ſome portfolios full of beautiful drawings or prints, and Sir George reads a play in a manner the moſt delightful. On Saturday evening it was 'As You Like It,' and I never heard the 'ſeven ages' ſo admirably read before. Laſt evening, Sun-

ſplendid hall lighted from the ceiling. Round the hall is a ſuite of rooms fitted up in the moſt elegant manner. The rooms above are chiefly bed rooms, while at the top of all is the painting room of Sir George himſelf. * * * The country around is pictureſque and rather richly wooded; and as we have the advantage of ſeeing it from an eminence, the diſtance ſoftens it to the eye, and helps to render it leſs rugged than any other part of the country we came through between this and London." Wilkie alſo ſpeaks of a ruined abbey in the neighbourhood, rendered intereſting by being the birth-place of Beaumont who wrote in conjunction with Fletcher, and whoſe brother was an anceſtor of Sir George.

day, he read a ſermon, and a good deal of Wordſworth's 'Excurſion.' Some of the landſcape deſcriptions in it are very beautiful. About nine, the ſervant comes in with a little fruit, and a decanter of water, and at eleven we go to bed. I always find a fire in my room, and make out about an hour longer, as I have every thing there, writing deſk, &c. and I grudge a moment's unneceſſary ſleep in this place. You would laugh to ſee my bedroom; I have dragged ſo many things into it, books, portfolios, prints, canvaſſes, pictures, &c."

"November 9th. How glad I was, my dear love, to receive your laſt kind letter, giving a good account of yourſelf and our dear babies. * * * Nothing ſhall, I hope, prevent my ſeeing you this week; indeed I am quite nervous about my abſence, and ſhall ſoon begin to feel alarmed about the exhibition. * * * I do not wonder at your being jealous of Claude. If any thing could come between our love, it is him. I am faſt advancing a beautiful little copy of his ſtudy from nature of a little grove ſcene. If you, my deareſt love, will be ſo good as to make yourſelf happy without me for this week, it will, I hope, be long before we part again. But, believe me, I ſhall be the better for this viſit as long as I live. Sir George is never angry, or pettiſh, or peeviſh, and though he loves painting ſo much, it does not haraſs him. You will like me a great deal better than you did. To-morrow Southey is coming, with his wife and daughter. I know you would be ſorry if I were not to ſtay and meet him, he is ſuch a friend of Gooch's; but the Claudes, the Claudes, are all, all, I can think of here. * * * The weather is ſo bad that I can ſcarcely ſee out of the window, but Friday was lovely. I ſhall hardly be able to make you a ſketch of the houſe, but I ſhall bring much, though in little compaſs, to ſhow you. * * * Thurſday was Sir George's birth-day. Sixty-nine, and married almoſt half a century. The ſervants had a ball, and I was lulled to ſleep by a fiddle."

"November 18th. My deareſt love, * * * I was very glad to hear a very nice account of you and my dear babies. * * * I ſhall finiſh my little Claude on Thurſday; and then I ſhall have ſomething to do to ſome of Sir George's pictures, that will take a day or two more, and then home. * * * I ſent you a haſty ſhabby line by Southey, but all that morning I had been engaged on a little ſketch in Miſs Southey's album, of this houſe, which pleaſed all parties here, very much. Sir George is loath to part with me. He would have me paſs Chriſtmas with him, and has named a ſmall commiſſion which he wiſhed me to execute here, but I have declined it, as I am ſo deſirous to return. Sir George is very kind, and I have no doubt, meant this little picture to pay my expenſes. I have worked ſo hard in the houſe, that I never went out of the door laſt week, ſo that I am getting quite nervous. But I am ſure my viſit here will be ultimately of the greateſt advantage to me; and I could not be better employed to the advantage of all of us by its making me ſo much more of an artiſt. * * * The breakfaſt bell rings. I now haſten to finiſh, as the boy waits. I really think ſeeing the habits of this houſe will be of ſervice to me as long as I live. Every thing ſo punctual. Sir George never looks into his painting room on a Sunday, nor truſts himſelf with a portfolio. Never is impatient. Always rides or walks for an hour or two, at two o'clock; ſo will I with you, if it is only into the ſquare. I amuſe myſelf, every evening, making ſketches from Sir George's drawings about Dedham, &c. I could not *carry* all his ſketch books. * * * I wiſh I had not cut myſelf out ſo much to do here,—but I was greedy with the Claudes."

In his next letter to his wife, Conſtable deplores the facility with which he allowed his time to be conſumed by loungers in his painting room, an evil, his good nature to the laſt entailed on him. Mrs. Conſtable in one of her letters had ſaid, "Mr. * * * * was here nearly an hour on Saturday, reading the paper, and talking to himſelf. I hope you will not admit him ſo often. Mr. * * * *, another lounger, has been here once or twice."

"Cole-Orton Hall, November 21ſt. My deareſt love, I am as heart ſick as ever you can be at my long abſence from you, and all our dear darlings, but which is now faſt drawing to a cloſe. In fact, my greedineſs for pictures made me cut out for myſelf much more work than I ought to have undertaken at this time. One of the Claudes would have been all that I wanted, but I could not get at that firſt, and I had been here a fortnight before I began it. To-day it will be done, with perhaps a little touch on Saturday morning. I have then an old picture to fill up ſome holes in. But I fear I ſhall not be able to get away on Saturday, though I hope nothing ſhall prevent me on Monday. I can hardly believe I have not ſeen you or my Iſabel, or my Charley, for five weeks. Yeſterday there was another very high wind, and ſuch a ſplendid evening as I never before beheld, at this time of the year. Was it ſo with you? But in London nothing is to be ſeen, worth ſeeing, in the *natural* way."

"I certainly will not allow of ſuch ſerious interruptions as I uſed to do, from people who devour my time, brains, and every thing elſe. Sir George ſays it is quite ſerious and alarming. Let me have a letter, on Sunday, my laſt day here, as I want to be made comfortable on my journey, which will be long and tireſome, and I ſhall be very nervous as I get near home; therefore, pray let me have a good account of you all. I believe ſome great folks are coming here in December, which Sir George dreads, as they ſo much interfere with his painting habits; for no artiſt can be fonder of the art."

"November 25th. My very dearest love, I hope nothing will prevent my leaving this place to-morrow afternoon, and that I shall have you in my arms on Thursday morning, and my babies; O dear! how glad I shall be. I feel that I have been *at school*, and can only hope that my long absence from you may ultimately be to my great and lasting improvement as an artist, and indeed, in every thing. If you have any friends staying with you, I beg you will dismiss them before my arrival."

Though Sir George Beaumont and Constable agreed, generally, in their opinions of the old masters, yet their tastes differed materially on some points of art, and their discourse never languished for want of "an animated no." A constant communion with pictures, the tints of which are subdued by time, no doubt tends to unfit the eye for the enjoyment of freshness; and Sir George thought Constable too daring in the modes he adopted to obtain this quality; while Constable saw, that Sir George often allowed himself to be deceived by the effects of time, of accident, and by the tricks that are, far oftener than is generally supposed, played by dealers, to give mellowness to pictures; and, in these matters, each was disposed to set the other right. Sir George had placed a small landscape by Gaspar Poussin on his easel, close to a picture he was painting, and said, "Now, if I can match these tints I am sure to be right." "But suppose, Sir George," replied Constable, "Gaspar could rise from his grave, do you think he would know his own picture in its present state? or if he did, should we not find it difficult to persuade him that somebody had not smeared tar or cart grease over its surface, and then wiped it imperfectly off?" At another time, Sir George recommended the colour of an old Cremona fiddle for the prevailing tone of every thing, and this Constable answered by laying an old fiddle on the green lawn before the house. Again, Sir George, who ſeemed to conſider the autumnal tints neceſſary, at leaſt to ſome part of a landſcape, ſaid, "Do you not find it very difficult to determine where to place your *brown tree?*" And the reply was, "Not in the leaſt, for I never put ſuch a thing into a picture." But however oppoſite in theſe reſpects their opinions were, and although Conſtable well knew that Sir George did not appreciate his works,—the intelligence, the wit, and the faſcinating and amiable manners of the Baronet had gained his heart, and a ſincere and laſting friendſhip ſubſiſted between them.

During his viſit to Cole-Orton, beſides his admirable copies of the Claudes, he made a ſketch from a landſcape by Rubens, a large ſketch of the front of the houſe, and a drawing of the cenotaph erected to Sir Joſhua Reynolds.

Conſtable had never been, nor was he ever again, ſo long ſeparated from his wife and children, as on this occaſion; and his anxiety to return, and at the ſame time, his wiſh to complete the copies he undertook at Cole-Orton, confined him ſo much to his eaſel, that the viſit proved an injury inſtead of a benefit to his health.

"Saliſbury, December 12th. My dear Conſtable, * * * I know not how to adviſe you for the exhibition. The Waterloo depends entirely on the poliſh and finiſh given to it. If I were the painter of it, I would always have it on my eaſel, and work at it for five years, a touch a day.

"The great ſtorm played deſtruction at Gillingham. It blew down two of my great elms, bent another to an angle of forty-five degrees with the ground, and ſtripped a third of all its branches, leaving only one ſtanding entire. This I have taken down, and your wood exiſts only in your ſketches. The great elm in the middle of the turf is ſpared.

"Southey is a friend of the eſtabliſhment: but in one point I think him (with diffidence) wrong. He would adopt the Methodiſt preacher into the church as an inferior

CHAP. VII. 1823.

ſervant. This was the very cauſe of the corruptions and downfall of the Roman Catholic eſtabliſhment. For the ſake of peace and unity they adopted enthuſiaſts, received their errors into the creeds of the church, and then had to *defend* them. You cannot make uſe of the *men* without receiving their opinions.

"Varley is here teaching drawing to the young ladies. '*Principles*,' he ſays, 'are the thing. *The warm gray, the cold gray, and the round touch*.' John Fiſher."

"December 18th. My dear Fiſher. Your kind and welcome letter, as uſual, breathes nothing but good humour, friendſhip, and underſtanding. I wanted juſt ſuch a one; as almoſt, from the time of my return, I have been laid up and am quite diſabled by pains in the bones of my head and face, probably originating in the teeth. It began at Gillingham. However, they have condemned one this morning, who though not the principal, was ſtill an acceſſory before the fact. Perhaps I may look for ſome eaſe, but I have lived on ſuction for the laſt fortnight. * * * I ſhall now turn to your letter to ſee what requires noticing.

"Firſt. I am ſettled for the exhibition. My Waterloo muſt be done, and one other; perhaps one of Tinney's, Dedham, but more probably my Lock. I muſt viſit Gillingham again for a ſubject for the other next ſummer.

"Second. How much I regret the grove at the bottom of your garden. This has really vexed me. I had promiſed myſelf paſſing the ſummer hours in its ſhade.

"Third. I am glad the great elm is ſafe.

"Fourth. What you ſay of Southey is wiſe, juſt, moderate, and undeniable. Though he can ſay much, he cannot gainſay that ſhort ſentence of yours. It marks you maſter of your own profeſſion; and every hour's experience proves to me that no man, not educated, from his early youth, to a profeſſion, can fully and juſtly enter into it."

CHAPTER VIII.

1824.

Letter from Sir George Beaumont. Picture of the Opening of Waterloo Bridge. Lady Paintreſs. Sale of two large Pictures to a Frenchman. Picture of a Lock on the Stour. Deſcription of Brighton. Mr. Phillips. J. Dunthorne, Jun. Venetian Secret diſcovered by a Lady. Mr. Ottley. Waſhington Irving. Note from Mr. Brockedon. Archibald Conſtable. French Criticiſms on Conſtable's Pictures.

1824.

"TO John Conſtable, Eſq. Dear Sir, I am very ſorry to hear you have been ſo unwell ſince your viſit to Cole-Orton, and am afraid it aroſe from too intenſe application. You muſt do me the juſtice to tell Mrs. Conſtable, that I never failed daily propoſing riding or walking. I am quite ſure artiſts ſave time in the end, by allowing the neceſſary interruptions for air and exerciſe. However, now it is over, I hope it will be a warning, and in the mean time, I muſt ſay your time was not paſſed unprofitably, and your induſtry has acquainted you with many of the arcana of Claude's myſterious and magical practice. I thank you for the trouble you have taken in ſending my colours, &c. and finally, wiſh you ſucceſs in the application of the reſult of your ſtudies. I hope you feel no remains of your illneſs, and will go on merrily with your preparations for Somerſet Houſe; but remember, air and exerciſe, or you may be interrupted. At all events, it muſt injure you in the long run, for I am convinced that many artiſts bring on various complaints, and ſhorten their lives from inattention to this point. It does not ſurpriſe me to hear that Sir Thomas Lawrence has delivered an excellent diſcourſe, and it adds to my pleaſure to hear that it is to be printed, and alſo that with his uſual liberality of feeling and good taſte, he has ſpoken in high terms of Mr. Weſt. I beg my compliments to Mrs. Conſtable, and requeſt her to inform you from me, with her influence ſuperadded, that unleſs you take more air and exerciſe, you will never reach my age. I remain, my dear ſir, with every good wiſh, truly yours, G. Beaumont. Cole-Orton Hall, January 6th, 1824. How are your copies approved?"

Whatever good effects Sir George's advice may have produced, were not laſting, for Conſtable never adhered to any plan of regular exerciſe. In town, he was often obliged to quit his eaſel; but even when called out, ſo conſtantly was his attention drawn to paſſing objects, that he loitered rather than walked, and his pace could ſcarcely be quickened into exerciſe, unleſs he was late for ſome appointment.

A letter to Conſtable from the Biſhop of Saliſbury, dated January 6th, encloſing a draft, concludes thus, "Our new year opens under many pleaſing circumſtances; fine weather, returning plenty, public quiet, and the appearance of general peace. May you and yours have many happy returns of ſuch a year."

"January 17th. My dear Fiſher, The Frenchman who was after my large picture of 'The Hay Cart' laſt year, is here again. He would, I believe, have both that and 'The Bridge,' if he could get them at his own price. I ſhowed him your letter, and told him of my promiſe to you. His object is to make a ſhow of them at Paris, perhaps to my advantage. I ſhould like to adviſe with you about the large 'Waterloo;' it is a work that ſhould not be hurried. I am engaged on my upright 'Lock,' and I hope, one of Tinney's new ones. I only want to work harder to be comfortable. My ſucceſs in life ſeems pretty certain, but no man can get much by ſtudy, and the labour of his own hands."

"January 18th. My dear Conſtable. Thurtell ſaid,*— but, perhaps, you are as ſick of his name as you were of the queen's, ſo we will change the ſubject. * * * Let your 'Hay cart' go to Paris by all means. I am too much pulled down by the agricultural diſtreſs to hope to poſſeſs it. I would, I think, let it go at leſs than its price for the ſake of the éclat it may give you. The ſtupid Engliſh public, which has no judgment of its own, will begin to think there is ſomething in you if the French make your works national property. You have long lain under a miſtake; men do not purchaſe pictures becauſe they admire them, but becauſe others covet them. * * *

"Did you know the fact in natural hiſtory that rooks prefer to build in elm trees before all others, and that they ſeldom, or never frequent cheſnuts? When we were felling our elms at Gillingham, ſome rooks flew over and were clamorous. Whether deprecating our work of deſtruction or not, I cannot tell.

"In the new novel attributed to Sir Walter Scott, ('St. Ronan's Well,') is the following paſſage. 'There are very well bred artiſts, ſaid Lady Penelope, it is the profeſſion of a gentleman.'—'Certainly, anſwered Lady Binks; but the poorer claſs have often to ſtruggle with poverty and dependence. In general ſociety, they are like commercial people

* This is a humorous hit at the importance attached to every thing ſaid or done by a convicted murderer.

in preſence of their cuſtomers; and that is a difficult part to ſuſtain. And ſo you ſee them of all ſorts—ſhy and reſerved, when they are conſcious of merit—petulant and whimſical, by way of ſhowing their independence—intruſive in order to appear eaſy—and ſometimes obſequious and fawning, when they chance to be of a mean ſpirit.' Are either you or * * * * * acquainted with Sir Walter Scott?

"I am ſhut up in lodgings here,—the walls covered with *old maſters*. I ſuffer like the martyrs of old, who had their eyes put out with hot brazen baſins held before their faces. But I am relieved by one picture which I gueſs to be a genuine Vanderhayden. Is not that the name of the man who painted brick buildings ſo minutely? It is very true and delicate, and with pretty light and ſhadow, but the ſky looks as if it had been touched up. J. Fiſher."

"January 22nd. My dear Fiſher, * * * I have done the little 'Waterloo,' a ſmall balloon to let off as a forerunner of the large one." * * *

Mr. Fiſher in a letter dated, "Weymouth, February 12th," ſays, "I beg to congratulate you on the appearance of your name in the newſpapers. Do not deſpiſe them too much. They cannot give fame, but they attend on her. *Smoke* gives notice that the houſe is on fire. I ſhall be in town Wedneſday or Thurſday next."

"April 15th. My dear Fiſher, I have been for ſome time deſirous of writing to you, but I was never more fully bent on any picture than that on which you left me engaged. It is gone to its audit, and my friends tell me it is my beſt; it is a good ſubject, and an admirable inſtance of the pictureſque. I hear there are ſome fine pictures this year at the Academy, from ſome of the old, as well as ſome of the new Academicians. On Saturday I ſhall go for a few days into Suffolk; I wiſh to ſee what they are about, and Lady Dyſart wants me to look at the woods which ſhe has given into the care of my brother, that I may bring a report to her, as he cannot leave them. I have had the Frenchman again with me; we have agreed as to price, two hundred and fifty pounds the pair, and I give him a ſmall picture of 'Yarmouth' into the bargain."

"I dined the other day with * * * * *, to be introduced to a lady paintreſs, 'with whom I ſhould be much pleaſed.' I found a laughing, ignorant, fat, uncouth old woman; but very good-natured; and ſhe gave me no trouble, as ſhe wanted no inſtruction from me. When ſhe told me of an oil proper for painting, I told her it would not do, but ſhe aſſured me it would, and that ſhe could give me no greater proof of it, than that one of her pictures was painted entirely with it."

Conſtable exhibited but one picture this year. "A Boat paſſing a Lock."—The ſcene of this ſubject is cloſe to Flatford Mill, and was often painted by him from different points of view. An early picture of it, in which the lock is on the right of the foreground, forms one of the moſt complete ſubjects of the "Engliſh Landſcape." The little wooden bridge, a principal feature in the engraving entitled the "River Stour, Suffolk," is here introduced at a greater diſtance, with the whole of the pictureſque cottage near it.

"May 8th. Dear Fiſher, I have juſt depoſited my picture in its place, and oppoſite, and as a companion to one by Mrs. * * * * *.† To what honours are ſome men born! * * * * My Frenchman has ſent his agent with the money for the pictures; they are now ready, and look uncommonly well, and I think they cannot fail to melt the ſtony hearts of the French painters. Think of the lovely valleys and peaceful farm-houſes of Suffolk forming part of an exhibition to amuſe the gay Pariſians. My Lock is liked at the

† The lady deſcribed in the laſt letter.

Academy, and indeed it forms a decided feature, and its light cannot be put out, becaufe it is the light of nature, the mother of all that is valuable in poetry, painting, or any thing elfe where an appeal to the foul is required. The language of the heart is the only one that is univerfal; and Sterne fays, he difregards all rules, but makes his way to the heart as he can. But my execution annoys moft of them, and all the fcholaftic ones. Perhaps the facrifices I make for lightnefs and brightnefs are too great, but thefe things are the effence of landfcape, and my extreme is better than white-lead and oil, and *dado painting*. I fold this picture on the day of the opening for one hundred and fifty guineas, including the frame, to Mr. Morrifon. I do hope my exertions may tend towards popularity; but it is you who have fo long held my head above water. Although a good deal of the devil is in me, I do think I fhould have been broken hearted before this time but for you. Indeed, it is worth while to have gone through all I have for the hours and thoughts we have had together. I am in high favour with all the Seymour Street family, and I look continually back to the great kindnefs fhown to me in my early days, when it was truly of value to me; for long I tottered on the threfhold, and floundered in the path, and there never was any young man nearer being loft; but here I am, and I muft now take heed where I ftand."

"Gillingham, May 10th. My dear Conftable. I admire your lion-like generofity in paffing over my long filence without vituperation. I am glad you did not afk me for a reafon, for I can affign none, except that I was always thinking of you, daily intending to write, and daily neglecting to put my intention into execution. Your laft letter is evidently written in a tone of great exultation, and with reafon. Your fame and fortune are both advanced; and for both you are indebted but to Providence and your own exertions. I am not ſurpriſed that 'The Navigator' ſold on a firſt inſpection; for it was one of your beſt pictures. The purchaſe of your two great landſcapes for Paris, is ſurely a ſtride up three or four ſteps of the ladder of popularity. Engliſh boobies, who dare not truſt their own eyes, will diſcover your merits when they find you admired at Paris. We now *muſt* go there for a week. * * * I generally leave you wiſer than I came to you, and ſome of your pithy apothegms ſtick to my memory like a thorn, and give me a prick when I fall a dozing. 'A man is always growing,' you ſaid, 'either upwards or downwards.' I have been trying to grow 'upwards' ſince we parted. When I conſulted you about the Lancaſtrian Sunday School in my pariſh, you adviſed me to 'be quiet and do all the good I could.' I took your advice, and the quakers have, unſolicited, dropped the offenſive rules. J. Fiſher."

"Gillingham, May 11th. My dear Conſtable. * * * * They have had one or two ſmart bruſhes at the Church, in Parliament, but have been triumphantly defeated. One member ſaid, 'if half the induſtry had been uſed to bring to light the good done by the clergy, which has been uſed to malign them, the Church would need no defender.' However, I am indifferent to ſuch attacks. I am at my poſt, and intend to be found at it, happen what will. The people of this place are given to my charge, and I will diſcharge the duty, with or without the tithes. What has become of Waterloo? I am ready to receive you at Saliſbury at any moment. Will you go with me on my viſitation? J. Fiſher."

"My dear Fiſher, I have counted on the pleaſure of ſeeing Berkſhire again with you, but that is not poſſible this year; I have juſt now engaged to get ſeven pictures of a ſmall ſize ready for Paris by Auguſt. The large ones are to be exhibited at the Louvre, and my purchaſers ſay they are much looked for at Paris. The Director of the Academy at Antwerp, Mr. Vanbree, has been here; he ſays they will make an impreſſion on the Continent. * * * The world is rid of Lord Byron, but the deadly ſlime of his touch ſtill remains."

"Brighton, May 29th. The dignitary of the Church ſeems to have forgotten the dignitary of the eaſel. * * * I am buſy here, but I diſlike the place, and miſs any letter from you. I am, however, getting on with my French affairs; one of the largeſt is quite complete, and is my beſt in ſparkle with repoſe, which is my ſtruggle juſt now. Brighton is the receptacle of the faſhion and off-ſcouring of London. The magnificence of the ſea, and its, to uſe your own beautiful expreſſion, 'everlaſting voice,' is drowned in the din and tumult of ſtage coaches, gigs, flys, &c. and the beach is only Piccadilly or worſe by the ſea-ſide. Ladies dreſſed and undreſſed; gentlemen in morning-gowns and ſlippers, or without them or any thing elſe, about knee deep in the breakers; footmen, children, nurſery-maids, dogs, boys, fiſhermen, and Preventive Service men with hangers and piſtols; rotten fiſh, and thoſe hideous amphibious animals, the old bathing-women, whoſe language, both in oaths and voice, reſembles men, all mixed together in endleſs and indecent confuſion. The genteeler part, or Marine Parade, is ſtill more unnatural, with its trimmed and neat appearance, and the dandy jetty or Chain Pier, with its long and elegant ſtrides into the ſea a full quarter of a mile." (Here the writing is interrupted by a ſketch). "In ſhort, there is nothing here for a painter but the breakers and the ſky, which have been lovely indeed, and always varying.* The fiſhing-

* On the back of one of Conſtable's oil ſketches made in the ſummer of this year at the Weſt end of Brighton, is written, "The neighbourhood of Brighton conſiſts of London cow-fields, and hideous maſſes of unfledged earth called the country."

boats here are not ſo picturеſque as the Haſtings boats; the difference is this." (Here a ſketch). "But theſe ſubjects are ſo hacknied in the Exhibition, and are indeed ſo little capable of the beautiful ſentiment that belongs to landſcape, that they have done a great deal of harm. They form a claſs of art much eaſier than landſcape, and have, in conſequence, almoſt ſupplanted it. While in the fields, for I am at the weſt of this city, and quite out of it, I met with a moſt intelligent and elegant-minded man, Mr. Phillips. We became intimate, and he contributes much to our pleaſure here. He is a botaniſt, and all his works on Natural Hiſtory are inſtructive and entertaining, calculated for children of all ages; his 'Hiſtory of Trees' is delightful. We are at No. 9, Mrs. Sober's Gardens, ſo called from Mrs. Sober, the lady of the manor; ſhe has built a Chapel; and a man who was taken before the magiſtrates quite drunk, when aſked what he was, ſaid he was 'one of Mrs. Sober's congregation.' Laſt Tueſday, the fineſt day that ever was, we went to the Dyke, which is, in fact, the remains of a Roman encampment, overlooking one of the grandeſt natural landſcapes in the world, and conſequently a ſcene the moſt unfit for a picture. It is the buſineſs of a painter not to contend with nature, and put ſuch a ſcene, a valley filled with imagery fifty miles long, on a canvaſs of a few inches; but to make ſomething out of nothing, in attempting which, he muſt almoſt of neceſſity become poetical; but you underſtand all this better than I. My wife and children are delightfully well."

In June, Conſtable returned to London with young Dunthorne, leaving his family at Brighton. While in town, he kept a diary, which he ſent at intervals to Mrs. Conſtable, and from which the following are a few extracts: "Wedneſday, June 16th. * * * A French gentleman and his wife called; they were much pleaſed, could talk a little Engliſh, and we got on very well. He ordered a little picture, and wished to know if I would receive any commissions from Paris, where he said I was much known and esteemed, and if I would go there, the artists would receive me with great éclat. He was delighted with Tinney's picture, which now looks very beautiful on the easel; it is of service to me to have so good a work to show. Jackson told me that Lord Fitzwilliam would certainly have bought my picture, if it had not been sold to Mr. Morrison. Fisher called and dined. Leslie called to ask me to pass the evening with him. He staid to tea. Fisher and Leslie had a good deal of talk about Washington Irving. A new book of his just out. Fisher is quite pleased with Irving."

"21st June. * * * Collins called; he says I am a great man at Paris, and that it is curious they speak there of only three English artists, namely Wilkie, Lawrence, and Constable. This sounds very grand. He was quite struck with the look of Tinney's picture. He hopes it will go to the Gallery."

"June 22nd. * * * Had a letter from Paris. Mr. Arrowsmith informed me of the safe arrival of my pictures, and how much they were admired; he talks of coming again the end of next month; I shall be ready for him; his letter is flattering, but I have no wish to go to Paris."

"June 24th. * * * * * called. He did not want to see me, but had something to say to a man he had with him, and if I would give him leave, would take him into the parlour.—He easily makes himself at home."

"June 25th. After breakfast called on the Bishop by his wish. He had to tell me that he thought of my improving the picture of the Cathedral, and mentioned many things.—'He hoped I would not take his observations amiss.' I said, 'quite the contrary, as his Lordship had been my kind monitor for twenty-five years.' I am to have it home to-morrow. He ſays I muſt viſit the Colonel,* at Charleton, this or next month, for a day or two. I do not wiſh it, as I begin to be tired of going to ſchool. The good Biſhop had been at Dedham, and found the wretched * * * * 's all at daggers drawn. He reconciled them, and inſiſted on their ſhaking hands, which they did. Mr. Neave called this evening about five. He is always the moſt agreeable perſon in the world. He was quite aſtoniſhed at the picture on the eaſel (Tinney's) and hoped I would always keep to the picturesque, and thoſe ſcenes in which I am 'ſo entirely original.' Mrs. Hand tells me that Owen always ſpeaks ſo very highly of me, in every way, that it is quite delightful."

"June 28th. F. Collins called to aſk me to a party; but Sir George Beaumont had ſent me tickets for the Britiſh Inſtitution this evening, and I thought it would be a treat to Johnny Dunthorne to ſee ſo many fine ladies."

"June 30th. Sir George Beaumont called to know if I would undertake a ſingular commiſſion. There is a lady who has devoted herſelf to the diſcovery of what is called the Venetian ſecret of colouring. She has been at it theſe twenty years, and has at length written to the Secretary of State to deſire proper trials may be made of it by ſome eminent artiſts. Sir George aſked me to try it, ſaying I ſhould be paid for my time, &c. and thinking that as the lady is now at Brighton, it might not be inconvenient to me. I ſhall ſee him again to-morrow; the lady's name I forget."

"July 1ſt. I am glad to find the lady who has diſcovered the Venetian ſecret declines ſubmitting it to any one artiſt. She wants the Governors of the Britiſh Inſtitution to ſend many artiſts, and to offer very high premiums for their ſucceſs, ſo Sir George hopes there will be an end of it. Mrs. * * * * ſaw the Exhibition, and was delighted with my

* A relation of the Biſhop, an amateur landſcape painter.

Chap. VIII.
1824.

picture, which, she says, 'flatters the spot, but does not belie nature.'"

"July 2nd. Received a letter from the Institution offering prizes for the best sketches and pictures of the Battles of the Nile and Trafalgar; it does not concern me."

"July 3rd. Mr. Ottley called this morning. I was introduced to him by Sir George Beaumont. He was much pleased, and stayed a long time, and looked at a good many things. He is more of a connoisseur than an artist, and therefore full of objections. A good undoer, but little of a doer, and with no originality of mind. He invited me to drink tea with him.—Mr. Appleton, the tub-maker, of Tottenham Court Road, called to know if I had a damaged picture which I could let him have cheap, as he is fitting up a room up one pair of stairs. * * * Went to tea with Mr. Ottley. Saw some beautiful prints. Such a collection of Waterloo's etchings I never saw. There was also an abundance of his own things, which gave me a great deal of pain; so laborious, so tasteless, and so useless, but very plausible. They were all of the single leaf,* and chiefly laurels, weeds, hops, grapes, and bell vines; and ten thousand of them. He is a very clever writer and a good man. He says he has lost a great deal by his publications on art."

"July 7th. Took tea with Rochard. The Chalons and Newton there. A pleasant evening. Saw in a newspaper on the table, a paragraph mentioning the arrival of my pictures in Paris. They have caused a stir, and the French critics by profession, are very angry with the artists for admiring them. All this is amusing enough, but they cannot get at me on this side of the water, and I shall not go there."

"July 10th. Dressed to go to Leslie's to dinner. It is a

* He means that every single leaf was drawn without attention to the masses.

very fit houſe for an artiſt, but ſadly out of the way. But it is quite in the country. Willes and Newton there. After dinner took a walk in the fields and to the new church, St. John's Wood, where my poor uncle, David Pike Watts, is buried. Saw the tomb. A lovely evening."

In another part of this journal, Conſtable deſcribes the familiarity of ſome of his neighbour's pigeons. They came into a room where John Dunthorne was working, and perched on the eaſel; and he continues: "Mary Conſtable told me a funny ſtory of one of her ſwans and a duck that had young ones. He poked his long neck towards ſome of her brood, and ſhe attacked him with fury, and after a great to do, and ſplaſhing, and noiſe, and hiſſing, and flapping of wings, ſhe drove him off, and rode away in triumph on his back."

"Brighton, July 18th. My dear Fiſher, I have often attempted to write to you, but in London I have ſo many occupations and interruptions, that I was glad to put it off 'till I arrived here, whither I am come to ſeek ſome quiet with my family. * * * I have formed a plan of receiving no commiſſion under twenty guineas, however ſmall, as the picture muſt be complete, and the ſubject as good as one on a ſix-foot canvaſs. We have received a letter from the wiſe men of the Inſtitution; they offer a good thing; it is to receive ſome pictures from living artiſts which are in private hands, to form an Exhibition next year inſtead of the old maſters. I have to beg that Tinney's picture may be one, and as it is already in my poſſeſſion, it is convenient. * * * The French critics have begun with me, and that in the uſual way, by compariſon with *what has been done*. They are angry with the artiſts for admiring theſe pictures, which they 'ſhall now proceed to examine,' &c. They acknowledge the effect to be 'rich and powerful, and that the whole has the look of nature, and the colour, their chief excellence, to be true and harmonious; but ſhall we admire works ſo unuſual for theſe excellencies alone? what then is to become of the great Pouſſin?' They then caution the younger artiſts to 'beware of the ſeduction of theſe Engliſh works.' All this comes of being regular critics. The execution of my pictures, I know, is ſingular, but I like that rule of Sterne's, 'Never mind the dogmas of the ſchools, but get at the heart as you can;' and it is evident ſomething like this has been attained, by the impreſſion theſe pictures have made on moſt people who have ſeen them here and abroad. I have the paper, and will ſend it to you. I am planning ſome large landſcape, but I have no inclination to purſue my Waterloo; I am impreſſed with a notion that it will ruin me. I want to ſee you at Saliſbury, but how or when, I know not. I am looking for a month's quiet here, and have brought with me ſeveral works to complete. What a bleſſing it is thus to be able to carry my profeſſion with me. My wife is much better and ſtronger for the change."

Conſtable's youngeſt brother, Mr. Abram Conſtable, with whom he kept up a conſtant correſpondence, in a letter dated Auguſt 2nd, ſays: "I fully coincide in your opinion of John Dunthorne. He is certainly the moſt extraordinary young man within my knowledge. So clever, ſo active, ſo innocent,—'tis marvellous. I aſſure you I had not overlooked his conduct. * * * Johnny has made every inquiry about the elm called 'Buck's elm,' and no intention is entertained of its coming down at preſent; but a look out ſhall be kept to prevent it, if poſſible. 'Tis of no value when down, and I hope that circumſtance will prevent it. * * * John Dunthorne is too good to paſs his life among diſſolute workmen."

Immediately on alighting from the coach after one of his journeys either to or from Brighton, Conſtable made the beautiful ſketch from which the engraving in the "Engliſh Landſcape," called "Summer, afternoon after a ſhower," was taken; it was the recollection of an effect he had noticed near Red Hill.

"Gillingham, Shaftesbury, September 8th. My dear Constable. * * * You recollect, probably, a conversation we had with Leslie respecting Washington Irving. I said that Irving had not done justice to the present character of the clergy. That they were a class of men who much admired his works, and had literary reputation much at their disposal. In his new work, the 'Tales of a Traveller,' he has made us ample amends. I copy the following from page 316, vol. i. 'He was a good man: a worthy specimen of that valuable body of our country clergy, who silently and unostentatiously do a vast deal of good; who are, as it were, woven into the whole system of rural life, and operate upon it with the steady yet unobtrusive influence of temperate piety and learned good sense.' The rest of the volume is on the same subject, and gives a pretty picture of the serene tranquillity and decorum of a Cathedral city, and a most amiable hint at the character of a *Prebendary*. Is this accident?—Take an opportunity to let Leslie know that the compliment has not been lost on the body. * * * I have a great mind to dress up your description of Brighton and send it to John Bull. It *is* an odious place. J. Fisher."

"November 2nd. My very dear Fisher, I am determined to write to you, though scarcely equal to it. * * * All my indispositions have their source in my mind. It is when I am restless and unhappy that I become susceptible of cold, damp, heats, and such nonsense. I have not been well for some weeks, but I hope soon to get to work again. * * *"

"November 2nd. My dear Constable. Association of ideas is sometimes very singular. What is there in common between you and Alderman Wood? and yet seeing his name at the head of a paragraph in a newspaper, made me think of you. I found that his son had been elected to some living

CHAP. VIII. 1824.

in the city, and that J * * * * * had been a rival candidate. The name of J * * * * * called that of Conſtable to my mind by an intimate aſſociation, and ſo I ſtole a few moments to write to you on the ſpur of the recollection.—November 4th. I had written thus far, when, yeſterday, I received your diſtreſſing letter. I was very ſorry to perceive both from the matter and the hand writing that you were very much out of order. But I truſt the cold weather, and your temperate habits, will ſoon reſtore nature to her healthy action. * * * Every body has been ill. Abernethy ſays, that there is not a healthy man in London; ſuch is the ſtate of the atmoſphere and mode of life. * * * I copy you a paſſage from 'D'Iſraeli's Anecdotes,' in the abſence of news. 'In all art, perfection lapſes into that weakened ſtate too often dignified as claſſical imitation. It ſinks into manneriſm, wantons into affectation, or ſhoots out into fantaſtic novelties. When all languiſhes in a ſtate of mediocrity, or is deformed by falſe taſte, then ſome fortunate genius has the glory of reſtoring another golden age of invention.' Hiſtory of the Caracci. J. Fiſher."

"November 13th. My dear Conſtable. This moiſt muggy weather ſeems to have deranged every body; and among others, your humble ſervant. I have been, as the old women ſay, 'quite poorly,' this laſt week, and not equal to the energy of a letter. * * * I hope you will diverſify your ſubject this year as to *time* of day. Thomſon, you know, wrote not four Summers, but four Seaſons. People get tired of mutton at top, mutton at bottom, and mutton at the ſide, though of the beſt flavour and ſmalleſt ſize. When you write again, give us a little hiſtory of your wife and children. J. Fiſher."

"Charlotte Street, November 17th. My dear Fiſher, Thank you for your letter of yeſterday * * * John Dunthorne is here; he cheers and helps me ſo much, that I could wiſh to have him always with me; he forwards me a good deal in ſubordinate parts, ſuch as tracing, ſquaring, &c. This morning a gentleman called on me who has nine teleſcopes; you may judge how thick they ſoon got;* it is John's forte, he is to ſee them to-morrow. I am planning a large picture, and I regard all you ſay; but I do not enter into that notion of varying one's plans to keep the public in good humour. Change of weather and effect will always afford variety. What if Vander Velde had quitted his ſea pieces, or Ruyſdael his waterfalls, or Hobbema his native woods. The world would have loſt ſo many features in art. I know that you wiſh for no material alteration; but I have to combat from high quarters, even from Lawrence, the plauſible argument that *ſubject* makes the picture. Perhaps you think an evening effect might do; perhaps it might ſtart me ſome new admirers, but I ſhould loſe many old ones. I imagine myſelf driving a nail; I have driven it ſome way, and by perſevering I may drive it home; by quitting it to attack others, though I may amuſe myſelf, I do not advance beyond the firſt, while that particular nail ſtands ſtill. No man who can do any one thing well, will be able to do any other different thing equally well; and this is true even of Shakſpeare, the greateſt maſter of variety. Send me the picture of the ſhady lane when you like. Do you wiſh to have any other? The ſketch-book I am buſy with for a few days; it is full of boats and coaſt ſcenes. Subjects of this ſort ſeem to me more fit for execution than for ſentiment. I hold the genuine paſtoral feeling of landſcape to be very rare, and difficult of attainment. It is by far the moſt lovely department of painting as well as of poetry. I looked into Angerſtein's the other day; how paramount is Claude! * * *

* Young Dunthorne, who was very ingenious, was fond of aſtronomy. His father ſhowed me, in 1840, the remains of a large teleſcope made by him.

CHAP. VIII. 1824.

Can any thing exceed the villany of the newſpapers? after having ſaid every thing bad of ——, moſt of which is true, they are now endeavouring to turn juſtice from its courſe. I met Sir —— ſeveral times at Brighton. He is a ſtrong, ſenſible, ſtupid, clever, fooliſh, vulgar dog; very amuſing, no doubt a great liar, has long been carried about on the ſhoulders of the world, and his mind is filled with all the dirt of life. I fear you will be annoyed by this ill-written rigmarole letter. But forgive it, as it has afforded much amuſement to my mind to write it. My wife wants ſome account of Mrs. Fiſher and your children."

"My dear Conſtable, You will find in the encloſed ſome remarks upon your pictures at Paris. I returned laſt night and brought this with me. The French have been forcibly ſtruck by them, and they have created a diviſion in the ſchool of the landſcape painters of France. You are accuſed of careleſsneſs by thoſe who acknowledge the truth of your effect; and the freſhneſs of your pictures has taught them that though your means may not be eſſential, your end muſt be to produce an imitation of nature, and the next exhibition in Paris will teem with your imitators, or the ſchool of nature *verſus* the ſchool of Birmingham. I ſaw one man draw another to your pictures with this expreſſion, 'Look at theſe landſcapes by an Engliſhman,—the ground appears to be covered with dew.' Yours very ſincerely, William Brockedon. 11, Caroline Street, Bedford Square, December 13th."

Conſtable told me of a ſingular practice of a nameſake of his, who was not, however, a relation. Archibald Conſtable, the Edinburgh publiſher, called on him, I think in this year, and introduced himſelf, ſaying that, wherever he was, he made it a point to call on every perſon he could find, bearing his own name, whom he had not previouſly known.*

* I did not meet with the following account of the origin of the name, in

" Charlotte Street, December 17th. My dear Fisher, * * * How much I ſhould like to paſs a day or two with you at Bath; but after ſuch an interrupted ſummer, and ſo much indiſpoſition in the autumn, I find it quite impoſſible to leave London, my work is ſo much behind hand. We hear of ſad illneſſes all round us, cauſed, no doubt, by the exceſſive wet. I have juſt received a letter from Sir George Beaumont; he has been ſeriouſly ill, and quite unable until lately to touch a pencil. Every thing which belongs to me belongs to you, and I ſhould not have heſitated a moment about ſending you the Brighton ſketch-book, but when you wrote, my Frenchman was in London, we were ſettling about work, and he has engaged me to make twelve drawings, to be engraved here, and publiſhed in Paris, all from this book. I work at theſe in the evening. This book is larger than my others, and does not contain odds and ends, but all regular compoſitions of boats or beach ſcenes; there may be about thirty of them. If you wiſh to ſee them for a few days, tell me how I am to ſend them to you. My Paris affairs go on very well. Though the Director, the Count Forbin, gave my pictures very reſpectable ſituations in the Louvre in the firſt inſtance, yet on being exhibited a few weeks, they advanced in reputation, and were removed from their original ſituations to a poſt of honour, two prime places in the principal room. I am much indebted to the artiſts for their alarum in my favour; but I muſt do juſtice to the Count,

time to place it, where it ſhould have appeared, in the firſt chapter. " The ſurname of Conſtable firſt took its riſe from an office of great truſt ſo called in former times, as the conſtable of Cheſter, the conſtable of Richmond; and at this time there is a conſtable of the Tower of London, which office was introduced into England by the Normans. Some of this ſort of offices were in Bretagne, in France, whence many of William the Conqueror's army came into England with him, among whom we find one Conſtable, the firſt of that name, as appears by the liſt or table of Battle Abbey, in the Tower of London, printed in How's Chronicle, p. 138."—*Poulſon's Hiſtory of Holderneſs*, vol. ii.

who is no artiſt I believe, and thought that as the colours are rough, they ſhould be ſeen at a diſtance. They found the miſtake, and now acknowledge the richneſs of texture, and attention to the ſurface of things. They are ſtruck with their vivacity and freſhneſs, things unknown to their own pictures. The truth is, they ſtudy (and they are very laborious ſtudents) pictures only ; and as Northcote ſays, 'They know as little of nature as a hackney-coach horſe does of a paſture.' In fact, it is worſe, they make painful ſtudies of individual articles, leaves, rocks, ſtones, &c. ſingly ; ſo that they look cut out, without belonging to the whole, and they neglect the look of nature altogether, under its various changes. I learnt yeſterday that the proprietor aſks twelve thouſand francs for them. They would have bought one, 'The Waggon,' for the nation, but he would not part them. He tells me the artiſts much deſire to purchaſe and depoſit them in a place where they can have acceſs to them. Reynolds is going over in June to engrave them, and has ſent two aſſiſtants to Paris to prepare the plates. He is now about 'The Lock,' and he is to engrave the twelve drawings. In all this I am at no expenſe, and it cannot fail to advance my reputation. My wife is tranſlating for me ſome of the criticiſms. They are amuſing and acute, but ſhallow. After ſaying 'It is but juſtice to admire the truth, the colour, and the general vivacity and richneſs of ſurface, yet they are like preludes in muſic, and the full harmonious warblings of the Æolian lyre, which *mean nothing* ;' and they call them 'orations and harangues, and high flowery converſations affecting a careleſs eaſe,' &c. However, it is certain they have made a ſtir, and ſet the ſtudents in landſcape to thinking. Now you muſt believe me, there is no other perſon living but yourſelf to whom I could write in this manner, and all about myſelf ; but take away a painter's vanity, and he will never touch a pencil again."

The following is part of Mr. Fisher's reply to this letter. "I am pleafed to find they are engraving your pictures, becaufe it will tend to fpread your fame: but I am almoft timid about the refult. There is, in your pictures, too much evanefcent effect, and general tone, to be expreffed by black and white. Your charm is colour, and the cool tint of Englifh daylight. The burr of mezzotint will never touch that."

CHAPTER IX.

1825.

Brighton Sketches. Family Picture at Woodmanſtone. Picture of "The Jumping Horſe." Gold Medal awarded to Conſtable by the King of France. Duc de Choiſeul. Paley. Sharon Turner. Picture of "The Lock." Opinion expreſſed of it by S. W. Reynolds. Conſtable's Pictures in the Exhibition at the Academy. Sale of two Pictures to Mr. Darby. Exhibition, at the Britiſh Gallery, of a Selection of the Works of Living Artiſts. Illneſs of Conſtable's eldeſt Son. Picture of "The White Horſe," ſent to Liſle. Dinner at Lady Dyſart's. Northcote. Cat and Chickens. Mr. Banniſter. J. Dunthorne's Deſcription of "The Devil and Dr. Fauſtus."

1825.

IN a letter dated January 5th, 1825, Conſtable ſpeaks of ſending ſome of his Brighton oil ſketches to Fiſher, and ſays, "Perhaps the ſight of the ſea may cheer Mrs. Fiſher," (who was then very ill;) he adds, "I am writing this haſty ſcrawl in the dark before a ſix-foot canvaſs, which I have launched with all my uſual anxieties. It is a canal ſcene, my next ſhall contain a ſcratch with a pen."

"January 22nd. My dear Fiſher, I am uneaſy that I have not heard from you. I hope your invalids have neither relapſed nor increaſed in number. I write from Woodmanſtone, a village ſix miles ſouth-eaſt of Croydon. I am painting a group of three children with a donkey, the grand-children of Mr. Lambert, whose anceftors lived here in 1300. It is to go to the parents in the Eaft Indies. The children are here for their education, and fpoke the language imperfectly on their arrival. The butcher was driving home a calf in his cart, when one of the boys exclaimed, 'Aunt, what for one *gentleman* take away *cow* in *gig*.' You may fuppofe I left home to execute this commiffion very unwillingly.—The large fubject on my eafel is promifing; it is a canal, and full of the buftle incident to fuch a fcene when four or five boats are paffing in company; with dogs, horfes, boys, men, women and children, and beft of all, old timber, props, water plants, willows, ftumps, fedges, old nets, &c.—I fhall not object, if you do not, to your picture going to the Gallery, but I fhall try for Tinney's when the time comes, as I think it has more qualities for exhibition among other pictures.—I had this morning a letter from Paris, informing me that on the King's vifit to the Louvre, he was pleafed to award me a gold medal for the merit of my landfcapes. At the fame time he made Sir Thomas Lawrence a Knight of the Legion of Honour. I have a pride and fatisfaction in mentioning this to you; but I can truly fay that your early notice of me, and your friendfhip for me in my obfcurity, was worth more, and is looked back to by me with more heartfelt fatisfaction than this, and all the other notice I have met with, put together. —I left home on Thurfday, and fhall be back by the end of the week. My little group is on the canvass, and makes a pretty picture. In the background is Woodmanftone Church." (here follows a pen fketch of the picture). "Mr. Lambert is the old country fquire. His ftudy contains pictures of racers and hunters, guns, gaiters, gloves, turn-fcrews, tow, gun-flints, &c. You cannot think how much I regret being here to the neglect of my large landfcape; but I muft not quarrel with kind friends, and kick down the ladder."

"Bath, January, 27th. My dear Conſtable, You have but too well gueſſed the cauſe of my ſilence. Two of my children have been ill with fever and inflammation of the windpipe. * * * My wife, thank God, is entirely recovered; and for my own part, I have not been ſo well for years. —Your package arrived ſafe. Your Brighton ſketches carried us down to Oſmington in imagination. I ſhewed them to an artiſt living here: he wiſhed to know what colours you uſed. The Choiſeul Gallery has been of the greateſt comfort to me. I have copied, in lead pencil, Oſtade's butcher ſelling the ox, the boy looking out of window into the ſunſhine, and a Vanderheyden. Thanks to you for giving me the *ſixth* ſenſe, the power of receiving pleaſure from the chiaroſcuro. It has whiled away many an anxious hour.—I was impatient to hear how you fared at the viſit of the King of France to the Louvre. Your medal could not have given you greater exultation than it did me. Indeed I always conſider your fame as mine, and, as you riſe in ſlow and permanent eſtimation, pride myſelf that I have formed as permanent a friendſhip with a man of ſuch talent. But theſe things are better felt than ſaid.—I ſhall be running up to London ſoon, when I ſhall get a ſight of your new ſix-foot canvaſs. My wife obſerved that your enumeration of objects 'carried her down to the river ſide.' I ſhould like to ſee my picture at the Gallery. —I do think that an impreſſion of your Cathedral would ſell at Saliſbury; but it entirely depends upon the brilliancy of the engraving. * * * * * I began this letter two days ago; ſince then I have carried my two ſick boys to a houſe on the top of Lanſdown, and they begin to recover."

"I have been reading much, lately, on the ſubject of the French revolution. The Duc de Choiſeul was principally, but ignorantly, perhaps, inſtrumental in bringing it about, protecting and abetting Voltaire and Co. He little thought, that in patronizing their licentious pens, he was laying the foundation of the bloody inſurrection which was to diſperſe his gallery of pictures, and ſend them to be ſold to the 'Nation of ſhopkeepers.' He it was who baniſhed the Jeſuits, the firſt and neceſſary ſtep to ſucceſs in bringing about the change. He died the year before the volcano burſt. * * * John Fiſher."

"Bath, April 8th. My dear Conſtable, I rode yeſterday out of the white atmoſphere of Bath, into the green village of Bath-Eaſton, and found myſelf by inſtinct at the *mill*, ſurrounded by wiers, back-waters, nets and willows; with a ſmell of weeds, flowing water, and flour in my noſtrils. I need not ſay that the ſcene brought you to my mind and produced this letter."

Mr. Fiſher, after ſpeaking of the ſerious illneſs of Mrs. Fiſher, continues, "I will ſend you in a week or ſo, your ſketches back. In the ſame box I ſhall encloſe two volumes of Paley's poſthumous ſermons, which you may read to your family of a Sunday evening. They are fit companions for your ſketches; being exactly like them, full of vigour, freſh, original, warm from obſervation of nature, haſty, unpoliſhed, untouched afterwards. There is, prefixed to a new edition of his works, a life of Paley, by his ſon, in which the inner man is laid open. If you can get it, there are parts that will delight you. He appears to have been a ſtrong-minded, guileleſs, ſimple-hearted man, who told the truth and declared his honeſt opinion to every man he met with, friend or foe. Hence he was ſometimes in ſcrapes. I hope to be able to get a peep at the metropolis and your picture about the 20th of June. * * * In a letter I had from the Charter Houſe, it was mentioned that you were out of ſpirits, ſeemingly, and had loſt your uſual glee in converſation. What cog of the wheel wanted greaſe? J. Fiſher."

Conſtable's anſwer to this letter is miſſing, but its tenor may, in part, be ſeen by Mr. Fiſher's reply. "Bath, April

10th. My dear Conftable, * * * We are going on for the prefent very profperoufly. * * * My mind and fpirits have been much fhaken; and I received your voluntary offer, to come down to Ofmington, with an exhilaration that I have been long unufed to. We will wander home from the fhore about dufk to the remnants of dinner, as heretofore, and fpend the evening in filling up fketches. There is always room for you. Will you accompany me on my vifitation, the 14th, 15th, 16th June, and return with me to Ofmington? * * * Why was not your picture on your eafel a few weeks longer? I have looked over your letter, but find no other obfervation to make on it, fo I will conclude with a quotation that will pleafe you. By the bye, you never anfwer my letters. You write as if you had not received them. My extract is from Sharon Turner's Hiftory of England, vol. i. page 424, 4to. He is fpeaking of our claffical education, that it ftunts originality, contracts the mind, and makes men knowing only in *words*. It is a complete illustration of your faying that 'a good thing is never done twice.'—

"'It has been remarked that great excellence has been ufually followed by a decline. No fecond Auguftan age is found to occur. A Virgil emerges, and if he caft on his countrymen an everlafting fpell, no future Virgil appears,—no fecond Homer or Euripides,—no fucceeding Pindar, Horace, Demofthenes, Thucydides, Tacitus, or Cicero. The fact is remarkable. But it is accounted for, not in a want of talent, but from the deftruction of talent by injudicious education. It is in literature as in painting: if we ftudy departed excellence too intenfely, we only imitate; we extinguifh genius, and fink below our models. If we make ourfelves copyifts, we become inferior to thofe we copy. The exclufive or continual contemplation of preceding merit contracts our faculties within, *greatly within*, its peculiar circle, and makes even that degree of excellence unattainable which we admire and feed upon.'

"There is more on the ſubject, equally good, if you turn to the book. It is a highly amuſing work. Quite original itſelf. J. Fiſher."

"Charlotte Street, April 13th, 1825. My dear Fiſher, Thank you for your ſecond letter. You ſay you 'are going on proſperouſly,' and this has relieved me from a ſad feeling which has haunted me ever ſince I read the ſecond paragraph in your firſt. * * * It is true I do not anſwer your letters, but I read them over and over, and they generally form anſwers to mine. All your quotations are good, and make for my grand theory. It is the rod and ſtaff of my practice, and can never fail or deceive its profeſſor.

"They are overwhelmed with large pictures at the Academy; what will become of mine I know not, but I am told it looks bright. * * * My 'Lock' is now on my eaſel; it is ſilvery, windy, and delicious; all health, and the abſence of every thing ſtagnant, and is wonderfully got together; the print will be fine. * * * I am ſo haraſſed and interrupted that I muſt now conclude almoſt as abruptly as I did my laſt. * * * The viſit to Oſmington I much look to. Nothing ſhall readily occur to prevent it. I will give up Paris firſt. * * * I have rather a cheering account of my picture at Somerſet Houſe. Its original feeling will ſupport me through all inaccuracies. But they ſhould not be there, to make it more *academical*, and to prevent the *learned vulgar*, in our art, from blowing their noſes upon it. * * * I am ſummoned to tea with my wife and new baby."*

Conſtable's deſcription of his picture of the Lock, and ſome paſſages from other letters in a ſimilar ſtrain of exultation, have been retained contrary to the advice of a gen-

* His third daughter.

Chap. IX. 1825.

tleman with whoſe opinion on many points I am ſo fortunate as to coincide. It appeared to me that in making ſelections from letters not intended for publication, if all that might ſeem egotiſtical were omitted, the intereſt would be greatly and unneceſſarily leſſened, and by this impreſſion I have been guided throughout my undertaking. The utterance of a man's real feelings is more intereſting, though it may have leſs of dignity than belongs to a uniform ſilence on the ſubject of ſelf, while the vanity is often no greater in the one caſe than in the other. In the preſent inſtance, the artiſt's exultation to his moſt intimate friend at the accompliſhment of his aim in one of his moſt important works, is ſo natural, and the qualities he had kept ſteadily in view while engaged on it are ſo well deſcribed by him, that I cannot think I am doing as much injuſtice to his memory by preſerving the paſſage as I ſhould do by its omiſſion. I am enabled to add to what he has himſelf ſaid of "The Lock," the opinion of another perſon, Reynolds, the admirable engraver, who was a good judge of pictures, and whoſe praiſes of it in the following letter were ſincere, for he had undertaken to engrave it at his own riſk.

"To Mr. J. Conſtable. My dear Sir, I have, ſince the arrival of your picture, been before it for the laſt hour, the light of a cheerful day through the clean windows falling full upon it. It is, no doubt, the beſt of your works, true to nature, ſeen and arranged with a profeſſor's taſte and judgment. The execution ſhows in every part a hand of experience; maſterly without rudeneſs, and complete without littleneſs; the colouring is ſweet, freſh, and healthy; bright not gaudy, but deep and clear. Take it for all in all, ſince the days of Gainſborough and Wilſon, no landſcape has been painted with ſo much truth and originality, ſo much art, ſo little artifice. Yours very truly S. W. Reynolds."

Reynolds was interrupted in the execution of his plate

by illneſs, and did not live to complete it; but the ſame ſubject, from a ſecond picture, has ſince been moſt admirably engraved, on a larger ſcale, by Mr. Lucas, and forms the companion to his print of "The Corn Field."

Conſtable exhibited three pictures this year at the Academy, of which the one mentioned by him as the Canal ſcene was the largeſt. The chief object in its foreground is a horſe mounted by a boy, leaping one of the barriers which croſs the towing paths along the Stour (for it is that river, and not a canal), to prevent the cattle from quitting their bounds. As theſe bars are without gates, the horſes, which are of a much finer race, and kept in better condition than the wretched animals that tow the barges near London, are all taught to leap; their harneſs ornamented over the collar with crimſon fringe adds to their pictureſque appearance, and Conſtable, by availing himſelf of theſe advantages, and relieving the horſe, which is of a dark colour, upon a bright ſky, made him a very impoſing object. His other works at the Academy were both landſcapes, one of which was deſcribed in a newſpaper as "A ſcene without any prominent features of the grand or beautiful, but with a rich broken foreground ſweetly pencilled, and a very pleaſing and natural tone of colour throughout the wild green diſtance."

Theſe two laſt pictures were purchaſed by Mr. Francis Darby, of Colebrook Dale. Conſtable was highly delighted that they had attracted the notice of an entire ſtranger to him.

In the ſummer of this year, the Directors of the Britiſh Inſtitution, inſtead of their annual diſplay of works of the old maſters, collected, as they had propoſed, ſome of the beſt pictures of living artiſts, and Conſtable was enabled by the kindneſs of Mr. Fiſher and Mr. Tinney to ſend to this exhibition, "The White Horſe" and "Stratford Mill."

Among Mr. Fiſher's letters, I found a ſheet of paper dated,

CHAP. IX.
1825.

"Osmington, Weymouth, August 12th," and containing, only a pen sketch of an hour glass with wings. That Constable was at this time in a state of extreme anxiety on account of his eldest son, who was very ill, will be seen by Mr. Fisher's next letter, dated, "Osmington, August 24th," in which he says, "It struck me after I had dispatched my blank memorandum, that the illness of yourself, or some of your family, was the cause of your non-appearance here. Your letter with its uncomfortable details has just reached me. If you can get the consent of the mother, bring your poor boy down here directly; or send him to my house at Salisbury and we will meet him there. He shall have the best advice the country affords, with sea air, sea bathing, and good food. You must exonerate me from any responsibility if any thing happens: and if he does well we will see what can be done for him in the way of education. This will relieve the mind and spirits of your wife, who is not strong, and will give you more leisure for your easel. * * * Bring your boy down yourself by easy stages, or if you prefer it, bring one of your healthy boys and leave him here to take his chance. As for money matters do not make yourself uneasy. Write for any thing you want, and send me any picture, in pledge, you think proper. Your family or yourself shall have the *difference* whenever it is called for. Whatever you do, Constable, get rid of anxiety. It hurts the stomach more than arsenic. It generates only fresh cause for anxiety by producing inaction and loss of time. I have heard it said of generals who have failed, that they would have been good officers if they had not harassed themselves by looking too narrowly into *details*. Does the cap fit? It does *me*. * * * I would have come to Hampstead had I been able. I could sooner do it now and at this distance, and *will* come if it will do you any good.

"Pity me. I am sitting in the shade with my children

by me, writing to you, with a quiet ſtomach and cool head; and I am obliged to leave all this to go ten miles to eat veniſon and drink claret with a brother officer, whoſe head is filled with the ſame ſort of materials that his veniſon paſty is made of. Let me hear from you again ſoon, and believe me always faithfully yours, John Fiſher. * * * You want a *ſtaff* juſt at preſent. Lean upon me, *hard*."

"Charlotte Street, September 10th. My very dear Fiſher, I was overcome by your kind and moſt friendly letter, which ſome changes here have prevented my anſwering ſooner. Your offer to receive my dear boy, indeed, all your friendly ſuggeſtions are fully appreciated by my wife and me, and we cannot ſufficiently expreſs our ſenſe of them; but the diſtance at which you are from us is ſo great, and you have ſuch a charge of your own, that we know not what to do. We determined to give our poor boy the chance of the ſea, and about a week ago I took them all to Brighton. I am now quietly at my eaſel again; I find it a cure for all ills. My commiſſions preſs in on me, and I have ſent for Johnny Dunthorne, who wiſhes to be here again. * * * But I crave your forgiveneſs on a ſerious matter; your large picture, 'The White Horſe,' is now exhibiting at the city of Liſle. Wilkie, Sir Thomas Lawrence, and myſelf were each applied to for pictures by the Mayor of that city, who, under Royal Authority, is the head of its eſtabliſhments. It will be ſafely returned about Chriſtmas. Lawrence has ſent ſome, but Wilkie is abroad."

From the diary which Conſtable kept with great regularity and minuteneſs, and ſent at intervals to Mrs. Conſtable, the following are a few quotations: "September 4th. Set off for Lady Dyſart's, and had a pleaſant ride in the Richmond coach. Received in the moſt agreeable manner, and found there Miſs Vernon, once maid of honour to Queen Charlotte, Mrs. Charles Tollemache and her daughter, and

Lady Laura. We all walked in the garden before dinner, at which I was placed at the bottom of the table, oppoſite Lady Dyſart. All ſorts of converſation, but not much that I remember. They talked of dreſs and of the new large ſleeves; Lady D. did not like them, nor the long waiſts that the ladies now wear. They ſaid I was very amuſing, and Lady D. gave me a ſovereign for old Fontaine,* and Mrs. Tollemache half-a-crown. After tea, Lady D. ſaid, 'We ſhall ſhock Mr. Conſtable, we are going to have a game of cards.'† They played a four game, I know not what; I walked about the grounds, and plucked as much fruit as I wanted.

"September 7th. Got up early. Set to work on my large picture,‡ took out the old willow ſtump by the horſe, which has improved the picture much; made one or two other alterations. Leſlie called and wanted to ſee old Fontaine, thinking from my deſcription he would make a good Don Quixote. Indeed he has the look of an old gentleman. * * * Called at Hamlet's for my medal, met there Richard Gubbins; he was looking at ſome beautiful bracelets, no doubt for his lady. My poor girl had none of theſe pretty things, but they go but a little way towards happineſs, nor do they always inſure a good huſband; but Richard will make a good huſband, he is ſo good a ſon. * * *

"September 13th. * * * In the evening went to Mr. Northcote's, and had a delightful converſation about painting, &c. It is wonderful to ſee him with all the energy of youth. His eye ſparkling ſo bright and ſo ſharp. * * *

"September 16th. This morning, a grand epoch, was uſhered in by a prodigious buſtle with the fowls in the gar-

* The Swiſs organiſt, who had become a regular penſioner of Conſtable.

† Conſtable never played. He ſaid he "conſidered the time ſpent at a card table as a vacuum in life."

‡ "The Leaping Horſe," which had met with no purchaſer.

den; the black hen making a great to do, the cock ſtrutting about, and Billy* looking at them in great aſtoniſhment from the back kitchen window. When all was a little quiet, I looked into the brewhouſe, and ſaw her on the neſt I had made, and at breakfaſt Elizabeth brought me a beautiful egg, probably the firſt ever laid in theſe premiſes. How much we have changed this houſe from what it was in Mr. Farrington's time; his attics turned into nurſeries, a beautiful baby born in his bedroom, his waſhhouſe turned into a brewhouſe, his back parlour, which contained all his prints, into a bedroom, and his painting rooms made habitable; well done! Billy is a moſt laughable cat; he plays with the kit, pulls it out of its baſket, toſſes it up, and holds it with his fore feet in a moſt ridiculous manner; the old Lady Hampſtead† looking on all the while, rather ſmiling than otherwiſe. Sir George Beaumont called; he liked what I was about, but wanted me to imitate pictures. * * * Took poor Mrs. H * * * her money. I was told ſhe was ill and in bed. How ſadly this poor artiſt's widow cloſes her days. Fortune ſeems indeed blind to give Miſs Mellon ſo much, and this poor widow, who is really a gentlewoman, ſo little. I went to the back drawing-room to ſee how Johnny was getting on, and a dear little Robin was waſhing himſelf in the pigeon's diſh at the window. Dipping himſelf all over, and making ſuch a daſhing, and ſhaking, and bobbing, and buſtle, that it was quite ridiculous. One comes to Mr. Bigg's garden, and ſings every night and morning quite loud and beautiful; does not this portend a hard winter? We do a great deal of painting, not going out, and I am getting my ſmall commiſſions off my hands as faſt as I can. I will do as you adviſe, 'not undertake little things, but keep to my large pictures.' But I muſt make my mind eaſy as to thoſe I have on hand,

* A cat. † The mother of the kitten.

CHAP. IX.
1825.

namely, 'Salisbury Cathedral,' Mr. Carpenter's picture, Mr. Ripley's, Mr. Arrowsmith's, and Mr. Mirehouse's picture to be altered. All these are paid for, and one more fortnight will clear them all off; how comfortable I shall then be. I am making my last picture saleable, getting the outline on the 'Waterloo,' &c.

"Sunday, October 2nd. Our dear blessed wedding day, owing to which we have five babies. * * *

"October 4th. * * * In the evening Mr. Stothard called; we walked to Islington together, he came back to tea with me, and I consulted him, fortunately, about the 'Waterloo Bridge,' in which he suggested a very capital alteration. It will increase its consequence, and do so much for it, that I am quite in spirits. Your father wanted me to go to St. Martin's Court to see three pictures by Morland, one at nine shillings, the others at twelve each. If I considered them to be original, I was to purchase them for him, as he thought them very pretty paintings. I went and found three coloured and varnished engravings from Morland, Mr. Bigg, and Wheatley. The boxing ring is much on the decline: let us hope it will become extinct. I am at work on my large 'Waterloo' on the *real canvass*; in the evening we are busy setting my portfolios in order, &c. Waterloo promises delightfully."

In one of Mrs. Constable's letters to her husband, she says, "I have no treat like your journal and letters. * * * I hardly allow myself to wish for you, knowing how well and profitably you are employed; but I endeavour to make myself happy, as the separation is for our mutual good. But when you do come, I trust we shall enjoy our rides and walks.—I long to go with you to the Dyke, and to watch with you the flying shadows on the downs. The Darbys are quite delighted with our cottage. They say we have Hampstead with the addition of the sea."

" Oſmington, September. My dear Conſtable. * * * I deſpair of ever ſeeing you out of London, but I repeat that I have bed and board at your ſervice. The news is, that Mat. Parham's (alias Perne's) mill is burnt to the ground, and exiſts only on your canvaſs. A huge miſſhapen, new, bright, brick, modern improved, patent monſter is ſtarting up in its ſtead.—Do you recollect the ſituation of Talbot's barn behind the old Manor Houſe, near the church at Oſmington? It took fire on the 28th September, when it was ſurrounded by fourteen large ricks at the diſtance of no more than twenty yards. No water,—no engines,—ſtraw on every ſide,—the barn full of wheat,—and thatched cottages, and cornſtacks in every direction. Talbot loſt his preſence of mind, and every body was at fault. The occaſion called me out of my uſual indolence. I took the command, gave plenty of beer and good words, worked hard myſelf, and in twenty minutes we ſmothered the fire with no other loſs than that of the barn. It was diſtreſſing to hear the poor rats ſqualling at one end of the barn as the fire approached them. They could not eſcape."

" Charlotte Street, November 12th. My dear Fiſher, * * * What you ſay of Mrs. Fiſher, and yourſelf and family makes me very happy. I am juſt returned from Brighton, and am glad that I can give you a good account of my wife and children; my poor boy has gained ſtrength and compoſure. I have been only occaſionally with them, being very buſy here, where I have done a great deal. I am hard at my 'Waterloo,' which ſhall be finiſhed for the next Exhibition, ſaving only the fatalities of life. I have nearly completed a ſecond Cathedral, and I think you will perhaps prefer it to the firſt, but I will ſend it to Saliſbury for your inſpection. I have much more to ſay about pictures, but you ſay I never anſwer your letters. Your laſt delighted me. The account of the fire and the rats intereſted John Dunthorne and me alike. How fortunate that you were there. I am vexed at the fate of the poor old mill. There will ſoon be an end of the pictureſque in the kingdom. I deſire to come to Saliſbury, if only for two days, to renew our friendſhip in thoſe walks where it firſt took ſo deep a root. I *will* come. How did the fire originate? Write for me when you wiſh for me. You ſet my mind at reſt by the way in which you ſpeak of your picture being at Liſle; they have ſent to know the price; I have ſet them right on that head. I am uncommonly well; never in better health or ſpirits."

"Charlotte Street, November 19th. My dear Fiſher. * * * My expectation of the happineſs of ſeeing you at Saliſbury will be but a viſion. I am ſo hard run in every way that I know not which canvaſs to go to firſt. My 'Waterloo,' like a bliſter, began to ſtick cloſer and cloſer, and to diſturb my reſt at nights. But I am in a field that knows no favour or affection: 'Go on,' is the only order heard. * * * My name will not appear at the opening of the noble inſtitution in Edinburgh. I ſhould like to have ſtruck a blow in that quarter; but I muſt ſubmit to circumſtances. * * * John Dunthorne and I are delighted at the full occupation we have here. He is calm, gentle, clever, induſtrious, full of prudence, and free from vice."

"November 26th. My dear Fiſher, My new picture of Saliſbury is very beautiful, and I have repainted entirely that belonging to Mr. Mirehouſe: but when I thus ſpeak of my pictures, remember it is to *you*, and only in compariſon with myſelf. Theſe pictures of the Cathedral have cauſed me of late to be almoſt abiding with you. My finances are ſadly deranged, and this, I fear, will cauſe me to give up my large work. I have juſt had a viſit from Mr. Banniſter* to requeſt a landſcape; he has long deſired one of me, from which, as he ſays, 'he can feel the wind blowing on his face.' Two

* The inimitable "Jack Banniſter."

chimney ſweepers were at my door, 'What?' he ſaid, 'brother bruſh.'"

In the journal written for his wife Conſtable ſays, "November 25th. Painted all day on Mr. Mirehouſe's little picture of 'The Cathedral,' making in all three 'Cathedrums,' as pretty Minna* calls them. Miſs Bigg was here to know what we paid for aſſes' milk, as they charge ſix ſhillings a quart at the *Wellington Aſs Shop* in the New Road. Mr. Strutt called to ſay they had orders for the play, Drury Lane, and aſked me to join them to ſee 'Dr. Fauſtus and the Devil.' I declined, ſo he was kind enough to take Johnny Dunthorne, and he was much pleaſed, though 'it was very terrible.' The Devil was of a flaming red, and had a diabolical countenance, and it was ſhocking to ſee how he led on his victim to perpetrate every crime, till he was involved in Hell at laſt."

"November 28th. Maſter Billy kicked up a terrible rumpus in the yard to-day; he wanted to have a game of play with the fowls, but they took it in earneſt, and made a great noiſe, eſpecially the cock. John and I went to their aſſiſtance. Mr. Balmanno called, and was ſo delighted with my 'Waterloo' (though he only ſaw the ſketch and outline), that he ſays it will be my triumph, and that I ſhall 'certainly ſet the Thames on fire, if any body can.' I am now finiſhing a copy of my 'Lock,' which rejoices me a good deal; it is a very lovely ſubject. Mr. Banniſter called, and ſaw all my goings on. He is fond of my landſcapes, and ſays he muſt have one. I think he likes the 'Lock' ſo much, that I ſhall reduce it to the ſize of Fiſher's old mill; how I ſhall pleaſe him, or when, I do not know. He ſays 'he breathes the open air in my pictures, they are more than freſh, they are exhilarating.

Miſs Arnott called to aſk me, with her mother's compliments, to dine there on Chriſtmas Day. I told her I had a wife, and muſt needs go and ſee her."

* His eldeſt daughter.

CHAPTER X.

1826-1827.

Return of the "White Horſe" from Liſle. Gold Medal voted to Conſtable. Letters of N. Pouſſin. Conſtable's Picture of "The Cornfield." Letter from Mr. Phillips. Mr. Fiſher's Deſcription of the Valley of Sutton and Preſton. Anecdote of one of Mr. Fiſher's Children. Exhibition at the Royal Academy. 1826. *Deſcription of a ruined Man. Paul Pry. Ludicrous Occurrence to the Ghoſt in Hamlet. "The Brighton Gazette." "The Glebe Farm." Mr. Fiſher and Biſhop Burgeſs. Northcote. Picture by Ruyſdael. Exhibition at the Academy.* 1827. *Conſtable removes his Family to a Houſe in Well Walk, Hampſtead.*

1826.

"CHARLOTTE Street, January 14th, 1826. My dear Fiſher, I begin this haſty note by wiſhing you a happy new year, hoping Mrs. Fiſher and all your children are well, and bearing up againſt this, to me, dreadful weather. All my family are at Brighton, and I left them well on Thurſday. I ſtaid a fortnight with them, and painted there one of my beſt pictures, the ſubject, the Mill (Perne's) at Gillingham; it is about two feet, and is ſo very rich and pleaſing that if you are at Saliſbury, and would like to ſee it, I will beg the proprietor, Mr. Hand, to let me ſend it to you; Mere Church is in the diſtance. 'The White Horſe' did me great credit at Liſle.

I am honourably mentioned in the final difcourfe of the Prefect, and a gold medal was voted to me, which I received yefterday. The difcourfe is curious; he fpeaks of the 'racinefs and originality of the ftyle, which being founded entirely in nature, is capable of much beauty, but dangerous to all imitators.' So far the Exhibition has extended my reputation, and I truft you will forgive what I did. There are generally among the works of an artift, one, two, or three pictures, on which hang more than ufual intereft; this is one of mine. All things confidered, the medal fhould be yours. Much pleafure had I at Brighton, mixed with a fentiment of melancholy, by a book in French which my wife read to me while I was painting the Mill; 'The Letters of Nicolo Pouffin,' now firft publifhed, having hitherto lain undifcovered. They are written to his employers in Paris, and are to me replete with intereft. My wife has difcovered that painters now and painters then are little different. The letters contain apologies to friends for not finifhing their pictures fooner, anxieties of all kinds, infults from ignorance, &c.; one of them fpeaks of 'ftrange news from England, the beheading of King Charles,' &c. My large picture is at a ftand owing to the ruined ftate of my finances. You richly deferve all I think of you for your kindnefs about your picture. * * * I am executing all my commiffions, amounting in all to four hundred pounds; two months will complete them. J. Dunthorne is painting portraits in the country."

"Charlotte Street, February 1ft. * * * My dear Fifher, Your picture is now ftanding in my room, and without a fpeck of injury; do not hurry its departure. All this morning I have been engaged with a fitter; a diffenter, but without knowing why, only that his wife will not let him go to Church."

"Ofmington, February 5th. My dear Conftable. I plead guilty to neglect, and feel much humbled by the forgiving tone of your laft letter. The truth is, my mind has been

Chap. X. 1826.

unufually occupied for the laft fix months. I do not affect the plea that I could not find *time*, but I could not find the *difengaged mind*. When I write to you, I do it with all my heart, and when its impulfes are obftructed with care or bufinefs, I have no appetite for our agreeable correfpondence. * * * Bifhop Burgefs has, in a moft flattering manner, reinftated me in my old fituation as chaplain, and I am juft where I was in my uncle's time. This is a very tall feather in my cap, and I am not a little elevated by it. I fit at the bottom of the old table, but, I confefs, I painfully mifs old faces. * * * I fhall be at Salifbury for fome days at the end of this month, and I fhould like much to have Perne's Mill there to look at. J. Fifher."

Having laid afide the 'Waterloo,' Conftable was engaged on a fubject more congenial to his tafte, "The Corn Field," now in the National Gallery. It had been feen by Mr. Phillips of Brighton, who fuggefted fome materials for its foreground in a letter of which the following is a part: "March 1ft. My dear Sir, I think it is July in your green lane. At this feafon all the tall graffes are in flower, bog-rufh, bullrufh, teafel. The white bindweed now hangs its flowers over the branches of the hedge; the wild carrot and hemlock flower in banks of hedges, cow parfley, water plantain, &c.; the heath hills are purple at this feafon; the rofe-coloured perficaria in wet ditches is now very pretty; the catchfly graces the hedge-row, as alfo the ragged robin; bramble is now in flower, poppy, mallow, thiftle, hop, &c."

"April 8th. My dear Fifher. I fhould not have remained fo long filent after your laft kind and friendly letter, had I been wholly without news of you and yours. I am glad to find from my friends in Seymour Street, that you are all well, and that I may expect to fee you for fome continuance of time in London, 'after the lilacs have bloffomed at Ofmington."

"I will endeavour to anſwer your letters in future, but when I write to you, I am always full of myſelf, which is indeed abominable; but you muſt thank yourſelf for taking a greater intereſt in all that concerns me than any other human being. * * * I have diſpatched a large landſcape to the Academy, upright, of the ſize of the 'Lock,' but a ſubject of a very different nature: inland corn fields, a cloſe lane forming the foreground; it is not neglected in any part; the trees are more than uſually ſtudied, the extremities well defined, as well as the ſtems; they are ſhaken by a pleaſant and healthful breeze at noon:

'while now a freſher gale
Sweeping with ſhadowy guſts the fields of corn, &c.'

I am not, however, without my anxieties, though I have not neglected my work, or been ſparing of my pains. * * * I, at this moment, hear a rook fly over my painting-room, in which I am writing; its call tranſports me to Oſmington, and makes me think I am ſpeaking and not writing to you; it reminds me of our happy walks in the fields, ſo powerful is the voice of nature. My picture occupied me wholly: I could think of and ſpeak to no one. I felt like a relation of mine in the battle of Waterloo. He ſaid he 'dared not turn his head right or left, but always kept it ſtraight forward, thinking of himſelf alone.' I hear of ſome fine pictures that are gone; Callcott has three; Ward, a battle; Collins's, I hear, are very fine, but I have not ſeen them; Lawrence has but one whole length, Shee only one, Jackſon but one, and Phillips none, ſo there will be a dearth of large canvaſſes. I am not writing in the beſt of ſpirits. To-day my boy has gone to Brighton to ſchool; John Dunthorne is gone with him. I ſaw him as far as Charing Croſs, and then left him to his fate. I hope for the beſt, and that the air will do him good. I am much worn, having worked hard, and have now

CHAP. X.
1826.

the confolation of knowing I muft work a great deal harder, or go to the workhoufe; I have fome commiffions, however, and I do hope to fell this prefent picture. * * * threatens me with having to paint his portrait:

'Angels and minifters of grace defend me!'

He is hofpitable, but there is a coarfenefs about him that is intolerable."

"To Mr. Samuel Lane. I am juft returned from Suffolk. I left London by the mail of Wednefday night in great anxiety and alarm for the ftate of my brother, who was fuddenly attacked by fever. I returned on Sunday morning. He was better, and I hope free from danger. 15th April."

"Ofmington, April 22nd. My dear Conftable. With this I fend you your fketch books, fo long detained. But they have propagated your name in heavy foils, where your pictures would never have taken root. My wife, to fave the books from rubbing, fends fome little memoranda of kindnefs to our god-children. * * * I had rather fee you here than in London; this is a country that the more you live in it, the more you difcover its beauties. Did you ever look down the little wooded valley of Sutton and Prefton from the fpring heads in the little amphitheatre formed by the hills? It has a peep of the blue bay, with Portland in the diftance, and two old forlorn afh trees in the foreground; the place is very fequeftered, and is frequented by kingfifhers and woodcocks; but fellows from Weymouth with padded chefts and vacant faces come there and let off guns, and difturb the quiet genius of the place; this in return for your rook. When your pet, Belim,* repeats his Catechifm, we cannot make him fay otherwife than, 'And walk in the *fame fields* all the days of my life;' he might have a worfe idea of happinefs."

* William.

"Charlotte Street, April 26th. My dear Fiſher, I received your letter and the books; and the kind recollections of Mrs. Fiſher and yourſelf towards your Godchildren have afforded me great pleaſure. I ſhall proceed to *anſwer* your letter. Firſt, to ſay that you may have the comfortable room next ours, with either a feather-bed or mattraſs, as you pleaſe, and for as long as you pleaſe. Secondly, the ſpot you ſpeak of, I well recollect, is lovely; the expanſe around, contraſted with the deep receſſes and ſolitudes below; but in general theſe ſubjects deceive on canvaſs. The anecdote of dear Belim is very pretty; depend on it, the love of nature is ſtrongly implanted in man. I have lately been into Suffolk, and have had ſome delightful walks 'in the *ſame fields*.' Bleſs the dear boy! our ideas of happineſs are the ſame, and I join with you in praying that he may never ſeek it in leſs hallowed places."

"When my mind is diſturbed it ſtirs up the mud. How could circumſtances ever place me in ſuch a ſituation as to write ſo much ſtuff to an *Archdeacon!*" *

"I am now buſy at the Academy, and am writing early, as after breakfaſt I muſt be there. My wife is very good, and is at the breakfaſt-table by eight; ſhe is now there, and as I have much to do, I will put this letter into my pocket, and finiſh it at Somerſet Houſe. It is quite out of my power to deſcribe the ſcene of diſmay and deſolation the rooms preſent. I could quote Dante and Milton:

'Dire was the toſſing, &c.'

but it is a delightful ſhow. Turner never gave me ſo much pleaſure or ſo much pain before. Callcott has a fine picture of a pictureſque boat driven before the wind on a ſtormy ſea; it is ſimple, grand, and affecting. He has another large

* Conſtable here alludes to parts of his correſpondence with Mr. Fiſher relating to a third perſon, and which for that reaſon are not publiſhed.

work, not ſo good, rather too quakeriſh, as Turner is too yellow; but every man who diſtinguiſhes himſelf ſtands on a precipice. Sir Thomas Lawrence's portraits of Peel and Canning are very fine. He has a lady playing on a guitar hanging by Turner, and you ſeem to hear its imperfect ſounds over his 'wide watered ſhore.' 'Canning' is over the fire-place, 'An Entombment' by Weſtall at the bottom of the room, and Etty's 'Judgment of Paris,' on the weſt ſide centre; the details of this ſhow we ſhall ſoon analyze together. Chantrey loves painting, and is always up ſtairs. He works now and then on my pictures, and yeſterday he joined our group, and after exhauſting his jokes on my landſcape, he took up a dirty palette, threw it at me, and was off. Preſently he came back and aſked me if I had ſeen a beaſtly landſcape by * * * It is ſo indeed. The voice in my favour is univerſal, it is my 'beſt picture.'

"* * * * has ſome of his heartleſs atrocious landſcapes in Seymour Street, and has ſent to conſult me on them. How ſhall I get out of ſuch an infernal ſcrape? Truth is out of the queſtion. What part can I then play?"

Conſtable exhibited, with "The Cornfield," a ſmaller landſcape, but I do not remember the ſubject.

"Charlotte Street, July 7th. My dear Fiſher. You will receive Dunthorne's Wilſons to-morrow; Mrs. Fiſher cannot fail to be pleaſed with them.—I have added a little to your batch of Waterloos, making, I think, a nice bargain for ten guineas. Have you done anything to your walls? they were of a colour formed to deſtroy every valuable tint in a picture. * * * A poor, wretched man called to ſee me this morning; he had a petition to the Royal Academy for charitable aſſiſtance: it was * * *. His appearance was diſtreſs itſelf, and it was awful to behold to what ill-conduct may bring us; yet calamity has impreſſed even on this man an air of dignity; he looked like Leſlie's Don Quixote. When I knew him at the Bishop's he wore powder, had a soft subdued voice, and always a smile, which caused him to show some decayed teeth, and he carried a gold headed cane with tassels. Now, how changed! his neck long, with a large head, thin face, nose long, mouth wide, eyes dark and sunken, eyebrows lifted, hair abundant, straight, erect, and very greasy; his body much emaciated and shrunk away from his dismal black clothes, and his left arm in a sling from a fall, by which he broke the left clavicle; I shall try the Artist's Fund for him. I cannot efface the image of this ghostly man from my mind. * * * Poor Mr. Bicknell is in a sad state; he had an attack of apoplexy about ten days ago; it was coming on when you saw him. * * * I have made several visits to the terrace at Lord Pembroke's; it was the spot of all others to which I wanted to have access.* I have added two feet to my canvass. My wife and all here are well. I trust we shall not need a country excursion, in which we leave this convenient house, and pay four guineas a week for the privilege of sleeping in a hen-coop, for the sake of country air."

"September. My dear Leslie, On returning to town this morning, and once more perusing your note, I find myself quite mistaken. I had missed the date, and consequently missed 'Paul Pry,' a serious loss to me; but the word 'to-morrow,' instead of naming the precise day, often leads to such mistakes on the side of the reader, the writer being fully aware of what he means; but it is my loss, and I assure you I had not a little reckoned on seeing such a master of humour, in company with yourself. I write in the forlorn hope that possibly you and Mrs. Leslie did not go."

Few persons more thoroughly relished good acting than did Constable, when he could be prevailed on to witness it. Yet so

* Part of Lord Pembroke's house and terrace form the nearest objects in the picture of "The Opening of Waterloo Bridge."

ſeldom did he viſit the theatres, that he never ſaw either Kean or Liſton, though I had ſeveral times propoſed to accompany him when thoſe great maſters of their art were to perform.

I have heard him give a ludicrous account of an accident that happened during one of the few viſits he ever paid to a theatre. The play was "Hamlet," and the ghoſt, from ſome derangement of the machinery, ſtopped in his deſcent, and remained for a conſiderable time preſenting a half-length figure, ſhaken occaſionally by the efforts of the carpenters to complete his exit, which was at length accompliſhed more rapidly than was deſirable, amidſt roars of applauſe. Conſtable happened to mention the circumſtance, ſome years afterwards to his neighbour, Mr. Pope, adding, "I ſhall never forget it," when the latter ſaid, "Neither ſhall I, for I was that unlucky ghoſt."

"Charlotte Street, September 9th. My dear Fiſher, It is a very long time ſince I have heard from you, and I have now no means of hearing of you elſewhere. Let me have a line ſoon to diſpel the thought that any thing may be amiſs, or any part of your family out of health. You once ſaid 'life is ſhort,' let us make the moſt of friendſhip while we can. I have little to ſay of what belongs to myſelf, but that little is good. My children are well, and my wife, for her, very tolerable; they are in a ſmall houſe on Downſhire Hill, to which it is an eaſy walk from home. I have juſt come back from a day or two at Brighton, where I had been to return my boy to Mr. Phillips. John Dunthorne is ſtill in Suffolk very buſy; his laſt job is a large ſign of the Duke of Marlborough. I have written to haſten him; he is wanted here by myſelf and others. My laſt landſcape is a cottage ſcene with the Church of Langham, the poor Biſhop's firſt living; it is one of my beſt in colour, freſh and bright, and I have pacified it into tone and ſolemnity. My friend Mr. Phillips is commencing a literary journal at Brighton: he wants me to contribute ſome paper on Art, landſcape, of courſe. What do you ſay? * * * Rochefoucault ſays, 'Lovers are never tired of each other's company, becauſe they always talk of themſelves.'"

The cottage with Langham Church was a pet ſubject with Conſtable; he repeated it frequently, and left one or two unfiniſhed pictures and ſketches of it with conſiderable variations. His beſt picture of this pretty ſubject, and one of his moſt perfect works, is that from which the engraving in the "Engliſh Landſcape," with the title of "The Glebe Farm" is taken. The riſing ground and trees on the right hand are imaginary, as the ground, in reality, deſcends rather ſteeply on that ſide of the Church.

"Cloſe, Saliſbury, July 1ſt. My dear Conſtable. The two pictures arrived ſafe on Friday, and within an hour were up in their places; 'The White Horſe' looking very placid, and not as if juſt returned from the continent. It is wonderfully improved by Dunthorne's coat of varniſh. The Cathedral looks ſplendidly over the chimney-piece. The picture requires a room full of light. Its internal ſplendour comes out in all its power, and the ſpire ſails away with the thunder clouds."

"Maidenhead, September 27th. My dear Conſtable. Do not accuſe me of neglect. You were never more occupied in the month of April preparing for the exhibition, than I have been ſince the month of Auguſt. Laſt week there was an ordination, and I preached the ſermon which you will ſoon ſee in print. * * * I write this ſitting in commiſſion upon a diſpute between a clergyman and his pariſhioners, and compoſe while the parties argue. There is a brother parſon arguing his own caſe, with powder, white forehead, and a very red face, like a copper veſſel newly tinned. He is mixing up, in a tremulous tone, with an eager blood ſhot eye, accuſations,—apologies,—ſtatements,—refervations,—and appeals, till his voice ſounds on my ear, as I write, like a diſtant waterfall. * * *

"I am doubtful about your 'Brighton Gazette.' You are in poſſeſſion of ſome very valuable and original matter on the ſubject of painting, particularly on the poetry of the art. I ſhould be ſorry to ſee this ſeed ſown on an unviſited field, where it would bloſſom in forgetfulneſs, while ſome thriving author, like a ſparrow, would fly off with a ſample, and take the credit from you. Throw your thoughts together as they ariſe, in a book, that they be not loſt; when I come to ſee you, we will look them over, put them into ſhape, and do ſomething with them. Pray do not forget to put together the hiſtory of your life and opinions, with as many remarks on men and manners as may occur to you. *Set about it immediately; life ſlips.* It will perhaps bring your children in a hundred pounds in a day of ſhort commons, if it does nothing elſe; beſides, I have been all along deſirous of writing your life and riſe in the art. * * *

"I live with the new Biſhop as ſon with father, or brother with brother. Our habits of life ſimilar, our purſuits ſimilar, our modes of thought ſimilar, or only ſufficiently different to increaſe the pleaſure of communication. * * * I have been unconſciouſly acquiring, at Oſmington, in long winter evenings, a greater ſhare of knowledge than I was myſelf aware of; and find that I have no reaſon to be diſcontented with the uſe I have made of my time. The Biſhop improves me and drives me on in my claſſical acquirements; while in general divinity and comprehenſive views of hiſtory, I find myſelf 'in eaſy circumſtances.' He is urging me to overcome my indolence and ſhow myſelf in print, and before I die I ſhall be out. I have got my nerves ſteadier, and my underſtanding more under my controul. My ambition is ſtrongly awakened, and I ſee glimpſes of light through the wood."

"Charlotte Street, November 28th. My dear Fiſher, The rumour may have reached you that I have another boy; the number of my children is now ſix, being three of each.

"I gloried in your letter. Its friendſhip for me was, if poſſible, forgot in the delight of ſeeing you at length properly appreciating yourſelf. You need never fear indulging too much in the exulting tone it breathes. Take care that you launch your boat at the appointed time, and fearleſſly appear before the world in a tangible ſhape. It is the only way to be cured of idle vapours and uſeleſs faſtidiouſneſs.

"My wife is at Hampſtead, and both ſhe and the infant are doing well. I am endeavouring to ſecure a permanent ſmall houſe there, and have put the upper part of this houſe into an upholſterer's hands to let, made my painting room warm and comfortable, and have become an inhabitant of my parlours. I am three miles from door to door, and can have a meſſage in an hour. I ſhall be more out of the way of idle callers, and above all, ſee nature, and unite a town and country life, and to all theſe things I hope to add a plan of economy. * * *

"I paſſed laſt evening with Northcote; he enjoys a green old age, and is as full of vivacity as ever; he is always inſtructive and amuſing. Talking of excellence, he ſaid, 'It ſhould be the aim of an artiſt to bring ſomething to light out of nature for the firſt time. Something like that for which in mechanics a patent would be granted; an original invention or a decided improvement; patents are not given for making a time-piece or a teleſcope, as long as it differs not from others.' He ſays, 'The failures, and difficulties of ſucceſs, in the arts and literature are for the moſt part cauſed by our early habits and education. Virgil is driven into boys as the height of excellence, whereas he is but a farthing candle compared with Shakſpeare.' The firſt book he (Northcote) ever read was 'Jack the Giant-killer,' and he ſtill believes it unequalled.

CHAP. X.

1826.

"I have taken your advice, and not written any thing for the 'Brighton Courier.'—I have ſeen an affecting picture this morning by Ruyſdael; it haunts my mind, and clings to my heart, and ſtands between you and me while I am talking to you; it is a water-mill; a man and boy are cutting ruſhes in the running ſtream (the tail-water); the whole ſo true, clear, and freſh, and as briſk as champagne; a ſhower has not long paſſed.—I am delighted to ſee how you live with the Biſhop; that you avail yourſelf of his great worth and underſtanding, and that he does not uſe his rank nor the wiſdom of age, to trip up and overbear the valuable qualities, the vigour and energy, to be found in youth and middle age."

1827.

In 1827, Conſtable ſent to the Academy a large picture of "The Marine Parade and Chain Pier at Brighton," and two ſmaller ones, "A Water Mill at Gillingham, Dorſetſhire," and "Hampſtead Heath." To the Britiſh Inſtitution he ſent his "Corn Field," and "The Glebe Farm."

"Sunday Evening, Auguſt 26th. My dear Fiſher, We ſadly neglect much happineſs that lies within our reach. Weeks and months have paſſed ſince we met, and no communication. I know not where you are, and you know not what I have been ſo long about. Your cares lay far and wide apart, and I am not wholly without mine. Still we do amiſs to remain inactive towards each other for both our ſakes. No worſe account can be given of life than to have neglected the ſocial duties. * * * We are at length fixed in our comfortable little houſe in Well Walk, Hampſtead, and are once more enjoying our own furniture, and ſleeping in our own beds. My plans in ſearch of health for my family have been ruinous; but I hope now that our moveable camp no longer exiſts, and that I am ſettled for life. So hateful is moving about to me, that I could gladly exclaim, 'Here let me take my everlaſting reſt!' The rent of this houſe is fifty-two pounds per annum, taxes, twenty-five, and what I have ſpent on it, ten or fifteen. I have let Charlotte Street at eighty-two pounds, retaining my two parlours, large front attic, painting room, gallery, &c. This houſe is to my wife's heart's content; it is ſituated on an eminence at the back of the ſpot in which you ſaw us, and our little drawing room commands a view unſurpaſſed in Europe, from Weſtminſter Abbey to Graveſend. The dome of St. Paul's in the air ſeems to realize Michael Angelo's words on ſeeing the Pantheon: 'I will build ſuch a thing in the ſky.' We ſee the woods and lofty grounds of the Eaſt Saxons to the north-eaſt. I read 'Turner's Hiſtory' continually, for two reaſons: firſt, I think thereby of you, and ſecondly, its information is endleſs, and of the beſt kind. I have Burnet's book on colour for you from Carpenter's; where ſhall I ſend it, or ſhall I meet you at Sarum during your durance, and make a few autumnal ſketches on ſpots endeared to us both? My 'Brighton' was admired on the walls, and I had a few nibbles out of doors. I had one letter from a man of rank, inquiring what would be 'its *ſelling* price;' is not this too bad? but this comes of the bartering at the Gallery. My Dr. † * * * has paid, but nothing more; no one will buy a ſchoolmaſter, for who would hang up a picture of the keeper of a treadmill, or a turnkey of Newgate, who had been in either place? Mr. Banniſter is my neighbour here; a very fine creature he is; very ſenſible, natural, and a gentleman.

"Lord De Tabley's Engliſh pictures have lately ſold for eight thouſand pounds; two thouſand more than he gave for them: a landſcape by Wilſon, five hundred pounds; query, had he fifty for this truly magnificent and affecting picture? 'May this expiate!' John Dunthorne has completed a very pretty view of your lawn and prebendal houſe, with the

† An engraving from one of his portraits.

great alder and the Cathedral. He is now in Suffolk, painting a portrait of * * *, whoſe uglineſs is portentous; how John will get on with him I know not. We long to hear news of you and Mrs. Fiſher and your children. We are well here. My pretty infant ſoon after you ſaw him was ſeized with whooping cough. I find medical men know nothing of this terrible diſorder, and can afford it no relief, conſequently it is in the hands of quacks. I have been adviſed to put him *three times over and three times under a donkey*, as a certain cure. * * * I have painted one of my beſt pictures here."

"Cloſe, Saliſbury, September 3rd. My dear Conſtable, * * * I am elected a member of the Royal Literary Society, and muſt appear in London, in December, to be inſtalled. I ſhall then have an opportunity of ſeeing you at the bottom of Well Walk. The arrangement is good in one particular. You will be leſs diſturbed by morning flies than in Charlotte Street. * * * I am worn to death with the inceſſant viſiting of the ſame perſons, and the ſame prate of this buſy-idle place. The whole of the dioceſe is on my hands, I educate my own boys, and there you have ſufficient reaſons why I write ſo ſeldom. J. Fiſher."

Conſtable paſſed the remainder of this year happily with his family at Hampſtead, where he painted ſeveral ſmall landſcapes.

CHAPTER XI.

1828—1829.

Illneſs of Mr. Abram Conſtable, and of Mrs. Conſtable. Birth of Conſtable's youngeſt Child. Pictures of Dedham Vale, and of Hampſtead Heath. Death of Mr. Bicknell. His Beqeuſt to Mr. and Mrs. Conſtable. Exhibition at the Royal Academy, 1828. Death of Archdeacon Coxe. Illneſs of Mrs. Conſtable. Her Death. Conſtable ill. Receives a commiſſion to paint a Sign. Elected an Academician, 1829. Congratulations from ſome of his Friends. Sir Thomas Lawrence and Conſtable. Picture of Hadleigh Caſtle. Conſtable engaged in preparing the "Engliſh Landſcape" for publication. Mr. David Lucas.

1828.

IN the ſpring of 1828, Conſtable was called to Flatford by an illneſs of his brother Abram, Mrs. Conſtable being at the ſame time extremely unwell.

The following note to Mr. Samuel Lane muſt have been written at this time. "My dear Lane, I am glad to hear of your return. I hope we ſhall meet ſoon. My poor wife is ſtill very ill at Putney, and when I can get her home I know not. We talk of Brighton, but we only talk of it. She can't make ſuch a journey. I am glad to remain quiet at my work, as I want to rid my mind of ſome troubleſome jobs. I am juſt returned from Suffolk, where I was again called to ſee my brother, but I left him ſo much better that I am cheered. I advifed him to fend away all his doctors. They have left him in poffeffion of his purfe, only,—now empty,—and of himfelf, only his fkeleton."

"Charlotte Street, June 11th. My dear Fifher, Is it poffible that I fhould have had little or no tidings of you fince we parted in November? We do fad injuftice to our friendfhip. This filence is a bad thing, and I am determined not to let this (my birthday) pafs without emancipating myfelf from what appears almoft a fpell, for I never felt a greater defire to write, nor ever had in reality more to fay to you, at leaft of myfelf, than now. This has been to me a moft eventful year, for half of it has not yet paffed, and three things of moment to myfelf have occurred: firft, the birth of a baby boy, whom we have named Lionel Bicknell, 2nd of January: fecondly, I have painted a large upright landfcape, perhaps my beft; it is in the Exhibition, and noticed as 'a redeemer' by 'John Bull,' and another, lefs in fize but equal in quality, purchafed by Chantrey: thirdly, and laftly, though *not leaft*, Mr. Bicknell has left us a fortune that may be twenty thoufand pounds!—This I will fettle on my wife and children, that I may do juftice to his good opinion of me. It will make me happy, and I fhall ftand before a fix-foot canvafs with a mind at eafe, thank God!

"The Exhibition is poor; but though the talent is fmall, its produce in money has been very great; a hundred and fifty pounds per diem, perhaps, on an average. I have little time to fpeak of it. Lawrence has many pictures, and never has his elegant affettuofa ftyle been more happy. Jackfon is the moft of a painter, but he does not rank with Lawrence in general talent. Turner has fome golden vifions, glorious and beautiful; they are only vifions, but ftill they are art, and one could live and die with fuch pictures. Some portraits that would petrify you. Newton has 'The Vicar of Wakefield,' moft affecting." * * *

"My wife is ſadly ill at Brighton; her letter to-day is however cheerful. Hampſtead, ſweet Hampſtead, is deſerted. I am at work here, and ſhall take my boy and pretty Minna to Brighton on the 20th."

The upright picture-mentioned in this letter, was a view of "Dedham Vale," and the ſmall one, the "Hampſtead Heath."

"Saliſbury, June 19th. My dear Conſtable. * * * Your legacy gave me as much pleaſure as it could have communicated to yourſelf. You will now be relieved from the carking cares of leaving a young family to privation and the world. You will feel that your fame and not your bread is dependant upon your pencil. * * * Mr. Bicknell has paid you a high moral compliment. * * * My plan of proviſion is to leave a home, and bread to eat, round which the weak and unſucceſsful of my family may rally. Perhaps this ſhould be your plan.

"Poor Coxe, as you probably know from Peter, is no more. He died of old age.—A more irreproachable, friendly man did not exiſt. He was always benevolently employed, and at his funeral, the congregation diſturbed the ſervice with ſobs. After a great dinner, he uſed to ſteal into his kitchen and give his cook a guinea. His domeſtics never left him. A ſilent but ſtrong compliment. His regard to truth was remarkable. He is the author of twenty-four quarto volumes, and has hardly been convicted of a miſtake. He was quoted as an authority in his life time, an event of rare occurrence. * * * J. Fiſher."

Conſtable returned with his wife to Hampſtead, from whence he wrote on the 22nd of Auguſt to John Dunthorne, Jun. who was at Bergholt, "I do hope things are not going on worſe here. On the contrary, I believe Mrs. Conſtable to be gaining ground. Her cough is pretty well gone and ſhe has ſome appetite, and the nightly perſpirations are, in a great meaſure, ceaſed. All this muſt be good, and I am a great deal

Chap. XI.
1828.

cheered. Still I am anxious,—ſhe is ſo ſadly thin and weak. I am determined to try and get her out. * * * The Neyland buſineſs can ſoon be decided upon.* *I hope you will do it*, but only in conjunction with your father. I think it requires not a moment's heſitation. Take care of cold. Work with the door and windows of the church open, even if that ſhould make it colder. It will drive out damp and ſmell of graves, &c. Nothing ſo bad as the air of a large apartment, as it never changes itſelf, and it always flies to the heart, liver, and lights. I was nearly killed, copying Sir Joſhua, at Lady Dyſart's, Hyde Park corner. * * * Remember Claude painted ſham architecture in churches, and it did not prevent his becoming a painter. But he fell off a ſcaffold."

In a letter to Mr. Dominic Colnaghi, dated September 15th, Conſtable writes: "I am greatly unhappy at my dear wife's illneſs; her progreſs towards amendment is ſadly ſlow, but ſtill they tell me ſhe does mend; pray God this may be the caſe! I am much worn with anxiety." And in a note to Mr. S. Lane, dated October 2nd, he ſays: "* * * My dear wife continues much the ſame; I do hope ſhe is not worſe, and home may yet do wonders."

The letter, to which the following is a reply, is miſſing. It, no doubt, contained a deſponding account of the ſtate of Mrs. Conſtable's health. "Cloſe, Saliſbury, October 4th. My dear Conſtable, Your ſad letter has juſt reached me, and I grieve to ſay, at a time when I fear I cannot move. I am expecting to be called into reſidence at this place, when I muſt be a fixture until January. But if this be not the caſe, and I can get my liberty, I will come and ſee you ſoon. I fear your friendſhip makes you over value the uſe I can be of to you; but what I can give, you ſhall have. * * * I began this letter

* This ſeems to have been that John Dunthorne ſhould paint ſome ornamental work in the interior of Neyland Church.

at Saliſbury and I finiſh it at Oſmington, and to-morrow I ſtart for Saliſbury again. Support yourſelf with your uſual manlineſs, and believe me always your moſt faithful and attached, John Fiſher."

Mrs. Conſtable's ſufferings, which ſhe endured with that entire reſignation to the will of Providence that ſhe had ſhown under every circumſtance of her life, were occaſioned by pulmonary conſumption. I was at Hampſtead a few days before ſhe breathed her laſt. She was then on a ſofa in their cheerful parlour, and although Conſtable appeared in his uſual ſpirits in her preſence, yet before I left the houſe, he took me into another room, wrung my hand, and burſt into tears, without ſpeaking. She died on the 23rd of November.

"Oſmington, Weymouth, November 29th. My dear Conſtable, I write with the hope and intention of giving you comfort, but really I know not how; yet if there be any conſolation to the heart of man to know that another feels with him, you have that conſolation. I do ſympathize with you, my old and dear friend, moſt truly, and I pray God to give you fortitude. I am additionally grieved that I cannot come and ſay this in perſon, but I am ſo entangled with my family and numerous affairs, that I cannot reach London until December. Our new but eſtimable friend, Evans,* paid me a moſt flattering viſit. He travelled one hundred miles out of his way to come and ſee me in my Arcadia for twelve hours only. He arrived over night, and left me next day at noon; we had time, however, to exchange a great deal of mind. Our converſation turned, of courſe, much upon you; we agreed that for your comfort, during the trial upon you for the exerciſe of your patience, you ſhould apply yourſelf rigidly to your profeſſion. Some of the fineſt works of art, and moſt vigorous exertions of intellect, have been the reſult

* Mr. Evans of Hampſtead was the medical friend who had attended Mrs. Conſtable.

of periods of diſtreſs. Poor Wilſon painted all his fineſt landſcapes under the preſſure of ſorrow.

"Let us talk of other things. I met in Schlegel a happy criticiſm on what is called Gothic architecture. We do not eſtimate it aright unleſs we judge of it by the ſpirit of the age which produced it, and compare it with cotemporary productions. The Gothic Minſter was the work which gave birth to that phenomenon, the Cruſades, and realized that poetical beautiful monſter, the mailed knight, who went forth in purity and honour to preach the Goſpel with his mouth, while he broke its laws with his ſword. The Minſter was raiſed to hold ſuch worſhippers while alive, and to contain their gorgeous tombs when dead; and we never look at the Cathedral aright, unleſs we imagine mitred abbots and knights in chained armour, walking in proceſſion down its ſolemn aiſles. I have put Schlegel into our own language, and have enlarged a little on his notion, ſince he only hints the thing. What a propriety it gives to the tombs of the croſs-legged knights! The monkiſh prieſts exacted the tribute of putting off the knightly ſpur when the Cathedral was entered. Our choriſters fine any body at this day coming in with ſpurs.—I do not know what to go on writing to you about. I live here apart from the world, and run into contemplative habits. Socrates conſidered life only as a *malady* under which the nobler ſpirit was condemned for a time to linger, and called living, 'the learning how to die;' he meant that the vexations of life render death deſirable. The word *malady* explains the cock ſacrificed to Æſculapius; death was curing him of his *malady*, and he ſacrificed the fowl, in playful alluſion to this, to the god of phyſic. It is ſingular, but this notion has much helped me under ſome very vexatious circumſtances. Chriſtianity puts the argument higher, and makes the *malady* preparative to better and laſting *health* * * * J. Fiſher."

1828.

"Osmington, December 7th. My dear Conſtable, As ſoon as my mother is fixed at Hampſtead, I will come and pay you a viſit, and help you to bear your privation. * * * Evans's letter was ſo far ſatisfactory that he reported you to be in a ſtate of complete ſelf-poſſeſſion. I entreat you to retain it, for you have need only to look within yourſelf, and find ſatisfaction. I wiſh, if 'Brighton' is not out of your poſſeſſion, you would put it on your eaſel by your ſide, and mellow its ferocious beauties. Calm your mind and your ſea at the ſame time, and let in ſunſhine and ſerenity. I feel much for your ſituation, but cannot put theſe feelings into words. You have a treaſure in your new friend Evans, who is always at hand. * * * J. Fiſher."

1829.

"January 8th, 1829. My dear Conſtable, * * * The tone of your letter to me was very ſatisfactory. You appear to be ſmitten, but not caſt down. I will lend you any aſſiſtance, in my power, in the education of your children. There is a little book publiſhed by the Society for Promoting Chriſtian Knowledge, which is all you want for religious inſtruction, 'Croſſman's Introduction,' to which you may add 'Nelſon's Practice of True Devotion.' It is a moſt ſenſible book. * * * J. Fiſher."

Conſtable returned with his children to London, but retained the houſe at Hampſtead as an occaſional reſidence.

"Charlotte Street, January 21ſt. My dear Leſlie, Do not believe me to be either ungrateful or negligent in that I have not called on you, or taken any notice of your kind attentions to me on my coming hither. You know that I have my ſeven children here. This is a charge I pray God you may never feel as I do. Six of the ſeven are in lovely health, but I grieve to ſay my darling boy John is in a ſad ſtate. * * * In this ſweet youth I ſee very much that reminds me of his mother; but I muſt not truſt myſelf on this ſubject; my grievous wound only ſlumbers. I hope dear Mrs. Leſlie and your children are well. My thoughts are often on your infant, for I well remember, on its being brought into my drawing-room at Hampſtead, the gleam of joy that overſpread that countenance which is never abſent from my ſight. * * * I ſhould like to ſee you, and am anxious to paſs an evening with you. I ſend this note by a meſſenger, that you may appoint any afternoon that I can come to you. I have been ill, but I have endeavoured to get to work again, and could I get afloat on a canvaſs of ſix feet, I might have a chance of being carried away from myſelf. I have juſt received a commiſſion to paint a *mermaid* for a *ſign* to an inn in Warwickſhire. This is encouraging, and affords no ſmall ſolace after my previous labours in landſcape for twenty years. However, I ſhall not quarrel with the lady now, ſhe may help to educate my children." He then changes the ſubject, and after ſome pleaſantry, goes on to ſay, " I would not write this nonſenſe at all, were it not to prove to you, my dear Leſlie, that I am in ſome degree, at leaſt, myſelf again."

Conſtable made a very pretty and finiſhed ſketch of the Mermaid, but I do not think the matter ever went farther. He gave the ſketch to Mr. Evans.

On the 10th of February, he was elected an Academician. That this diſtinction ſhould not have been conferred on him at a much earlier period of his life is a proof that the progreſs of an original ſtyle of art, in the eſtimation even of artiſts, is very ſlow. Much as he was pleaſed at the attainment of this honour, he could not help ſaying, " it has been delayed until I am ſolitary, and cannot impart it." He did not add with Johnſon, " until I am known, and do not want it ;" for no painter of equal genius was ever leſs known in his own country. Wilkie, who had been for ſome time abroad, told me that when he ſaw Conſtable's pictures in the Louvre, he could not underſtand why the painter of ſuch magnificent works had not long been a full member of the Academy.

"Lodge, Charter Houſe, February 11th. My dear Conſtable, Although I fully expected the event, your note telling me that you are an Academician gave me the greateſt pleaſure. Your rewards are at laſt beginning to flow in upon you, although (as everything is ordained in a ſtate of trial) the painful is mixed with the ſweet. My mother ſends her congratulations, which are worth the having. To-morrow I go with you to call upon your friends. The event is in every way important to me, ſince my judgment was embarked in the ſame boat with your ſucceſs. Moſt faithfully yours, John Fiſher."

"My dear John Chalon. Accept my thanks for your kind meſſage to me by your brother. I greatly rejoice in the event of my election, as it is attended with ſo many gratifying circumſtances; but I aſſure you in none more ſo than the certainty that it cannot fail to promote and continue our eſteem for each other. I beg my kindeſt regards to your family. Believe me, dear Chalon, your brother's kind and conſtant ſupport of me has made an impreſſion on my mind never to be done away by time or circumſtances. After he left me laſt night, there came, 'though laſt, not leaſt,' Turner and Jones. We parted at one o'clock this morning, mutually pleaſed with one another. I ſhall take an early opportunity of calling at your houſe. * * * Ever, dear Chalon, believe me to be moſt ſincerely yours, John Conſtable. Charlotte Street, February 11th.

"34, Gerrard Street, Soho, February 11th. My dear Conſtable, Our friend Peter Coxe has juſt called in the higheſt glee to tell me of your good fortune, or rather of your having attained an honour which ought to have been conferred on you long ago. It is now ſomewhere about twenty-ſeven years ſince you and I firſt entered the Academy together as ſtudents. From that period, in much intercourſe, it is to me a gratifying reflection that never on any ſingle occaſion did any cloud interpoſe to interrupt the ſunſhine of our friendſhip, nor even the ſhadow of a cloud, yet you have produced many, but always painted them ſo well, that they have only increaſed my great admiration of your very original genius. Our uniform coincidence of opinions on men and things is equally remarkable.—Having gained this election, you have nothing higher to look up to in this world. I would, therefore, my dear friend, take this opportunity, and the privilege of a friend, to direct your attention more and more to another election which we are all too apt to loſe ſight of, our election to a glory far above and beyond all the kingdoms of this world, and to ſecure which, is the great purpoſe for which we are ſent into it. I ſhould have had the pleaſure of calling to congratulate you, but I am ſtill confined by illneſs. Believe me to remain on all occaſions, my dear Conſtable, ever affectionately yours, Andrew Robertſon."

Conſtable called, according to cuſtom, after the honour that had juſt been conferred on him, to pay his reſpects to Sir Thomas Lawrence, who did not conceal from his viſiter that he conſidered him peculiarly fortunate in being choſen an Academician at a time when there were hiſtorical painters of great merit on the liſt of candidates. So kind-hearted a man as Lawrence could have no intention to give pain; but their taſtes ran in directions ſo widely different, and the Preſident, who attached great importance to ſubject, and conſidered high art to be inſeparable from hiſtorical art, had never been led to pay ſufficient attention to Conſtable's pictures to become impreſſed with their real merit, and there can be no doubt but that he thought the painter of, what he conſidered, the humbleſt claſs of landſcape was as much ſurpriſed at the honour juſt conferred on him, as he was himſelf. Conſtable was well aware that the opinions of Sir Thomas were the faſhionable ones; he felt the pain thus unconſciouſly inflicted, and his reply intimated that he looked upon his election as an act of justice rather than favour. What occurred at this visit, as well as some ill-natured paragraphs in the newspapers, will explain a passage marked by italics in a note to me, dated "Hampstead, April 5th. Since I saw you I have been shut up here. I have forwarded my picture of Hadleigh Castle, which I shall send to Charlotte Street to-morrow morning. Can you oblige me with a call to tell me whether I ought to send it to the Exhibition? I am grievously nervous about it, as *I am still smarting under my election.* I have little enough either of prudence or self-knowledge, as you know, and I am willing to submit to what you and others whom I value may decide. I shall dine with the Dowager Lady Beaumont to-day, and I hope I shall meet you. I could hardly refuse; yet at this time (for I am in the height of agony about my crazy old walls of the Castle), I could rather wish myself at home. I beg an answer by bearer to tell me how you all are. My children are lovely, and all the better for being here. Last Monday we had a little party, it being the birthday of two of mine, and I sat down to table with fourteen, the eldest of whom was only eleven."

"Charlotte Street, April 23rd. My dear Fisher, I am glad that you can make this house serviceable to your family on any occasion. My housekeeper will provide all that is necessary, so that the sole attention of your servant can be devoted to your little boy.* They could not have come more conveniently; my own family having left this house to-day, where they have been passing Easter, the beds and rooms are well aired. Mrs. Savage,† who is anything but what her name implies, proposes that the front bed-room, being large

* Who was sent to town to undergo a slight operation, the removal of a spot from his lip.

† His housekeeper.

Chap. XI.
1829.

and having two beds, be theirs; one bed is ſo large that your boy can either ſleep with or from your ſervant; a fire can be kept conſtantly there or in the drawing-room for them for the day. I live down here, (in the parlour,) and ſhall not be put at all out of my way.

"I have juſt got a letter from the Academy. The Pandemonium opens on Saturday, in which we are allowed every exceſs for ſix days (Sunday excepted).*

"Your ſudden departure put me out a good deal and made me angry, and it was a diſappointment to my friends in the Academy. Propitiate them on your return, and then you may leave me to myſelf.—I was ſadly ill after you left me. I never had ſo bad a cold before. However, Hampſtead and a picture ſet me tolerably well up. I have ſent the great Caſtle, ſuch as it is, to the Exhibition, and a rich Cottage. Nothing ſhall prevent my coming to you at Saliſbury in the ſummer; Evans would be delighted, but he has ſuffering humanity on his hands. I paſſed a day or two with my children at Ham Houſe, the Counteſs of Dyſart's; ſhe was very kind to them, and pleaſed with them.

"Wilkie has eight pictures, Lawrence eight, Jackſon Phillips and Pickerſgill eight each. Callcott, though not eight, has one eight feet long,—a claſſical landſcape. Turner has four. They have an immenſe craſh† in the hall, and it is evident the Devil muſt vomit pictures over London. * * * Poor old Northcote was at the edge of death, but revived. I ſaw him yeſterday."

"Oſmington, April 27th. My dear Conſtable, I ſhall be at Eton with my boy Oſmond on the 1ſt May, and muſt ſtay there a fortnight.—I thank you, moſt gratefully, for your kindneſs in receiving my little boy Frederick and his nurſe.

* The varniſhing days allowed to the members of the Academy.
† He alludes to the quantity of pictures rejected.

* * * I beg your pardon for uſing you ſo ill when in London. But the cold, bitter, north-eaſt winds kept me in ſuch a ſtate of irritation, the whole of my ſtay, that I ſhould have been a moſt unpleaſant inmate to you, and have diſturbed your ſerenity. I felt this, and ſtaid purpoſely away. I gave you all of my company that I *dare;* and at laſt ſuddenly left London, and its windy ſtreets, in a precipitate fit of deſperation. I have not yet recovered it. There is a deep cellar in the infernal regions reſerved for the moſt deſperate. London, in March, is a type of it. See Milton's *Cold* Hell. Why did you turn out into an unwholeſome room on my account? I cannot hold myſelf reſponſible for ſuch inſtances of unwiſe hoſpitality. Your life is valuable.

"Will you run down to Windſor for a few days, between May 1ſt and 14th? You will find me there in lodgings. Pray do; and let us walk over thoſe delicious ſcenes again of natural and artificial magnificence; where parſons eat, and ſtuff, and dream of preferment; where pedagogues flog little boys, talk burly, and think themſelves great men in three-cornered hats; where ſtateſmen * * * *; and where every body ſeems indifferent to the ſplendid ſcenes that ſurround them. Ever yours, ſomewhat cynically, J. Fiſher."

"Oſmington, April 30th. My dear friend, I diſcovered in an old pocket book, this day, an extract from Milton's proſe works. *When* I made it, and from *which* of his works, I forget. But this I remember, that I meant to ſend it to you, ſaying what I now ſay; that it is the principle upon which my friendſhip for you is founded. You know that I do not uſe words in mere flattery.—'As to other points, what God may have determined for me I know not. But this I know, that if he ever inſtilled an intenſe love of moral beauty into the breaſt of any man, he has inſtilled it into mine. Ceres, in the fable, purſued not her daughter with a greater keenneſs of inquiry, than I have, day and night, the

CHAP. XI. 1829.

idea of Perfection. Hence, whenever I find a man despising the false estimates of the vulgar, and daring to aspire, in sentiment, language, and conduct, to what the highest wisdom, through every age, has taught us as most excellent, to him I unite myself by a sort of necessary attachment. And if I am so influenced, by nature or by destiny, that by no exertion or labour of my own, I may exalt myself to the summit of worth and honour, yet no powers of heaven or earth will hinder me from looking with reverence and affection upon those who have thoroughly attained to that glory.' * * * My dear Constable, ever yours faithfully, John Fisher."

The Hadleigh Castle, Constable's principal picture in the exhibition of 1829, received rather rougher usage than usual from the newspaper critics; but it finely embodied to the eye the following lines from "Thomson's Summer," with which its title was accompanied in the catalogue of the Exhibition:

> "The desert joys
> Wildly, through all his melancholy bounds,
> Rude ruins glitter; and the briny deep,
> Seen from some pointed promontory's top,
> Far to the blue horizon's utmost verge,
> Restless, reflects a floating gleam."

I witnessed an amusing scene before this picture at the Academy on one of the varnishing days. Chantrey told Constable its foreground was too cold, and taking his palette from him, he passed a strong glazing* of asphaltum all over that part of the picture, and while this was going on, Constable, who stood behind him in some degree of alarm, said to me "there goes all my dew." He held in great respect Chantrey's judgment in most matters, but this did not prevent his carefully taking from the picture all that the great sculptor had done for it.

* Glazing is the process of using transparent colour alone.

"Charlotte Street, July 4th. My dear Fiſher. I was moſt happy to receive Mrs. Fiſher's very kind letter, in which you are ſo kind as to wiſh to ſee me with my children. I have taken places in the coach for Wedneſday next, the 7th, and we *three* ſhall be with you to *tea*;—I am told, before ſix o'clock, ſo that we ſhall be able to walk over the bridge before dark.—The weather may be more ſettled by the time I come to you, but the fine effects of ſuch a ſeaſon make ample amends for its inconvenience. My children are all well, and I think I never felt in better health, thanks to Evans.

"I took a farewell look with him at the Academy on Thurſday.—He is impreſſed with my Caſtle. * * * He will be delighted to join us at Saliſbury.—His intellect and cultivation are, as you diſcovered, of the firſt claſs, and his integrity invaluable. I have juſt done a ſmall portrait of his mother.—If you have not your book of Claude's etchings at Saliſbury, will you procure it?—as it contains his epitaph and ſome memoranda, and I am engaged to give a ſketch of his character to prefix to a book of engravings, now making from the National Gallery.

"I paſſed the afternoon of yeſterday with Jackſon at his villa alone. He uſed a definition which was uſeful and comprehenſive.—He ſaid, 'The whole object and difficulty of the art (indeed, of all the fine arts) is to *unite imagination with nature*. We were talking of * * * * * and * * * * * * &c. &c.—The art is now filled with *Phantaſmagoria*.—More when we meet.—"

"Saliſbury, September 3rd. My dear Conſtable. Many thanks for your continual remembrance of me, which is worth more than all; but neverthelefs many thanks for your outward ſigns of remembrance, your veniſon, and your revification of the Claude.—I ſhall be at Windſor on Saturday night, September 5th, with my boy. Now either let me ſee you there, or hear from you.—I yearn to ſee you tran-

CHAP. XI. 1829.

quilly and collectedly at work on your next great picture, undisturbed by gossips good and ill-natured; at a season of the year when the glands of the body are unobstructed by cold, and the nerves in a state of quiescence. You choose February and March for composition, when the strongest men get irritable and uncomfortable, during the prevalence of the N.E. winds, the great destruction of the frame in England.

" Minny* is the nicest child in the house possible. Nobody would know of her existence if she were not seen. She improves in French and music,—(her ear is perfect,) and she dances quadrilles with the chairs, like a parched pea on a drum head.

" * * * and * * * have been together on the visitation for three weeks. They have neither broken bread nor spoken together, nor, I believe, seen one another.—What a mistake our Oxford and Cambridge Apostolic missionaries fall into when they make Christianity a stern haughty thing. Think of St. Paul with a full blown wig—deep shovel hat—apron—round belly—double chin—deep cough—stern eye—rough voice—and imperious manner,—drinking port wine, and laying down the law as to the best way of escaping the operation of the Curates' Residence Act. I need not, I believe, sign my name. My hand is pretty well known to you."

Constable was now engaged in preparing the " English Landscape" for publication, having secured the valuable assistance of Mr. David Lucas; and it led to the magnificent engravings that gentleman afterwards executed of " The Corn Field," " The Lock," which Reynolds had contemplated, and the " Salisbury Cathedral from the Meadows," on a large scale, and the " Stratford Mill" and " Hadleigh Castle" of a lesser size. A prospectus of the " English Land-

* Maria Constable.

ſcape" was printed, ſaying, " It is the deſire of the Author in this publication to increaſe the intereſt for, and promote the ſtudy of the rural ſcenery of England, with all its endearing aſſociations, and even in its moſt ſimple localities; of England with her climate of more than vernal freſhneſs, in whoſe ſummer ſkies and rich autumnal clouds, ' in thouſand liveries dight,' the obſerver of nature may daily watch her endleſs varieties of effect." He was by this time fully aware of the obſtacles that exiſted to a juſt eſtimation of his art, and he drew up a preface to his work, in which the following paſſage ſeems to me to be a true ſtatement of the caſe between the public and himſelf. " In art, there are two modes by which men aim at diſtinction. In the one, by a careful application to what others have accompliſhed, the artiſt imitates their works, or ſelects and combines their various beauties; in the other, he ſeeks excellence at its primitive ſource, nature. In the firſt, he forms a ſtyle upon the ſtudy of pictures, and produces either imitative or eclectic art; in the ſecond, by a cloſe obſervation of nature, he diſcovers qualities exiſting in her which have never been portrayed before, and thus forms a ſtyle which is original. The reſults of the one mode, as they repeat that with which the eye is already familiar, are ſoon recognized and eſtimated, while the advances of the artiſt in a new path muſt neceſſarily be ſlow, for few are able to judge of that which deviates from the uſual courſe, or are qualified to appreciate original ſtudies."

In the year 1814, when a collection of pictures by Wilſon, Hogarth, and Gainſborough, was exhibited at the Britiſh Gallery, in the preface to the catalogue it was ſaid, " The merit of Wilſon's works is now juſtly appreciated; and we may hope that ſince the period of his deceaſe, the love and knowledge of art have been ſo much diffuſed through the country, that the exertion of ſuch talents may never again remain unrewarded during the life time of him who may

Chap. XI.
1829.

possess them."—Who would not say Amen to this?—And yet, long after it was penned, Constable was as much neglected as Wilson had been, and so will it again happen with genius equally original and natural, in Landscape, until that branch of the art shall be better understood, with reference to nature, than it is yet by our dispensers of fame.

In one of Constable's sketch-books, there is a draught of a letter to Mr. Fisher, in which he says, "I know not if the landscapes I now offer to your notice will add to the esteem in which you have always been so kind as to hold me as a painter; I shall dedicate them to you, relying on that affection which you have invariably extended to me under every circumstance."—In another part of this memorandum he mentions Mr. Lucas, of whom he says, "His great urbanity and integrity are only equalled by his skill as an engraver; and the scenes now transmitted by his hand are such as I have ever preferred. For the most part, they are those with which I have the strongest associations—those of my earliest years, when 'in the cheerful morn of life, I looked to nature with unceasing joy.'"

Mr. Fisher died before the work was published, and it appeared without a dedication.

The first plate engraved was of "Dedham Mill," from a very slight sketch; but Constable did not again place anything so unfinished in the hands of Mr. Lucas. A few of the many notes he wrote to that gentleman while the work was in progress, will shew how much he was disquieted by the undertaking, though in itself of no great magnitude, owing to his fastidiousness in the choice and execution of the subjects, (five plates that were finished being rejected by him), and to his discovering as he proceeded, that all chances of remuneration for the time and money he was spending upon it were hopeless. Indeed the "English Landscape" proved in the end to be, as Coleridge said of a work of his own, "a ſecret confided to the public, and very faithfully kept."

"September 15th. Dear Lucas, A total change has again taken place; Leſlie dined with me yeſterday; we have agreed on a long landſcape, evening, with a flight of rooks, as a companion to the 'Spring,' and the 'Whitehall Stairs,' in place of 'The Caſtle.' Prithee come and ſee me at ſix this evening, and take the things away, leſt I change again. However, I like all the laſt affairs if you do. I will tell you the reaſons for ſo changing. Pray come at ſix. Bring ſomething in your hand, I don't care what."

The "Autumnal Sunſet," the ſubject mentioned in this note was ſketched in his favourite fields near Bergholt. In the diſtance towards the right is the tower of Stoke Church, and on the left are Langham Hill and Church.

CHAPTER XII.

1830-1831.

*Picture of "Bergholt Church Yard." Death of Sir Thomas Lawrence. Mr. Shee elected President of the Royal Academy. Notes to Mr. Lucas. Constable on the Committee of Arrangement at the Academy. Picture of "A Dell in Helmingham Park" exhibited in 1830. Illness of George IV. Jackson. Bannister. Constable Visitor in the Life Academy. Etty. Wilkie. Illness. Large Picture of "Salisbury Cathedral from the Meadows" exhibited, 1831. Death of Jackson. Death of Northcote. Watteau. Greuze. John Varley. Coronation of King William IV. and Queen Adelaide. Lord B * * * * * * m. Lord Lyttelton and the Ghost. Old Sarum. Illness. Reform Bill. E. Landseer.*

1830.

HAD asked Constable to allow my sister to copy the small picture of "The Porch of Bergholt Church," which has been described in the first chapter, and it came to us with the following note: "January, 1830. My dear Leslie, I send the 'Churchyard,' which my friends in Portman Place are welcome to use for any purpose but to go into it. * * * The motto on the dial is, 'Ut umbra, sic vita.'"—This note was singularly followed by his next: "January 8th. My dear Leslie, I have just received the distressing intelligence of the death of poor Sir Thomas Lawrence. This sad event took place last night in consequence of internal inflammation. I could not help sending to you; the council is called in consequence."

Constable, though always on friendly terms, had never been very intimate with Sir Thomas Lawrence, but he felt in common with every artist in the kingdom the magnitude of the loss of so eminent a painter, cut off with such apparent suddenness; at a time, too, when he was pursuing his art with all the energy of youth, though in his sixty-first year; and when, indeed, so far from betraying any diminution of power, he seemed to be improving on himself. This, I think, was acknowledged by all who had an opportunity of seeing the, scarcely finished but very fine, portrait of the Earl of Aberdeen in the exhibition at the Academy that followed the death of its President.

When the painting materials of Sir Thomas were sold, Constable purchased a palette which had belonged to Sir Joshua Reynolds, and had been given by him to Sir George Beaumont, who gave it to Lawrence. He presented this interesting relic to the Academy, with its history inscribed on a silver plate inlaid upon it.

"January 26th. My dear Lane. Mr. Shee was elected last night by a large majority of the Academy; we expect much from his self devotion and chivalrous sense of honour. * * * Yours, ever truly, J. C." Constable lived long enough to witness the ample fulfilment of the highest expectations formed on this occasion.

"January 31st. My dear Leslie. I hope your toothache is better. It is an entire illness with me whenever I am so visited. It was a grievous disappointment to all of us, not seeing you and Mrs. Leslie. My little girls were all in 'apple-pie order,' to be seen. My dear Maria had been practising her steps and music all day that she might appear to advantage. All my boys were in their best, and had allowed a total clearance of the drawing room of their numerous ſhips, caſtles, books, bricks, drawings, &c. &c. &c. I miſſed you by going to the Gallery where I had invited Newton and Landſeer to meet you, neither of whom came; though, as I claſs them with the nobility, they having adopted their habits, I ſat up till twelve to receive them. Not having *a tongue* of my own, I had ordered one, with two lovely fowls for you, and our beſt ſilver candleſticks for your ſiſter. My pretty Minna had ready a little preſent for my God-daughter, and to prove to you and Mrs. Leſlie that though our diſappointment was ſevere, we are not angry, ſhe begs to ſend it this afternoon."

"Charlotte Street, February 26th. Dear Lucas. I am anxious to ſee you, to have farther talk about the plates. Firſt, I want to know how forward the 'Evening' is, and the retouched 'Stoke.' I have not the wiſh to become the poſſeſſor of the large plate of the 'Caſtle,'* but I am anxious that it ſhould be fine, and will take all pains with it. It cannot fail to be ſo, if I may judge from what I have ſeen. I have taken much pains with the laſt proof of 'The Summerland,' but I fear I ſhall be obliged to reject it. It has never recovered its firſt trip up, and the ſky with the new ground is and ever will be rotten. I like your firſt plates far, very far, the beſt; but I allow much for your diſtractions ſince, with thoſe devils, the printers, and other matters not in uniſon with that patient toil which ought always to govern the habits of us both. Do not neglect 'The Wood,'† as I am almoſt in want of the picture. Bring me another large 'Caſtle,' or two, or three, for it is mighty fine, though it looks as if all the chimney ſweepers in Chriſtendom had been at work on it, and thrown their ſoot bags up in the air. Yet every body likes it; but I ſhould recollect that none but friends ſee my things; I have no doubt the world deſpiſes

* "Hadleigh Caſtle."   † "Helmingham Park."

them. Come early to-morrow evening, and bring what you can, and an account of the next; I am nervous and anxious about them. I have made the upright windmill quite perfect. I ſhould like the book to conſiſt of eight; pray tell the writer not to complete his ſketch of the title; I have made another."

The engraving of the "Evening," one of the fineſt of his ſmall pictures, is the leaſt ſucceſsful of all Mr. Lucas's plates. The ſcene is near Bergholt, with Stoke and Langham in the diſtance. This plate, the "Summerland," and the "Autumnal Sunſet," all repreſent the ſame fields, and from points of view not far diſtant from each other.

"March 2nd. Dear Lucas, * * * Shall I ſee you on Thurſday? Alfred Chalon ſays, 'The Caſtle is a fine looking thing.' I am anxious to ſee a firſt proof of the 'Evening;' but take your time; I will be very good and patient in future. I long to ſee the Church, now that it is removed to a better ſpot—two fields off. Take care to avoid rottenneſs, it is the worſt quality of all. Leſlie has not the 'Stoke;' take him one when you next prove it, with the laſt alteration."

"Dear Lucas, I ſend the 'Jaques' in a flat, yet feel aſſured you will not make a *flat* of him. I am much pleaſed with what we are about ſo far, only I fear if we do not mind, we ſhall not have enough of the paſtoral. Leſlie has juſt been here, and likes much the ſketch in a lane, which I ſend for you to look at. It is a lovely ſubject, rich and novel, and what is better than all, *natural;* it would be a glorious full ſubject." The 'Jaques' mentioned by Conſtable in this note was a water-coloured drawing of the often painted ſcene, the wounded ſtag. Of this ſubject he made many ſketches, and contemplated a large picture, the only imaginary landſcape he ever thought of painting.

As a newly elected Academician, he was now on the committee of arrangement of the Exhibition, and in a note to

Mr. Lane he ſays, "I am ſadly haraſſed, and not being able to call on you is moſt vexatious. I cannot go out, leſt my picture and my fire ſhould *go out* too. How get you on? * * * I ſhall be overwhelmed with pictures, eſpecially portraits, the painters of them all believing they can eaſily fill the ſhoes of Lawrence."

In a note to me written ſoon after, he ſays, "I regret the entire confinement I have been in ſince I ſaw you. My picture has been, and is, plaguing me exceedingly, for it is always impoſſible to know what a picture really wants till it comes to the laſt. However, it ſhall go. It would amuſe you to ſee how I am beſet; I have poets—earls—dukes—and even royalty at my feet; all painted canvaſs, of courſe." His own pictures this year were, the "Dell in Helmingham Park," a ſmall landſcape, and "A view of Hampſtead Heath." While aſſiſting in the arrangement, he found much trouble from the exceſſive ſize of ſome of the frames; and on remonſtrating with an exhibiter on this point, who defended himſelf by ſaying that his frames were made exactly on the pattern of thoſe of Sir Thomas Lawrence, he could not help replying, "It is very eaſy to imitate Lawrence in his *frames*."

I have often obſerved with ſurpriſe, how readily Conſtable would make alterations in his pictures by the advice of perſons of very little judgment. While finiſhing the picture of the Dell, he was one day beſet with a great many ſuggeſtions from a very ſhallow ſource, and after adopting ſome of them, he felt inclined to make a ſtand, which he did by ſaying to his adviſer, "Very true; but don't you ſee that I might go on, and make this picture ſo good, that it would be good for nothing."

"May. My dear Leſlie, Can you take a chop with me at five, or a diſh of tea at ſix, on your way to the Academy to the general meeting, where I hope you will be. The debate muſt be learned, as we are to decide whether *plaſter* *casts* come under the head of *marbles*, which they were not able to do at Edinburgh; I shall get there by seven to look round the Exhibition. I feel like the old woman who kept a stall at a fair, who 'hoped the King would not die during the show.' "*

"August. My dear Leslie, Will this fine weather tempt you to a walk over the fields to my pretty dwelling in Well Walk? If it should, and you can make it the afternoon to dinner, you will find Mr. Bannister and Newton. Prithee come; life is short (and so is my notice); we meet too little."

Mr. Bannister was unable on this occasion to dine with Constable, who received from him the following characteristic note: "August 17th. My dear Sir, To prevent my place being unsupplied, pray allow me to send you a *lame* excuse. Certain gouty symptoms convince me that I shall not be able to join your party. My apprehension, however, of mortification, my surgeon says, 'is a mere farce;' and adds, 'Can't you be contented with the gout?' My only *mortification* will be in declining your kind invitation. Believe me, my dear friend, yours most truly, J. Bannister."

A young friend of mine, a student of the Academy, whom I had introduced to Constable, had called to ask his advice on the subject of engaging himself as an assistant to an eminent portrait painter; and to this matter the following note chiefly alludes: "Charlotte Street, December 29th. My dear Leslie. K. F * * * calling on me this morning on his way to you, I send you my second number of the 'Landscape,' the first yet sent out. I have carefully looked out a fine one, and beg you will receive all these trifles as marks of my affection, and if so, they are no longer trifles in my estimation. Poor F * * * has much to say to you about himself and * * *. I know not how to advise. * * * is an honourable man, and his

* This was written during the last illness of George IV.

1830.

art is ſound and good, but what F * * * will be able to earn with him, will, I fear, but ill requite the loſs of time. Theſe kind of engagements are ſeldom attended with ſatisfaction to either party, becauſe they both want to make all they can of each other. I was much delighted with my day at your houſe on Sunday, and to complete it, I paſſed the evening with Turner at Tomkiſon's."

Though Conſtable ſtrenuouſly objected to any ſtyle in art however excellent, being looked at as an object to be attained, rather than as a means towards the attainment of what is always better than the beſt ſtyle, *nature*, yet he well underſtood how important it is that the ſtudent ſhould be directed to nature by the aſſiſtance of previous art. In the month of January, 1831, he was viſitor in the Life Academy. It is the duty of the viſitors to determine the attitude of the model, and to give advice to the ſtudents; and he placed every figure, during his attendance, from ſome well known one by a great maſter, beginning with an Eve from Raphael, and allowed no evening to paſs without a ſhort lecture addreſſed to the ſtudents.

1831.

"Dear Leſlie, I ſet my firſt figure yeſterday, and it is much liked; Etty congratulates me upon it; do, dear Leſlie, come and ſee it. I have dreſſed up a bower of laurel, and I told the ſtudents they probably expected a landſcape background from me. I am quite popular in the Life; at all events I ſpare neither pains nor expenſe to become a good Academician. My garden of Eden coſt me ten ſhillings, and my men were twice ſtopped coming from Hampſtead with the green boughs, by the police, who thought (as was the caſe) they had robbed ſome gentleman's grounds. * * * The fun is, my garden at the Academy was taken for a Chriſtmas decoration, holly and miſletoe. Wilkie called yeſterday; I was unfortunately at the Academy; but he good-naturedly came in, and aſked to ſee my children, and was delighted with my dear girl, who was teaching the leſſer ones; he 'hoped they were all good children.' Jackſon alſo called. I leave home at half-paſt five every evening, at the lateſt. Come and walk down with me. It is no ſmall undertaking to make a Paradiſe of the Life Academy." In another note, Conſtable ſays, "I ſhall look for you this evening at five, or you will look in on me in my *den;* but I muſt ſay my *lions* are exceedingly well behaved. Saſs and Etty are never abſent; they ſet an excellent example. * * * I have been reading an amuſing lecture to my children over the print of your 'Sir Roger De Coverley going to Church.' I was delighted to find how much I was agreeably reminded of poor dear old Bigg."*

Conſtable ſet two male figures at the Academy from The Laſt Judgment of M. Angelo;—he afterwards ſet a female figure which he called an Amazon.—"January 27th, My dear Leſlie, I hope you will find an evening to come down to the Academy and ſee my Amazon. My labours finiſh there on Saturday. This figure is liked beſt of all. Etty is ſo delighted, that he has aſked me to breakfaſt, to meet ſome friends, among them Mr. Stothard."

Mr. Lucas was interrupted in the work he was engaged on, by the illneſs of Mrs. Lucas and one of his children, and in a note to him, dated January 4th, Conſtable ſays, "I am ſo very anxious to hear how things are going on in your houſe, that I ſend my man, who I truſt will bring me ſome better account, though for the poor little fellow I cannot feel ſanguine. I feel for your diſtreſs, and I truſt you have ſeen Dr. Davis; for if human means can avail they are his. Don't think of me or my concerns for a moment; your buſi-

* Mr. Bigg, R.A. ſat to me for the face of Sir Roger. I thought him an admirable ſpecimen both in look and manner of an old faſhioned Engliſh gentleman. A more amiable man never exiſted.

nefs is with yourfelf. I mention this only to relieve your mind from all other anxiety, as I well know your great integrity, and that you are always too ready to devote yourfelf to others, or at leaft to me."

The early part of the fpring of every year was a time of anxiety to Conftable, as it is to moft of our artifts, who are juft then finifhing their works for the Exhibition. He too often found himfelf behind hand, and the redoubled application that his pictures demanded, as the time of fending them to the Academy drew near, fatigued his mind, and this, with the effects of the eafterly winds of the feafon, and the increafed irregularity of his meals generally difordered his health. His ufual time for dining was in the middle of the day, but when very bufy it varied, and I have known him eat a few oranges while at work, and fit down to dinner ill with exhauftion, when it was too dark to paint. In addition to all this, his uneafinefs about his book had now a fhare in producing the illnefs of which the next note fpeaks. "March 12th. Dear Lucas, My indifpofition fadly worries me, and makes me think (perhaps too darkly) on almoft every fubject. Neverthelefs, my feven infants, my time of life and ftate of health, and other ferious matters, make me defirous of lightening my mind as much as poffible of unneceffary oppreffion, as I fear it is already too overweighted. I have thought much on my book; and all my reflections on the fubject go to oppress me; its duration, its expenfe, its hopeleffnefs of remuneration; added to which, I now difcover that the printfellers are watching it as their lawful prey, and they alone can help me. I can only difpofe of it by giving it away. My plan is to confine the number of plates to thofe now on hand; I fee we have about twenty. The three prefent numbers contain twelve; others begun are about eight or ten more, fome of which may not be refumed, and we muft begin the frontifpiece. It haraffes my days, and difturbs my reſt at nights. The expenſe is too enormous for a work that has nothing but your beautiful feeling and execution to recommend it. The painter himſelf is totally unpopular, and ever will be on this ſide the grave; the ſubjects *nothing but the art*, and the buyers wholly ignorant of that. I am haraſſed by the lengthened proſpect of its duration; therefore I go back to my firſt plan of twenty, including frontiſpiece and vignette, and we can now ſee our way out of the wood. I can bear the irritation of delay (from which I have ſuffered ſo much that I attribute my preſent illneſs in part to it) no longer; conſider, not a real fortnight's work has been done towards the whole for the laſt four months. Years muſt roll on to produce the twenty-ſix prints, and all this time I ſhall not ſell a copy. Remember, dear Lucas, I mean not, nor think one reflection on you. Every thing, with the plan, is my own, and I want to relieve my mind of that which haraſſes it like a diſeaſe. Do not for a moment think I blame you, or that I do not ſympathize with you in thoſe lamentable cauſes of hindrance which have afflicted your home. Pray let me ſee you ſoon. I am not wholly unable to work, thank God! I hope poor Mrs. Lucas is better. Dr. Davis has been to ſee me and my poor boy John, who is very ill. Mr. Drew gives me pills, ſo that both their medicines (which I take together) may get me well in double quick time."

"March 23rd. Dear Lucas, Let me know when I ſhall ſee you. I am very anxious that you ſhould call, as I am ſadly lonely, and do not get well; but I am very much better. I have formed the wiſh to add a windmill to the ſet, leaving the title and vignette diſtinct, and to be given in, which will look handſome. I have made a drawing of the title for you to ſee, and I wiſh you to chooſe the windmill. I have made a great impreſſion on my large canvaſs. * * * Beechey was here yeſterday, and ſaid, 'Why, d—n it, Conftable, what a d—d fine picture you are making; but you look d—d ill, and you have got a d—d bad cold!' fo that you have evidence *on oath* of my being about a fine picture, and that I am looking ill. I hope Mrs. Lucas is better, and yourfelf well."

With the large picture of "Salifbury Cathedral from the Meadows," the one fpoken of in the laft note, and which will often again be mentioned, Conftable exhibited at the Academy this feafon, a fmaller one of "Yarmouth Pier," and when the anxiety of preparing for the Exhibition was over, his health improved.

Britifh art, which had fo recently fuftained great loffes by the deaths of Owen and Lawrence, now again fuffered heavily by the death of Jackfon, who had ftood with them, and occafionally perhaps before either of them, in the firft rank of portraiture.* He had lingered for fome time in a decline, and as his refidence was near mine, Conftable heard of his death from me.

"June 2nd. Dear Leflie, Your note this morning firft informed me of the departure of poor dear Jackfon. One is fo apt to believe that all things which give us pleafure are always to continue, that when thefe fad events do come, and come they muft, we are the more appalled and afflicted. It feems impoffible that we are to fee that dear fellow no more. He is a great lofs to the Academy and to the public. By his friends he will be for ever miffed, and he had no enemy. He did a great deal of good, much more, I believe, than is generally known, and he never did harm to any creature living. My fincere belief is, that he is at this moment in Heaven.

* His portrait of Canova, painted for Chantrey, and the one of Northcote, painted for the Earl of Carlifle, will, I think, bear me out in faying this. As a colourift, Lawrence certainly never approached him.

"The papers ſtill abuſe the Exhibition and the painters. A book, 'The Library of the Fine Arts,' has been juſt left here, in which they ſpeak very properly of your pictures, and perhaps fairly of my 'Chaos,' as they term the Saliſbury; they ſay, after much abuſe, 'It is ſtill a picture from which it is impoſſible to turn without admiration.' I ſhall hope to ſee you very ſoon, but Hampſtead breaks me up; I will, if I can, walk round to-morrow: I want to ſee Lord Groſvenor's Gallery by you. I muſt ſay I like to ſee my friends in difficulties; no good comes without them; but I can hardly underſtand what yours can be; I cannot believe your patron and you have choſen a canvaſs ſufficiently large to do you juſtice, but I will not pre-judge. I hear a good account of Fiſher; he is preaching at Saliſbury."

"July 5th. My dear Leſlie, I returned from Suffolk yeſterday to attend the Council. I left my little girls with my family there, very happy and 'comfordil.' Nothing can exceed the beauty of the country; it makes pictures appear ſad trumpery, even thoſe that have moſt of nature; what muſt thoſe be that have it not?"

The following letter is addreſſed, not to the eminent Academician but to another gentleman of the name of Ward, who was at that time practiſing portrait painting in London: "Charlotte Street, July 22nd. Dear Ward, Our mutual loſs in poor Northcote makes one cling to what is left, and I now more than ever value the ſtores you poſſeſs of his delightful converſation. Do you (as I truſt you do) ever mean to give them to the world; they contain a maſs of information, eſpecially on the art. I do think in that reſpect they are above all things calculated to be uſeful in guiding ſtudents in the right way of thinking and regulating their lives and habits. Let me have the pleaſure of ſeeing you ſoon. I am, dear Ward, always ſincerely yours, John Conſtable."

I had aſked Conſtable to look at a copy of a Watteau,

" The Ball," from the Dulwich Gallery, on which I was then engaged at the Academy; and to this his next note alludes.

" Dear Leſlie, I miſſed you on the day we ſhould have met at the ſchool of painting by about half an hour. Your Watteau looked colder than the original, which ſeems as if painted in honey; ſo mellow, ſo tender, ſo ſoft, and ſo delicious; ſo I truſt yours will be; but be ſatisfied if you touch but the hem of his garment, for this inſcrutable and exquiſite thing would vulgarize even Rubens and Paul Veroneſe. * * * My dear little girls are beautifully bronzed; they have had a happy viſit. We are all here. Come to us to-morrow evening."

" Auguſt. My dear Leſlie, * * * Lady Dyſart has ſent me half a buck; and I hope to ſee the Preſident and Howard and Mr. Banniſter to partake of it about the middle of next week; will you come? One thing I much want your help in; a requeſt is made to me by a lady, (a relation), to make a copy of Mr. Wells's picture of 'The Girl and Pigeon' by Greuze. This friend of mine had a dear little daughter taken from her; ſhe pines for her child. The picture is the exact image of the ſoft lovely girl, of whom ſhe is bereft without any memorial. Give me your advice how to act. I called on Landſeer, who is now, I find, on a viſit to Mr. Wells, and might poſſibly aid me. Could the picture be left with me after the cloſe of the Gallery, I would copy it, and enſure its ſafety. * * * I looked into the National Gallery yeſterday. Carr's Rembrandts are fine, and the large Gaſpar magnificent; indeed, no where does landſcape ſtand higher than under that roof. * * *"

" Auguſt 22nd. My dear Leſlie, On Thurſday next at ſix o'clock they tell me Lady Dyſart's haunch will be in perfection; at all events it will be on my table at that hour.—It is indeed very kind of you to name my gallery to * * * *

But ſhould your endeavours draw him into it, can you give him underſtanding? 'One man may lead a horſe to the pond, &c.' I ſhould be delighted, however to have him in my room, as it would be nuts, to me, to ſee him ſo puzzled. Lord N * * * * * * * * is a better creature, but he eſteems 'our own Glover' too much to like our *diſowned* Conſtable. One picture he had of Glover, the foreground of which conſiſted of one hundred flower pots all in a row as thus," (here a ſketch,) "the ſun was ſhining bright, but they caſt no ſhadow.

"Varley, the aſtrologer, has juſt called on me, and I have bought a little drawing of him. He told me how to '*do* landſcape,' and was ſo kind as to point out all my defects. The price of the drawing was 'a guinea and a half *to a gentleman*, and a guinea only to an *artiſt*,' but I inſiſted on his taking the larger ſum, as he had clearly proved to me that I was no artiſt."

"September 9th. My dear Leſlie, My ſervant told you of my being at the Coronation. I was in the Abbey eleven hours, and ſaw with my own eyes the crown of England put on the head of that good man, William IV.; and that too in the chair of a ſaint! I ſaw alſo the gentle Adelaide crowned, and I truſt, what may now be called the *better half* of England's crown has ſought its own wearer in this inſtance. I ſaw alſo B * * * * * * m with his crown on, a ſight than which nothing could be more ridiculous, for as his coronet was perched on the top of an enormous wig, he bore the external ſhape of a Jack in the Green, as he ſtood with his back towards me a full hour." (Here the writing is interrupted by a ſketch). "I ſat ſo that I commanded a view of all the peers placed in raiſed ranks in the ſouth tranſept. The moment the King's crown was on, they all crowned themſelves. At the ſame inſtant the ſhouts of 'God ſave the King,' the trumpets, the band, the drums of the ſoldiers in the nave, and laſt, though not leaſt, the artillery, which could be diſtinguiſhed amid all this din, and the jar even felt, made it eminently impoſing. The white ermine of the peers looked lovely in the ſun; I ſhall ſketch ſome of the effects; the tone of the walls was ſublime, heightened, no doubt, by the trappings, like an old picture in a newly gilt frame."

"September 12th. My dear Leſlie. Accept my third number with my beſt regards. I hope Mrs. Leſlie was not the worſe for her viſiters yeſterday. Her dear infant has never been a moment from my ſight ſince I left you; they were happy days with me when I had infants. Will you come any day when we can look at the old maſters in Pall Mall together? I ſleep in town to-night. I am glad I ſaw the ſhow in the Abbey; it was very delightful, and I can now ſay I have ſeen a Coronation. Every body ſeemed amuſed with B * * * * * * m; the annoyance to him muſt have been great."

"September 26th. My dear Leſlie. I have been paſſing a day or two with Digby Neave at Epſom. I ſlept on Friday night in the room in which Lord Lyttelton ſaw the ghoſt.* But I neither ſaw nor heard anything of the lady or the bird. It is a beautiful and romantic old houſe; deeply fixed in

"Thomas, the ſecond Lord Lyttelton had great parts and ambition. He had all his father's foibles, but without his ſound principles of religion and morality; for want of which he fell into great enormities and vices. His pleaſures were reſtrained by no ties of relationſhip, friendſhip, or decency. He was a great lover of gaming; in his younger years he was unſucceſsful, but he afterwards became more artful, and at his death he was ſuppoſed to have acquired thirty thouſand pounds by play. His conſtitution was feeble, and by his vices ſo enervated, that he died an old man at the age of thirty-five. He was like his father a believer in ghoſts, and many ſtories are told, with conſiderable confidence, which have relation to his death. About three days before he died, a female figure with a bird on her hand appeared to him, as he imagined, and told him he ſhould die in three days. The day of this ſuppoſed appearance he went to the Houſe of Lords, and ſpoke with great earneſtneſs on ſome buſineſs trees and dells and filled with marble ſtatues, dolphins, cupids, &c. * * * This morning I have ſeen * * * * * * * * 's ſtudies in Italy and Greece; temples, trees, ſtatues, waterfalls, figures, &c. &c.; excellent of their kind, and done wholly for the *underſtanding;* bald, and naked,—nature diveſted of her chiaroſcuro, which ſhe never is under any circumſtances, for we never ſee but through a medium. Yet theſe things have wonderful merit, and ſo has *watch-making.*"

One of Conſtable's ſketch books contains a beautiful drawing in water colours, of the houſe, formerly Lord Lyttelton's, now belonging to Digby Neave, Eſq. The view is taken from the lawn, which is decorated with ſtatues, urns, &c.

Among the engravings made for the "English Landſcape" which Conſtable afterwards rejected, when he came to arrange them with the others, was a very powerful one, a view on the Orwell, with two veſſels hauled up on the beach, and of this plate the next note ſpeaks. "September 27th. Dear Lucas, I fear that we muſt now engrave the 'Waterloo.' The ſhips are too common-place and vulgar, and will never unite with the general character of the book. Though I

then in agitation. The next day he went to a villa he had at Epſom, apparently as well as he had been for ſome time before. The ſucceeding day he continued there, and was in as good health and ſpirits as uſual, though the apparition ſtill hung upon his mind. He ſpent the evening in company with the Miſs Amphletts, Admiral Woleſely, Earl Forteſcue, and ſome other perſons; he ſeemed perfectly well, and pulling out his watch ſaid jocularly it was ten o'clock, and if he lived two hours he ſhould *jockey* the ghoſt. In about an hour he retired to his chamber, and ordered his valet to bring his powder of rhubarb which he frequently took at night. His ſervant brought it, and forgetting to bring a ſpoon was going to ſtir it with a key; upon which his Lordſhip called him a dirty fellow and bid him fetch a ſpoon. Accordingly he went, and returning in a few minutes, found his Lord in the agonies of death."—*Supplement to Naſh's Hiſtory of Worceſterſhire.*

Chap. XII. 1831.

want variety, I don't want a hotch-potch. We muſt not have one uncongenial ſubject; if we have, it cannot fail to tinge the whole book." In another note he ſays, "Dear Lucas, You will be ſurpriſed and pleaſed with the touch proofs; they quite tempt one to proceed, ſo clever and artful is the devil!"

Conſtable was now beginning to feel ſymptoms of what ſoon proved a very ſerious illneſs; and in a note to Mr. Lucas, dated October 27th, he writes, "I think myſelf better, but don't much care; it gives me an excuſe to be idle. Keep the new 'Old Sarum' clear, bright, and ſharp, but don't loſe ſolemnity."

A city turned into a landſcape, independently of the hiſtorical aſſociations with Old Sarum, could not but be intereſting to Conſtable; and not ſatisfied with Mr. Lucas's firſt engraving of it, in which its mounds and terraces were not marked with ſufficient preciſion, he incurred the expenſe of a ſecond plate. Sir Thomas Lawrence, who had ſeen the firſt, greatly admired the treatment of this ſubject, and told Conſtable he ought to dedicate it to the Houſe of Commons.

The plate of "Old Sarum" was accompanied with letter-preſs, of which the following are paſſages: "This ſubject, which ſeems to embody the words of the poet, 'Paint me a deſolation,' is one with which the grander phenomena of nature beſt accord. Sudden and abrupt appearances of light —thunder clouds—wild autumnal evenings—ſolemn and ſhadowy twilights 'flinging half an image on the ſtraining ſight'—with variouſly tinted clouds, dark, cold and gray— or ruddy and bright—even conflicts of the elements heighten, if poſſible, the ſentiment which belongs to it.

"The preſent appearance of Old Sarum, wild, deſolate, and dreary, contraſts ſtrongly with its former ſplendour. This celebrated city, which once gave laws to the whole kingdom, and where the earlieſt parliaments on record were convened, can only now be traced by vaſt embankments and ditches, tracked only by ſheep-walks. 'The plough has paſſed over it.' In this city the wily Conqueror in 1086, confirmed that great political event, the eſtabliſhment of the feudal ſyſtem, and enjoined the allegiance of the nobles. Several ſucceeding monarchs held their courts here; and it too often ſcreened them after their depredations on the people. In the days of chivalry, it poured forth its Longſpees and other valiant knights over Paleſtine. It was the ſeat of the eccleſiaſtical government, when the pious Oſmond and the ſucceeding biſhops diffuſed the bleſſings of religion over the weſtern kingdom; thus it became the chief reſort of eccleſiaſtics and warriors, till their feuds and mutual animoſities, cauſed by the inſults of the ſoldiery, at length occaſioned the ſeparation of the clergy, and the removal of the Cathedral from within its walls, which took place in 1227. Many of the moſt pious and peaceable of the inhabitants followed it, and in leſs than half a century after the completion of the new Church, the building of the bridge over the river at Harnham diverted the great weſtern road, and turned it through the new city. This laſt ſtep was the cauſe of the deſertion and gradual decay of Old Sarum. The ſite now only remains of this once proud and populous city, whoſe almoſt impregnable caſtle, with its lofty and embattled towers, whoſe churches, with every veſtige of human habitation, have long ſince paſſed away. The beautiful imagination of the poet Thomſon, when he makes a ſpot like this the haunt of a ſhepherd with his flock, happily contraſts the playfulneſs of peaceful innocence with the horrors of war and bloodſhed, of which it was ſo often the ſcene:

'Lead me to the mountain's brow,
Where ſits the ſhepherd on the graſſy turf
Inhaling healthful the deſcending ſun.
Around him feeds his many-bleating flock,
Of various cadence; and his ſportive lambs,

CHAP. XII.
1831.

> This way and that convolved, in friſkful glee,
> Their frolics play. And now the ſprightly race
> Invites them forth ; when ſwift the ſignal giv'n
> They ſtart away, and ſweep the maſſy mound
> That runs around the hill, the rampart once
> Of iron war.' "

In a note to Mr. Benjamin Dawſon of Hampſtead, Conſtable, ſpeaking of Old Sarum ſays: "Who can viſit ſuch a ſolemn ſpot, once the moſt powerful city of the Weſt, and not feel the truth and awfulneſs of the words of St. Paul: 'Here we have no continuing city!' "

Towards the end of October Conſtable became very unwell, and was greatly depreſſed in ſpirits. I had called on him, and found him in a ſtate of mind which magnified every anticipation of evil. The Reform fever was then at its criſis, and he talked much of all that was to be feared from the meaſure. I endeavoured to quiet his mind, but fearing that I had done him more harm than good by prolonging the converſation, I wrote to him a day or two afterwards: "My dear Conſtable, I have heard of you twice ſince I ſaw you; once from Lucas, and once from Vaughan, and I now want to hear that you were not the worſe for attending the Council. I came away from you with the uncomfortable feeling that I had excited you to talk too much, and on an irritating ſubject. I have not a doubt but that at the preſent time, as it always has been when parties have run high, the evils on both ſides are tremendouſly exaggerated, and I truſt you will ſoon find your fears about the ſecurity of the funds to be groundleſs. * * * It is grievous to me to think that a mind like yours may be haraſſing itſelf with uſeleſs apprehenſions of the future, to no other end than that of impairing your health, which is of the greateſt conſequence to yourſelf, your children, and your friends. There is no evil more certain than the dread of uncertain ones. Don't trouble yourſelf by writing to me unleſs, as I ſincerely hope, you are a great deal better; but ſend me word that you did not ſuffer by going to the Academy."

"Dear Leſlie, Greatly do I lament going to the Academy. I am much worſe than when you and Mrs. Leſlie were here. The truth is, I have long been getting ill, and it will ſurpriſe you to hear that I have always had the *worſt tongue* poſſible. The miſchief that has been ſo long hatching has at length come to a head. Evans tells me I muſt take great care of my health for my children's ſake; I much doubt if my life is of any uſe to them, but I love them, and they love me, ſo the parting, at leaſt, will be ſad. * * * What makes me dread this tremendous attack on the conſtitution of the country, is, that the wiſeſt and beſt of the Lords are ſeriouſly and firmly objecting to it; and it goes to give the government into the hands of the rabble and dregs of the people, and the devil's agents on earth, the agitators. Do you think that the Duke of Wellington, the Archbiſhop of Canterbury, and Copley, and Eldon, and Abbot, and all the wiſeſt and beſt men we have, would oppoſe it, if it was to do good to the country? I do not. No Whig government ever can do good to this peculiar country."

"Charlotte Street, November 4th. My dear Leſlie, I know not how enough to thank you and dear Mrs. Leſlie for the kind intereſt you both take in me. I am now, perhaps, quite well, and I can give you no greater proof of it than by telling you that the Reform Bill now gives me not the leaſt concern. I care nothing about it, and have no curioſity to know whether it be dead or alive, or if dead, whether it will revive from its aſhes. I hope to paſs a quiet and domeſtic winter. My illneſs was much increaſed by fretting and pining for my children, of whom I ſaw little or nothing. I ſhall now call Hampſtead *my home*, Charlotte Street *my office*. Only think, I had the children here only three or four months all laſt year, and then took them to Hampſtead look-

Chap. XII. 1831.

ing like parboiled rabbits. I have begun the copy of Mr. Wells's picture."

"November 26th. My dear Leslie, I am sending to poor Lucas, fearing he must be ill, as I have not heard of him so long. * * * I shall bring my children to Charlotte Street at Christmas, where I shall have a pleasant party, and I hope often to see you and Mrs. Leslie. I was delighted to have Edwin Landseer on Sunday at my retreat; besides, he fell in love with my eldest daughter, and I could not say nay; it was to paint her."

"Well Walk, December 17th. My dear Leslie, I cannot let Lucas depart, without a wretched line or two to you. I have not been in London since we parted last at the Academy. My sad illness has a good deal returned, and the worst is, it is accompanied by an attack of acute rheumatism which has quite disabled me. Thank God, this right hand is left me entire; reminding me, if I could ever forget it, of your dear child's surprise at 'the poor gentleman who was all shot away but his hand;'* but my left side and arm prevented my working by pain and helplessness. Fourteen leeches, however, on that shoulder, dislodged part of the enemy, but only that he should make a lodgement in my knee, and now I can't stand; but I am so much better in general health, that I bear it with a tolerable grace, *for me*."

"Charlotte Street, Tuesday, December 28th. My dear Leslie. * * * I have parted with my dear little Maria for a week on a visit to Putney, a great sacrifice on my part; I miss her exceedingly; she is so orderly in all her plans, and so full of method,—so lady-like by nature, and so firm, and yet so gentle, that you cannot believe the influence this heavenly little monitor has on this whole house, but most of all on me, who watch all her dear ways with mingled smiles and

* On seeing an engraving of an antique fragment.

tears. This calls to my recollection two lines of an epitaph in a country churchyard, written by a gentleman on his wife:

> 'The voice of all who knew her this confeſt,
> But chief the voice of him who knew her beſt.'

Should I live, and this dear image of her mother be ſpared to me, what a bleſſing and comfort to my old age; I have, indeed, much to be thankful for. * * * I muſt put Mrs. Leſlie's name to this paper, or how can I convey to you and her my ſincere good wiſhes of the ſeaſon? I hope you and ſhe may be happy for many many Chriſtmaſes. For myſelf, I am always happy if my children are well, which, thank God, is the caſe now."

"December 29th. I ſhall try all I can to get well, and come to you on Monday with my two little girls, who I am ſure will be much delighted. But I am ſtill a poor devil; however, to-day I have been painting, and to-morrow I hope to get the Greuze finiſhed. My pretty Minna dreſſed up my mantel-piece with Chriſtmas boughs, and ſet out a little table in the dining-room, that I might look pretty in her abſence, which I ſcrupulouſly forbid to be diſturbed."

CHAPTER XIII.

1832.

Illneſs. Turner. Claude. Hobbema. Gainſborough. Stanfield. Picture of Waterloo Bridge. Mr. Lawley. Callcott. Conſtable's Mode of Proceeding with his Pictures. The Palette Knife. Exhibition at the Academy 1832. *Conſtable's eldeſt Daughter dangerouſly Ill. Illneſs of John Dunthorne, Jun. New Apartments for the Academy. Death of Archdeacon Fiſher. Copy of de Hooge. Death of J. Dunthorne, Jun. Conſtable attends his Funeral at Bergholt. Vale of Dedham. E. Landſeer. Mr. George Conſtable. Picture of "Englefield Houſe." The Meſſrs. Chalon. Palette Knife-painting.*

1832.

"AMPSTEAD, January, 1832. My dear Leſlie, We intend reaching Charlotte Street, pack and package, with my ſeven children, about Thurſday. I am not certain, however, of myſelf, for Evans ſays I may not be fit for removal by that time. He is a ſkilful and honeſt doctor, a very ſenſible man with great acquirements, and a moſt ſincere friend, ſo that I have many bleſſings yet. I am not ſorry to have miſſed the viſitorſhip in the Life this year, and next year I ſhall be ineligible; my youth being gone, I can hardly ſtand the fags I lay on myſelf. I hope all is well with you."

The painful illneſs from which Conſtable had lately ſuffered ſo ſeverely, had not yet left him. I had written from Petworth deſcribing ſome of the pictures there, and received the following letter, dictated by him, for he was diſabled by rheumatiſm in his hand from holding a pen: "From my bed, Charlotte Street, January 14th. My dear Leſlie, Accept my thanks for your kind letter. I rejoice to hear that you and Mrs. Leſlie and the dear children got through your journey ſo comfortably. For myſelf, I have had rather a ſevere relapſe, but I paſſed laſt night almoſt wholly free from pain, the firſt, I believe, for theſe three weeks. I had great pleaſure in ſeeing my brother, by whom I was much excited on family matters, he entering with great cordiality into all my wiſhes regarding my children. The exertion was, no doubt, too great for me, but Evans aſſured me, laſt night, he had not ſeen me ſo well. I am much intereſted with your account of the pictures at Petworth. I remember moſt of Turner's early works; amongſt them was one of ſingular intricacy and beauty; it was a canal with numerous boats making thouſands of beautiful ſhapes, and I think the moſt complete work of genius I ever ſaw. The Claude I well know; grand and ſolemn, but cold, dull and heavy; a picture of his old age. Claude's exhilaration and light departed from him when he was between fifty and ſixty, and he then became a profeſſor of the 'higher walks of art,' and fell in a great degree into the manner of the painters around him; ſo difficult it is to be natural, ſo eaſy to be ſuperior in our own opinion. When we have the pleaſure of being together at the National Gallery, I think I ſhall not find it difficult to illuſtrate theſe remarks, as Carr has ſent a large picture* of the latter deſcription. Hobbema, if he miſſes colour, is very diſagreeable, as he has neither ſhapes nor compoſition.

* The ſubject of this picture, which is called "Sinon before Priam," is evidently David at the cave of Adullam.

Chap. XIII.
1832.

Your mention of a ſolemn twilight by Gainſborough has awakened all my ſympathy; do pray make me a ſketch of it of ſome kind or other, if it is only a ſlight ſplaſh.

"As to meeting you in theſe grand ſcenes, dear Leſlie, remember the Great were not made for me, nor I for the Great; things are better as they are. My limited and abſtracted art is to be found under every hedge and in every lane, and therefore nobody thinks it worth picking up; but I have my admirers, each of whom I conſider an hoſt. My kindeſt regards to Mrs. Leſlie."

"My dear Leſlie, After three weeks inability to hold my pen, I reſume it for the firſt time to write to you. * * * So far had I written when your letter arrived. I am now recovering, I may ſay faſt, and am beyond the fear of relapſes; but certainly, as you ſay, 'excitement under illneſs is a much worſe thing than is generally imagined.' I ſat up yeſterday, dreſſed, by the fire, and ate a ſmall fiſh for my dinner, to the great delight of Alfred, who would dine with me, as he it was, he ſaid, (and truly,) 'who nurſed me ſo well.' How heavenly it is to wake, as I now do, after a good night, and ſee all theſe dear infants about my bed, all up early to know how papa paſſed the night. Even little Lionel puts out his little face to be kiſſed, and ſmacking his lip, ſays, 'Are you well, better to-day?' I am often inquired after by kind friends, and the ſympathy of my real, own, and dear friends is great indeed. I have got my 'Church' from Hampſtead, to hang at the foot of my bed to amuſe me.

"How kind of you to think of the Gainſborough;* the 'Lord Rodney'† I remember at Mr. Bigg's, who did it up very well, and of whom Lord Egremont bought it. Bigg had it to ſell for a gentleman; he ſhowed it to Lord Egre-

* Of which I was making a ſketch for him.
† By Sir Joſhua Reynolds, one of his fineſt pictures.

mont, who ſeemed hardly to notice it, but on going away, he ſuddenly turned round at the door, and ſaid, 'You may ſend me the Admiral.' I knew the grandſon of Lord Rodney, who was enough like the picture to have ſat for it.

"I had a terrific viſit from K. F * * * on Sunday morning. He was bruſhed up and 'bearded like the pard,' and going to hear Irving, who, he ſaid, was the only man to preach the Bible, explain the prophecies, &c. I cautioned him againſt enthuſiaſm in religion, which, as it has no foundation, is apt to ſlip from under a man, and leave infidelity or madneſs; but I talked to a tree. However, touching his picture of 'Circe' told better, and he went away with a ghaſtly ſmile, nearly cruſhing my hand in that graſp of his. This viſit really did excite me, and I fell into a paſſion, which did me good. * * * P * * * * * has juſt been here, accompanied by Newton's dog, who has preſented me with two fleas, leſt I ſhould now ſleep. God bleſs you all. Alfred cloſe at my elbow. * * * Jones likes my preface. * * * I have ſeen Stanfield, and am much ſtruck with him altogether as a ſound fellow; he has great power."

"March 3rd. My dear Leſlie, Many thanks for your viſit yeſterday. I have got my large Waterloo beautifully ſtrained on a new frame, keeping every inch of canvaſs. It gives me much pleaſure in the preſent occupation, but how long that will laſt, I know not. Archdeacon Fiſher uſed to compare himſelf in ſome ſituations to a lobſter in the boiler; very comfortable at firſt, but as the water became hotter and hotter, grievouſly perplexed at the bottom. P * * * * * called yeſterday.* I joked with him at firſt on the folly of fighting with windmills, but he is quite confirmed in the boundleſs

* A friend of Conſtable and of mine, whoſe good heart and ſtrong underſtanding ſhould have kept him aloof from that claſs of politicians, who would overturn the eſtabliſhed inſtitutions of the country.

notions he entertains *on the wrong ſide of every thing.* My beſt regards; I ſhall ſoon come and ſee you; I am quite tired and out of patience at being ſo long ill and diſabled."

"March 4th. My dear Leſlie, I have not the power to come ſo far as your houſe, but I want much to ſee you, and to thank Mrs. Leſlie for her very kind note of yeſterday, of which Alfred has taken poſſeſſion for his 'real own,' as he ſays it was intended for him, for he is mentioned in it. Mrs. Leſlie was ſo good as to ſpeak of me in the uſual kind way in which you are both pleaſed to conſider me, to Mr. Lawley,* who called yeſterday afternoon, and nothing could be more agreeable than we both were to one another; he admiring my pictures, and I admiring him for doing ſo; but he has not admired only, he has taken a great fancy to my 'Heath,' and to my book, which is now aſſuming a tangible ſhape. * * * He deſired the India copies of my book to be put up for him, and he will ſend one of his 'lazy fellows' for them on Monday morning; all this is very delightful to me. He was much pleaſed with my *Harlequin's jacket*, and ſaid he ſhould often call and ſee it, for it was 'a moſt amuſing picture, the houſes—the bridge—St. Paul's—the numberleſs boats—&c. I wiſh I could get to your houſe, but my knee is ſo bad, I could not walk to the top of my own ſtreet."

In a note to Mrs. Leſlie, dated March 28th, Conſtable, ſpeaking of Alfred Chalon's very fine water colour drawing, the whole length portrait of Mrs. la Touche, ſays, "Has Leſlie ſeen Chalon's old lady in black? it is the grandeſt 'Il Penſeroſo' ever done in the world."

"April 9th. My dear Leſlie, I hope you get on with your picture to your liking; I am in a dreadful ſtate about mine, for I am determined to ſend it. I ſhould like much

* Now Sir Francis Lawley.

Painted by J. Constable. Engraved by D. Lucas.

Little Roxalana,

DAUGHTER OF JOHN CONSTABLE.

to ſee yours, but that has not been poſſible, as you will do me the juſtice to believe. I met Callcott at dinner the other day; he ſaid he regretted much that you had determined not to ſend the 'Sterne;' I regret it alſo; he ſaid it 'was quite fit, and very fit for the Exhibition;' I think ſo too. At all events, I thought you might like to hear his opinion, and I aſſure you it was the only one in which we did agree during the evening. He thinks I do not believe what I ſay, and only want to attract attention by ſingularity; but my pictures being my acts, ſhow to my coſt that I am ſincere, for

'He who hangs, or beats his brains,
The devil's in him if he feigns.'

But he is on the ſafe ſide. * * * My boys are all here. I ſaw my little girls on Sunday, all well—ſo the world is light as a feather to me."

"Charlotte Street, April 24th. My dear Leſlie, All my little girls are here. Can Mrs. Leſlie and your ſiſter and yourſelf come and paſs an hour with us on Thurſday at ſeven or ſo. On Wedneſday, the levee, which they are to view from a window in St. James's Street. If they ſee only the ſoldiers, they are worth the ſeeing, and 'little things are great to little minds.' I have never been more reſtleſs about a picture than with the premature diſmiſſal of this, and it has not even my redeeming quality, the rural."

Two oppoſite modes of proceeding are adopted by painters in the execution of their works. With ſome it is the practice to finiſh part by part as the picture proceeds, ſo that while it is in progreſs, portions entirely or very nearly completed are ſeen on a canvaſs, the remainder of which is blank. Other artiſts carry on the whole together; beginning with a faint dead colour, in which the maſſes only are laid in, and proceeding with the details gradually, and without ſuffering one part to advance much beyond the reſt, until the whole is

CHAP. XIII. 1832.

finiſhed. The firſt mode is the moſt favourable to preciſion of touch, the laſt to richneſs of ſurface and truth of tone. I need not ſay this was the mode adopted by Conſtable. Indeed, in landſcape it ſeems impoſſible that thoſe almoſt imperceptible gradations of colour and light and ſhadow which form ſo much of its charm, ſhould be obtained by any other proceſs. It has, however, the diſadvantage of tempting the artiſt at times to ſacrifice parts too much to the general effect. With Conſtable chiaroſcuro was the one thing to be obtained at whatever coſt. "I was always determined," he ſaid, "that my pictures ſhould have chiaroſcuro, if they had nothing elſe." In the purſuit of this indiſpenſable quality, and of that brightneſs in nature which baffles all the ordinary proceſſes of painting, and which it is hardly poſſible to unite with ſmoothneſs of ſurface, he was led by degrees into a peculiar mode of execution, which too much offended thoſe who were unable to ſee the look of nature it gave at the proper diſtance. In the "Waterloo Bridge" he had indulged in the vagaries of the palette knife, (which he uſed with great dexterity) to an exceſs. The ſubject challenged a compariſon with Canaletti, the preciſion of whoſe execution is wonderful, and the compariſon was made to Conſtable's great diſadvantage; even his friend, Mr. Stothard, ſhook his head and ſaid, "Very unfiniſhed, ſir," and the picture was generally pronounced a failure. It was a glorious failure, however; I have ſeen it often ſince it was exhibited, and I will venture to ſay, that the noonday ſplendour of its colour, would make almoſt any work of Canaletti, if placed beſide it, look like moonlight. But ſuch pictures ought not to be compared, each has its own excellence, and nothing can be more true than Conſtable's remark, that "*fine pictures neither want nor will bear compariſon.*"* It might be at this time that

* In the following chapter.

he wrote what I found on a ſcrap of paper among his memoranda: "My art flatters nobody by *imitation*, it courts nobody by *ſmoothneſs*, it tickles nobody by *petiteneſs*, it is without either *fal de lal* or *fiddle de dee*, how then can I hope to be popular?"

With the "Waterloo Bridge," Conſtable exhibited a very ſmall picture of "Sir Richard Steele's Cottage, Hampſtead;" with two others, "A Romantic Houſe, Hampſtead," and "Moonlight," and four drawings, among which was the "Jaques and the wounded ſtag."

When the following note was written, every thought of art was baniſhed from Conſtable's mind by the ſudden illneſs of his eldeſt daughter with ſcarlet fever: "Charlotte Street, June 22nd. My dear Leſlie, Thank you for your kind note. I knew you would be anxious, and I regret to ſay this note of mine will not allay your anxiety. My dear child is alarmingly ill; her pulſe to-day is at a hundred and fifty. My hope is this may be the worſt day, ſo Evans hopes alſo. Mr. Haines ſays her throat is not worſe to-day than yeſterday, but God only knows how it will terminate. I have, as you and Mrs. Leſlie know, looked to this ſweet infant as the hope and comfort of my old age; but hope is futile, and on what joy can we reckon on this ſide the grave? * * * I am alſo very anxious about the two other little dears, who muſt remain at ſchool, it being not adviſable to have them home or even away. All our endeavour is to keep this moſt cruel diſorder out of the way of my boys. How providential it was that ſhe was not already at home; ſhe is managed fai better where ſhe is, but it is a caſe of hard neceſſity, and poor Roberts* is crying all day at not being able to adminiſter to the dear darling child's comfort. Poor John Dunthorne† is getting daily, nay hourly worſe; he cannot long

* Her nurſe.

† Conſtable's young friend had been for ſome time ſuffering from a diſeaſe of the heart.

remain to me. I do not contemplate a happy old age even if I ſhould attain it."

"June 24th. My dear Leſlie, I ſend you a packet which I had made up laſt night for Lucas to take to you, but he did not come. I think I have rather a better account to ſend you of my little girl; it is not impoſſible but the worſt is paſt. To-day her pulſe is leſſened and her throat better, but ſhe is in a fearful ſtate. It is cruel I cannot ſee her, and it is hard for the other little girls that they cannot come home; but little Emily told Miſs Noble that it was not 'near ſo diſagreeable and naſty to ſtay the holidays as ſhe expected.'"
* * *

"June 25th. Dear Lucas, I ſend you the picture with my beſt hopes and wiſhes, and which I aſſure you are not ſlight nor diſintereſted; but I am more anxious for your ſake than my own; anxious that your enthuſiaſm may not be thrown away nor prove unpropitious. My dear little girl is better, God be praiſed! and with His bleſſing ſhe may recover. She got ſome ſweet ſleep yeſterday, but otherwiſe it was my moſt anxious day, though the fever was greateſt (pulſe one hundred and fifty) on Friday. I am full of anxiety about the other two little dears, who of neceſſity muſt be left at the ſchool, but apart from her."

The picture mentioned in this note was "The Corn Field," now in the National Gallery, which Mr. Lucas undertook to engrave at his own riſk; the plate was afterwards purchaſed and publiſhed with its companion, "The Lock," by Mr. Moon.

I received the following letter at Brighton: "July 6th. My dear Leſlie, I was much delighted with your letter this morning, and loſe no time in replying to it. My dear child, thank God, is wonderfully recovered; I can take her away ſafely to herſelf, though not to others, next week. Which to do, I know not, take her to Brighton or Suffolk. I fear moſt for my boys. Poor dear John Dunthorne is very much worſe; he had ſeveral doctors with him yeſterday, who have relieved him a little, but this ſtate of things cannot laſt long. It makes me ſadly melancholy; I ſhall loſe a ſincere friend, whoſe attachment to me has been like that of a ſon, from his infancy. He is without fault, and ſo much the fitter for Heaven. I wake in the night about him. * * * Pray make my kindeſt regards to Mrs. Leſlie, and God bleſs the dear children! I truſt you have not thrown the lovely baby into the ſea; it has been the ruin of thouſands of young infants. * * * Some noble pictures at the Gallery, along with a good deal of rubbiſh."

"July 9th. My dear Leſlie, Our meeting at the Academy was to addreſs the King on his 'happy and providential eſcape.'* The plan of a new houſe is quite flouriſhing, and at preſent there is no obſtacle ſave what may be apprehended from the Commons' Houſe, it being poſſible it may be filled with *common* minds. K. F * * * was with me when your letter was put into my hands. He ſeemed amuſed at your mode of life; he, chivalrous man, goes on

'Scorning delights, living laborious days;'

and ſo far he realizes the poet's words, in that he finds 'no guerdon.' He is an excellent fellow. His drawings are now before me, and he certainly ſees and feels the grandeur of the great painters in the Gallery. I have preſented him with a ſet of proofs of my work. I ſhall ſend my little girl to Brighton as ſoon as ſhe is able to be removed. Miſs Noble will go with her and take charge of her, in a poſt-chaiſe, as I ſhould not like any other dear child who might be in a ſtage-coach, to take any harm. To-day I thought

* A ſtone had been thrown at the King at Epſom.

ſhe looked like herſelf; this is only the ſecond time of my ſeeing her. The other little priſoners are as yet well * * * Evans is to be married on Saturday. No man deſerves more happineſs, and ſo far as we ſhort-ſighted mortals can promiſe it to ourſelves, he has every proſpect of it; but as Archdeacon Fiſher's father's coachman told him, 'It is all a myſtery, this ſame matrimony.' * * * Poor dear John Dunthorne is ſo very ill, that I do fear his time is now ſhort indeed. My viſits to him are ſo melancholy, that I do not get over them all day; ſtill he works a little. A nice friend and relative is now ſtaying with him, and this is a great comfort."

While Conſtable's mind was agitated by the near proſpect of loſing John Dunthorne, to whom he had been a uſeful patron, having aſſiſted to eſtabliſh and to procure him employment as a picture cleaner, he heard of the death of that friend who had been his own and only patron, when patronage was of the greateſt importance to him.

September 4th. My dear Leſlie, You will be grieved to hear that I have loſt my dear friend, Archdeacon Fiſher. He went with Mrs. Fiſher to Boulogne, hoping there to find ſome relief from a ſtate of long and ſevere ſuffering. He was benefited at firſt, began to take an intereſt in what was about him, and poor dear Mrs. Fiſher was cheered with the proſpect of his being ſpeedily reſtored to health and ſpirits, when on Friday, Auguſt 24th, he was ſeized with violent ſpaſms, and died on the afternoon of Saturday, the 25th. This ſudden and awful event has ſtrongly affected me. The cloſeſt intimacy had ſubſiſted between us for many years; we loved each other, and confided in each other entirely, and his loſs makes a ſad gap in my worldly proſpects. He would have helped my children, for he was a good adviſer, though impetuous, and he was a truly religious man. I cannot tell you how ſingularly his death has affected me.

I ſhall paſs this week at Hampſtead, to copy the 'Winter,'* for which, indeed, my mind is in a fit ſtate. Evans has returned with his nice bride."

Hoping to amuſe Conſtable, I had ſent him a copy of a ſmall picture by De Hooge, of which a ſunbeam, and that alone, may be conſidered the ſubject; but it ſhines through a window on the wall of a clean little Dutch room, from which it is reflected on the return of the wall and other objects with extreme elegance, and a degree of truth perfectly illuſive.

"September 22nd. My dear Leſlie, I came here laſt evening, and ſaw the pictures. I am delighted with the copy of De Hooge. How completely has he overcome the art, and trampled it under foot, yet how full of art it is. No painter that ever lived could change a ſingle thing in it, either in place, or light or dark, or colour, warm or cold. Such things are in ſhort quite above the art, and it is a bleſſing they are done. I muſt take the De Hooge to Hampſtead."

"October 1ſt. Dear Lucas, * * * I have ſad accounts, indeed, of poor John Dunthorne from Suffolk. He will never ſee London again. He is confined to his bed and cannot write."

"Dear Lucas, I have added a *Ruin* to the little Glebe Farm,† for not to have a ſymbol in the book of myſelf, and of the work which I have projected, would be miſſing the opportunity. The proof of the new Old Sarum looks well this morning, half paſt ſeven. October 2nd, J. C."

"November 6th. My dear Lucas, I go to Suffolk on

* By Ruyſdael, belonging to Sir Robert Peel.

† This was a plate rejected by Conſtable, and which its general maſſes enabled him to turn into a view of Caſtle Acre Priory. It was not publiſhed, though I believe he intended it, with ſome other plates, to form an appendix to the book.

Thurſday to attend the laſt ſcene of poor John Dunthorne; but he 'fought a good fight,' and I think muſt have left the world with as few regrets as any man of his age I ever met with. * * * His fond father, who has been here to-day, is gone back entirely broken hearted; he was ſo proud of him, and well he might be. Do not cut the plate of the new Old Sarum yet. I have touched another proof to-day, and it looks ſo well, I think you may like it, and perhaps adopt it. I did it on ſeeing poor John Dunthorne's rainbow this morning. * * * They like the Stonehenge. I mean Leſlie, and the gentleman who lectured on it, and tried to prove it antediluvian; the thing was ingenious."

"Well Walk, November 14th. My dear Lucas, I returned laſt night, after ſeeing the laſt of poor John; no one can ſupply his place with me. God's will be done! The text of the ſermon of the Rev. D. C. Rowley for poor John, was from Iſaiah, chap. iv. ver. 2: 'In that day ſhall the branch of the Lord be beautiful and glorious, and the fruit of the earth ſhall be excellent and comely for them that are eſcaped of Iſrael.' * * * To-day is dear Alfred's birthday, and they have kept me a willing gueſt. * * * An angry neighbour has killed my fine black cat, who uſed to call me up in the morning, but ſhe had been naughty, and killed one of his ducks. * * * In the coach yeſterday, coming from Suffolk, were two gentlemen and myſelf, all ſtrangers to each other. In paſſing the vale of Dedham, one of them remarked, on my ſaying it was beautiful, 'Yes, ſir, this is Conſtable's country.' I then told him who I was, leſt he ſhould ſpoil it."

The lovely engraving, in the Engliſh Landſcape, called "Summer Morning," is a view of Dedham vale, very much as it is ſeen from the high road. Its foreground and ſky were greatly altered by Conſtable while the plate was in progreſs. The plough, the two cows, and the milkmaid, were introduced in the place of a ſingle figure of a man with a ſcythe on his ſhoulder.

"Well Walk, November 20th. My dear Leſlie, My man is going from here to Lucas, and I avail myſelf of the opportunity to return the De Hooge, which has afforded me much pleaſure. Theſe mutual communications of ſtudy are a great help to the happineſs of life. * * * I ſhall ſend my God-daughter Biſhop Horne's ſermon on a kiſs when ſhe is a little bigger."* I was in Charlotte Street, fortunately, yeſterday, when Newton called with his wife, and was pleaſed to ſee a lady ſo genteel and ſo amiable, and ſo free from affectation or falſe pride. * * * It is delightful to ſee Landſeer's unaffected kindneſs to his ſiſters."

Conſtable's eldeſt ſon ſeemed now to have outgrown the ailments that had cauſed ſo much anxiety to his parents, and in a note to me, dated December 4th, he ſays, "This is dear John's birth-day.—Poor dear Maria, if ſhe could ſee him now! * * *."

"Charlotte Street. My dear Leſlie, It is long ſince I have ſeen you, or heard of you and Mrs. Leſlie; but we have got ſettled here after the agony of three days' moving. The firſt detachment of my forces went off with Roberts, and conſiſted of all my boys, and a ſervant or two beſides, and I followed with my girls and innumerable boxes—ſhips—dolls—fire engines—pictures—eaſels—and other uſeleſs lumber; and now we are all looking round with aſtoniſhment at having been ſo long away from ſo comfortable a houſe as

* In the following year he preſented her with the firſt and beſt book ever written expreſſly for children, "Dr. Watts's Songs." It is illuſtrated by wood cuts from Stothard, and Conſtable not only coloured them very beautifully, but added ſome deſigns of his own, as a bird ſinging over its neſt to the ſong againſt quarrelling, and a bee ſettling on a roſe to that on induſtry; while over the lines beginning, "Let dogs delight to bark and bite," he wrote with a pencil, "For Landſeer."

Chap. XIII.
1832.

this. I am in poſſeſſion of half a doe, which I ſhall not at all enjoy unleſs you and Mrs. Leſlie and your ſiſter partake of it. My wiſh is to entrap Newton and his bride. I have not been out into the ſtreet ſince my return, but have finiſhed, or ſhall to-morrow, a ſmall wood, and a head, both commiſſions of long ſtanding, and ſo far I ſecure ſome peace of mind. As to the exhibition, the 'Houſe that Jack built' will be enough to me."

Conſtable had recently formed an acquaintance with a gentleman of his own name, though not a relation, Mr. George Conſtable of Arundel, and this was the beginning of a warm friendſhip which contributed much to the happineſs of the laſt years of his life. The next letter is addreſſed to this gentleman; "Charlotte Street, December 14th. My dear Sir, I beg to ſend the copies of my work for your choice. The proofs that are ſealed have had my cloſe inſpection; but I ſend thoſe you had laſt evening to compare with the India ones. I ſend alſo the prints, which are equally good, for all are printed by ourſelves.* I ſhould feel happy in the belief that my book ſhould ever remunerate itſelf, for I am gratifying my vanity at the expenſe of my children, and I could have wiſhed that they might have lived on me, not the reverſe. My only conſolation is, that my fortune has not ſheltered me in idleneſs, as my large canvaſſes, the dreams of a happy but unpropitious life, will prove. Pray forgive the unreſerved tone of this haſty ſcrawl. I remain, my dear ſir, always your obliged ſervant, John Conſtable."

He was now engaged on a portrait of Englefield Houſe, Berkſhire, for its poſſeſſor, Mr. Benyon de Beauvoir; and of which, though the ſubject was unpromiſing, he made a beautiful picture. The commiſſion had been obtained for

* Mr. Lucas had fitted up a preſs in his own houſe.

him by the recommendation of Mr. Samuel Lane.

"December 17th. My dear Leſlie, I was ſadly diſappointed at miſſing you and Mrs. Leſlie here on Tueſday. I am glad Bonner ſhowed you what I am about with the houſe, as it produced your very kind note. It reached me at tea time that day, and before bed time I had made all the cows in the foreground of the houſe picture bigger, and put in another bigger than all the reſt. This has had the effect you anticipated, and ſent the houſe back, and alſo much recovered and helped to realize my foreground, which indeed this blank canvaſs wants to aid it; but I muſt try at one of the elements, namely, air, and if that include light, I ought not to deſpair. What you ſay generally of my canvaſſes is too delightful for me to diſpute; I ought to be ſatisfied that you think ſo; to pleaſe *one* perſon is no joke, now-a-days."

CHAPTER XIV.

1833.

Meſſrs. Chalon. The Palette Knife. Mr. Seguier. Mr. Beauchamp's Eſtabliſhment. Picture of the Cenotaph erected by Sir G. Beaumont to the Memory of Reynolds. Conſtable viſited by a Connoiſſeur. Lady Morley. Letters to Mr. George Conſtable. Stothard. Letter to Mr. Thomas Dunthorne. Exhibition at the Royal Academy. Picture of Englefield Houſe. Alluſion to the Loſs of the Abergavenny, Captain Wordſworth. The Author's Viſit to America. Conſtable's Firſt Lecture on the Hiſtory of Landſcape. Captain Cook. Letters to Mr. George Conſtable. Notes to Mr. Lucas. Picture of Waterloo Bridge.

1833.

"Y dear Leſlie. * * * I called on the Chalons; John's landſcape is very promiſing, one of his beſt. As to Alfred's 'Samſon,' it is juſt what Paul Veroneſe would have made it, if he could have combined expreſſion with colour; it is full of power, full of ſplendour. They are both adopting the palette knife, while I have laid it down, but not till I had cut my own throat with it. The Dalilah is lovely in her ſupplicating poſture. January 7th, 1833."

The dexterity with which Conſtable uſed the palette knife has been mentioned, and when he ſpeaks of having "cut his own throat with it," he alludes to a recent charge brought againſt his pictures, that they conſiſted "only of palette knife painting." But if he had now laid the knife down, he very ſoon took it up again.

"January 11th, 1833. My dear Leſlie, * * * I have had a friendly viſit from a much greater man than the Duke of Bedford—Lord Weſtminſter—Lord Egremont—the Preſident of the Royal Academy—or even the King himſelf,—Mr. Seguier!* He ſeemed rather aſtoniſhed to find ſo good an appearance, or rather, an appearance ſo far beyond his expectation, and beſtowed much praiſe, ſuch as, 'Did you do this? really! Who made that drawing, you? really! very good indeed.' * * * John Chalon has ſpread a report reſpecting myſelf that has reached me from two or three quarters much to my advantage, namely, that he actually ſaw four ſmall ſable pencils in my hand, and that I was bonâ fide uſing them in the art of painting. * * * I muſt give up —— on Saturday morning, as I have much to do to the great 'Saliſbury,' and am hard run for it. I have written to * * * to beg off hearing for the hundredth time that his are the beſt pictures in the world."

I had introduced Conſtable to Mr. Beauchamp, to whoſe manufactory of Britiſh plate in Holborn, he paid a viſit with his ſons, of which he gave me the following amuſing account: "January 20th. My dear Leſlie, I went with John and Charles to Mr. Beauchamp's laſt evening; their delight was great, not only at the very great kindneſs of Mr. and Mrs. Beauchamp and their boys, but at the ſight of all that was to their heart's content; forges—ſmelting pots—metals—turning lathes—ſtraps and bellows—coals—aſhes—duſt—dirt—and cinders; and every thing elſe that is agreeable to boys.

* Mr. Seguier was ſuppoſed to be the principal director of the taſte of the nobility and gentry in all that related to pictures. He was a good-natured and honeſt man.

CHAP. XIV. 1833.

They want me to build them juſt ſuch a place under my painting-room; and had I not better do ſo, and give up landſcape painting altogether? Poor Mrs. Beauchamp was ſuffering with the tooth-ache, but her politeneſs made her aſſure me that I ſucceeded in talking it off.

"I have called on poor * * * *. I did not think his things were quite ſo bad. They pretend to nothing but an imitation of nature; but then it is of the coldeſt and meaneſt kind. He is immerſed in white lead, and oil, and black, all of which he daſhes about the canvaſs without the ſmalleſt remorſe. All is, thence, utterly heartleſs."

"Charlotte Street, February 13th. Dear Leſlie, * * * May I beg of you to let your ſervant take the little parcel to Edwin Landſeer; it is my firſt number, in which is the 'Mill' he wanted. I have ſent it with the four other prints, which is like getting rid of a bad ſhilling among half-pence."

In a note to me, not dated, but written in the early part of this year, Conſtable ſays, "I have laid by the Cenotaph* for the preſent. I am determined not to haraſs my mind and health by ſcrambling over my canvaſs as I have too often done. Why ſhould I? I have little to loſe and nothing to gain. I ought to reſpect myſelf for my friends' ſake, and my children's. It is time, at fifty-ſix, to begin, at leaſt, to know oneſelf,—and I do know what I am *not*." * * * He then ſpeaks of the qualities at which he chiefly aimed in his pictures,—"light—dews—breezes—bloom—and freſhneſs; not one of which," he adds, "has yet been perfected on the canvaſs of any painter in the world."

"April 2nd. Dear Leſlie, Do not paſs my door if you come to town. I have bruſhed up my 'Cottage' into a pretty look, and my 'Heath' is almoſt ſafe, but I muſt ſtand

* He had begun a picture of the Cenotaph erected by Sir George Beaumont to the memory of Reynolds.

or fall by my 'Houſe.' I had on Friday a long viſit from Mr. * * * alone; but my pictures do not come into his rules or whims of the art, and he ſaid I had 'loſt my way.' I told him that I had, 'perhaps, other notions of art than picture admirers have in general. I looked on pictures as *things to be avoided*, connoiſſeurs looked on them as things to be *imitated*; and that, too, with ſuch a deference and humbleneſs of ſubmiſſion, amounting to a total proſtration of mind and original feeling, as muſt ſerve only to fill the world with abortions.' But he was very agreeable, and I endured the viſit, I truſt, without the uſual courteſies of life being violated.—What a ſad thing it is that this lovely art is ſo wreſted to its own deſtruction! Uſed only to blind our eyes, and to prevent us from ſeeing the ſun ſhine—the fields bloom—the trees bloſſom—and from hearing the foliage ruſtle; while old—black—rubbed out and dirty canvaſſes take the place of God's own works. I long to ſee you. I love to cope with you, like Jaques, in my 'ſullen moods,' for I am not fit for the preſent world of art. * * * Lady Morley was here yeſterday. On ſeeing the 'Houſe,' ſhe exclaimed, 'How freſh, how dewy, how exhilarating!' I told her half of this, if I could think I deſerved it, was worth all the talk and cant about pictures in the world."

Conſtable often did himſelf harm by attempting to ſet right thoſe whom he might have known, from the very conſtitution of their minds, it was impoſſible to ſet right, in matters of taſte. Such ſtrong expreſſions, as thoſe mentioned in the laſt letter, though eaſily comprehended by the few who underſtood his views of art, only gained him the character of a dealer in paradox with thoſe who did not. An affronted taſte is very unforgiving, and he not only waſted his time, but too often made enemies by attempting to "cut blocks with a razor."

"To Mr. George Conſtable. April 12th. My dear Sir,

I am delighted to hear of the ſteady improvement of your health, and I moſt ſincerely hope it will continue to improve; the coming ſeaſon is in your favour. I have always heard of the autumn being the *painter's ſeaſon*, but give me the ſpring, though

'With tears and ſunſhine in her fickle eyes.'

I ſend the drawing by Varley, and I venture to accompany it with two others; they all belonged to my poor friend * * *, who died in the autumn, leaving a widow and dear little girl; the diſpoſal of theſe drawings would eſſentially ſerve them. That by Varley is ſix pounds, the others two pounds each; they would be pretty accompaniments to the 'Curfew' on a mantel-piece; they are by Ziegler. * * * I beg my beſt compliments to Mrs. Conſtable, and believe me, my dear ſir, with ſincere regards, yours truly, John Conſtable."

"To Mr. George Conſtable. April 17th. My dear ſir, Accept my beſt thanks for your very kind letter which I received this morning, encloſing ten pounds, which with great pleaſure I tranſmitted to Mrs. * * *. I feel aſſured your friend will never repent the poſſeſſion of thoſe very beautiful drawings. I hear the Exhibition will be excellent; the quantity ſent exceeds all precedent; Wilkie and Leſlie are ſtrong, Phillips and the Preſident are ſtrong, Landſeer is ſtrong, and ſo on; but perhaps you wiſh me to ſpeak of myſelf; Conſtable is weak this year. We ſhall probably all know our fate on Thurſday ſe'nnight, and the public may ſabre us at their pleaſure on the firſt Monday in May. * * * I paſſed an hour or two with Mr. Stothard on Sunday evening. Poor man! the only Elyſium he has in this world is found in his own enchanting works. His daughter does all in her power to make him happy and comfortable. Lucas has been ſo buſy about the portrait of Sir Charles Clark, that till now he could not take up my appendix, which I ſhall be happy to present to you when ready. I am, my dear sir, always your obliged friend, John Constable."

"To Mr. Thomas Dunthorne.* April 19th. Dear sir. I was prepared to receive the melancholy account of the death of poor Mrs. Folkard,† which Mr. Wright has just told me of. How truly melancholy is the history of all this excellent family! How well I remember the birth of all of them;—Ann—James—poor John—and Hannah;—little thinking I should live to lament the death of every one. My poor old friend, the father of this hapless race, must be in a fearful condition. But since the death of poor John I well know he has made up his mind to every thing that can happen. He now neither cares to stay or go. He told me he did not care how soon he was laid in the same grave with poor John.‡ There seemed an unsoundness in the constitution of all; from the mother probably. There has been a young lady here to enquire for John, to whom he gave lessons. She wished to know if anything was owing to him, and had he been living, to have had more lessons. * * * With the kindest regards, I am truly yours, J. Constable."

"April. Dear Leslie. I send Pitt to know how you are all getting on. R * * * assured me that * * * and all of them did all in their power to help me to a change of the place of my picture, but could not manage it. They have immense trouble this year, but I am easy now, and they all say it looks very well. But S * * * and H * * * are so strictly academical that they deny the painter the power of making a picture out of nothing, or out of a subject not to their liking, though they do not deny it to the poet. The frames have annoyed them beyond measure, and the cold blooded selfish-

* Brother of Constable's early friend, J. Dunthorne, Senr.

† A daughter of J. Dunthorne, Senr.

‡ Mr. Dunthorne survived until October 1844.

neſs of * * * more than all. The council have written to him two mild letters entreating to change a monſtrous piece of gilded wood, as it ruined the hopes of, at leaſt five others who only look for the crumbs that fall from the Academic table, while at the ſame time it ſpoiled his own picture,—but he would not comply. * * *'s frames are ſhameful, or rather *ſhameleſs*. The council are determined to regulate theſe things next year. My Heath is admired, and is well placed."

"Dear Leſlie. I ſend to know how your dear family and yourſelf get on. * * * John Chalon has juſt been here. He is full of anxiety about his picture. I told him I would change places with him at a venture. * * * Thank you, dear Leſlie, for your kind note.—One ambition I *will* hold faſt. I am determined never to deſerve the praiſe of S * * *, H * * *, C * * *, D * * *, W * * * R * * *, &c. &c. &c.

Conſtable's pictures at the Academy, this year, were "Englefield Houſe, Berkſhire, morning;—a Heath, ſhowery, noon;—Cottage in a Cornfield;—Landſcape, ſunſet," and three drawings in water colours, namely, "An old Farm houſe;—a Miller's houſe;" and "A Windmill, ſqually day."

"May 14th. Dear Lane. Thank you for your admiration of my book; the intention is good. I wiſh it gave me the ſame unalloyed pleaſure; but the extravagant, uſeleſs, and ſilly expenditure I have been led into diſtracts me, now that the hour of reflection is come. * * * The 'Morning Poſt' ſpeaks beautifully of my 'Houſe.' S * * * told me it was 'only a *picture of a houſe*, and ought to have been put into the Architectural Room.' I told him it was 'a picture of a ſummer morning, *including a houſe*.'"

Mrs. Leſlie had ſeen in Charlotte Street a proof impreſſion of the "Weymouth Bay," in ſome reſpects imperfect, but in others very beautiful, and had expreſſed a wiſh to have it, to which I objected, thinking it was of value to Conſtable. He ſent it the next day with the following note: "Dear Mrs. Leſlie. I have no idea that huſbands ſhould control their wives, any more than that wives ſhould control their huſbands, at leaſt, in trifles; I therefore make no ſcruple to ſend you what is good for nothing. It is, I hope, a ſufficient excuſe for me that you expreſſed a wiſh for it, and I felt at the ſame time aſſured that its being uſeleſs was the reaſon of your doing ſo; thus 'much ado about nothing.' I ſhall now, to give value to the fragment I ſend you, apply to it a line of Wordſworth:

'This ſea in anger, and that diſmal ſhore.'*

I think of Wordſworth, for on that ſpot periſhed his brother in the wreck of the Abergavenny."

That Conſtable's next note may be underſtood, I muſt mention that I contemplated taking my family to America, with the probability of remaining there.

"June 11th. My dear Leſlie. As it may not be ordained that I write to you again on my birthday, (at leaſt in England), I cannot omit the occaſion, though the pleaſure is a melancholy one in every way to me. * * * The loſs of you is a cloud caſting its ſhade over my life, now in its autumn. I never did admire the autumnal tints, even in nature, ſo little of a painter am I in the eye of common-place connoiſſeurſhip. I love the exhilarating freſhneſs of ſpring. My kindeſt regards to Mrs. Leſlie; I hope all your children are well. * * * Remember I play the part of Punch on Monday at eight, at the aſſembly-room at Hampſtead."

"The part of Punch" alludes to his firſt appearance as a

* From "Elegiac Stanzas, ſuggeſted by a picture of Peele Caſtle, in a ſtorm, painted by Sir George Beaumont." The death of Captain Wordſworth is alſo alluded to, in another moſt affecting poem, by his brother, addreſſed "To the Daiſy."

lecturer. His subject was "An outline of the History of Landscape Painting," which he afterwards filled up in a course of four lectures delivered in London.

"June. Dear Leslie. * * * My Godchild is a delightful little creature, and I shall be glad to live long, if it is only to cross the Atlantic to give her away. When Captain Cook stood sponsor for a little girl in Barking Church, he said, 'If this infant lives, I will marry her;' he fulfilled his promise, and she was living until lately. Only think of the vicissitudes of life; what may we not hope and almost expect? you may return. Don't separate any ties in this country. Keep your diploma."

"Well Walk, August 16th. My dear Leslie. I have wished much to write to you. I have not thanked you for your long and delightful letter, but I am not now so much master of that cœur de joie which used to cheer me, especially when I took pen in hand to write to you. The thought that I am to be deprived of the consolations of your and Mrs. Leslie's society—of such happy hours as you and I have passed together—and of our communications on art, and every thing else, weighs heavy on me; so much so, indeed, as to depress my mind, and prevent the enjoyment of even the little that remains of our personal intercourse; this is not right on my part, I know.

"I had a delightful visit into Suffolk. We ranged the woods and fields, and searched the crag-pits for shells, and the bones and teeth of fossil animals for John; and Charles made drawings, and I did nothing at all, but I felt happy to see them enjoy themselves. All my family were very kind to the boys. * * * I have just lost a valuable Suffolk friend, Sir Thomas Ormsby, who would have served me always. He was son-in-law to General Rebow, an old friend of my father's; thus I am almost daily bereft of some friend or other. * * * I am glad you are going to Lord Egremont's; he is really a great patron of art. * * * I can hardly write for looking at the ſilvery clouds; how I ſigh for that peace (to paint them) which this world cannot give, (to me at leaſt.) Yet well I know 'happineſs is to be found any where or no where;' but this laſt year, though, thank God, attended with no calamity, has been moſt unpropitious to my happineſs. To part with my dear John is breaking my heart, but I am told it is for his good."

Conſtable's two eldeſt ſons were about to leave him for a ſchool at Folkſtone.

"To Mr. George Conſtable. Well Walk, December 9th. My dear Sir. I am grieved at the letter I have received from you. To have had ſuch a ſerious accident,* and at a time, too, when your health was ſo much improving, is extremely diſtreſſing, as it muſt prevent your general habits of enjoying the air, and of exerciſe. Gigs are bad things, one is ſo much at the mercy of the horſe. I hope, however, from the almoſt cheerful tone in which you have dictated your letter, that all will do well with you, and that your next letter will bring ſatisfactory accounts; at leaſt, that the inflammation is gone, and the bone ſet. The former is much within the reach of the profeſſors, our friends of the ditches, the leeches. Theſe humble creatures have the power and the will, too, to render mankind eſſential benefits; and this grateful argument will hold good of everything in nature, more or leſs. I have been ſadly ill, and during the laſt week, particularly ſo; ſtill I have ventured to embark on a large canvaſs, and have thus ſet forth on a ſea of troubles, but it is a ſea that generally becalms as I proceed; I have choſen a rich ſubject. * * * To-morrow I paſs a long evening at the Academy; the 10th being its anniverſary. We give

* Mr. G. Conſtable had been thrown out of a gig, and his left arm was broken above the elbow.

CHAP. XIV.
1833.

the prizes for all kinds of art. I lament to ſay we muſt give away an abundance of our beautiful medals to little purpoſe. How are we to account for this? perhaps as Fuſeli once told me, 'as the conveniences and inſtruments of ſtudy increaſe, ſo will always the exertions of the ſtudents decreaſe.' Now, my dear ſir, how can I oblige you, or contribute to your amuſement during your ſad calamity? Can I ſend you anything to look at?

"To Mr. George Conſtable. Well Walk, Hampſtead, December 17th. My dear ſir. I would not have kept you ſo long in ſuſpenſe, had it been in my power to do otherwiſe; but I can't get well. I have been long in a diſordered ſtate of health, and my ſpirits are not as they uſed to be. I have not an idea that I ſhall be able to part with the 'Salisbury;'* the price will of neceſſity be a very large one, for the time expended on it was enormous for its ſize. I am alſo unwilling to part with any of my ſtandard pictures; they being all points with me in my practice, and will much regulate my future productions, ſhould I do any more large works. The picture by Cuyp which you ſend is agreeable, and its colour and ſunſhine will no doubt pleaſe many; I wiſh not, however, to add any more old pictures to my ſtock. If you wiſh for any information about its money value, I can get ſome profeſſional friends to ſee it; of that I am no judge; I only know *good* from *bad* things in art, and that goes but little way in being of uſe to my friends. I ſhall greatly rejoice to hear that you are ſo far recovered as to be out again. I will look for ſome little matters to return with the Cuyp, when you deſire to have it."

"To Mr. John Conſtable. Arundel, December 18th. * * * I ſincerely wiſh I could prevail on you to take a trip

* One of his repetitions of the beautiful picture of the Cathedral from the Biſhop's Grounds.

to Arundel, I am ſure you would derive great benefit from it. I am from experience quite ſatisfied that the occaſional removal from the monotony of domeſtic ſcenes and circumſtances, is very beneficial both to mind and body. * * * Reſpecting one of your pictures, I ſhall certainly do my utmoſt to poſſeſs what I think your beſt in ſome reſpects, the 'Saliſbury Cathedral;' but more on this ſubject when I have the pleaſure of ſeeing you. Could you without much trouble encloſe me a bit of your ſparkling colour to copy, I ſhould be more than I can expreſs obliged. I am, my dear ſir, your ſincere friend, George Conſtable."

"To Mr. George Conſtable. Well Walk, Hampſtead, December 20th. My dear Friend. I thank you moſt ſincerely for your kind and friendly letter. I am ſadly out of order, but you ſeem determined that I ſhall not knock under. I am too unwell to go to town, but my friend Bonner has juſt ſet off to Charlotte Street to pack your picture and forward it; it is a beautiful repreſentation of a ſummer's evening; calm, warm, and delicious; the colour on the man's face is perfect ſunſhine. The liquid pencil of this ſchool is replete with a beauty peculiar to itſelf. Neverthele ſs, I don't believe they had any *noſtrums*, but plain linſeed oil; '*honeſt linſeed*,' as old Wilſon called it. But it is always right to remember that the ordinary painters of that day uſed, as now, the ſame vehicle as their betters, and alſo that their works have all received the hardening and enamelling effects of time, ſo that we muſt not judge of originality by theſe ſigns always. Still your picture has a beautiful look; but I ſhall not collect any more. I have ſent moſt of my *old men* to Mr. Davidſon's Gallery in Pall Mall to be ſold. I find my houſe too much encumbered with lumber, and this encumbers my mind. My ſons are returned from Folkſtone for Chriſtmas. John is delighted with the collection* you have

* Of foſſils.

CHAP. XIV. 1833.

ſent him; he ſays they are very valuable indeed, and he highly prizes them. To me theſe pieces of 'time-mangled matter' are intereſting for the tale they tell; but above all, I eſteem them as marks of regard to my darling boy, the darling, too, of his dear mother."

Perhaps the following notes to Mr. Lucas, without date, may not be far from their proper place here.

"Dear Lucas. Poor, infatuated printer, * * *† has done nothing for me for three weeks: not a ſingle India copy nor one plain one can I get. But he has ſent me a large piece of wedding-cake, and this, too, juſt as he has been begging aſſiſtance to buy bread and butter! The devil undoubtedly finds much fun in this town, or we never ſhould hear of ſuch acts of exceeding folly."

"Dear Lucas. All who have ſeen your large print like it exceedingly; it will be, with all its grandeur, full of detail. Avoid the ſoot-bag, and you are ſafe; Rembrandt had no ſoot-bag, you may rely on it. Be careful how you etch it, that you do not hurt the detail; but there is time enough. I hope you will not injure your family by ſo large a print."

"Dear Lucas. I ſhould think the Yarmouth would make by far the beſt companion to Old Sarum. At the ſame time Old Billy Lott's Houſe, if it could be regrounded at the ſides, is a lovely ſubject. The Lord Mayor's ſhow, I do believe is too good a joke to be received into *our* church. Nothing can made it either Apoſtolic or canonical, ſo uncongenial is any part of this hideous Gomorrah. J. C.—And yet, after all, the Waterloo is a famous compoſition, and ought to give much pleaſure;—but it is the devil,—and I am ſore perplexed."

By the "Lord Mayor's Show," he means the "Opening of Waterloo Bridge," (his lordſhip's barge being a conſpicu-

† The printer of the letter-preſs to the "Engliſh Landſcape."

ous object in that picture).—The reader cannot fail to have obſerved how uncertain Conſtable always felt, of the ſucceſs of this compoſition. In the year 1819, it firſt entered his mind to paint it; and between that time and 1832 (when it was exhibited) it was often taken up and as often laid aſide, with many alternations of hope and fear. The expanſe of ſky and water tempted him to go on with it, while the abſence of all rural aſſociations made it diſtaſteful to him; and when at laſt it came forth, though poſſeſſing very high qualities,—compoſition, breadth, and brightneſs of colour, it wanted one which generally conſtituted the greateſt charm of his pictures—*ſentiment*,—and it was condemned by the public; though perhaps leſs for a deficiency which its ſubject occaſioned, than for its want of finiſh. What would he have felt, could he foreſee that, in little more than a year after his death, its ſilvery brightneſs was doomed to be clouded over by a coat of *blacking*, laid on by the hand of a picture dealer!—Yet that this was done, by way of giving *tone* to the picture, I know from the beſt authority, the lips of the operator, who gravely aſſured me that ſeveral noblemen conſidered it to be greatly improved by the proceſs. The blacking was laid on with water, and ſecured by a coat of maſtic varniſh.

CHAPTER XV.

1834—1835.

Illneſs of Conſtable and his eldeſt Son. Death of Lady Beechey. Conſtable again ill. Mr. Purton. Pictures at the Britiſh Gallery and at the Academy 1834. *Viſit to Arundel. Mr. George Conſtable. Petworth. Lord Egremont. Large Picture of Saliſbury Cathedral. Lady Dyſart. Gainſborough. Ham Houſe. Pictures there. Cuyp. Viſit to Petworth. Cowdry Caſtle. Old Mills. Barns. Farm Houſes. Conſtable's Habits. Conflagration of the Houſes of Parliament. Large Picture of Saliſbury Cathedral. Wilkie's "Columbus." Picture called "The Valley Farm" exhibited at the Academy,* 1835, *and purchaſed by Mr. Vernon. Cozens. Pictures by David. Second Lecture at Hampſtead. Attacks on the Academy. Committee of the Houſe of Commons, etc. Charles Conſtable. Mr. Vernon's Picture. Bryan's Dictionary.*

1834.

"WELL Walk, January 20th, 1834. My dear Leſlie. I have been ſadly ill ſince you left England, and my mind has been ſo much depreſſed, that I have ſcarcely been able to do any one thing, and in that ſtate I did not like to write to you. I am now, however, buſy on a large landſcape; I find it of uſe to myſelf, though little noticed by others. Still the trees and the clouds ſeem to aſk me to try and do ſomething like them. Poor John has been very ill; walking in his ſleep at ſchool, he fell and brought on eryſipelas; he was ſix weeks in bed, and on his return to Hampſtead for the holidays, he took a rheumatic fever, and was confined for a month. I do not think I ſhall ſend the boys again to Folkſtone. Bonner is ſtill with me, and Alfred and Lionel are getting on in their ſtudies with him. * * * I dined with Mr. Banniſter, who is much delighted with your print of 'Uncle Toby and the Widow.'† * * * Poor Sir William Beechey has loſt Lady Beechey; ſhe was taken ill on a Saturday, and died the next day; but ſo happy a death, it was more like a tranſlation; ſhe ſaid, 'Now I have no more to do or to ſay. I have done my beſt for you all here, and I will go and ſee my three dear children in Heaven;' thoſe ſhe had loſt early. * * * The Chalons were here on the Heath for ſix weeks, and it was delightful weather. * * * I have been buſy in making a fly-leaf to each of my prints, and I ſend a ſpecimen or two that are ready, to know what you think of that plan. Many people can read letter-preſs who cannot read mezzotinto. I ſhall ſend you my *diſcourſe*. They want me to preach again in the ſame place. * * * I dine with Sir Martin to-morrow; Chalon will be there."

Conſtable had another, and very painful illneſs, which is thus deſcribed by Mr. Evans in a note addreſſed to Mr. Wm. Purton of Hampſtead: "It was a ſevere attack of acute rheumatiſm, (or rheumatic fever, as it is uſually called), which began in February, and laſted for the greater part of two months. In the early part of this period the ſuffering was very great; all the joints became the ſeat of the diſeaſe two or three times over, and the pain and fever were of the moſt aggravated kind. Theſe ſufferings he bore with great patience for one of ſo ſenſitive a frame; and on the occaſion of my viſits to him, his cheerfulneſs was generally reſtored, and his converſation was of the ſame delightful character

† Mr. Banniſter ſat for the face of Uncle Toby.

which you know ſo well. I only wiſh I could recollect all that I heard from his lips on theſe and all ſimilar occaſions. I think he was never ſo well after this ſevere illneſs; its effects were felt by him, and ſhowed themſelves in his looks ever afterwards; ſo that I think it may be ſaid to have had ſome ſhare in his removal from us."

Among the moſt valuable friendſhips Conſtable formed during the laſt years of his life, was that with the gentleman to whom Mr. Evans's note is addreſſed. Fond of devoting his leiſure hours to landſcape painting, and wholly uninfluenced by that "cant of criticiſm," againſt which Conſtable waged unceaſing war, Mr. Purton was led by the ſtudy of nature alone, to form a juſt eſtimate of the art of his new friend.

In 1834, Conſtable exhibited three pictures at the Britiſh Gallery, "A Cottage in a Field of Corn," "A Heath," and the "Stour Valley, with Dedham and Harwich in the diſtance;" theſe had all been exhibited before. His long continued ill health diſabled him from ſending any large work to the Academy, where he exhibited drawings only; three in water colours, "The Mound of the City of Old Sarum," "Stoke Pogis Church, the Scene of Gray's Elegy," "An Interior of a Church," alſo an illuſtration of the Elegy,* and a large drawing in lead pencil, "A Study of Trees made in the grounds of Charles Holford, Esq. at Hampſtead." I returned to England in time to ſee this exhibition.

"To Mr. George Conſtable. Charlotte Street, July 2nd. Your prompt and very kind reply to my dear boy makes us quite happy; he is exceedingly impatient to be with you, and to be introduced to his young friend.† I am ſorry that a meeting of The Artiſts' General Benevolent Fund, of which

* Theſe beautiful drawings of the Church were purchaſed by Mr. Rogers.
† Mr. George Conſtable's ſon.

I am a Vice-Prefident, will take place on Monday evening. It is for the relief of cafes, many of which are of my own recommendation; and if I am not prefent, it may be materially to their difadvantage; therefore I can't come to you on the day you name; but we have arranged, if it is quite agreeable to yourfelf and Mrs. Conftable, to take a place for John on Saturday, and that I follow him on Tuefday, by which he will get two or three days the ftart of me in the pleafure of our vifit. I am brufhing up my 'Waterloo Bridge,' and fhall make it look like fomething before I have done with it. The difficulty is to find a fubject fit for the largeft of my fizes; I will talk to you about one; either a canal or a rural affair, or a wood, or a harveft fcene; which, I know not, but I could hardly choofe amifs; certainly not, if, as Wilkie fays, it could be 'painted well.'* I rejoice to hear fuch a good account of your health."

"Arundel, July 16th. My dear Leflie. In all my walks about this delightful fpot I think of you, and how much I fhould like you to enjoy with me the beautiful things that are continually croffing my path. The chalk cliffs afford John many fragments of oyfter fhells and other matters that fell from the table of Adam, in all probability. Our friend, Mr. George Conftable, is fond of all matters of fcience, and he has won John's heart by a prefent, (the arrival of which in Charlotte Street I fhall dread,) of an electrifying machine. The Caftle is the chief ornament of this place; but all here finks to infignificance in comparifon with the woods and hills. The woods hang from fteeps and precipices, and the trees are beyond every thing beautiful. Some parts of the Caftle, fuch as the keep and fome of the old walls, are as grand as poffible, but the more modern part is not unlike a

* If a young artift confulted Wilkie as to what he fhould do to a picture, his ufual anfwer was, "Paint it well."

London ſhow place. The Baron's hall is a grand room, though ſtrangely vulgarized by ſome hideous figures larger than life on painted glaſs; theſe ruffian-looking fellows look like drunken bargemen dreſſed up as Cruſaders, and are meant to repreſent the 'Barons bold,' the former lords of the eſtate, who ſpread the Engliſh name over Paleſtine; but 'how are the mighty fallen!' you would take them to be the very men who are watering the ſtreets of London this hot weather. Theſe things make true what Horace Walpole ſays, in ſpeaking of the painters of the middle or *dark* ages, as we call them: 'It would not be eaſy to know where to go to order a painted window' like one he was deſcribing. The meadows are lovely, ſo is the delightful river; and the old houſes are rich beyond all things of the ſort; but the trees are above all, yet every thing is beautiful. Only laſt night I ſtumbled on an old barn ſituated amid trees of immenſe ſize, like this;" (here the writing is interrupted by a ſketch;) "it is of the time of King John.

"But we have been to Petworth, and I have thought of nothing ſince but that vaſt houſe and its contents. The Earl was there; he aſked me to ſtay all day, nay more, he wiſhed me to paſs a few days in the houſe. I excuſed myſelf, ſaying, I ſhould like to make ſuch a viſit when you were there, which he took very agreeably, ſaying, 'Be it ſo, then, if you cannot leave your friends now;' he came to us two or three times. I had a very kind letter of introduction to him from Phillips."

On his return to London, in a letter of thanks to his amiable hoſt at Arundel, Conſtable ſpeaks of his viſit as one of the moſt happy and intellectually delightful he ever paid. "You thought," he ſays, "of everything you could to make John and me happy, and the ſame motive actuated every member of your delightful and kind family."

"35, Charlotte Street, July 29th. My dear Purton.

Should you have time to look in to-morrow or next day, I ſhould be glad. I have done wonders with my great Saliſbury; I have been preparing it for Birmingham, and I am ſure I have much increaſed its power and effect; I do hope you will ſay ſo. I ſhould much like you to ſee it, becauſe as you are ſo good as to look at my things at all, I argue you ſee ſomething to admire in them, and I have no doubt of this picture being my beſt now. * * * I am, dear Purton, yours moſt truly, John Conſtable."

In September, Conſtable accepted an invitation to Petworth, where I was at that time with my family, ſharing with other gueſts, among whom were Mr. Phillips, R.A. and his family, Lord Egremont's hoſpitality.

"My dear Leſlie. I was happy to receive your kind letter, and I hope in a few days to avail myſelf of Lord Egremont's kindneſs. I have been two days at Ham. Lady Dyſart is old, and rather more infirm, but well. You and I muſt go there together. It ſeems as if its inmates of a century and a half back were ſtill in exiſtence, and on opening the doors ſome of them would appear. * * * I ſhall write to ſay when I hope to be at Petworth, which, as they want to ſee me again at Ham on Sunday or Monday, will, I think, be about Wedneſday or Thurſday. How I long to be again in that houſe of art where you are. I amuſed Lady Dyſart with the ſtory of the ſky-rocket; at all events it proved ſhe had been taught where God was to be found.† * * * The Gainſborough was down when I was there. I placed it as it ſuited me, and I cannot think of it even now without tears in my eyes. With particulars he had nothing to do; his object was to deliver a fine ſentiment, and he has fully ac-

† Conſtable alludes to my having told him of the exclamation of one of my children on ſeeing ſome fire-works in Petworth Park. As the rockets aſcended ſhe ſaid, "Won't God be ſhot?"

complished it; mind, I use no comparisons in my delight in thinking of this lovely canvass; nothing injures one's mind more than such modes of reasoning; no fine things will bear, or want comparisons; every fine thing is unique."

"September 6th. My dear Leslie. I hope nothing will happen to prevent my being with you on Tuesday. Perhaps it is now unnecessary to write to Lord Egremont to say that I am coming, but if you think I ought, write on the receipt of this. You see how awkward I am with the great folks. * * * I wish I had said nothing about pictures in my letter. So much has expression to do with words, that writing and talking are not the same thing. I did not in the least misunderstand you. I should like to have *a keen eye** for myself and for my friends, as a thing I should prize above all the attributes of our profession; only I don't think in that I deserve your good opinion to the degree you believe. How beautifully, how justly does Dr. Johnson somewhere speak of epistolary correspondence;† but he cautions the writers against complimenting each other, and warns them of the danger of its self-deception. See what the evangelicals have done to one another in this way, till at last they have forgotten the first principles of Christianity, and treated the rest of the world with contempt. I am going to-morrow to Ham; we must see it together. I expect always in wandering through the rooms there, to meet either King Charles II., or the Duke of Marlborough, or Addison. It has the art, in portraiture, on its walls, from Cornelius Jansen to Sir Joshua Reynolds, including Hopkins and Cooper in miniature. There is there a truly sublime Cuyp; still and tran-

* I was painting a picture at Petworth for Lord Egremont, and I had said in my reply to Constable's last letter, "I do not think I shall shew you what I am about, as I fear your keen eye."

† He probably alludes to a passage in "The Life of Pope."

quil, the town of Dort is ſeen with its tower and windmills under the inſidious gleam of a faint watery ſun, while a horrid rent in the ſky almoſt frightens one, and the lightning deſcends to the earth over ſome poor cottages with a glide that is ſo much like nature, that I wiſh I had ſeen it before I ſent away my 'Saliſbury.'"

September 8th. My dear Leſlie. Calculating from your letter that there was a coach to Petworth every day, I ſent for a place for Tueſday, when I found the coach was on alternate days, therefore I have taken one for Wedneſday next. I have not thought it worth while to trouble Lord Egremont about this trifling change of a day, and I hope you will ſet the matter right for me. I have my picture back from Worceſter, and my houſe is now full of old jobs and lumber. My glaſs is very low, but I hope we may ſtill have fine weather. I ſhall put off Worceſter, as I hope to be better engaged. I have almoſt determined to attack another canal for my large frame.—How beautiful did old Father Thames look yeſterday, ſcattered over with ſwans above Richmond! and when they flew over the water, the clapping of their wings was very loud indeed.—How lovely the trees are juſt now!"

"To Mr. George Conſtable. Petworth, September 14th. I am much obliged by your kind letter. If I can ſee you at Arundel before I leave this, I ſhall be delighted, but of that, as my time is ſhort, I can ſay nothing. I am glad you are ſo well, but how could you ſend your boys to France? I don't think I could; but I dare ſay you are right, I act ſo ſadly always on my prejudices.—Leſlie has commenced a picture here, a companion to his 'Ducheſs.'—Mr. Phillips leaves this place in a few days. Mrs. Phillips is going to take me to ſee a caſtle about five miles off. Yeſterday I viſited the river banks, which are lovely indeed; Claude nor Ruyſdael could not do a thouſandth part of what nature here

Chap. XV.
1834.

presents. Yours, my dear sir, always truly, John Constable."

Lord Egremont, with that unceasing attention which he always paid to whatever he thought would be most agreeable to his guests, ordered one of his carriages to be ready every day, to enable Constable to see as much of the neighbourhood as possible. He passed a day in company with Mr. and Mrs. Phillips, and myself, among the beautiful ruins of Cowdry Castle, of which he made several very fine sketches; but he was most delighted with the borders of the Arun, and the picturesque old mills, barns, and farm-houses that abound in the west of Sussex. I recollect spending a morning with him, he drawing the outside, while I was sketching the interior, of a lonely farm-house, which was the more picturesque from its being in a neglected state, and which a woman we found in it told us was called "wicked Hammond's house;" a man of that name, strongly suspected of great crimes, having formerly been its occupant. She told us that in an old well in the garden some bones had not long ago been found, which the "doctor said were the arm bones of a *Christian*."—While at Petworth, where Constable spent a fortnight, he filled a large book with sketches in pencil and water colours, some of which he finished very highly.

It was on this occasion only, that as an inmate of the same house, I had an opportunity of witnessing his habits. He rose early, and had often made some beautiful sketch in the park before breakfast. On going into his room one morning, not aware that he had yet been out of it, I found him setting some of these sketches with isinglass. His dressing-table was covered with flowers, feathers of birds, and pieces of bark with lichens and mosses adhering to them, which he had brought home for the sake of their beautiful tints. Mr. George Constable told me that while on the visit to him, Constable brought from Fittleworth Common, at leaſt a dozen different ſpecimens of ſand and earth, of colours from pale to deep yellow, and of light reddiſh hues to tints almoſt crimſon. The richneſs of theſe colours contraſted with the deep greens of the furze and other vegetation on this pictureſque heath, delighted him exceedingly, and he carried theſe earths home carefully preſerved in bottles, and alſo many fragments of the variouſly coloured ſtone. In paſſing with Mr. G. Conſtable ſome ſlimy poſts near an old mill, he ſaid, "I wiſh you could cut off, and ſend their tops to me."

On the 16th of October the Houſes of Parliament were burnt; and Conſtable witneſſed the ſcene from a hackney coach, in which, with his two eldeſt ſons, he took a ſtation on Weſtminſter Bridge. The evening of the 31ſt he ſpent with me; and while deſcribing the fire, he drew with a pen, on half a ſheet of letter paper, Weſtminſter Hall, as it ſhowed itſelf during the conflagration; blotting the light and ſhade with ink, which he rubbed with his finger where he wiſhed it to be lighteſt. He then, on another half ſheet added the towers of the Abbey and that of St. Margaret's Church,—and the papers, being joined, form a very grand ſketch of the whole ſcene.

He was now again at work on the "Saliſbury from the Meadows." This was a picture which he felt would probably in future be conſidered his greateſt; for if among his ſmaller works there were many of more perfection of finiſh, this he conſidered as conveying the fulleſt impreſſion of the compaſs of his art. But it met with no purchaſer. "December 4th. My dear Leſlie, I have never left my large 'Saliſbury' ſince I ſaw you. It would much delight me, if in the courſe of to-day or to-morrow you could ſee it for a moment. I cannot help trying to believe that there may be ſomething in it that in ſome meaſure, at leaſt, may warrant your too high opinion of my landſcape in general."

"December 15th. My dear Leslie, I write to beg of you to let me put off our visit to * * * for a little. I was all day on Saturday at Ham, and shall be all this day with Wilkie, and I can hardly spare so much of my valueless time, for though my life and occupation are useless, still I trifle on in a way that seems to myself like doing something; and my canvass soothes me into a forgetfulness of much that is disagreeable. I could not get on with * * *; how could I? you will say." * * * Constable was at this time disturbed by some transactions with the last person mentioned in this note, and with some other unpleasant occurrences, and which, as it generally happened, his imagination magnified, and he continued: "Every gleam of sunshine is withdrawn from me, in the art, at least. Can it be wondered at, then, that I paint continual storms:*

'Tempest o'er tempest roll'd;'

Still the darkness is majestic, and I have not to accuse myself of ever having prostituted the moral feeling of the art. * * * I saw Mr. Bannister yesterday, so well, so happy, and more delightful than ever. I told him I had venison in the house, and that I wanted you and Mrs. Leslie to dine with me, if he would but come; he did not say no."

"December 17th. My dear Purton. I am obliged to you for the quotations; the second is excellent,† and shall be used in the title-page of my book; but I must take care of being an author, it is quite enough to be a painter. I beg my best respects to Mrs. Purton. I shall like to see what you are doing, and will try to catch a glimpse by daylight, but I am

* One of the objections made to his pictures by those who could not deny them nature. He was fond of representing the passing shower, but I know of no other instance in his pictures of a storm, and here it is breaking away.

† From Crabbe. "It is the soul that sees; &c." Constable made use of this in the third lecture he delivered at the Royal Institution.

in a terrible turmoil with all my things. I ſeem fooliſhly bent on a large canvaſs. I was at Wilkie's all day on Monday; he has painted a noble picture, Columbus with the monk, when he ſhews him his plan for overtaking another world."

Conſtable had been aſked by Wilkie to ſit for one of the heads in the picture of "Columbus," that of the phyſician Garcia Fernandez. Among his papers I found a ſlight pencil ſketch of the whole compoſition of that fine picture, no doubt made from recollection while deſcribing the ſubject to ſome friend. Wilkie alſo aſked Conſtable to ſit to him for a portrait, and it is much to be regretted that he declined doing ſo.

The following letter to Mr. Dunthorne accompanied a preſent of Mr. Lucas's large engravings of "The Lock," and "The Cornfield." "My dear friend. I hope you will receive the prints ſafe. Mr. Lucas bids me tell you that he ſhall ſend two more which he is now about, 'Saliſbury' and 'Stratford Mill.' If you can lend me two or three of poor John's ſtudies of the aſhes in the town meadow, and a ſtudy of plants that grew in the lane below, Mr. Coleman's, near the ſpouts which ran into the pond, I will take great care of them and ſend them ſafe back to you ſoon. I am about an aſh or two now. The prints will come to you from Flatford, as I have ſent a pair to Abram. Yours very truly, John Conſtable. Charlotte Street, February 14th."

"March. My dear Leſlie, Our friend Bonner* is on his way to bid my children good bye at Hampſtead. He is going to Germany, whence his family originates, and he cannot leave England without ſhaking you by the hand. I have been wholly ſhut up, ſo much ſo that I do not know

* Mr. Bonner had been for ſome time domeſticated with Conſtable as private tutor to his ſons.

what is going on ſince you have been here. My picture muſt go, but it is wofully deficient in places. Yeſterday Mr. * * * called, and though he ſaid, 'perhaps it is a little better,' yet he added, 'you know I like to be honeſt;' but, fortunately for me, I am ſure it was not at all to his liking. Mr. Vernon called ſoon after with the Chalons; he ſaw it free from the muſtineſs of old pictures, he liked its daylight, and bought it; it is his, only I muſt talk to you about it; he leaves all to me." * * * Conſtable told me that Mr. Vernon aſked him if the picture on his eaſel was painted for any particular perſon; to which he replied: "Yes, ſir, it is painted for a *very particular* perſon,—the perſon for whom I have all my life painted."

"To Mr. George Conſtable. April 8th. Your trips to France muſt be delightful, and John bids me tell you that of all things he ſhould like to go with you at ſome time or other. At preſent, however, it is impoſſible, as all his lectures now are in regular courſe; he is a pupil of Faraday's at the Inſtitution in Albemarle Street on chymiſtry, he is alſo a pupil at the London Univerſity in ſurgery and phyſiology, and he is attending a courſe of lectures on anatomy in Windmill Street. To all theſe things he is as regular as a clock; all I pray for is, that his health will continue to bear it; nevertheleſs, he muſt take ſome trips in the ſummer, and he, as well as I look with great pleaſure to a repetition of our moſt unalloyed and delightful viſit to Arundel. Having ſpoken of the young chymiſt and ſurgeon, let me ſpeak of the old landſcape painter. I have got my picture into a very beautiful ſtate; I have kept my brightneſs without my ſpottineſs, and I have preſerved God Almighty's daylight, which is enjoyed by all mankind, excepting only the lovers of old dirty canvaſs, periſhed pictures at a thouſand guineas each, cart greaſe, tar, and ſnuff of candle. Mr. * * *, an admirer of common place, called to ſee my picture, and did not like it at all, ſo I am ſure there is ſomething good in it. Soon after, Mr. Vernon called, and bought it, having never ſeen it before in any ſtate."

This beautiful work, a view of Willy Lott's houſe from an early ſketch, had the rare luck, when exhibited, of pleaſing even ſome of the newſpaper critics; it was the only picture Conſtable ſent to the Academy this year.

"To Mr. George Conſtable. Charlotte Street, June 6th. John has declared this morning, that if I defer writing to you any longer, he will never ſpeak to me again. I have had almoſt every ſort of occupation, and if I do not write almoſt directly to any letter I receive, I am too apt to delay it for a very long time, as you, my dear friend, have ſo often experienced, and ſo often been kind enough to forgive. The Exhibition is a ſucceſsful one, it is profitable and productive; I ſpeak now of pictures under the line, the large pictures are very ſo ſo. * * * But there are ſome excellent works of art on the walls. 'Columbus and his little Son,' the 'Gulliver,' 'The Scotch Drovers,' and Eaſtlake's 'Pilgrims.'—Turner's light, whether it emanates from ſun or moon, is exquiſite.—Collins's ſkies and ſhores are true, and his horizons always pretty."

"My dear William Carpenter. Some years ago, a lady got away my copy of 'Bryan's Dictionary,' and this has ever ſince been an inconvenience to me. I want to know when the younger Cozens* was born; his name was John, and he was the greateſt genius that ever touched landſcape. He was

---

* "This artiſt was the ſon of Alexander Cozens, a Ruſſian by birth, who eſtabliſhed himſelf in London as a landſcape painter and drawing maſter about the year 1770. He followed the ſame profeſſion, and with great ability and elegance. He produced ſome drawings which poſſeſſed extraordinary merit, executed in a ſtyle which was afterwards adopted and improved by the ingenious Mr. Girtin. He died in 1799."—*Bryan's Dictionary*, Appendix, Vol. II. p. 680. In an octavo edition of "Pilkington's Dictionary" printed in

Chap. XV. 1835.

the ſon of Alexander Cozens, drawing-maſter of Eaton, and John died in 1796, ſtill rather young. I want this for my lecture on Monday to be given at Hampſtead. My beſt regards to your father. Very truly yours, J. Conſtable. Perhaps Days or Edwards mentions his birth." What Conſtable here ſays of Cozens, is ſtartling, although all who are acquainted with the beautiful works of that truly original artiſt, will admit that his taſte is of the higheſt order; but the reader muſt have obſerved that in other inſtances Conſtable ſpeaks in ſimilar unqualified terms of admiration of that which at the moment engaged his attention.

"The longeſt day. My dear Leſlie. 'Tis true we have got you back from America, but you are ſtill too far away, too far for indolent friends like me. * * * Alfred, to my ſurpriſe and delight, ſeems quite happy at Mr. Brooks's. He plays firſt fiddle there at every thing but his book. But, poor dear boy, his whole life has been one of affliction,* which, as well as his drollery, has endeared him to me, perhaps unduly. I have been cloſely ſhut up doing—nothing. Lord N * * * ſaw my pictures at Tiffin's; he wanted the 'Church,' and offered his Hobbema for it. I dare ſay his Hobbema is good for nothing. All this time the painter is to be had, but they ſtill wait for his quiet departure. * * * I have ſeen David's pictures; they are indeed loathſome, and the room would be intolerable but for the urbane and agreeable manners of the Colonel. David ſeems to have formed his mind from three ſources, the ſcaffold, the hoſpital, and a brothel. * * * I give my lecture at Hampſtead

1829, ſpeaking of John Cozens, it is ſaid, "His drawings were ſold at Chriſtie's in 1805 for five hundred and ten pounds. He died in a ſtate of mental derangement in 1799." I think Pyne, in thoſe articles he contributed to "The Literary Gazette" under the title of "Wine and Walnuts," gave ſome notices of Cozens.

* From ill health.

to-morrow evening at a quarter before eight. I have ſent up young Uwins's beautiful copy of Ruyſdael; it will be of infinite ſervice to me; alſo Partridge's 'Peter Martyr.' I have written little, and ſhall depend moſt on being converſational. I have got a lovely drawing of young Bone's of Guido's 'Aurora.' * * * I never ſaw the elder buſhes ſo full of bloſſom, and ſome of the flowers, fore-ſhortened as they curve round, are extremely elegant; it is a favourite of mine, but 'tis melancholy; an emblem of death."

The pictures by David mentioned in this letter were of Buonaparte croſſing the Alps, Mars and Venus, The Death of Marat, and ſome drawings of revolutionary ſcenes which were exhibited in Leiceſter Square; and "the Colonel" was a French gentleman who attended in the room during the exhibition.

Of Conſtable's ſecond lecture delivered at Hampſtead I have preſerved no notes; but the reader will find much of it incorporated with what I have been able to preſerve of thoſe he gave in London. I remember that the ſky was magnificent on the day on which it was delivered; and as I walked acroſs the Weſt End fields to Hampſtead, towards evening, I ſtopped repeatedly to admire its ſplendid combinations and their effects over the landſcape, and Conſtable did not omit in his lecture to ſpeak of the appearances of the day.

Mr. Lucas was now proceeding with his large plate of the "Saliſbury Cathedral from the Meadows," which Conſtable had commiſſioned him to undertake, and it is of this the next note ſpeaks: "June 30th. Dear Lucas. I ſhould be glad if you would leave the plate here a day or two. Leſlie is ſo much impreſſed with the proof, that he would give any money to poſſeſs one; ſo am I, and would give any thing to poſſeſs two at leaſt. Now would you mind printing a few, five or ſix? would it hurt the plate? I know you don't like

Chap. XV.
1835.

to do ſo, but I would gladly pay all expenſes. It never can nor will be grander than it is now: it is awfully ſo. You ſhall be amply paid for this indulgence. I do think with you, it is well to ſtay your hand with my works when theſe large ones are all done, and pauſe for ſome time; and if you take up a portrait or ſo, it may be adviſable, leſt that branch of the art ſhould be ſhut out from you, and your forming a connexion that way be cut off. All this I meant to ſay yeſterday, but you availed yourſelf of Rembrandt's light and ſhadow, and were loſt."

Mr. Lucas had parted from Conſtable in a crowded exhibition room containing the drawings by Rembrandt, which formed part of the Lawrence collection.

"To Mr. George Conſtable. 35, Charlotte Street, July 2nd. I had the pleaſure of ſeeing the lady yeſterday bearing your note, in which you ſpeak ſo highly of the ſervices ſhe has rendered your dear children. I can, indeed, well appreciate ſuch benefits, as my own dear girls have received them at the hands of my friend, Miſs Noble, for ſeven, eight, and nine years. I agree with you in its being the leaſt we can do to expreſs our gratitude to ſuch benefactors. This excellent lady introduced herſelf to me by ſaying ſhe had 'had two hundred and fifty children;' I was alarmed,—but an explanation ſoon took place, and I told her the contents of your note. My poor boy John and myſelf are panting for a little freſh air. He is gone to Hampſtead to look for a mouthful, leaving me with a promiſe that I write to you this evening, to ſay that if it is quite agreeable to yourſelf and Mrs. Conſtable, he and I will come to you on Tueſday to paſs a few days, and if alſo agreeable, I will bring my eldeſt girl with me. I long to be among your willows again, and in your walks and hanging woods; among your books of antiquities, and enjoying your ſociety as I did before; without reſerve, reſtraint, coldneſs, or form. I am much worn with a long and hard winter and ſpring campaign, though a ſucceſsful one. I gave my lecture laſt Monday week at Hampſtead, and did it much better this time; I was thanked by the committee; it was all converſational; but all this wears me; and to crown the whole, I was led up to the ſtake in a court of juſtice (for it proved one in this inſtance) to give evidence about a Claude."

"To Mr. George Conſtable. Auguſt 3rd. I have been ſadly vexed with myſelf for not writing to you long ago; but I am ſorely perplexed with ſundry matters which day after day eat up my time. I have been with Maria to Kingſton, and have juſt brought her home; and now that all my girls and my little boys are ſafely depoſited at ſchool, I begin to breathe, and to recollect that I was a week or two ago at Arundel, paſſing a moſt delightful time with my dear friends, and amid moſt heavenly ſcenery; or was it a dream? for it ſeems much like one. John was determined that this day ſhould not paſs without my writing to you; his words are, 'Papa, remember how happy you were, and how kind Mr. and Mrs. Conſtable were.'—I have no news, excepting that the Exhibition was proſperous. But the attacks on the Royal Academy have commenced, and a Mr. Foggo has written a pamphlet, and a committee in the Houſe of Commons are enquiring into our affairs. I ſhould ſay, that the country, ignorant and ungrateful as it is in all liberal matters, does not deſerve the Academy.—My picture is in my room; it is going to its deſtination in Mr. Vernon's great houſe in Pall Mall."

The thoughts and wiſhes of Conſtable's ſecond ſon, Charles, had been turned towards the ſea from his childhood; he ſeemed, indeed, to have been born a ſailor as certainly as his father was born a painter. It coſt Conſtable many pangs to conquer his repugnance to ſuch a deſtiny for his boy, but he found it fruitleſs to oppoſe it, and placed him under the

CHAP. XV. 1835.

care of Captain Hopkins of the Buckinghamſhire, Eaſt Indiaman.

" Dear Leſlie, I ſend you a proof of the great ' Saliſbury' in its priſtine grandeur. My poor Charley's time is now very ſhort in the land of comfort. The ſhip ſails this week, and the houſe has been long in a ſtir with his outfit. There is no end to his wants. What would Diogenes, or an old ſow, (much the ſame thing), ſay to all the diſplay of trowſers, jackets, &c. by dozens, blue and white ſhirts by ſcores, and a ſupply of rattlin for his hammock, as he expects to be often cut down !—Poor dear boy! I try to joke about him, but my heart is broken at parting with him."

" To Mr. George Conſtable. Charlotte Street, September 12th. John's return, and ſo exceedingly well, has made me quite happy; he is delighted with his tour, and with your and Mrs. Conſtable's great kindneſs to him. I know not how I can be ſufficiently thankful to you and her. It has ſet up his health, and it is eſſential to his enſuing winter's ſtudies that he ſhould be ſtrong enough to meet the fag. I have had, as you may ſuppoſe, a moſt anxious and buſy time with Charles. I have done all for the beſt, and I regret all that I have done, when I conſider that it was to bereave me of this delightfully clever boy, who would have ſhone in my own profeſſion,* and who is now doomed to be driven about on the ruthleſs ſea. It is a ſad and melancholy life, but he ſeems made for a ſailor. Should he pleaſe the officers and ſtick to the ſhip, it will be more to his advantage than being in the navy,—a hateful tyranny, with ſtarvation into the bargain. Barrow told me not long ago, that they had twelve hundred midſhipmen they did not know what to do with at the Admiralty. In the midſt of my perplexities I have made a good portrait, and finiſhed and ſold my little ' Heath.' Mr.

* Charles Conſtable drew and etched beautifully for ſo young a practitioner.

Vernon has luckily paid me, for it has coſt me two hundred pounds to get Charles afloat. My pictures have come back from Worceſter; I wiſh I could get off going there to lecture, eſpecially as C * * * * has been drivelling a parcel of ſad ſtuff in the Worceſter paper in the name of Lorenzo; God knows, not Lorenzo de Medici; but it is all about *ideal art*, which in landſcape is ſheer nonſenſe, as they put it. Even Sir Joſhua is not quite clear in this."

"Charlotte Street, September 14th. My dear Leſlie, Nothing but my almoſt entire occupation within doors by my poor Charley, and various other matters, could have cauſed me ſo long to delay writing to you.* I have ſeveral letters from Charles from the ſhip, and at length a final one off Start Point, when the ſhip was leaving the land. He is a true ſailor, and makes up his mind to combat all difficulties in calms or ſtorms with an evenneſs of mind that little belongs to me, a landſman. They have had a rough buſineſs of it ſo far. He ſays Captain Hopkins is a delightful man. * * * Poor Charles hung about me when I parted from him; Roberts and Alfred were with me; he aſked if I could ſtay in the ſhip till next day, but I knew we muſt part, ſo we ſhook hands, and I ſaw him no more. It is a noble ſhip, the ſize of a ſeventy-four. * * * John is returned from France, much pleaſed and wonderfully ſtrong and well, ready and willing for a winter fag in London, where he enters his courſe of chymiſtry, anatomy, and materia medica. He was amuſed with France, but with the food he was annoyed, as he ſays they put vinegar into everything they eat and drink. I have made a beautiful drawing of Stone Henge; I venture to uſe ſuch an expreſſion to you.—I called on Mr. Banniſter, who is well, but ſadly low about the poor young men who were drowned; they were brothers of his ſon's wife.—The

* I was then out of town.

Academy has given Mrs. * * * forty pounds, ſo I hope Parliament will not put it down.—I muſt go to Worceſter, or they will think me ſhabby and a charlatan. I have got my picture back; they tell me I played firſt fiddle. John tells me of Lord Egremont ſhooting three brace of partridges and a hare on the 1ſt of September; wonderful at his age.

"To Mr. J. J. Chalon. October 29th. I much regret not ſeeing you laſt night, but I want moſt to ſee you by daylight, as I have been very buſy with Mr. Vernon's picture. Oiling out, making out, poliſhing, ſcraping, &c. ſeem to have agreed with it exceedingly.' The 'ſleet' and 'ſnow' have diſappeared, leaving in their places, ſilver, ivory, and a little gold. I wiſh you could give me a look, as it will go in a few days. I am glad you are all on the return, and I was exceedingly glad to hear you are all well."

"To Mr. George Conſtable. November 11th. We ſhall be delighted to ſee your ſon and any part of your family; John has a bed to ſpare in his own room. For myſelf, I only wiſh to be left to my painting-room. I do not think of much canvaſs this year; a ſize ſmaller will be better, and more of them; ſuch as will ſuit my friends' pockets; though 'tis too late in life for me to think of ever becoming a popular painter. Beſides, a knowledge of the world, and I have little of it, goes farther towards that than a knowledge of art."

"December 1ſt. My dear Leſlie, Will you be ſo kind as to call in your way to-morrow, ſo that we may go to the Academy together, and this will give me a fair opportunity of begging you to look at Mr. Vernon's picture by daylight. I don't wonder at your working ſo much on the ſame picture, now that I ſee what can be done by it. I want you, of all things, to ſee it now, for it has proved to me what my art is capable of when time can be given ſufficient to carry it home. So much you will take from me."

"December 9th. My dear Leſlie, I have had a letter from your ſiſter, with another from Mr. Carey, who has deſired me to ſend him a picture which I have not got, nor ever had. Through the kindneſs of your ſiſter, he has ſeen my book, and has taken a liking to 'The Sea Beach,' thinking, no doubt, it was done from ſomething more than a ſketch. I know not what to ſay, perhaps you will call on me to-morrow evening, and we will go together to hear Sir Martin. Mr. Vernon's picture is not yet gone to him; he wants it, but it never was half ſo good before, and I will do as I like with it, for I have ſtill a greater intereſt in it than any body elſe."

"To Mr. William Carpenter. Dear Sir, Accept my beſt thanks for the book, 'James's Italian School,' which I return. The 'Dictionary' is a moſt valuable work, but as I go on referring to it, I occaſionally meet with errors; and how can it be otherwiſe, when the ſources from whence the information is derived are ſo often erroneous? I ſhall not fail, however, to make memoranda when I meet with them to ſubmit to you. My character of Ruyſdael I have not yet found, but I can always write it for you, and better and better.*—I have never ceaſed to work on Mr. Vernon's picture ſince I ſaw you; it is at preſent with him in Pall Mall, but is coming back by the bearer for 'more laſt words.'—My painter's library is now getting very conſiderable.—I wrote a long note to you the other day, full of nonſenſe, which my man loſt by the way."

"To Mr. George Conſtable. Charlotte Street, December 16th. We ſhall be delighted to ſee you and any of your family; our own plans are thus. My daughters come home to-morrow, and will go in a few days to their aunt at Wimbledon. John and I have engaged to eat our Chriſtmas dinner

* I regret to ſay it was not found among his papers.

Chap. XV. 1835.

at Bergholt with my own family. We ſhall leave town on the 24th, and ſtay a week; in the ſecond week of January, therefore, we ſhall look for you. Can you bring with you the little Gainſborough, and the ſketch I made of your 'Mill?' John wants me to make a picture of it. I had a nice excurſion to Worceſter, and got on quite well with my ſermons; you will ſee my placards, and how well they are arranged. I would make a book, but I recollect the ſaying, 'O that mine enemy would write a book!' John is now at the door, by which I know it is exactly ten minutes paſt four."

CHAPTER XVI.

1836—1837.

Mr. Vernon's Picture. Contemplated Pictures of Arundel Mill, and of Stoke. Deſcription of Stoke Church. Engraving of "Saliſbury." Breakfaſt with Mr. Rogers. Lectures at the Royal Inſtitution. Exhibition of 1836. *Picture of "The Cenotaph erected by Sir George Beaumont to Sir J. Reynolds." Drawing of Stone Henge. Conſtable's two eldeſt Sons. Clouds and Skies. Death of Weſtall. Conſtable Viſitor in the Life Academy. Picture of Arundel Mill. Engraving of "Saliſbury Cathedral from the Meadows." Probable Cauſes of the decline of Conſtable's Health. His Death. His Funeral.*

"TO Mr. George Conſtable. January 12th, 1836. * * * I have never left my picture till now, when Mr. Vernon has allowed it to go to the Britiſh Gallery, and I am glad to get it there in its preſent ſtate, as you will be able to ſee it. When you come, will you bring the little ſketch of Arundel mill, as I contemplate a picture of it of a pretty good ſize."

1836.

"Charlotte Street, February 6th. My dear Purton. I am ſure theſe dear children would be diſappointed were they not to have the pleaſure of joining the young folks at your party on Saturday. We all, therefore, gladly avail ourſelves of your and Mrs. Purton's kind invitation, and will be with you at four o'clock that day, John, myſelf, and the ſailor; though

CHAP. XVI.
1836.

for myſelf there is always an uncertainty, I like to be poking about among my lumber, and loathe to go from home. I am glad you encourage me with 'Stoke.' What ſay you to a ſummer morning? July or Auguſt, at eight or nine o'clock, after a ſlight ſhower during the night, to enhance the dews in the ſhadowed part of the picture, under

'Hedge row elms and hillocks green.'

Then the plough, cart, horſe, gate, cows, donkey, &c. are all good paintable material for the foreground, and the ſize of the canvaſs ſufficient to try one's ſtrength, and keep one at full collar. Now pray keep to your canvaſs, and get up a heath ſcene, to which you are now fully competent, having the advantage of previous experience of that kind of practice on your large picture.* I am happy with theſe boys about me. My monitor, John, I always give up to, he is always in the right. Charley is a good boy, but a ſtraw will draw him aſide,—his character is eaſily miſtaken. He is every other night with his navigation maſter. Both boys are now reading their ſtudies by my ſide."

The large picture of Stoke was never painted; but a ſketch of the ſubject furniſhed a plate for "The Engliſh Landſcape." Of his intention in this ſketch, Conſtable ſays, "The impreſſive ſolemnity of a ſummer's noon, when attended as it often is during the heats of the ſeaſon, by thunder clouds, is attempted to be expreſſed in this picture; at the ſame time, the appearance of a noon-day rainbow is hinted at, when the arc it deſcribes is at its loweſt.—Suffolk, and many of the other eaſtern counties, abound in venerable Gothic churches, many of them of a ſize which cannot fail to ſtrike the ſtranger with admiration and ſurpriſe; and a

* Conſtable ſaid to Mr. Purton, "A large canvaſs will ſhew you what you cannot do, a ſmall one will only ſhew you what you can."

melancholy but ſtriking characteriſtic of theſe churches is, their being found in ſituations now comparatively lonely, ſome of them ſtanding in obſcure villages containing a few ſcattered houſes only, and thoſe but ill according with ſuch large and beautiful ſtructures; but it is thus accounted for: theſe ſpots were the ſeats of thoſe flouriſhing manufactories once ſo numerous in theſe counties, where they had from a remote period been eſtabliſhed, and were during the reigns of Henry VII.* and VIII. greatly increaſed by the continual arrival of the Flemings, who found here a refuge from the perſecutions of the Low Countries; as well as afterwards in the reign of Elizabeth, whom the courſe of events had raiſed to be the glory and the ſupport of Proteſtant Europe. The vaſt ſize of theſe noble ſtructures, with the charm that the mellowing hand of time has caſt over them, gives them an aſpect of extreme ſolemnity and grandeur, and they ſtand laſting monuments of the power and ſplendour of our eccleſiaſtical government, as well as of the piety and ſkill of our anceſtors. Stoke, though by no means one of the largeſt, certainly ranks with the churches alluded to. It was probably erected about the end of the thirteenth century. The length of the nave, with its continuous line of embattled parapet, and its finely proportioned chancel, may challenge the admiration of the architect, as well as its majeſtic tower, which from its commanding height may be ſaid to impart a portion of its own dignity to the ſurrounding country. In the church are many intereſting monuments; and here, as well as at Neyland, are many of the tombſtones of the clothiers; being moſtly laid in the pavement, they are much defaced, but are known to belong to them by the ſmall braſſes ſtill remaining."

* Dedham Church was built by Margaret Tudor, the mother of Henry VII. and bears her initials in many of its ornaments.

"February 15th. My dear Lucas. The 'Salisbury' is much admired in its present state, but still it is too heavy, especially when seen between 'The Lock' and 'The Drinking Boy.' Yet we must not break it up, and we must bear in recollection that the sentiment of the picture is that of solemnity, not gaiety; nothing garish, but the contrary; yet it must be bright, clear, alive, fresh, and all the front seen."

"March 18th. My dear Leslie. I never had such a morning in my life as that which I passed with Mr. Rogers. I long to see you, but the grievous place in which you are, cuts off everything. All that know you agree that the spot is fatal to your friendships; you will justly say, What are such friendships worth? But I am angry because I have wanted of late so very much to see you. Mr. Rogers thinks I am in the right road in my pursuit of landscape. He likes my plan of its history, and says 'nobody can do it so well;' this is encouraging. He was pleased with my pointing out the falling or shooting star in his exquisite Rubens.* But he is very quiet in his likes and dislikes; a delightful man, all intelligence, all benevolence and justice, and a generous upholder of art, living and dead. What pictures he has got! the best in London; and he has some noble old wood-cuts. It was pleasing to see him feed the sparrows while at breakfast, and to see how well they knew him. But he has some melancholy ideas of human nature. He said 'it is a debt genius must pay to be hated.'—I doubt this in general, but there is something like it in nature. I told him if he could catch one of those sparrows, and tie a bit of paper about its neck, and let it off again, the rest would peck it to death for being so *distinguished*."

* A moonlight; a scene of such perfect stillness, that the entire orb of the moon is reflected in a pool of water. There is a horse in the foreground, and you seem to hear him cropping the grass.

"March 26th. My dear Leſlie. I ſend you a few ſkies, ſuch as we thought might ſuit your picture. Perhaps a mountain aſh among the ſhepherds might be uſeful; I ſend a rough ſketch of one I made from a bed-room window where I ſlept; they are pretty with the berries. * * * I am ſorely perplexed with concerns not my own, in the picture way; I have in my houſe ſeveral works ſupplicating for places in the Exhibition; they are ſent to me becauſe it is well known what a fool I am.† * * * What ſtuff I am writing to you, but the worſt is, I am really ſerious in all I aſk of you. I encloſe a card of the Royal Inſtitution, that you may be convinced of my folly and activity, but I am not yet ſelling ſpruce beer in the ſtreets, like * * *."

"To Mr. George Conſtable. May 12th. I am pretty full handed, and ſorely perplexed for time, owing to the numerous irons I have put in the fire. I have engaged to deliver four lectures, as the card I encloſe will let you ſee; they will comprehend a pretty full account of the hiſtory of landſcape. * * * I got up a tolerably good picture for the Academy, not the Mill, which I had hoped to do, and which was prettily laid in as far as chiaroſcuro, but I found I could not do both; and ſo I preferred to ſee Sir Joſhua Reynolds's name and Sir George Beaumont's once more in the catalogue, for the laſt time at the old houſe. I hear it is liked, but I ſee no newſpaper, not allowing one to come into my houſe. I ſend you a catalogue, and marked, I believe, pretty fairly. The Exhibition is much liked. Wilkie's pictures are very fine, and Turner has outdone himſelf; he ſeems to paint with tinted ſteam, ſo evaneſcent and ſo airy. The public think he is laughing at them, and ſo they laugh at him in return. The non-members are very powerful; Charles Landſeer, Herbert, Partridge, Knight, and

† I was then on the arranging committee at the Academy.

Roberts. The Prefident was never better, but his health gives way under his duties. I dined with Wilkie laft week, and met Allan, who is very entertaining. Wilkie recommended to me to paint a large picture for over the line next year."

The picture mentioned in the beginning of this letter was of the Cenotaph erected by Sir George Beaumont to the memory of Reynolds. It might feem as if Conftable had confulted the tafte of his late friend in choofing the autumnal tints for the foliage of a fcene taken from Sir George's grounds, but his doing fo arofe naturally from his having made his ftudies from it late in the autumn. In this fine picture, every way worthy of fo interefting a fubject, Conftable introduced nothing living, except a deer in the foreground, and a robin red-breaft perched on one of the angles of the monument. In defcribing "The Cenotaph" in the catalogue, he quoted the lines infcribed on it, written by Wordfworth at Sir George Beaumont's requeft:

"Ye lime trees ranged before this hallow'd urn,
Shoot forth with lively power at fpring's return;
And be not flow a ftately growth to rear
Of pillars branching off from year to year,
Till they have learn'd to frame a darkfome aifle,
That may recal to mind that awful pile
Where Reynolds, 'mid our country's nobleft dead,
In the laft fanctity of fame is laid.
There, though by right the excelling painter fleep
Where death and glory a joint fabbath keep,
Yet not the lefs his fpirit would hold dear
Self-hidden praife and friendfhip's private tear:
Hence in my patrimonial grounds have I
Raifed this frail tribute to his memory;
From youth a zealous follower of the art
That he profeff'd, attach'd to him in heart;
Admiring, loving, and with grief and pride
Feeling what England loft when Reynolds died."

Conftable exhibited with this picture a magnificent drawing

in water colours of Stone Henge, of a large ſize.

He was now wholly occupied in preparing the lectures which he delivered in the ſummer of this year at the Royal Inſtitution, Albemarle Street, beginning on the 26th of May. The ticket mentioned in the following note was an admiſſion to theſe lectures.

"Dear William Carpenter, I ſend a ticket, as you requeſted, to Mrs. Carpenter; and if your ſon is, as I ſincerely hope, better, he may accompany her and yourſelf, as both may poſſibly be included among her friends. Don't trouble yourſelf about Lanzi any farther, as I have now pretty well done with him. He is an old twaddler, but the labour he ſpares is immenſe, and certainly his arrangement, his hiſtory, and the marking of the epochs is admirable and very uſeful. Yours truly, J. Conſtable."

"To Mr. George Conſtable. Charlotte Street, September 16th. My dear Friend. It is a very long time ſince I have written to you, or ſince I have had the pleaſure of hearing from you. I am anxious to know how you and Mrs. Conſtable and all your family are, and what have been your occupations in the way of the arts, in antiquities, and in natural hiſtory. My dear John is always engroſſed with ſome ſtudy or other; he is remarkably well, and is wholly devoted to Latin and Greek. I know not, nor does he know himſelf, exactly, what he will ultimately be, but either a clergyman or a phyſician. He is bruſhing up for Cambridge; this I regret, but it is a ſelfiſh feeling; I cannot bear to part with him. I live a life of more ſolitude than you would ſuſpect for the midſt of London, and in ſuch a purſuit, ſo wide a field as the arts. My ſon Charles is returned from the Eaſt Indies; the voyage has been a hard one, but it is all for the beſt. All his viſionary and poetic ideas of the ſea and a ſeaman's life are fled, the reality only remains; and a ſad thing the reality is. But in the huge

CHAP. XVI.
1836.

floating mafs there is an order, and an habitual good conduct, which muft be of advantage to a youth of ardent mind, and one who has never been controlled. Charley is preparing for another voyage, and the fhip fails in the middle of November for China. * * * I have not been out of town once this year, but for an hour or two. I diflike to leave home, but enjoy an excurfion very much when I am away. I have an invitation to the Ifle of Wight, but I dare fay I fhall not go. I muft go into Suffolk, and take my failor boy with me. John was there this fummer for five weeks; he was a great favourite with his aunts and my brothers; indeed, John is fure to win his way, for he never gives offence to any living creature. I have lately painted a Heath that I prefer to any of my former efforts; it is about two feet fix, painted for a very old friend, an amateur, who well knows how to appreciate it, for I cannot paint down to ignorance. Leflie was here to-day; he is going to Petworth in ten days. I have never feen fuch fcenery as your country affords; I prefer it to any other for my pictures;—woods—lanes—fingle trees—rivers—cottages—barns—mills—and, above all, fuch beautiful heath fcenery."

"October 29th. My dear Leflie. It feems a very long time fince we met, or that I have heard from you. I fhould, as you will believe, be delighted to have a letter, if it is only to give me a hint of what is going on at Petworth. I truft you will hardly quit fo hofpitable a roof till this ebullition of premature winter is paffed; the fnow is very deep indeed, and all fince four o'clock this morning. My boys are very good boys. I have not left home for a day, nor can I till John is at Cambridge and Charley at fea. O what a melancholy, dirty life is a failor's! but he is going out again with the fhip to China. There are to be twelve or thirteen midfhipmen, and where they find a pighole for fo many, I know not. * * * I hear a fad account of poor Mr. Bannifter, who will never leave his room again, nor fee any more of his friends, nor fing any more of his delightful fongs."

"My dear Leflie. * * * My poor Charley has had fad weather in his progrefs to the Downs, where he is now pof-fibly wind bound. The frightful gale on Tuefday is well defcribed by him. The fhip was anchored by the Nore light, and rode out the ftorm with little damage; but the wrecks around and within two hundred yards were fhocking; one large fhip floated paft, bottom upwards, and after the gale he faw feven large hulls in tow with fteam boats. In their paffage to the Downs they faw fome on the Goodwin Sands, and fome on the beach under the Foreland."

"December 8th. My dear Leflie. * * * Mr. Sheep-fhanks means to have my 'Glebe Farm' or 'Green Lane,' of which you have a fketch; this is one of the pictures on which I reft my little pretenfions to futurity. * * * I hope you are all well, and fafely returned, and the better for the excurfion. Will you come to the laft lecture given in the old houfe? if fo, call and dine here. * * * Poor Weftall!"

"To Mr. George Conftable. December 12th. I return the book which you lent me fo long ago. My obfervations on clouds and fkies are on fcraps and bits of paper, and I have never yet put them together fo as to form a lecture, which I fhall do, and probably deliver at Hampftead next fummer. I wifh I had fecured your fine old willow, which you fay is now no more, (what a pity), for my lecture on trees. If you want anything more about atmofphere, and I can help you, write to me. Fofter's is the beft book; he is far from right, ftill he has the merit of breaking much ground. * * * Poor Weftall! I went to his funeral on Sa-turday."

"December 30th. My dear Leflie. I am vexed with myfelf for having fo long delayed to write to you, to thank you for your kind invitation to these dear children. This fearful weather intimidates me, but it seems little likely to change; and all my dreads, and all I can say about the danger of such an *excursion into the country* at such a time, gives no alarm whatever to the children, and they insist on my coming out of my lurking place, where I thought I had lain up for the winter, and so I must accompany them to your house on Monday to keep new year's day. Now all this I do, and let them do, only on condition that Mrs. Leslie and you dine with me on Wednesday. We have venison from my old friend, Lady Dysart, and are almost alone; only Mr. and Miss Spedding, very old and esteemed friends of my poor wife. Prithee come, '*life is short, friendship is sweet;*' these were the last words of poor Fisher to me in his last invitation.—My month in the Life School is March. I have concluded on setting the three figures of the 'St. Peter Martyr,' for I am determined to sift that picture to the bottom.* I have by me a very old print of the subject five years before Titian's picture, done from the one which occupied the same place in the Dominican Church. The picture was by Jacopo del Fiore, or 'Jemmy of the flower;' the flower stands for his name in the print, forming a very expressive figure."

The invitation contained in this letter was Constable's last written one to me. Without attaching to coincidences such as these, any superstitious importance, they are too affecting to pass unnoticed. The expression, also, which follows, with regard to March, which proved to be the last month of his life, is very remarkable.

In a note to Mr. Lucas, after thanking him for some proofs of the "Salisbury," and making some remarks on

* His lectures, in which he says much of the 'Peter Martyr,' will explain this.

1836.

them, he continues: "God preserve your excellent wife, and give her a happy hour; I have not forgotten my own anxieties at such times, though they are never to return. I beg to thank you again and again for the most lovely winter piece I ever saw.* You have caused the last of the old year to slip away from me with pleasurable feelings; we have now only a quarter of an hour left of the year 1836! Farewell."

1837.

"January 19th, 1837. Dear Lucas. We must keep this proof as a criterion, and get as much of it as we can. The bow is grand whole, provided it is clear and tender. How I wish I could scratch and tear away with your tools on the steel, just as old * * *† wanted to fly up to Langham hill, and tear the trees and hedges all up by the roots; but I can't do it, and your quiet way is, I well know, the best and only way."

"To Mr. George Constable. February 17th. * * * I cannot give much account of myself, but we have all been well, and have escaped this sad influenza, which has been the desolation of so many hundreds of all ages. John is the most tender of us all; he works hard, as he wishes so much to get himself fit for Cambridge. I believe he goes in October. As the spring gets up he would be delighted to pass a few days with you; he looks for an hour at his old fishing place near the Black Duck. For myself, I am at work on a beautiful subject, Arundel Mill, for which I am indebted to your friendship. It is, and shall be, my best picture; the size, three or four feet; it is safe for the Exhibition, as we have as much as six weeks good. We hold our first general

* An impression of the "Salisbury" taken when the plate was imperfectly filled with ink, and which had accidentally the appearance of winter. Mr. Lucas had sent it to Constable as a curiosity.

† A farmer, who by his restless grasping disposition having made some of his neighbours as well as himself very uncomfortable, uttered this singular wish.

meeting at the new houſe on Monday, and a very noble houſe it is.* I am viſitor next month in the Life Academy, which I regret, as it cuts up my time; but I relieve, by exchange, Turner. My great Saliſbury print is done; I ſhall call it 'The Rainbow;' you ſhall ſoon receive a proof of it. Remember me moſt kindly to Mrs. Conſtable, and all your family. Pray write to me ſoon; I long to know that all is well with you."

"February 25th. My dear Leſlie. I know not how to reply to your kind requeſt to come to you on Monday, as I am engaged with my *aſſaſſin* on that day, and ſhall be employed with him all the week; in other words, I commence my viſitorſhip at the Academy, and I ſhall ſet Titian's figure of the aſſaſſin in the 'Peter Martyr.' I ſhall turn Fitzgerald into the *fallen ſaint*, and the remaining figure of the monk I give to Emmet, who is an obliging and well behaved man, and anxious for a turn at the Academy; will not this flying monk ſicken him? I have been ſadly hindered, and my picture is not worth any thing at preſent. Roberts was at Hampſtead on Thurſday. All my little girls are well and happy, and I really believe they cannot be in better hands than with that excellent woman, Miſs Noble."

"March 18th. Dear Lucas. Mr. Cook, the Academician, ſaid yeſterday, that the 'Saliſbury was a grand looking thing.' I hope that obliging, and moſt ſtrange and odd ruffian, your printer, will be allowed to have juſt his own way in printing the plate, for I now ſee we muſt not be too full, otherwiſe it will, as he ſays, 'only be fit for a parcel of painters.'"

No date. "Dear Lucas. The print is a noble and beautiful thing; entirely improved and entirely made perfect;

* Conſtable never joined in the popular cry againſt the architect of the National Gallery, for not building a larger houſe than the ground given for the purpoſe permitted.

the bow is noble, and is now a neck or nothing bufinefs; it is ftartling and unique. I have mentioned to your clever and agreeable ruffian, who is in high good humour, two things; the light on the tower under the trees muft be made thus" (here a fketch) "inftead of thus;" (another fketch;) "alfo the little fpot on the cloud your ruffian will fhew you, and he pointed out a good way of doing it; half an hour will alter both. Thank you for the pains you have taken with the bow; it is lovely. I hope you are better. I muft now difmifs the ruffian, for he is getting too knowing for John and me."

"Dear Lucas. Your man has told me that there is every reafon to know that the 'Salifbury' will print both full and rich. Tone, tone, is the moft feductive and inviting quality a picture or print can poffefs; it is the firft thing feen, and like a flower, invites to our examination of the plant itfelf. * * * Your man is a droll fellow. I have given him two fhillings, but it was before he had told me that he 'is given to break out of a Saturday night, but it does not laft long, and generally goes off on the Sunday morning.' He cannot help it, he cannot even account for it, but fo it is. This is his own gratuitous account of himfelf. What a creature is man, either cultivated or not, either civilized or wild! I offered him fome rum and water, and gin and water, all of which he refufed almoft with loathing; perhaps his hour is not yet come."

"To Mr. Samuel Lane. March. My dear Lane. * * * Pray keep your children within doors this grievous weather; I am told nothing breeds whooping cough fo much as fuch bitter eafterly winds as are now prevailing. I am out every evening from five to nine at the old Academy, vifitor in the Life."

The recollection that Conftable was very fenfitive to atmofpheric influences, and that his health had many times fuffered in the early part of the ſpring, recalls to my mind the paſſage from Shakſpeare I have moſt often heard him repeat :

> " daffodils,
> That come before the ſwallow dares, and take
> The winds of March with beauty,—"

they were, now, indeed, winds of ominous import to him.

He was the laſt viſitor who officiated in the Life Academy within the walls of Somerſet Houſe. On the concluding evening of his attendance, he made a ſhort addreſs to the ſtudents, pointing out to them the many advantages our Academy affords, and cautioning them not to be in too great haſte to exchange theſe for inſtruction in the ſchools of France, Germany, or Italy. He was of opinion that the beſt ſchool of art will always exiſt in that country where there are the beſt living artiſts, and not merely where there are the greateſt number of works of the old maſters. He did not admit that the French excel the beſt of the Engliſh artiſts in drawing, a point generally conceded to them; and in ſupport of his own opinion he quoted that of Mr. Stothard, who ſaid, " The French are very good *mathematical* draughtſmen, but life and motion are the eſſence of drawing, and their figures remind us too much of ſtatues. In the ſlighteſt pen and ink ſketches of Raphael, however irregular the proportions, you have the real principle of good drawing, —his figures live and move."

This is but a recollection, at ſome diſtance of time, of what Conſtable told me he ſaid. I wrote to Mr. Macliſe, who was then a ſtudent in the Life School, to aſk if he could help me to anything more, and that gentleman very kindly ſent me the following note, encloſing a pencil ſketch he had made of Conſtable in the Academy.

" 14, Ruſſell Place. My dear ſir. I cannot call to mind the ſubſtance of any particular addreſs of Conſtable when he was viſitor, but I recollect that he conſtantly addreſſed us collectively; or rather, whatever obſervation he had to make, he made aloud; and this was very frequent. Every evening he ſaid ſomething, generally relating to the model he had ſet, and in favour of certain pictureſque accompaniments which he thought might always be introduced with propriety;* he was, with the ſtudents, a moſt popular viſitor. The little ſketch was made under the diſadvantage of my being on the upper and back ſeat, looking down on him as he ſat on the front and lower one in the Life School, and muſt have been when he ſet the Eve, although I ſhould not have thought it was ſo long ago as 1830.—I remain, very faithfully yours, D. Macliſe."

"March 29th. Dear Lucas. I am greatly pleaſed to ſee how well you are preparing for the new bow;† the proof is about what I want; I mean that you took hence. I took from the elder buſh a bloſſom to the left, you will poſſibly do the ſame. Go on as you think proper. I go to a general meeting on Thurſday, to-morrow evening, and I dine at the

* This reminds me of what I have often heard Conſtable ſay, that he "never could look at any object unconnected with a background or other objects," and he thought the ſtudents might very advantageouſly to themſelves be taught at an early age to look at nature in this way. For this reaſon all his figures were ſet with backgrounds and other accompaniments. A difference of opinion exiſts as to the expediency of this method of teaching, and it is one of the charges brought againſt the Academy, that the ſtudents are placed under the care of various inſtructors, who have each their own notions; and yet this may poſſibly be an advantage, when it is conſidered that the opinions of any one man can ſcarcely be right on all points; and alſo that the Life is the higheſt ſchool in the Academy, and that in which the ſtudents may be ſuppoſed to have arrived at an age to judge in ſome meaſure for themſelves; and that they are not placed under more than one maſter until they have entered the Life School.

† From the manner in which this is expreſſed, it would appear that the rainbow had been taken out, and a new one was to be put in, but this was not the caſe; the "new bow" was the one with which Conſtable had before expreſſed himſelf ſo much pleaſed.

Charter Houſe on Saturday. We cannot fail with a proper bow. The ruffian is ſo delightful, that no one would for a moment judge him to be one; ſo bland, ſo delighted with John, and John with him; they are both in the room."

This note may, perhaps, be the laſt Conſtable ever wrote. The engagement mentioned in it to dine with Dr. Fiſher, the father of Archdeacon Fiſher, at the Charter Houſe, was for Saturday, the 1ſt of April, but the dawn of that day he never ſaw. His conſtitution was undermined to a degree of which he was not himſelf aware, far leſs his friends, for ſedentary and irregular as were his habits, he had not the look of a valetudinarian, nor would his age have been eaſily gueſſed from his appearance. Not long before the time of which I am writing, I had remarked to him that I ſhould gueſs him to be younger than he really was, to which he anſwered,

> "In my youth I never did apply
> Hot and rebellious liquors to my blood, &c."

But the reader has ſeen how far his mind was from being an equable one. In reference to his art, he would ſometimes ſay he "thanked Heaven he had no imagination," though in reality, few men ever had more; and if it heightened all his enjoyments, it greatly deepened all his ſorrows. He had fully proved the truth of Burns's lines:

> "Dearly bought the hidden treaſure
> Finer feelings can beſtow;
> Chords that vibrate ſweeteſt pleaſure
> Thrill the deepeſt notes of woe."

Had Conſtable been even leſs ſenſitive, the perpetual activity of a mind that could not reſt muſt have affected his conſtitution at no very late period. His very amuſements conſiſted of ſtudy. I do not think he ever read a novel in his life. It was on no narrow principle that he objected to works of fiction, but they did not intereſt him. I remember ſoon after the death of Mrs. Conſtable, when books were propoſed to him as a relief to his mind, he ſaid, "I ſhould be delighted to read 'Tom Thumb,' if it could amuſe me." If her loſs had been but that of an aſſiſtant in his parental duties, and a partaker of the cares of a family, he muſt have felt it daily; how much more heavy, then, muſt have been his affliction for the loſs of a wife in whom no hope formed by him during the days of courtſhip had been diſappointed, excepting the hope of her longer continuance on earth. His married years were unqueſtionably the happieſt of his exiſtence. In Fiſher and the younger Dunthorne, he was alſo bereft of friends whoſe places were never ſupplied to him; and his profeſſional life had been a continual ſtruggle for the eſtimation which he felt he deſerved, but which he had now ceaſed to expect. If his intimate friends were but imperfectly acquainted with the real ſtate of his feelings, thoſe who knew him but ſlightly, and who ſeldom ſaw him unleſs ſurrounded by ſmiles of his own creating, could not have believed how much he was now a prey to melancholy and anxious thoughts; thoughts, no doubt, in part, both the cauſe and effect of declining health. The reader will remember a paſſage in one of his letters to Mr. Fiſher, in which he ſays, "all my indiſpoſitions have their ſource in my mind. It is when I am reſtleſs and unhappy that I become ſuſceptible of cold, damp, heats, and ſuch nonſenſe."

On Thurſday, the 30th of March, I met him at a general aſſembly of the Academy, and as the night, though very cold, was fine, he walked a great part of the way home with me. The moſt trifling occurrences of that evening remain on my memory. As we proceeded along Oxford Street, he heard a child cry on the oppoſite ſide of the way; the griefs of childhood never failed to arreſt his attention, and he croſſed over to a little beggar girl who had hurt her knee; he gave her a ſhilling and ſome kind words, which, by ſtopping her tears, ſhowed that the hurt was not very ſerious, and we continued our walk.—Some pecuniary loſſes he had lately met with had diſturbed him, but more becauſe they involved him with perſons diſpoſed to take advantage of his good feelings, than from their amount. He ſpoke of theſe with ſome degree of irritation, but turned to more agreeable ſubjects, and we parted at the weſt end of Oxford Street, laughing.—I never ſaw him again alive.

The whole of the next day he was buſily engaged finiſhing his picture of Arundel Mill and Caſtle. One or two of his friends who called on him ſaw that he was not well, but they attributed this to confinement and anxiety with his picture, which was to go in a few days to the Exhibition. In the evening, he walked out for a ſhort time on a charitable errand connected with the Artiſts' Benevolent Fund. He returned about nine o'clock, ate a hearty ſupper, and feeling chilly, had his bed warmed, a luxury he rarely indulged in. It was his cuſtom to read in bed; between ten and eleven he had read himſelf to ſleep, and his candle, as uſual, was removed by a ſervant. Soon after this, his eldeſt ſon, who had been at the theatre, returned home, and while preparing for bed in the next room, his father awoke in great pain, and called to him. So little was Conſtable alarmed, however, that he at firſt refuſed to ſend for medical aſſiſtance; he took ſome rhubarb and magneſia, which produced ſickneſs, and he drank copiouſly of warm water, which occaſioned vomiting; but the pain increaſing, he deſired that Mr. Michele, his near neighbour, ſhould be ſent for, who very ſoon attended. In the mean time Conſtable had fainted, his ſon ſuppoſing he had fallen aſleep; Mr. Michele inſtantly ordered ſome brandy to be brought, the bed room of the patient was at the top of the houſe, the ſervant had to run down ſtairs for it, and before it could be procured, life was extinct; and within half an hour of the firſt attack of pain.

A poſt mortem inveſtigation was made by Profeſſor Partridge in the preſence of Mr. George Young and Mr. Michele, but ſtrange to ſay, the extreme pain Conſtable had ſuffered could only be traced to indigeſtion; no indications of diſeaſe were any where diſcovered ſufficient, in the opinion of thoſe gentlemen, to have produced at that time a fatal reſult. Mr. Michele, in a letter to me, deſcribing all he had witneſſed, ſays, "It is barely poſſible that the prompt application of a ſtimulant might have ſuſtained the vital principle, and induced reaction in the functions neceſſary to the maintenance of life."

Conſtable's eldeſt ſon was prevented from attending the funeral by an illneſs, brought on by the painful excitement he had ſuffered; but the two brothers of the deceaſed and a few of his moſt intimate friends followed the body to Hampſtead,* where ſome of the gentlemen reſiding there, who had known Conſtable, voluntarily joined the proceſſion in the churchyard. The vault which contained the remains of his wife was opened, he was laid by her ſide, and the inſcription which he had placed on the tablet over it,

"Eheu! quam tenui e filo pendet
Quidquid in vita maximè arridet!"

might well be applied to the loſs his family and friends had now ſuſtained. The funeral ſervice was read by one of thoſe friends, the Rev. T. J. Judkin, whoſe tears fell faſt on the book as he ſtood by the tomb.

* I cannot but recall here a paſſage in a letter to Mr. Fiſher, written by Conſtable nearly ten years before his death, in which, after ſpeaking of having removed his family to Hampſtead, he ſays, "I could gladly exclaim, here let me take my everlaſting reſt!"

CHAPTER XVII.

Picture of Arundel Mill and Castle exhibited, 1837. Presentation of the Picture of "The Cornfield" to the National Gallery. Letter from Mr. Andrew Robertson. Constable and Hogarth compared. Traits of Constable's Character described by Mr. George Field. Farther Particulars. Selections from Constable's miscellaneous Memoranda. Note from Mr. Collins. Pictures injured by cutting, enlarging, &c. Forgeries of Constable's Pictures. Recollections of his Sayings and Opinions. The Author's Visit to East Bergholt, in company with Mr. Purton and John Constable, Junior. Mr. Purton's Remarks on Constable's Art. Sketch Books.

BY a law of the Royal Academy works, not before exhibited, of a deceased artist are allowed to appear in the first exhibition, and that one only, which follows his death; and Constable's picture of "Arundel Mill and Castle" was considered by his friends sufficiently completed to be sent to the Academy. He had begun two smaller pictures, but they were not forward enough to be admitted even as sketches; and the "Mill" was therefore the only work of his pencil that graced the Exhibition of 1837, the first in Trafalgar Square. The scene was one entirely after his own heart, and he had taken great pains to render it complete in all its details; and in that silvery brightness of effect which was a chief aim with him, in the latter years of his life, it is not ſurpaſſed by any production of his pencil. It remains in the poſſeſſion of his children, being one of thoſe reſerved from the ſale of his works, by his eldeſt ſon.

Before the property Conſtable left, in pictures, was diſperſed, it was ſuggeſted by Mr. Purton that one of his works ſhould be purchaſed by a ſubſcription among the admirers of his genius, and preſented to the National Gallery. He propoſed that the large picture of " Saliſbury from the meadows," ſhould be choſen as being from its magnitude, ſubject, and grandeur of treatment, the beſt ſuited to the public collection. But it was thought by the majority of Conſtable's friends that the boldneſs of its execution rendered it leſs likely to addreſs itſelf to the general taſte than others of his works, and the picture of " The Corn Field," painted in 1826, was ſelected in its ſtead.—As I felt much intereſted in this proceeding, I wrote on the ſubject to thoſe of Conſtable's friends whom I thought likely to join in it, and from among the replies I received, I truſt Mr. Andrew Robertſon will forgive the publication of his.

" 19, Berners Street, Auguſt 21ſt, 1837. My dear Sir, I have had this day the melancholy gratification, if I may combine ſuch terms, of again viſiting the gallery of our lamented friend Conſtable. The great number of his works left in his poſſeſſion proves too clearly how little his merits were felt by thoſe who could afford, and ought to have poſſeſſed them; and that unleſs ſome ſuch a meaſure had been adopted as that which, to the honour of his friends, has been carried into effect, it is too probable that his works would have fallen into the hands of artiſts only, for a mere trifle, and remained comparatively buried, till dug up, as it were, and brought to light in another age. Much, indeed, ſhould I regret to have loſt the opportunity of having my name enrolled in the liſt of thoſe who bear teſtimony to the merits of genius ſo original, ſo Engliſh, ſo alive to the beauties of ſimple nature, and of whom it may be ſaid ſo truly, that he was

'Nullius addictus jurare in verba magiſtri.'

He had his peculiarities, but they were not in conception, nor in the way in which he looked at nature; he ſaw clearly, and not through a glaſs darkly, nor through other men's eyes. His peculiarities were only in his execution, and in the admirable picture ſelected for his monument in the National Gallery, we find all his truth of conception, with leſs of the manner that was objected to, than in moſt of his later works. I remain, my dear Sir, always truly and ſincerely yours, A. Robertſon."

In ſome points of Conſtable's character a ſtriking reſemblance may be traced to that of Hogarth. Though their walks of art were wide apart, yet each formed a ſtyle more truly original than that of any of his cotemporaries, and this in part, prevented each from enjoying the fame to which he was entitled.* They both incurred the imputation of vanity, perhaps from much vainer men, becauſe they vindicated their own merits.—Hogarth expreſſed in a witty etching ("The Battle of the Pictures") his ſenſe of the injuſtice he ſuffered from the connoiſſeurs, and Conſtable ſpoke his opinions openly of the critics; and with point, truth, and freedom, as did Hogarth, of cotemporary artiſts, and each by ſo doing, made bitter enemies.—In concluſion, they were both genuine Engliſhmen; warmly attached to the character and inſtitutions of their country; alike quick in detecting cant and quackery, not only in Religion and Politics, but in Taſte and in the Arts; and though they ſometimes may have carried the

* Hogarth's prints were popular; for his wit, his ſatire, and his matchleſs power of expreſſion were felt;—but the taſte and richneſs of his compoſitions, and the beauty of his colour, in other words *his art*, was not. One circumſtance alone proves this,—he could not obtain for the ſix pictures of the "Marriage-à-la-Mode," together, more than one hundred and ten guineas.

prejudices of their John Bull-iſm too far, they each deſerved well of their country, as ſteady opponents to the influence of foreign vice, folly, and bad taſte; in which, however, Hogarth's claſs of ſubjects enabled him to exert himſelf with far the moſt effect.

The object I have endeavoured to keep in view throughout the preceding pages being to give an account of Conſtable's life and occupations as much as poſſible in his own words, my extracts from his letters have been neceſſarily limited to paſſages relating chiefly to himſelf; but had not this, and the reſerve due to other perſons, prevented my quoting theſe papers more at length, it would be ſeen that in very many of them his own affairs occupied the leaſt part of his attention. Many indeed of his notes and letters have been entirely unavailable to me on this account, excepting in as far as they have added to the high opinion I had before formed of the kindlineſs of his nature.

My friend, Mr. George Field, who knew him long and intimately, ſays, in a letter to me, "Of Conſtable's benevolent feelings and acts a volume of inſtances might be recorded, and no better proof of his genuine worth can be adduced than that affluence did not ſpoil the artiſt, while it very much improved the man."

In another of his obliging communications to me, Mr. Field ſays, "At all times of the day, at night, and in all ſeaſons of the year, Conſtable had inexpreſſible delight in viewing the works of nature. I have been out with him after all colour of the landſcape had diſappeared, and objects were ſeen only as ſkeletons and maſſes, yet his eye was ſtill active for his art. 'Theſe were the things,' ſaid he, 'that Gainſborough ſtudied, and of which we have ſo many exquiſite ſpecimens in his drawings.'* Conſtable found undeco-

* Several very fine ſketches by Gainſborough, in black and white chalk, hung in Conſtable's parlour.

Chap. XVII.

rated beauties in the nakedneſs of winter when he laviſhed admiration on the anatomy of trees, &c. He well knew the *language* of a windmill, and by its expreſſions could tell you of the winds, and of the ſkies, and beſides this he knew many other tongues that are not written, and are too little ſtudied and underſtood for the boundleſs authorities they furniſh to artiſts, to poets, to philoſophers, and all true lovers of the wiſdom of nature. To this attachment to nature and averſeneſs to factitious ſtudies, he probably owed the originality of thought, expreſſion, and manners by which he was diſtinguiſhed; which, however ſometimes ſavouring of ruſticity and deſtitute of the artifice and convention of ſociety, were marked by an unreſtrained amiableneſs and real refinement which were his own. This claſh of nature and artifice appears alſo to have given riſe to the inceſſant workings of a humorous ſatire, by which he continually levelled the pretenſions of others, which although not entirely inoffenſive was generally juſt, and few ventured to face it. It ſubjected him and his peculiarities, however, to aſſailments from anonymous, injudicious, and pointleſs criticiſm, which a leſs genuine and more courtly carriage might have ſaved him from, or transformed into praiſe or fame, patronage or profit. Theſe anonymous attacks ſerved him for a ſpur, and his ſatirical humour for a theme, with which he entertained his friends at the time, although his heart was naturally too affectionate to all the world to be inſenſible to praiſe, for affection ſeeks affection, and praiſe is love. It is remarkable of our moſt eminent landſcape painters, in common with genius in other ſhapes, that they have been ſubjected by this natural independence of thought and action to frequent miſpriſe and neglect during their lives, and the incomparable Wilſon was an inſtance of it. But in him this quality wrought more aſperity than in Conſtable. Was this to be attributed to difference in the circumſtances of fortune or of diſpoſition in theſe great painters?"

Theſe extracts from the letters of Mr. Field, contain but a part of the aſſiſtance with which he has favoured me.

In the winter ſeaſons, after he could afford it, Conſtable frequently ſent clothes and blankets to be diſtributed among the poor of his native village; indeed no feature of his character was more amiable than his ſympathy with the ſufferings of the humbler claſſes, and his conſideration for their feelings in all reſpects. He poſſeſſed that innate, and only real gentility, of which the teſt is conduct towards inferiors and ſtrangers; he was a gentleman to the pooreſt of his ſpecies,——a gentleman in a ſtage coach, nay more,——a gentleman at a ſtage coach inn dinner.

A mind like Conſtable's, united to a nervous temperament ſo ſenſitive, could not be indifferent to muſic. In his youth he was a good flute player, but he laid the inſtrument aſide as he found that painting required his whole attention. Preferring ſimplicity and expreſſion to an oſtentatious diſplay of art, I remember that at a muſical party during a trio in Italian, with which his ears were ſtunned, and which was only fit for the vaſt area of the Opera Houſe, he whiſpered to me, "I dare ſay it is very fine, for it is very diſagreeable; but if theſe people were to make ſuch a noiſe before your door or mine, we ſhould ſend for the police to take them away."

The following may be placed here as connected with this ſubject. I found it among his papers in his hand writing; and it was no doubt a draught of a paragraph inſerted by him in a provincial newſpaper.

"Died on the 29th ult. at Great Wenham, Thomas Cheverton, aged 48 years, leaving a widow and nine children. This individual, although in the humble condition of a day labourer, may fairly claim ſome further notice in our obituary from the circumſtance of his being gifted with a moſt extraordinary voice; one of the fulleſt, richeſt, and ſweeteſt counter tenors ever, perhaps, heard. He could with eaſe aſcend to D, and even to E in Alt. His knowledge in the ſcience of muſic was by no means inconſiderable, and his appearance in the humble choirs of the village churches in his immediate neighbourhood was always hailed with ſilent ſatisfaction even by the beſt educated people. He was gentle and affectionate to his family, who are now thrown on a world, too buſy, it is feared, to caſt a look on beings ſo humble, or to extend the hand of charity to objects ſo unobtruſive and friendleſs. Auguſt 1ſt, 1831."

Among the papers with which I found this, were many ſeparate ſcraps, containing notes, memoranda, and quotations, many of them, no doubt, intended to aſſiſt him in his lectures. The following are ſelections from them, and from a few of his unpubliſhed letters.

"When young, I was extremely fond of reading poetry, and alſo fond of muſic, and I played myſelf a little; but as I advanced in life and in art, I ſoon gave up the latter; and now after thirty years, I muſt ſay that the ſiſter arts have leſs hold on my mind in its occaſional ramblings from my one purſuit than the ſciences, eſpecially the ſtudy of geology, which, more than any other, ſeems to ſatisfy my mind. November 10th, 1835."

"The difference between power and truth is very material in painting, as it is in other matters of taſte. It may be illuſtrated by an anecdote of Barry and Garrick. Few actors had more power than Barry; indeed, he was able for ſome time to divide the admiration of the town with Garrick. They played Lear in competition fifty nights; but the public were ſet right by an epigram, which placed the diſtinction between them in the proper light, the laſt line of which was

'To Barry we give loud applauſe, to Garrick only tears.'"

"'Syſtem can by no means be thrown aſide. Without ſyſtem, the field of nature would be a pathleſs wilderneſs; but ſyſtem ſhould be ſubſervient to, not the main object of, our purſuit.'—WHITE *of Selborne*."

"This imitation of an elegantly touched drawing by Waterloo was one of my earlieſt inſtructors.—J. C.—Preſented to me by J. T. Smith, 1798."—(Written on the back of a pen drawing.)

"Connoiſſeurs think the art is already done."

"I have never ſeen anything in the art yet with which I have been entirely ſatisfied. The leaſt mannered, and conſequently the beſt pictures I have ſeen, are ſome of the works of De Hooge, particularly one of an out-door ſubject, at Sir Robert Peel's. His in-doors are as good, but leſs difficult, as being leſs luſtrous."*

"The world is wide; no two days are alike, nor even two hours; neither were there ever two leaves of a tree alike ſince the creation of the world; and the genuine productions of art, like thoſe of nature, are all diſtinct from each other."

"In ſuch an age as this, painting ſhould be *underſtood*, not

* Conſtable would not have ſaid that ſuch works were the greateſt achievements of art; he merely meant that they were the moſt perfect, in the ſenſe in which ſome minor poems may be conſidered more perfect than "The Iliad," or the "Paradiſe loſt."

looked on with blind wonder, nor confidered only as a poetic afpiration, but as a purfuit, *legitimate*, *fcientific*, and *mechanical*."

"The old rubbifh of art, the mufty, common place, wretched pictures which gentlemen collect, hang up, and difplay to their friends, may be compared to Shakfpeare's

> 'Beggarly account of empty boxes,
> Alligators ftuffed,' &c.

Nature is any thing but this, either in poetry, painting, or in the fields."

"Barry thought, to be great he muft reject the attributes of painting; hence the iron-bound outline and brazen lights of his pictures in the Adelphi."

"The moft perfect of all mafters of real chiarofcuro, are Claude and Oftade. The chiarofcuro of Rembrandt is decidedly an artificial feature in his works; he painted exprefsly for it; it was his own peculiar language, and ufed by him to exprefs the fentiment."

"What were the habits of Claude and the Pouffins? though furrounded with palaces filled with pictures, they made the fields their chief places of ftudy."

"Cowper numbered it among his advantages as a compofer that he had read fo little poetry; for 'imitation,' faid he, 'even of the beft models is my averfion; it is fervile and mechanical; a trick that has enabled many to ufurp the name of author, who could not have written at all, if they had not written upon the pattern of fomebody indeed original.' "*

* The laft book Conftable had been reading, and on which his attention had

"The folly of imitation is well ſhown in the fable of 'The Aſs and the Lap-dog.'"

"'I hate e'en Garrick when at ſecondhand.'—CHURCHILL."

"Mr. W * * * * * * is conſcious of being a great manneriſt, and that he is thought ſo. He was told how much trouble his picture had given the Council on that account, for that it would hang with nothing elſe; he was hurt, and ſaid, 'manner might be either good or bad;' but Fuſeli makes the true diſtinction between *ſtyle* and *manner*."

"Lord Bacon ſays, 'Cunning is crooked wiſdom. Nothing is more hurtful than when cunning men paſs for wiſe.' —This is manneriſm in painting. The manneriſts are cunning people; and the misfortune is, the public are not able to diſcriminate between their pictures and true painting."

"Manner is always ſeductive. It is more or leſs an imitation of what has been done already,—therefore always plauſible. It promiſes the ſhort road, the near cut to preſent fame and emolument, by availing ourſelves of the labours of others. It leads to almoſt immediate reputation, becauſe it is the wonder of the ignorant world. It is always accompanied by certain blandiſhments, ſhowy and plauſible, and which catch the eye. As manner comes by degrees, and is foſtered by ſucceſs in the world, flattery, &c. all painters who would be really great, ſhould be perpetually on their guard againſt it. Nothing but a cloſe and continual obſervance of nature can protect them from the danger of becoming manneriſts."

---

probably been engaged little more than an hour before his death, was a volume of Southey's Life of Cowper, containing the poet's letters.

"'Is it not folly,' ſaid Mr. Northcote to me in the Exhibition, as we were ſtanding before * * * 's picture, 'for a man to paint what he can never ſee? is it not ſufficiently difficult to paint what he does ſee?'*—This delightful leſſon leads me to aſk, what is painting but an imitative art? an art that is to *realize*, not to *feign*. I conſtantly obſerve that every man who will not ſubmit to long toil in the imitation of nature, flies off, becomes a phantom, and produces dreams of nonſenſe, and abortions. He thinks to ſcreen himſelf under 'a fine imagination,' which is generally, and almoſt always in young men, the ſcape-goat of folly and idleneſs."

"'Rien eſt beau que le vrai.'—BOILEAU."

"'Obſerve that thy beſt director, thy perfect guide is Nature. Copy from her.—In her paths is thy triumphal arch. She is above all other teachers; and ever confide in her with a bold heart;—*eſpecially when thou beginneſt to feel that there is a ſentiment in drawing*.—Day after day never fail to draw ſomething, which however little it may be, will yet in the end be much; and do thy beſt.'

"Extracted from Cennino Cennini's book on painting written four hundred years ago, now firſt printed in 1821, from the manuſcript in the Vatican. He was a pupil of Angiolo Gaddi, whoſe father painted under Giotto twenty-four years."

"None of the greateſt painters were eccentric in their works. They were too conſiſtent with themſelves to merit ſuch an epithet; too ſenſible of what they were about."

* Northcote's objection did not apply to the *ſupernatural* in painting, but to the *unnatural*. The picture before which they ſtood profeſſed to be a real ſcene, but treated in what the artiſt conceived to be a poetic manner.

"The rage of what may be called *protégé-iſm* among the rich and great, ariſing from the expectation either of being the firſt to diſcover genius in obſcurity, or of turning ſome young man of ordinary talent into a genius, though it may now and then be of uſe, is far more often prejudicial to the real intereſts of art, and even to the individual ſo patronized. Very worthy men, poſſeſſed with this vanity, become completely blinded to the injuſtice they commit to all who have fairly won the field, and whom they would not heſitate to drive from it, to make room for ſome favourite of their own, who is, by their *inſtruction* as well as patronage, to be placed on the pinnacle of fame.—Thus, Raſſelas, in recalling the viſions he had indulged in of a perfect government when he ſhould come to the throne, acknowledges that he afterwards was ſtartled to think with how little regret he had contemplated the death of his father and elder brothers."

"There ſhould be a moral feeling in the art, as well as in every thing elſe, and it is not right in a young man to aſſume great daſh, or great completion, without ſtudy or pains."

"There has never been a boy painter, nor can there be. The art requires a long apprenticeſhip, being *mechanical*, as well as intellectual."

"It was at Rome Claude became the real ſtudent of Nature. He came there a confirmed mannered painter. But he ſoon found it neceſſary to 'become as a little child,' and he devoted himſelf to ſtudy with an ardour and a patience of labour perhaps never before equalled. He lived in the fields all day, and drew at the Academy at night, for after all Art is a plant of the conſervatory, not of the deſert."

"'D. O. M.*
CLAUDIO . GELLEE . LOTHARINGO .
EX . LOCO . DE . CHAMPAGNE . ORTO .
PICTORI . EXIMIO .
QUI . IPSOS . ORIENTIS . ET . OCCIDENTIS .
SOLIS . RADIOS . IN . CAMPESTRIBUS .
MIRIFICE . PINGENDIS . EFFINXIT.
HIC . IN . URBE . UBI . ARTEM . COLUIT,
SUMMAM . LAUDEM . INTER . MAGNATES .
CONSECUTUS . EST.
OBIIT . IX . KALEND . DECEMBRIS . MDCLXXXII.
AETATIS . SUAE . ANNO . LXXXII.
JOANN . ET . JOSEPHUS . GELLEE .
PATRUO . CHARISSIMO . MONUM . HOC .
SIBI . POSTERISQUE . SUIS .
PONI . CURARUNT.'

"'To Claude Gellée Lorraine, a moſt eminent painter, born in the province of Champagne, who, in painting landſcape, repreſented to admiration the very rays of the riſing and ſetting ſun. In this city, where he practiſed his art, he obtained the higheſt celebrity among the great. He died the 9th of the Kalends of December, 1682, (i. e. 23rd of November), aged 82.

"'John and Joſeph Gellée, cauſed this monument to be erected to their beloved uncle, for themſelves and their poſterity.'

"The above inſcription was on the monument of Claude Lorraine (now deſtroyed) in the Church of the Trinità al Monte at Rome. Sir George Beaumont, who had ſeen it, and again ſought for it when there about 1820, informed

* Diis omnibus manibus. "To all the infernal Gods." So the ancient Romans inſcribed their monuments. This inſcription was turned by the Chriſtians into Deo optimo maximo, "To the good and great God," thus preſerving the ſame initial letters.

me that it was mural, and moderately ornamented, having a palette and pencils carved on it. Had he been succefsful in finding the fragments, it was his intention to have brought them to his feat at Cole-Orton, and put them up in the Church or on his grounds."*

Conftable feldom failed to penetrate the real characters of men through the difguifes of manner. In an unpublifhed letter he fays, of one of a clafs of perfons not very uncommon, "More *overbearing meeknefs* I never met with in any one man."

To thefe few gleanings from Conftable's papers, I will add fome recollections of his fayings. His manner of talking was perpetually digreffive, yet he never loft fight of the fubject with which he fet out, but would always return to it, though often through a long and circuitous path. This rambling habit made his talk, which was amufing enough in itfelf, fometimes ftill more fo, but it unfitted him in a great degree, for an extemporaneous lecturer. His converfation might be compared to a diffected map or picture, of which the parts, as feen feparately, appear to have no connection, yet each is capable of being fo placed as to form a complete whole.

In reply to an application to my friend Collins for his affiftance in this part of my undertaking, I received the following note:

"Dear Leflie, I have been cudgelling my brains on the

* My friend, Mr. T. Uwins, has obliged me with the following account of the deftruction of Claude's monument: "When the French republican troops devaftated Italy in 1798, their great delight was to turn out the monks and nuns from the convents and other religious houfes, which houfes they converted into barracks. This happened to the Church and Convent of the Frati Minori on the Trinità al Monte at Rome, and it was during this barbarous occupation that Claude's monument was obliterated."

ſubject of the Conſtable anecdotes, and the reſult is, the recollection of a great number of good things, calculated, alas, only for table-talk among friends. This, as I told you, I feared would be the caſe. The great charm of our lamented friend's converſation upon art, was not only its originality, but its real worth, and the evidence it afforded of his heartfelt love of his purſuit, independent of any worldly advantages to be obtained by it. * * * I mentioned to you his admirable remark upon the compoſition of a picture, namely, that its parts were all ſo neceſſary to it as a whole, that it reſembled a ſum in arithmetic; take away or add the ſmalleſt item, and it muſt be wrong. His obſervations, too, on chiaroſcuro, were all that could be made on that deep ſubject. How rejoiced am I to find that ſo many of the great things he did, will at laſt be got together for the benefit of future ſtudents."

The compariſon mentioned by Mr. Collins of a picture to a ſum in arithmetic, was intended by Conſtable to expoſe the unpardonable liberties ſometimes taken by the poſſeſſors of the works of deceaſed artiſts, in cutting, enlarging, or otherwiſe altering them. "Would you take from or add," he would ſay, "to a phyſician's preſcription?" * * * Another proceeding, perhaps not more juſtifiable, may be here adverted to,—the employment of artiſts to finiſh pictures left incomplete by their predeceſſors. The beſt painters know that a work of any value can only be carried through by the head and hand of him who planned it, and conſequently, thoſe only undertake to complete unfiniſhed pictures who are the leaſt capable of divining the intentions of their authors.* Some of Conſtable's ſketches have thus been *finiſhed* into worthleſſneſs, and what is a ſtill greater injury to his reputation, entire forgeries have been made of his works. Mul-

* I have known ſome deplorable inſtances of the *finiſhing* of Wilkie's incompleted pictures, and many more of works, ſo left, by Lawrence.

titudes of theſe I have ſeen, and with aſtoniſhment that their wretchedneſs ſhould impoſe upon purchaſers. But they are put forth, in ſafe reliance on the little real knowledge of his ſtyle that, at preſent, exiſts among our connoiſſeurs.

To return from this digreſſion to the more agreeable ſubject of Conſtable's converſation, I remember to have heard him ſay, "When I ſit down to make a ſketch from nature, the firſt thing I try to do is, *to forget that I have ever ſeen a picture*."* He well knew that, in ſpite of this endeavour, his knowledge of pictures had its influence on every touch of his pencil, for in ſpeaking of a young artiſt who boaſted that he had never ſtudied the works of others, he ſaid, "After all, there *is* ſuch a thing as the art."

On hearing ſomebody ſay of the celebrated collection of Raphael's drawings that belonged to Sir Thomas Lawrence, "They inſpire," he replied, "They do more, they inform."

The amiable but eccentric Blake, looking through one of Conſtable's ſketch books, ſaid of a beautiful drawing of an avenue of fir trees on Hampſtead Heath, "Why, this is not drawing, but *inſpiration*;" and he replied, "I never knew it before; I meant it for drawing."

"My pictures will never be popular," he ſaid, "for they have no *handling*. But I do not ſee *handling* in nature."

He ſaid alſo, "Whatever may be thought of my art, it is my own; and I would rather poſſeſs a freehold, though but a cottage, than live in a palace belonging to another."

* A curious proof of the ſtillneſs with which he had ſat one day while painting in the open air, was the diſcovery of a field mouſe in his coat pocket.

To a lady who, looking at an engraving of a houſe, called it an ugly thing, he ſaid, "No madam, there is nothing ugly; *I never ſaw an ugly thing in my life:* for let the form of an object be what it may,—light, ſhade, and perſpective will always make it beautiful. It is perſpective which improves the form of this."

Speaking of the taſte for the *prodigious* and the *aſtounding*, a taſte very contrary to his own, he made uſe of a quotation from the 1ſt Book of Kings. "A great and ſtrong wind rent the mountains, and brake in pieces the rocks before the Lord; but the Lord was not in the wind: and after the wind an earthquake; but the Lord was not in the earthquake: and after the earthquake a fire; but the Lord was not in the fire: and after the fire *a ſtill ſmall voice.*"

There were many occaſions on which Conſtable quoted the aphoriſm of Dr. Johnſon: "That which is *greateſt* is not always *beſt.*"

His fondneſs for children has been mentioned. I have often heard him ſay, but as a quotation (I think from Plato) "*Children ſhould be reſpected.*"

He was aſked how ſoon a reliſh for the works of Domenichino might be acquired, and replied, "In about the ſame time in which you may acquire a reliſh for the works of Homer."

An artiſt who undervalued every claſs of art but the heroic, ſaid in his preſence, "that he could not conceive to what Jan Steen owed his great reputation, unleſs to the high encomiums Sir Joſhua Reynolds had paſſed on his ſtyle;" "And could he," replied Conſtable, "owe it to a better authority?"

Chap. XVII.

He was ſtruck with a remark of Dr. Gooch, that he found "every individual caſe of diſeaſe a new ſtudy." Conſtable applied this to painting, and ſaid, "In like manner every truly original picture is a ſeparate ſtudy, and governed by laws of its own; ſo that what is right in one, would be often entirely wrong if transferred to another."

A friend of Conſtable expreſſing to him his diſſatisfaction at his own progreſs in art, received (as he told me) the greateſt encouragement to proceed he ever met with, in the following anſwer: "If you had found painting as eaſy as you once thought it, you would have given it up long ago."

He could not eaſily reſiſt the temptation of making an unexpected reply, and when Archdeacon Fiſher, one Sunday, after preaching, aſked him how he liked his ſermon, he ſaid, "Very much indeed, Fiſher; I always did like that ſermon." But Fiſher had too much wit himſelf not to reliſh this; and if he kept any account of ſuch hits with his friend, it was no doubt a fairly balanced one.

If Conſtable had occaſion to find fault with a ſervant or a tradeſman, it was ſeldom unaccompanied with a pleaſantry, though often a ſharp one. To the perſon who ſerved his family with milk, he ſaid, "In future we ſhall feel obliged if you will ſend us the milk and the water in ſeparate cans."

A picture of a murder ſent to the Academy for exhibition while he was on the Council, was refuſed admittance on account of a diſguſting diſplay of blood and brains in it; but he objected ſtill more to the wretchedneſs of the work, and ſaid, "I ſee no *brains* in the picture."*

* This recals to my recollection a ſaying, ſtill better, which is related of Opie, who, when a young artiſt aſked him what he mixed his colours with, replied, "*Brains*."

I regret that among his papers I have not met with the obſervations on ſkies and clouds, which he mentions in a letter to Mr. George Conſtable. I recollect hearing, at different times, remarks by him on atmoſpheric effects, but I can ſcarcely recall any thing he ſaid, with ſufficient diſtinctneſs to repeat it. I remember that he pointed out to me an appearance of the ſun's rays, which few artiſts have perhaps noticed, and which I never ſaw given in any picture, excepting in his "Waterloo Bridge." When the ſpectator ſtands with his back to the ſun, the rays may be ſometimes ſeen *converging* in perſpective towards the oppoſite horizon. Since he drew my attention to ſuch effects, I have noticed very early in the morning the lines of the rays diminiſhing in perſpective through a rainbow.

I have ſeen him admire a fine tree with an ecſtaſy of delight like that with which he would catch up a beautiful child in his arms. The aſh was his favourite, and all who are acquainted with his pictures cannot fail to have obſerved how frequently it is introduced as a near object, and how beautifully its diſtinguiſhing peculiarities are marked. I remember his pointing out to me in an avenue of Spaniſh cheſnuts, the great elegance given to their trunks by the ſpiral direction of the lines of the bark.

He would never admit of a diſtinction which is ſometimes made between poetry and truth. He felt that the *ſupernatural* need not be the *unnatural*.† Neither did he admit that the *conventional* in art, though it may be found in the works of the greateſt maſters, was to be conſidered in any other light than as an evidence of human imperfection. He looked upon the imitation by modern painters of that which is conven-

† Why do "the Gods of Homer continue to this day the gods of poetry," but becauſe they are endued with human paſſions? And for the ſame reaſon do the weird ſiſters, the Oberon, Titania, Puck, Ariel, and Caliban intereſt us.

tional in the works of their predeceſſors, as one great cauſe of the deterioration of art. "Raphael and Michael Angelo," he ſaid, "would be greatly aſtoniſhed could they riſe from their graves, at the theories on which it has been ſuppoſed their works were formed; as, for inſtance, that the charms of colour, or chiaroſcuro, would detract from the intellectual dignity of their inventions."* He has often pointed out to me, even in the imperfect engravings we have from the Siſtine Chapel, the admirable conduct of the light and ſhade; and he told me that Stothard, looking at theſe things with him, ſaid, "Michael Angelo always compoſed for chiaroſcuro." Conſtable conſidered that the union of various excellence propoſed by the Carracci, might not be impoſſible, but that their failure, where they did fail, was mainly owing to their attention being too much confined to the works of their predeceſſors. He preferred the advice given by Wilkie when conſulted by young artiſts, "*paint it well*," to the elaborate recommendations contained in the ſonnet of Agoſtino Carracci.† He conſidered the analogy to hold good in all reſpects between religion and taſte. He told me that one of Sir Joſhua Reynolds's Diſcourſes had been turned into a ſermon, and was found not to require any alteration in the general ſcope of the arguments.

When the opinions ſcattered through Conſtable's letters are compared with thoſe expreſſed in his lectures, it will not be neceſſary for me to ſay, that his love of nature did not blind him to the real value of art. I never remember to have ſtood with him before a fine picture, either ancient or modern, without his directing my attention to ſome excel-

* Such a theory, it appears to me, may be overturned at once by two remarks of Fuſeli: "The Jeremiah among the Prophets glows with the glow of Titian, but in a breadth unknown to Giorgione and him." And "The Eve under the Tree has the bland pearly harmony of Correggio."

† See Fuſeli's Second Lecture.

lence in it which I had not before noticed; and if his intimate acquaintance with nature made him more than usually fastidious in his admiration of pictures, it gave him a relish for the best, of which no mere connoisseur can form the least conception. But the light in which Constable considered works of art, was exactly that in which Lord Bacon places the sciences, when he says, "It is a fatal mistake to suppose that they have gradually arrived at a state of perfection, and then been recorded by some one writer or other; and that as nothing better can afterwards be invented, men need but cultivate and set off what is thus discovered and completed: whereas in reality, this registering of the sciences proceeds only from the assurance of a few, and the sloth and ignorance of many."—And again, "As water ascends no higher than the level of the first spring, so knowledge derived from Aristotle will at most rise no higher again than the knowledge of Aristotle. And therefore, though a scholar must have faith in his master, yet a man well instructed must judge for himself; for learners owe to their masters only a temporary belief, and a suspension of their own judgment till they are fully instructed, and not an absolute resignation, or perpetual captivity. Let great authors, therefore, have their due; but so as not to defraud time, which is the author of authors, and the parent of truth."

Need I mention how very little Constable cared for the usual classifications of art? he judged as all who have taste, and who give their taste fair play, judge of pictures, by their intrinsic merit alone. *Good art* was with him *high art*, however humble the subject; and mediocre art, let the attempt be ever so sublime, was in his estimation, *low art*.*

* All men of genius have something in common, however dissimilar their productions, but genius and mediocrity have nothing in common; Raphael and Ostade *may* be classed together, but never Raphael and Carlo Maratti. Since

In the ſummer of 1840, I accompanied Mr. Purton on an excurſion to Suffolk. We were received at Flatford with the greateſt hoſpitality by Mr. Abram Conſtable and his ſiſters, and were accommodated with facilities for exploring what to us was claſſic ground, in which we had the advantage of being accompanied by Conſtable's eldeſt ſon, and his nephew, the Rev. Daniel Whalley.

We viſited the houſe in which Conſtable was born.—It was a large and handſome manſion, at that time untenanted, and has ſince been pulled down. A view of the back of it forms the frontiſpiece to the "Engliſh Landſcape," with theſe lines inſcribed under it,

> "Hic locus ætatis noſtræ primordia novit
> Annos felices lætitiæque dies:
> Hic locus ingenuis pueriles imbuit annos
> Artibus et noſtræ laudis origo fuit."

Of which, in one of his ſketch books, is the following tranſlation by Mr. Fiſher.

> "This ſpot ſaw the day ſpring of my life,
> Hours of Joy and years of Happineſs;
> This place firſt tinged my boyiſh fancy with a love of the Art,
> This place was the origin of my Fame."

We found that the ſcenery of eight or ten of our late friend's moſt important ſubjects might be encloſed by a circle of a few hundred yards at Flatford, very near Bergholt; within this ſpace are the lock, which forms the ſubject of ſeveral pictures—Willy Lott's houſe—the little raiſed wooden bridge and the pictureſque cottage near it, ſeen in the pic-

this note was firſt printed, I have met with the following paſſage in Cunningham's Life of Wilkie. Speaking of Raphael and M. Angelo, Wilkie ſays, "They have that without which the Venus and Apollo would loſe their value, and with which the forms of Oſtade and Rembrandt become inſtructive and ſublime; namely expreſſion and ſentiment."

ture engraved for Meſſrs. Finden's work, and introduced into others—and the meadow in which the picture of "Boat-building" was entirely painted. So ſtartling was the reſemblance of ſome of theſe ſcenes to the pictures of them, which we knew ſo well, that we could hardly believe we were for the firſt time ſtanding on the ground from which they were painted. Of others, we found that Conſtable had rather combined and varied the materials, than given exact views. In the larger compoſitions, ſuch as "The White Horſe" and "The Hay Wain," both from this neighbourhood, he has increaſed the width of the river to great advantage; and wherever there was an opportunity, he was fond of introducing the tower of Dedham Church, which is ſeen from many points near Flatford. At Stratford we miſſed the pictureſque little water-mill, with which the picture given by Fiſher to Mr. Tinney had made us acquainted, in place of which now ſtands a large brick building. We viſited Stoke; and at Neyland, which adjoins it, we ſaw the altar-piece of the Saviour bleſſing the elements; we ſaw, likewiſe, the altar-piece at Brantham; and viſited Langham, where all is ſo much changed excepting the Church, that we could ſcarcely recognize it as the ſcene of "The Glebe Farm." The appearance of Dedham Mill is greatly improved in every picture Conſtable painted of it, by his ſhewing the water-wheel, which in reality is hidden.

In the education of an artiſt, it is ſcarcely poſſible to foreſee what circumſtances will prove advantageous, or the reverſe; it is on looking back only that we can judge of theſe things. Travelling is now the order of the day, and it may ſometimes prove beneficial,—but to Conſtable's art there can be little doubt that the confinement of his ſtudies within the narroweſt bounds in which, perhaps, the ſtudies of an artiſt ever were confined, was in the higheſt degree favourable; for a knowledge of atmoſpheric effects will be beſt attained by a conſtant ſtudy of the ſame objects under every change of the ſeaſons, and of the times of day. His ambition, it will be borne in mind, was not to paint many things imperfectly, but to paint a few things well.

The impreſſion made on the minds of Mr. Purton and myſelf by theſe beautiful ſcenes was, that Conſtable being born among them, and being born a painter, was almoſt of neceſſity born a landſcape painter. As we were leaving them, my companion made ſome remarks which ſeemed to me ſo juſt and ſo happily expreſſed, that I begged he would give them to me on paper, and his kind compliance with my requeſt enables me to add them to this brief account of our excurſion.

"In looking," ſays Mr. Purton, "at ſuch faithful tranſcripts of nature as are exhibited in the landſcapes of Conſtable, it would be difficult to point out any one quality or excellence which preeminently diſtinguiſhes them; and perhaps it will be found that this one-neſs or individuality conſtitutes their principal charm: one pervading animus, one ſingleneſs of intention runs through the whole; and this, it may be obſerved, has been pronounced on the beſt authority, the *ſine quâ non* in poetical compoſition:

'Denique ſit quidvis ſimplex duntaxat et unum.'*

Whether he portray the ſolemn burſt of the approaching tempeſt—the breezy freſhneſs of morning—or the deep ſtillneſs of a ſummer noon—every object repreſented, from the grandeſt maſſes to the ſmalleſt plant or ſpray, ſeem inſtinct with, as it were, and breathing the very ſpirit of the ſcene. His figures, too, ſeem naturally called forth by, and form part of, the landſcape: we never aſk whether they are well

* "In a word, it may be what you will, only let it be ſimple (or rather ſingle) and one."—HORACE *on the Art of Poetry*.

placed, there they are, and unlefs they choofe to move on, there they muft remain. His quiet lanes and covert nooks never ferve to introduce a romantic or fentimental epifode to divide, not heighten the intereft; all is made fubfervient to the one object in view, the embodying a pure apprehenfion of natural effect. Hence it is that the true lover of nature admires not at fight the beauty of the lines, or the truth of colouring difplayed in his works; his firft impulfe is, as with Fufeli, to call for his umbrella, or with Bannifter, he feels the breeze blowing on his face.† I do not prefume to point out what high qualities of art he muft have attained, or what difficulties overcome, before he could have effected fo deep a feeling of the natural; but I imagine that the higheft attainments of art, even all his patient ftudy had been vain, had they not been engrafted on the pureft and warmeft admiration and affection for the fcenes and effects which he reprefented."

An extremely interefting portion of Conftable's works is known only to his intimate friends,—I mean the contents of his numerous fketch books. In thefe are many complete landfcapes in miniature, often coloured, and when not tinted the chiarofcuro is generally given in lead pencil, fometimes with great depth of effect, and always with exquifite tafte.—The name of nearly every fpot fketched is added, and in looking through thefe books one thing is ftriking, which may be equally noticed of his pictures, that the fubjects of his works form a hiftory of his affections.—Bergholt and its neighbourhood—Salifbury—Ofmington—Hampftead—Gillingham—Brighton—Folkeftone, (where his boys were at fchool,)—and

* The reader will remember Mrs. Fifher's remark on the arrival of the "White Horfe" at Salifbury, that fhe carried her eye from the picture to the garden, and obferved "the fame fort of look in both;" and Lady Morley's exclamation on feeing the view of Englefield Houfe, "How frefh, how dewy, how exhilarating!" It was for thofe who feel and judge in this way Conftable painted; but connoiffeurs, and even artifts, are not always fuch judges.

ſcenes in Berkſhire viſited by him with Mr. Fiſher. With the exception of his excurſion in Derbyſhire, and afterwards to the Engliſh Lakes, he never travelled expreſſly for ſubjects. Chiaroſcuro, as I have ſaid, was an all important thing in his eſtimation. Many artiſts ſee it nowhere, but Conſtable ſaw it everywhere, and in all its beauty. Why then ſhould he go in queſt of ſubjects, when the ſpots endeared to him from his infancy, or from the aſſociations of friendſhip, had not only in general great attractions of their own, but where they had leaſt of beauty could be elevated by this power to ſublimity?

CHAPTER XVIII.

Notes of Six Leɛtures, delivered by Conſtable, on Landſcape Painting.

THE lectures Conſtable delivered at the Hampſtead Aſſembly Rooms,—at the Royal Inſtitution in Albemarle Street,—and at Worceſter, were never written. He prepared ſome brief notes only, but he depended more on a collection of copies and engravings from the pictures to which he had occaſion to allude, with large placards containing the names of the principal painters who had contributed to the advancement of landſcape painting, chronologically arranged. Theſe ſufficiently ſerved to refreſh a memory well ſtored with information on the ſubject of his lectures.—Many of his friends urged him after the delivery of the firſt diſcourſe to write it, and he probably intended to amplify the following abſtract which was found among his papers, and which, he ſays, "is little more than a recollection of a diſcourſe delivered at the Hampſtead Aſſembly Rooms in June 1833."

"In offering a few obſervations on the hiſtory of landſcape painting, to the members of the Literary and Scientific Society of Hampſtead, it will be neceſſary, before I proceed, to exonerate the gentlemen forming its Committee from blame for the appointment to this taſk of one ſo inefficient, at leaſt as a ſpeaker; and perhaps I cannot better excuſe their choice, nor illuſtrate the poſition in which both the committee and myſelf are placed, than by the following words of Lord Bacon.

" 'He who queſtioneth much, will learn much; and will content much; but eſpecially if he apply his queſtions to the ſkill of thoſe whom he aſketh; for he ſhall give them occaſion to pleaſe themſelves in ſpeaking.'—And again. 'There is ſmall doubt but that men can write beſt and moſt *really* and *ſincerely* on their own profeſſions; only there is one vice which accompanies them that write on their own profeſſions, that they magnify them in exceſs; but generally it were to be wiſhed as that which would make learning indeed ſolid and fruitful, that active men would or could become writers.'

" In tracing the hiſtory of landſcape, although my limits neceſſarily permit me to give but an outline, I ſhall endeavour to render it clear, uſeful, and intereſting, by pointing out the *epochs* which mark the development, progreſs, and perfection of this department of art,—a department than which there is none more efficient, impreſſive, or delightful,—none that has more completely ſucceeded in the attainment of its object.—My endeavour ſhall be to ſeparate it from the maſs of hiſtorical art in which it originated, and with which it was long connected. Conſidering, as I do, that landſcape has hitherto eſcaped a diſtinction to which it is entitled, I propoſe to trace it to its ſource, to follow its progreſs to its final ſucceſs, to ſhow how by degrees it aſſumed form until at laſt it became a diſtinct and ſeparate claſs of painting, ſtanding alone, when, from being the humble aſſiſtant, it became the powerful auxiliary to that art which gave it birth, greatly enriching the dignity of hiſtory.

" If we are to form any opinion of the ſtate of landſcape

painting among the ancients from the ſpecimens diſplayed on the walls of Herculaneum, the Baths of Diocletian, and in other places of more recent diſcovery, it would appear that, although they practiſed it with much grace and elegance, they merely ſeemed to conſider it as forming a part of their arabeſques. Trees, like candelabra, formally ſpread on a plain blue ſky, for inſtance;—but we have no ſpecimen in their landſcape in which we can trace any attempt at chiaroſcuro, without which it can never be rendered impreſſive. Yet if we are to believe Pliny and other ancient writers, chiaroſcuro as well as colour was thoroughly underſtood and practiſed by the great hiſtorical painters.

"All was, however, loſt in the general wreck of Europe; and it is hardly to be expected that in the early time of the middle ages any thing of ſo refined a character ſhould re-appear. The Bayeux tapeſtry, which is indeed little better than a Mexican performance, ſcarcely hints at it. The illuminated manuſcripts and miſſals, when they repreſent the agony of Chriſt, indicate the garden only by a flower, or a flower pot, the reſt of the field of the picture being dark. But when hiſtorical painting was attempted on a larger ſcale, and the Paſſion, the Crucifixion, and the Entombment of our Saviour afforded its moſt important ſubjects, landſcape, and even ſome of its phenomena, became indiſpenſable. The croſs muſt be fixed in the ground,—there muſt be a ſky,—the ſhades of night muſt envelope the garden, (the ſcene of the agony,)—and a more awful darkneſs the Crucifixion;—while rocks and trees naturally made a part of the accompaniments of the ſepulchre. Here, then, however rude and imperfect, we are to look for the origin of landſcape. It was firſt uſed as an aſſiſtant in conveying ſentiment, and being found completely ſucceſsful, was cultivated by ſucceeding painters, until at length it became a diſtinct branch of art.

"Pictures are books; and they were especially so considered in the earliest ages of painting in Europe, when so few even of the highest classes could either read or write. The great importance of painting, therefore, as a means of instruction, will account for the whole history of our Saviour being painted on one panel. The artists, very justly, considered themselves engaged in works of piety, and they employed all their powers to tell their stories with the greatest perspicuity. In the first simple ages of painting there was no display of the technicalities of art; they were indeed unknown. The holy truths of Christianity were told with sincerity, in pictures filled with natural expression and purity of sentiment. The works of Cimabue, Giotto, &c., were carried in procession to the churches, there to remain, to enlighten the ignorant, and to add to the fervours of the devout.

"It was fortunate, therefore, for landscape, destined as it was to become so material a feature of the art, that it originated and was in its infancy nursed in the hands of men who were masters of pathos. As early, I believe, as Cimabue, and certainly Giotto, landscape became impressive. I am told that in the Campo Santo at Pisa, the frescos exhibit wonderful proofs of its use and power. The names of Ghirlandaio, Barnardo, and Paolo Uccello (the first master of perspective,) follow. By these artists architecture, vistas, and other materials, were added with great intelligence; so much so, as to cause us not to be surprised at the future advance of landscape, as an accompaniment, in the hands of Raphael. In his early pictures, generally Holy Families, and many of which may be seen in England, it is most beautifully and appropriately introduced; the single leaves of plants, flowers, and that religious emblem the trefoil, in his foregrounds are very elegantly detailed; and the soothing solitudes of his middle distances find a corresponding serenity in the features of the benign and lovely subjects of these works. In the first of the grand ſeries of freſcos with which he adorned the chambers of the Vatican, he has placed the Euchariſt on the table in the open air. The low horizon juſt permits the tops of trees, ſpires, and gently riſing hills to be ſeen over the altar, and the ſerenity imparted to the picture by an exceedingly elegant landſcape, aids the religious feeling which reigns over the whole. In many of his ſmaller ſubjects in the Loggia of the Vatican, the landſcape backgrounds are of extreme beauty, and of great importance; and the lovely paſtoral ſcenery of that noble cartoon, 'the charge to Peter,' is probably familiar to all my auditors.

"Thus was landſcape cradled in the lap of hiſtory, at a time when its grandeur, ſimplicity, and powers of expreſſion were carried to their greateſt perfection by the ſchools of Italy; and it thus early gained a ſtrength and dignity which has never ſince wholly forſaken it.

"Although I ſhall have occaſion to notice its obligations at a later period to the German, Dutch, and Flemiſh colour* and delicacy of finiſh, it may be worth while to advert to what would probably have been the reſult, had its cultivation at the time at which we have arrived been carried on by the German and Dutch painters only. In their hands dignity of ſubject never excluded meanneſs, and the wretched material introduced into their hiſtorical pictures could have led to nothing, or worſe than nothing, impreſſive. The accompaniments even of the Nativity, were often, with them, an aſſemblage of the mean and ridiculous. An owl, ſeen through a hole in a thatched roof, ſitting on a beam juſt over the head of the Virgin, with a mouſe dangling by its tail from

* The exquiſite colour of the early Flemiſh art as ſeen in the works of Van Eyck, Hemmelinck, &c. is not more ſurpriſing than the ſtate of perfect preſervation in which the tints of their pictures, ſome of which are more than four hundred years old, ſtill remain.

his claw; pigs quarrelling at the trough, &c.—But Albert Durer and Lucas Van Leyden, though they have been guilty of theſe things, have, occaſionally rendered a very different account of landſcape. The back ground to the figure of 'Fortune' is a grand exception, as well as thoſe to the 'Prodigal Son' and the 'Armed Knight;' and indeed in all Albert Durer's landſcape, notwithſtanding the objections I have mentioned, there is much that is ſtriking.

"It was, however, at Venice, the *heart* of colour, and where the true art of imitation was firſt underſtood, that landſcape aſſumed a rank and deciſion of character that ſpread future excellence through all the ſchools of Europe. Giorgione and Titian, both hiſtorical painters, were early diſciplined in the ſchools of the brothers Bellini, where they were taught to imitate nature in what has been termed a ſervile manner. But it appears to have been the true way of proceeding if we may judge from the reſult; for afterwards, when thoſe great painters had attained the plenitude of their powers, they never loſt their reſpect for nature, nor for a moment wandered from the materials which were about them, and which they had been taught to copy ſo admirably, into the vacant fields of idealiſm. In the Venetian ſchool, landſcape formed a very important ſtudy, and whether ſeparate or united with hiſtory, it was here carried to a degree of perfection it had never before attained.

"In the year 1520, Titian, then in his fortieth year, produced his celebrated picture of the martyrdom of the Dominican Peter, the background of which, although not the model, may be conſidered as the foundation of all the ſtyles of landſcape in every ſchool of Europe in the following century. In this admirable union of hiſtory and landſcape, the ſcene is on the ſkirts of a foreſt, and the time verging towards the cloſe of day, as we may judge from the level and placid movement of the clouds on the deep blue ſky, ſeen under the pendent foliage of the trees which overhang the road. The choice of a low horizon greatly aids the grandeur of the compofition; and magnificent as the larger objects and maffes of the picture are, the minute plants in the foreground are finifhed with an exquifite but not obtrufive touch, and even a bird's neft with its callow brood may be difcovered among the branches of one of the trees. Amid this fcene of amenity and repofe, we are ftartled by the rufh of an affaffin on two helplefs travellers, monks, one of whom is ftruck down, and the other wounded and flying in the utmoft terror. At the top of the picture, through the loftieft branches of the trees, a bright and fupernatural light ftrikes down on the dying man, who fees in the glory a vifion of angels bearing the emblems of martyrdom; and illuminating in its defcent the ftems and foliage, contrafts with the fhadowy gloom of the wood.—The elder bufh, with its pale funereal flowers, introduced over the head of the faint, and the village fpire in the diftance, the object of his journey, increafe the intereft and add to the richnefs of the compofition. Admirable alfo is the contrivance of the tight drawn drapery, part of the garment of the martyr, which preffed by the foot of the affaffin, pins his victim to the earth.—The noble conception of this great work is equalled, I am told, by its breadth and its tone, while the extreme minutenefs and variety of its details no way impair the unity of its impreffion.

"However juftly the hiftoric art of the Bolognefe fchool may be termed 'eclectic,' the landfcape of the Caracci and Domenichino cannot be fo confidered, as each poffeffes a character of its own.—The landfcape of Annibal Caracci, though fevere, is grand and poetic, not to meddle with the ambiguous term *claffic*, and is admirably adapted to the fauns and fatyrs, and other mythological beings with which he peopled it, as may be feen in that moft felicitous conception of Pan and Apollo, in our National Gallery.

"The Bolognese landscape, although founded mainly on the Venetian, is not wholly so. Denis Calvart, born at Antwerp, in 1555, died at Bologna in 1619, having come to Italy as a landscape painter, on purpose to perfect himself in the study of the figure. He learned perspective under P. Fontana, studied at Rome, and left it to set up his school at Bologna, in which Albano, Domenichino and Guido became his pupils.

"The landscape of Domenichino is of the highest order; and although it bears the stamp of composition, yet we recognise the features and hues of nature in every part of it. His pictures in the National Gallery are poetic, but not of so high a character as the Orleans picture called "le Batelier," now in the possession of Lord Francis Egerton. The subject is pastoral; sheep flocking to a river, over which a romantic bridge discovers through its lofty arch a wide sheet of water falling into a lake. Two elegant ash trees gently overhang a neighbouring steep. The lake expands in the centre of the picture, on which the boatman is seen, and a group of figures recline on the grass on the near bank. The grandeur of the composition, and the urbanity of tone which pervades it, place this picture in the highest class of landscape.

"In the St. Jerome of Domenichino, the landscape is accessory only, yet most important. The subject of the picture is an aged and decrepit man, dying, attended by the ministers of religion. Through columns and a lofty arch are seen some religious buildings, perhaps often the scene of the dying saint's good works, on a gentle eminence, and overshadowed by a single group of trees. The placid aspect of this simple landscape seems like a requiem to soothe the departing spirit: its effect is like that of solemn music heard from an adjoining apartment. On the serene blue sky, hovering cherubs fill and complete the composition. This noble and

CH. XVIII.

pathetic picture, if not so startling as the Peter Martyr, leaves an impression as lasting.—Yet it was rejected by the authorities of the church for which it was painted, until Nicolo Poussin restored it to the world, and in a public harangue (the lecture of a painter) pointed out its beauties. It is mournful to reflect that neither age, worth, nor transcendent talents, could screen the virtuous Domenichino from the bad passions of intriguing cotemporaries, who blighted, and it is supposed, ultimately destroyed a life they had long embittered.*

"Although no distinct landscape is known by the hand of Guido, yet in a history of this particular branch it may not be improper to notice its immense importance as an accessory in his picture of Aurora. It is the finest instance I know of the beauty of natural landscape brought to aid a mythological story, and to be sensible of its value we have only to imagine a plain back ground in its stead. But though Guido has

---

* "Domenichino was so persecuted and overborne by the partisans of Guido, that his picture of the Communion of St. Jerome had been torn from its place in the church of San Girolamo della Carità, and thrown into a garret, where it remained forgotten, until the monks, desirous of having a new altar-piece, requested Poussin to paint one for them, and sent him Doménichino's picture as old canvass to paint it upon. He no sooner saw it, than, struck with its extraordinary merit, he carried it to the church for which it had been painted, and gave a public lecture upon it, in which he dared to compare it with the Transfiguration, and called these two, with the Descent from the Cross, by Daniel de Volterra, the three finest pictures in Rome. As to the accusation that the composition was a theft, from the sketch by the Caracci on the same subject, he showed that the Caracci had never finished their picture, and that as it was altered and improved in every particular, that was no ground for condemnation; for, far from injuring them by his appropriation of their idea, he had shown what a noble use might be made of it, and from it had composed one of the finest pictures in the world. The public had only to be roused by a steady and right-judging criticism; the elegant but weaker attractions of the rival school gave way, and Domenichino thenceforward was placed in his just rank among the great painters of Italy."—Life of Nicolo Poussin, by Maria Graham, afterwards Lady Callcott.—Domenichino was still living when his picture was restored to its place by Poussin. He died in 1641, it is supposed by poison.

placed us in the heavens, we are looking towards the earth, where ſeas and mountain tops are receiving the firſt beams of the morning ſun. The chariot of Apollo is borne on the clouds, attended by the Hours and preceded by Aurora, who ſcatters flowers; and the landſcape, inſtead of diminiſhing the illuſion, is the chief means of producing it, and is indeed moſt eſſential to the ſtory.

"Every walk of landſcape,—hiſtoric—poetic—claſſic—and paſtoral, were familiar to Nicolo Pouſſin; and ſo various were his powers, that each claſs, in his hands, vies with the reſt for preference. He was gifted with a peculiarly ſound judgment; tranquil, penetrating, and ſtudious of what was true rather than of what was novel and ſpecious. His beſt performances are perhaps to be found among what may be called his local landſcapes, compoſed often from the ſcenery near Rome, ſuch as the "Snake at the Fountain," and that admirable picture in the National Gallery, erroneouſly called "Phocian;" and if he did not often reach the lofty energy of the Caracci, or the ſentiment and romantic grandeur of Domenichino, yet in the poetry of art his Polyphemus remains unequalled, and in the awful ſublimity of the conception of his picture of Winter, generally known as the Deluge, he has ſurpaſſed every other painter who has attempted the ſubject; nor can there be a greater proof of the effective power of landſcape than that this portentous event ſhould have been beſt told by landſcape alone, the figures being few and entirely ſubordinate.

"My preſent limits do not allow me to dwell on Gaſpar Pouſſin, although a painter of exquiſite taſte; his ſtyle being for the moſt part compounded from that of his brother-in-law and Claude Lorraine. Perhaps his beſt works are his ſtorms, of which we have two noble ſpecimens in the national collection; the 'Dido and Æneas,' and its companion.

"It was reſerved for Paul Bril, who arrived at Rome

about the end of the ſixteenth century, bringing with him from Antwerp a ſtyle of landſcape peculiarly his own, and leſs ſevere than that of the Caracci, to exerciſe an influence on the art which was deſtined in the ſeventeenth century to extend through Bril's pupil, Agoſtino Taſſi, to Claude Lorraine, and to lead to that more minute imitation of particular nature which was the practice of the French and German artiſts of the time. By thus engrafting a certain portion of Flemiſh art on that of Italy, a more perfect and beautiful tranſcript of nature was achieved by the inimitable Claude, and conduced to the production of thoſe exquiſite works of his pencil which are wholly without rivalry in the quality which diſtinguiſhes them of placid brightneſs. In his ſea-views, his golden ſunſets, his wild and romantic ſhores, and his exquiſitely poetic paſtoral ſcenes, the luminous beauties of the painter are ſo clearly developed as to require leſs explanation than the qualities of many of the works already referred to. He has been deemed the moſt perfect landſcape painter the world ever ſaw, and he fully merits the diſtinction. The characteriſtics of his pictures are always thoſe of ſerene beauty. Sweetneſs and amenity reign through every creation of his pencil; but his chief power conſiſted in uniting ſplendour with repoſe, warmth with freſhneſs, and dark with light.—Although he was a painter of fairy land, and ſylvan ſcenery of the moſt romantic kind, he is nowhere ſeen to greater advantage than in his ſea ports, which, while they poſſeſs many of the moſt charming qualities of his more ſequeſtered landſcapes, are full of buſineſs and buſtle.

"The names of Salvator Roſa and Sebaſtian Bourdon, come next in an account of the art in which they ſo much excelled. The one, wild and terrific in his conceptions of natural ſcenery, formed his mind amid the ſavage receſſes of the Abruzzi, and painted ſubjects which beſt accorded with its character. The other equally romantic, but more viſionary, ſelected as the materials of his pictures ſolitudes among rocks, waterfalls, and ſolemn looking buildings which he peopled with monks and hermits.

"In following the art to Flanders we find the magnificent Rubens, with his numerous followers, Vadder, Fouquieres, Artois, Huyſman, Van Uden, &c. In no other branch of the art is Rubens greater than in landſcape;—the freſhneſs and dewy light, the joyous and animated character which he has imparted to it, impreſſing on the level monotonous ſcenery of Flanders all the richneſs which belongs to its nobleſt features. Rubens delighted in phenomena;—rainbows upon a ſtormy ſky,—burſts of ſunſhine,—moonlight,—meteors,—and impetuous torrents mingling their ſound with wind and wave. Among his fineſt works are a pair of landſcapes, which came to England from Genoa, one of which is now in the National Gallery.

"In Holland, Rembrandt's "Mill" is of itſelf ſufficient to form an epoch in the art. This is the firſt picture in which a ſentiment has been expreſſed by chiaroſcuro only, all details being excluded.—Nor muſt the names of Ruyſdael and Cuyp be overlooked as diſtinguiſhed from numerous other painters by traits peculiarly their own.

"On the death of theſe great men Landſcape rapidly declined; and during almoſt the whole of the ſucceeding century, little was produced beyond mannered and feeble imitations of their art,—the painters of this period adding nothing to the general ſtock, as their predeceſſors had done by original ſtudy, but referring always to the pictures of their maſters inſtead of looking to the aſpects of nature which had given birth to thoſe pictures. From this degraded and fallen ſtate it is delightful to ſay, that landſcape painting revived in our own country, in all its purity, ſimplicity, and grandeur, in the works of Wilſon, Gainſborough, Cozens, and Girtin.

"It is a ſtriking feature in the hiſtory of all the arts and

CH. XVIII. ſciences, though it has not perhaps been noticed in ours, that the great names by which they have each been ſupported are about equal in number in any given ſpace of time. The names of the painters I have mentioned and which have become points marking the epochs of landſcape, correſpond numerically with thoſe of the eminent men who have materially enlarged the boundaries of each of the other departments in art, literature, and ſcience. It will not be eaſy to add to thoſe I have enumerated, as forming the fixed ſtars in the hemiſphere of art; and although others of great talent crowd in, "Thick as autumnal leaves," to fill the interſtices, yet they all emanate from, or converge into thoſe which form the great points, and my limits do not permit an account of them here. Should, however, at any future time my humble ſervices be employed in any further inquiry of this kind, they muſt in juſtice be brought forward, as each brings in his hand a flower ſnatched by himſelf from the lap of nature.

"I ſhall conclude with a brief alluſion to a certain ſet of painters, who, having ſubſtituted falſehood for truth, and formed a ſtyle mean and mechanical, are termed manneriſts. Much of the confuſion of opinions in art ariſing from falſe taſte, is cauſed by works of this ſtamp, for *if the manneriſts had never exiſted, painting would always have been eaſily underſtood.* The education of a profeſſed connoiſſeur being chiefly formed in the picture gallery and auction room, ſeldom enables him to perceive the vaſt difference between the manneriſt and the genuine painter. To do this requires long and cloſe ſtudy, and a conſtant compariſon of the art with nature. So few among the buyers and ſellers of pictures poſſeſs any knowledge ſo derived, that the works of the manneriſts often bear as large a price in the market as thoſe of the genuine painters. The difference is not underſtood by picture dealers, and thus, in a mercantile way, has a kind of art been propagated and ſupported from age to age, deſerving only to be claſſed with the ſhowy and expenſive articles of drawing room furniture. To this ſpecies of painting belong the works that have marked the decay of ſtyles and filled the intervals between the appearances of the great artiſts. They are the productions of men who have loſt ſight of nature, and ſtrayed into the vacant fields of idealiſm; ſometimes, indeed, with talent, and even with power, as in Wouvermans,* Berghem, Both, Vernet, Zuccherelli, and Loutherbourg; but oftener with feebleneſs and imbecility, as in Jacob Moore, Hackert, &c."

* The great merit of Wouvermans only makes it the more important that the wide departure from nature in his highly wrought works ſhould be pointed out. No perfection of execution can atone for inky foregrounds, ſlaty trees and diſtances, and leaden ſkies; but it may well be doubted whether that execution ſhould be called perfect which reduces every object to a Lilliputian ſcale. They are exactly ſuch painters as Wouvermans, ſo near excellence in the minutiæ of a picture, and at the ſame time ſo falſe in the whole together, of whom Conſtable has well ſaid, "had they never exiſted, painting would always have been eaſily underſtood."

There is a claſs of the Dutch painters of familiar life, men of much talent, ingenuity, and patience, at the head of which Gerard Dow may be placed, whoſe works call forth the wonder of ignorance rather than the admiration of taſte, though from their ſcarcity they often command higher prices than the pictures of Jan Steen, Oſtade, Terburgh, Metzu, De Hooghe, and Nicholas Maas, the great maſters of familiar life of the Dutch ſchool, and in ſome of whoſe beſt works is perhaps to be found the moſt perfect art the world ever ſaw.

PREVIOUSLY to the delivery of Conſtable's lectures in London, the following card was printed:

"ROYAL INSTITUTION OF GREAT BRITAIN,

ALBEMARLE STREET, 23RD APRIL, 1836.

SYLLABUS

OF

A COURSE OF LECTURES,

ON

THE HISTORY OF LANDSCAPE PAINTING,

BY

JOHN CONSTABLE, ESQ. R.A.

TO BE DELIVERED ON THURSDAY, MAY 26TH, AND THE THREE FOLLOWING THURSDAYS AT THREE O'CLOCK.

"Lecture 1ſt, May 26th. The Origin of Landſcape—Coeval in Italy and Germany in its riſe and early progreſs—Farther advanced in Germany in the Fifteenth Century—Albert Durer—Influence of his Works in Italy—Titian impreſſed by them; in *his* hands Landſcape aſſumed its real dignity and grandeur, and entitled him to the appellation of the *Father of Landſcape*—The 'St. Peter Martyr.'

"Lecture 2nd, June 2nd. Eſtabliſhment of Landſcape—The Bologneſe School. By this School Landſcape was firſt made a ſeparate Claſs of Art—The Sixteenth and Seventeenth Centuries—The Caracci—Domenichino—Albano—Mola—Landſcape ſoon after perfected in Rome—The Pouſſins—Claude Lorraine—Bourdon—Salvator Roſa—The 'Bambocciate'—Peter de Laar—Both—Berghem—The Deterioration of Landſcape—Its Decline in the Eighteenth Century.

" Lecture 3rd, June 9th. Landſcape of the Dutch and Flemiſh Schools—Emanates from the School of Albert Durer, forming diſtinct branches—Rubens—Rembrandt—Ruyſdael—Cuyp—The marks which characterize the two Schools—Their decline, alſo, in the Eighteenth Century.

" Lecture 4th, June 16. The decline and revival of Art. Imitation of preceding excellence oppoſed to original ſtudy, the main cauſe of the decline—The Reſtoration of Painting takes place in England—Hogarth—Reynolds—Wilſon—Gainſborough—Weſt—When Landſcape at length reſumes its birthright, and appears with new powers."

LECTURE I.

May 26th.

" I AM here on the behalf of my own profeſſion, and I truſt it is with no intruſive ſpirit that I now ſtand before you; but I am anxious that the world ſhould be inclined to look to painters for information on painting. I hope to ſhew that ours is a regularly taught profeſſion; that it is *ſcientific* as well as *poetic;* that imagination alone never did, and never can, produce works that are to ſtand by a compariſon with *realities;* and to ſhow, by tracing the connecting links in the hiſtory of landſcape painting, that no great painter was ever ſelf taught.

" The art of painting may be divided into two main branches, hiſtory and landſcape; hiſtory including portrait and familar life, as landſcape does flower and fruit painting.

" Landſcape is the child of hiſtory, and though at firſt inſeparable from the parent, yet in time it went alone, and at a later period, (to continue the figure,) when hiſtory ſhowed ſigns of decrepitude, the child may be ſeen ſupporting the parent, as in the works of Pietro da Cortona. Although it was in the ſchool of the Caracci landſcape firſt ſtood quite alone, yet as early as the year 1546, there were diſtinct landſcape painters in Germany." Conſtable ſhowed an enlarged drawing from an engraving of a landſcape by Albert Durer, in which a cannon placed on an eminence overlooking an extenſive country, forms a foreground object. He pointed out the grandeur of this work, and ſaid, "There can be no doubt but that Titian had received early and deep impreſſions from the works of Albert Durer and other Germans."

"The writers on art employ the word *School* to denote a ſimilarity of feeling and practice in many individuals ariſing from the example of one powerful mind, yet by no means implying a want of originality in the reſt. The greateſt maſters were largely indebted to their predeceſſors. Each ſprang from, and in turn founded, a ſchool; but in the complicated art of painting ſo many avenues to excellence are open, that every painter, in every ſchool, whoſe fame has outlived his age, is diſtinguiſhed from all the reſt by ſome perfection which is to be found with himſelf only."

Near the commencement of this lecture, Conſtable exhibited a drawing from a very grand and ſimple compoſition by Paolo Uccello, of Noah and his family kneeling round an altar, while the birds and beaſts are leaving the ark, the whole arched by the rainbow. "Uccello was either the inventor or the perfector of parallel perſpective, and this new art is beautifully ſhown in the flight of the birds. Titian's Cornaro family ſomewhat reſembles this picture."

In ſpeaking of the "Peter Martyr" of Titian, he ſaid, "The monk, afterwards canonized as St. Peter, was a General of the Dominicans and an Inquiſitor. In the zeal diſplayed by him in the laſt of theſe offices he had given great offence to a powerful family, who employed an aſſaſſin to waylay and murder him. In the repreſentation of this ſubject Titian has brought together a rich aſſemblage of pictureſque objects producing a felicitous combination of the two moſt important walks of art,—hiſtory and landſcape; and contraſting them ſo as to enhance the ſentiment of each. We ſee a deed of horror perpetrated with the utmoſt energy of action, in a ſcene, hitherto one of ſtillneſs and repoſe." Conſtable then ſpoke of the probable manner in which Titian proceeded with the compoſition of the picture, and whether in every reſpect he gueſſed rightly or not, he accompliſhed his principal object, which was to ſhow that the greateſt works of genius are not thrown off as if by inſpiration, but on the contrary, are the reſult of patient labour, and often undergo many changes of plan during their progreſs. He ſhowed an old print bearing the name of Titian, in which the ſaint is looking down and writing with his finger on the ground the word *credo*, while the aſſaſſin who holds him by his drapery is about to ſtrike a death blow with his ſword. "This," he ſaid, "was poſſibly a mode in which it was ſuggeſted by the monks that the ſubject ſhould be treated, and the engraving may have been made from a firſt deſign. But Titian could not reſt contented with the unnatural incident of a man writing while in the graſp of an aſſaſſin, and he therefore turned the face of the victim towards the murderer, and afterwards ſtill more ſo, with an expreſſion of great horror." Conſtable here ſhowed a copy of an original ſketch by Titian, (one of the Lawrence collection,) in which the ſaint has the outlines of three heads drawn one over the other, the firſt looking down, the others more and more turned up, and ſaid,—"ſtill this made the ſubject nothing more than a common murder by the road ſide, and it wanted the dignity of a martyrdom. The compoſition was then heightened, the viſion of angels introduced, and the head of the ſaint again altered, ſo as to look up to the glory that now beamed down on him." Several ſketches ſuppoſed to be by Titian, ſeemed to confirm theſe conjectures, and by theſe it alſo appeared that the tall tree on the right of the picture, with ſmall round leaves, was an after thought, and made neceſſary by the additional height given to the picture; it is not in the ſketch of the landſcape alone. "It is ſtriking," ſaid Conſtable, "to obſerve with what conſummate ſkill the painter, like a great muſician, has varied his touch and execution from ſlow movements to thoſe of extreme rapidity. Thus the quick and vivid ſparks of light near and upon the aſſaſſin's arm, hand, and ſword, give inconceivable energy to his action, and contraſt finely with the ſolemn quiet of the retiring foreſt.*

"Reynolds has cenſured Count Algarotti for admiring the minute diſcrimination of the leaves and plants in the foreground, but Sir Joſhua was ſwayed by his own practice, of generalizing to ſuch a degree that we often find in his foregrounds rich maſſes of colour, of light and of ſhade, which, when examined, mean nothing. In Titian there is equal breadth, equal ſubordination of the parts to the whole, but the ſpectator finds, on approaching the picture, that every touch is the repreſentative of a reality; and as this carries on the illuſion, it cannot ſurely detract from the merit of the work.

"Mr. Weſt ſaid of the 'Peter Martyr,' that '*it had required three hundred years to produce ſuch a work*;' and this will be found to be about the time from the revival of the art in the middle ages to that in which it was painted.

* The murderer has the ſhirt ſleeve ſtripped from his right arm, as in the old pictures of decapitations by the ſword, the right arm of the executioner is bared. This circumſtance which makes the figure more pictureſque, aids the ſtory by ſhowing that the crime was premeditated. In the earlier deſign of the ſubject, the aſſaſſin is entirely dreſſed.

"Titian was by no means high in reputation when he produced this great work, and ſo inadequate was the remuneration he received for it, and for many others that had preceded it, that he was in a condition little removed from indigence. Albert Durer, who at that time viſited Venice, does not mention him in ſpeaking of the moſt eminent painters there; it was not, indeed, until through the praiſes beſtowed on his works by his friend Peitro Aretino, the poet, he was called to Bologna to paint the portrait of Charles V. in 1530, that he became the great idol of popularity in Italy, and indeed, of Europe."*

LECTURE II.

June 2nd.

CONSTABLE began this lecture with the Caracci, in whoſe ſchool landſcape firſt became *permanently* a diſtinct branch of the art, and recapitulated what he had ſaid at Hampſtead of Domenichino. He characterized alſo the art of Albano and Mola, but of this part of his diſcourſe I have no notes.

He ſpoke of Claude Lorraine as "a painter whoſe works had given unalloyed pleaſure for two centuries. In Claude's landſcape all is lovely—all amiable—all is amenity and re-

* In a note to Mr. Purton, dated May 28th, 1836, Conſtable ſays, "How did I get on? Faraday ſaid it pleaſed him; Sir Martin and Howard liked it; Phillips did not like my unbigoted mention of Sir Joſhua's obſervation on Algarotti, and ſaid I was wrong; I knew I was quite right. I truſt you will follow me through my ſermons, and help me in putting them together afterwards. I hope to murder Both and Berghem on Thurſday next at a quarter to four o'clock. The reſt that come after are not worth murdering."

poſe ;—the calm ſunſhine of the heart. He carried landſcape, indeed, to perfection, that is, *human perfection*. No doubt the greateſt maſters conſidered their beſt efforts but as experiments, and perhaps as experiments that had failed when compared with their hopes, their wiſhes, and with what they ſaw in nature. When we ſpeak of the perfection of art, we muſt recollect what the materials are with which a painter contends with nature. For the light of the ſun he has but patent yellow and white lead,—for the darkeſt ſhade, umber or ſoot.

"Brightneſs was the characteriſtic excellence of Claude; brightneſs, independent on colour, for what colour is there here?" (holding up a glaſs of water.)

"The 'St. Urſula,' in the National Gallery, is probably the fineſt picture of *middle tint* in the world. The ſun is riſing through a thin miſt, which, like the effect of a gauze blind in a room, diffuſes the light equally. There are no large dark maſſes. The darks are in the local colours of the foreground figures, and in ſmall ſpots; yet as a whole, it is perfect in breadth. There is no evaſion in any part of this admirable work, every object is fairly painted in a firm ſtyle of execution, yet in no other picture have I ſeen the evaneſcent character of light ſo well expreſſed.

"Claude, though one of the moſt iſolated of all painters, was ſtill legitimately connected with the chain of art. Elſheimer and Paul Bril opened the way to him, coming after the Caracci, with a ſofter and richer ſtyle than theirs.—Could the hiſtories of all the fine arts be compared, we ſhould find in them many ſtriking analogies. Corelli was to Handel what Elſheimer and Paul Bril were to Claude. Claude (as he is) could not have exiſted without them. He was, therefore, not a *ſelf-taught artiſt*, nor did there ever exiſt a great artiſt who was ſo. A *ſelf-taught artiſt* is one taught by a very ignorant perſon.

"Claude neglected no mode of ſtudy that was calculated

to extend his knowledge, and perfect his practice. His evenings were paſſed at the Academy, and his days in the fields; and though it is the faſhion to find fault with his figures indiſcriminately, yet in his beſt time they are ſo far from being objectionable, that we cannot eaſily imagine any thing elſe according ſo well with his ſcenes;—as objects of colour, they ſeem indiſpenſable. Wilſon ſaid to a friend who was talking of them in the uſual manner, 'Do not fall into the common miſtake of objecting to Claude's figures.'—In the little picture of Cephalus, and Procris, the expreſſion of the former is very touching; and, indeed, nothing can be finer than the way in which Claude has told that affecting ſtory throughout. Procris has come from her concealment to die at the feet of her huſband. Above her is a withered tree claſped by ivy, an emblem of love in death,—while a ſtag ſeen on the outline of a hill, over which the riſing ſun ſpreads his rays, explains the cauſe of the fatal miſtake. Claude's own figures always accord better with his ſcenes than thoſe ſometimes introduced for him by other artiſts. Painting does not readily admit of partnerſhip.

"But of Claude, it may be proper to remark, that his ſtyle and mode of execution, and even of thinking, varied much at different periods of life. Of his very early manner we know little; in middle age he appeared in the moſt perfect ſtate, and from which he faſt declined, ſo much ſo, that the dates of his pictures (which can for the moſt part be aſcertained) will ſerve as a criterion of their merit. Between the ages of forty and ſixty he produced moſt of thoſe works in which are ſeen his peculiar attribute, *brightneſs*, in its greateſt perfection. Some of his beſt pictures are in the National Gallery,—the 'Narciſſus,' painted at forty-four, the 'Hagar' at forty-ſix, and the 'St. Urſula,' under ſixty. Thoſe of his latter time are cold, heavy, and dark, though ſtately,—for he ſeemed as if trying to make up by grandeur of ſubject and conception, for the loſs of that excellence which, in the decline of life, and in the abſence of his former habits of inceſſant obſervation of nature, was now departing from him. It is in theſe laſt pictures that his figures are defective in their proportions; and though it muſt be admitted that ſome of his moſt important works (as the Doria and the Altieri,) were painted in his old age, ſtill with all their grandeur, they are in his black, his cold, or his green manner. There are undoubted productions of his pencil however, ſo deſtitute of his diſtinguiſhing excellence, that it may be ſaid purchaſers are not always buying *a Claude* when they are buying a picture painted by him.*

"The landſcapes of Sebaſtian Bourdon are all poetry; viſionary, romantic, abſtracted. Sir George Beaumont ſaid of this imaginative painter, that 'he was *the prince of the dreamers, yet not without nature.*'"—Conſtable ſhowed a drawing of ſome pine trees from nature, of peculiarly wild and eccentric forms, and compared them with trees extremely like them in an engraving after Bourdon, to prove that the latter were not imaginary.—He ſpoke of "The Return of the Ark" in the National Gallery as a very fine ſpecimen of the ſtyle of this painter.

"The circumſtances attending the life and education of Salvator Roſa were peculiar, and ſhow how his character and that of his art were formed, or rather *confirmed.* He was firſt placed with Franceſco Francanzani, and he then became one of the *deſperate* ſchool of Anniello Falcone, a battle painter, who formed the 'Company of Death' at Naples, in the revolt with Maſaniello. He was afterwards for a ſhort

* The ſtory ſo often repeated of Claude's apprenticeſhip to a paſtrycook, reſts on no foundation whatever. The beſt account of the little known of his early life is given by Mr. Smith, in his Catalogue Raiſonné of the works of the Dutch, Flemiſh, and French Painters.

time in the ſchool of Spagnoletto;—thus he had *ſavages* for his maſters in painting, and he painted *ſavage* ſubjects. Salvator Roſa is a great favourite with novel writers, particularly the ladies; and it has lately been attempted to ſhow that he deſerved the reputation to which he always aſpired, of a great hiſtorical painter. But there is a meanneſs in all his conceptions of hiſtory which muſt ever exclude him from its firſt ranks, and Fuſeli, with true judgment, admits him to be a great genius only in landſcape.

"A claſs of artiſts now appeared, in all reſpects the reverſe of the laſt, and whoſe ſtyle Salvator has ſatirized in one of his ſonnets with more juſtice than when he preſumed to cenſure Michael Angelo.

"Peter de Laar, who travelled from Holland into Italy, and was there ſurnamed 'Bamboccio,' probably from the claſs of ſubjects he painted, which were the various ſports of the populace and the tranſactions of vulgar life, gave riſe to a ſchool called by the Italians, 'The Bambocciate.' Of this ſchool were Both and Berghem, who, by an incongruous mixture of Dutch and Italian taſte, produced a baſtard ſtyle of landſcape, deſtitute of the real excellence of either. In their works, all the common-place rules of art are obſerved; their manipulation is dextrous, and their finiſh plauſible; yet their pictures carry us in imagination only into their painting rooms, not as the pictures of Claude and Pouſſin do, into the open air. They rarely approach truth of atmoſphere. Inſtead of freſhneſs they give us a clean and ſtony coldneſs, and where they aim at warmth they are what painters call *foxy*. Their art is deſtitute of ſentiment or poetic feeling, becauſe it is factitious, though their works being ſpecious, their reputation is ſtill kept up by the dealers, who continue to ſell their pictures for high prices.*

* After this lecture, one of Conſtable's auditors, a gentleman poſſeſſing a

CH. XVIII. Landſcape was afterwards ſtill farther debaſed by Vernet, Hakert,* Jacob Moor, and the Engliſh Wooton, the laſt of whom, without manual dexterity, left it in unredeemed poverty and coarſeneſs, until Hogarth and Reynolds arouſed the minds of our countrymen, and directed them to nature by their own ſplendid examples; then, with Wilſon and Gainſborough, the high and genuine qualities of landſcape appeared in England at a time when they were utterly unknown in any other part of the world.

"The deterioration of art has every where proceeded from ſimilar cauſes, the imitation of preceding ſtyles, with little reference to nature. In Italy, the taſte was for the beautiful, but the beautiful in the hands of the manneriſts became the inſipid, and from that deſcended to the unmeaning. In Germany a clumſy imitation of Italian art, and particularly of M. Angelo, produced inflation and bombaſt, as in the works of Goltzius and Spranghen; while in Flanders and Holland, the taſte for the pictureſque, when colour, chiaroſcuro, and execution were gone, left only the coarſe and the mean.

"The decline of hiſtory was parallel with that of landſcape. What is termed the 'French taſte,' (as oppoſed to good taſte) and which may be characterized as *romantic hyperbole*, began with Lucatelli, a pupil of Pietro da Cortona, who died about 1717. He was an Italian, and practiſed his art chiefly in Rome; but his ſtyle ſoon ſpread itſelf in France, where it deſtroyed whatever may have remained of the influence of Pouſſin, Le Sueur, or Sebaſtian Bourdon. He painted chiefly hiſtorical ſubjects for churches, and was like his maſter, a compendious painter—a manneriſt—a ſelf-wor-

fine collection of pictures, ſaid to him, "I ſuppoſe I had better ſell my Berghems," to which he replied, "No, ſir, that will only continue the miſchief, *burn them.*"

* Not Hackaert, a Dutch painter, born in 1635, but Hakert, a Pruſſian, born a century later.

ſhipper; he preferred forms of his own imagination to thoſe of nature. In his works may be ſeen the beginning of that prettineſs which ſoon afterwards in Marco Ricci, Paulo Panini, and Zuccherelli, and Vernet in landſcape, diſplayed itſelf ſo offenſively. In hiſtory, Mengs, Cipriani, Angelica Kauffman, &c. followed this emaſculated taſte, to the excluſion of all that is ſound in art.

"But the climax of abſurdity to which the art may be carried, when led away from nature by faſhion, may be beſt ſeen in the works of Boucher. Good temper, ſuavity, and diſſipation, characterized the perſonal habits of this perfect ſpecimen of the French School of the time of Louis the Fifteenth, or the early part of the laſt century. His landſcape, of which he was evidently fond, is paſtoral; and ſuch paſtorality! the paſtoral of the Opera houſe. But at this time, it muſt be remembered, the court were in the habit of diſperſing into the country, and ducheſſes were to be ſeen performing the parts of ſhepherdeſſes, milk maids, and dairy maids, in cottages; and alſo brewing, baking, and gardening, and ſending the produce to market.* Theſe ſtrange anomalies were played off on the canvaſſes of Boucher. His ſcenery is a bewildered dream of the pictureſque. From cottages adorned with feſtoons of ivy, ſparrow pots, &c. are ſeen iſſuing opera dancers with mops, brooms, milk pails, and guitars; children with cocked hats, queues, bag wigs, and ſwords,—and cats, poultry, and pigs. The ſcenery is diverſified with winding ſtreams, broken bridges, and water wheels; hedge ſtakes dancing minuets—and groves bowing and curtſying to each other; the whole leaving the mind in a ſtate of bewilderment and confuſion, from which laughter

* Vagaries like theſe were practiſed by Madame de Pompadour at the Parc-aux-cerfs to amuſe Louis the Fifteenth, and afterwards by Marie Antoinette at the Petit Trianon to amuſe herſelf.

alone can relieve it.*—Boucher told Sir Joſhua Reynolds, 'that he never painted from the life, for that nature put him out.'

"It is remarkable how nearly, in all things, oppoſite extremes are allied, and how they ſucceed each other. The ſtyle I have been deſcribing was followed by that which ſprung out of the Revolution, when David and his cotemporaries exhibited their ſtern and heartleſs petrifactions of men and women,—with trees, rocks, tables, and chairs, all equally bound to the ground by a relentleſs outline, and deſtitute of chiaroſcuro, the ſoul and medium of art."

Conſtable ſpoke of the want of ſenſe in David's large picture, in which the Romans and the Sabines are about to join battle, ſtark naked, but with helmets on their heads, and ſhields and ſpears in their hands. "What," he ſaid, "would be the impreſſion of a ſpectator of ſuch a ſcene, but that he ſaw before him a number of ſavages who had accidentally found and ſnatched up theſe weapons and accoutrements?"

* Watteau reconciles us by his natural grace and expreſſion, and his exquiſite colour, to an ideal union of the paſtoral and the faſhionable, and to which he alone gives an air of probability. The manners he painted were French, but his art is eſſentially Flemiſh, being founded on Rubens, whoſe "Garden of Love," no doubt, ſuggeſted a claſs of ſubjects in which Watteau has excelled all other painters. Boucher is Watteau run mad,—bereaved of his taſte and his ſenſe.

LECTURE III.

June 9th.

"I SHALL confider four works as marking four memorable points in the hiftory of landfcape, and all by hiftorical painters. The 'Peter Martyr' by Titian—'The Deluge' by Pouffin—'The Rainbow' by Rubens—and 'The Mill' by Rembrandt."

Having fpoken of the "Peter Martyr," Conftable fhowed an engraving of "The Deluge," and faid, "Towards the end of the life of Nicolo Pouffin, he was employed by Cardinal Richelieu to paint four pictures, each to reprefent a feafon. For the fpring, he chofe the terreftrial Paradife; for the fummer, the ftory of Boaz and Ruth; for the autumn, the two Ifraelites bearing the bunch of grapes from the promifed land; and for the winter, the Deluge. This picture, though fmall, and with little contraft of light and fhadow, and almoft no colour, ftands as much alone in the world as the Magdalen of Correggio. The good fenfe of Pouffin, which was equal to his genius, taught him that by fimplicity of treatment, the moft awful fubjects may be made far more affecting than by overloading them with imagery. In painting the Deluge, he has not allowed his imagination to wander from the Mofaic account, which tells us of rain only.* Human habitations, rocks, and mountains are gradually difappearing, as the water rifes undifturbed by earthquakes or tornadoes; and the very

* Pouffin feems to have reafoned as Coleridge did, who faid, "I think it abfurd to attribute fo much to the deluge. An inundation, which left an olive-tree ftanding, and bore up the ark peacefully on its bofom, could fcarcely have been the fole caufe of the rents and diflocations obfervable on the face of the earth."—COLERIDGE'S *Table Talk.*

few figures introduced, intereſt us the more deeply from the abſence of all violence or contortion of geſture. But of this picture Fuſeli ſays truly 'It is eaſier to feel than to deſcribe its powers. We ſee the element itſelf, and not its image. Its reign is eſtabliſhed, and by calm degrees ingulfs the whole. It mocks the food it feeds on. Its lurid haze has ſhorn the ſun of his beams. Hope is ſhut out, and nature expires!'

"By the Rainbow of Rubens, I do not allude to a particular picture, for Rubens often introduced it; I mean, indeed, more than the rainbow itſelf, I mean dewy light and freſhneſs, the departing ſhower, with the exhilaration of the returning ſun, effects which Rubens, more than any other painter, has perfected on canvaſs."—Conſtable deſcribed the large picture in the National Gallery, in which a fowler is ſeen watching a covey of partridges, as a fine ſpecimen of Rubens' power in landſcape, and lamented that it was ſeparated from its companion, "which had doubtleſs been painted to give more effect to it by contraſt." He ſaid, "When pictures painted as companions are ſeparated, the purchaſer of one, without being aware of it, is ſometimes buying only half a picture. Companion pictures ſhould never be parted, unleſs they are by different hands, and then, in general the ſooner they are divorced the better.

"The art of Rubens and Teniers* is eſſentially Flemiſh, and though it is uſual to ſpeak of the Dutch and Flemiſh ſchools as one, they are no more ſo than are the Lombard and Venetian ſchools. The Dutch art is more influenced by chiaroſcuro, the Flemiſh by colour, by brightneſs, and hilarity.

"Rembrandt's 'Mill'† is a picture wholly made by chiar-

---

* It muſt have been from inadvertence that Conſtable omitted any farther mention of the younger Teniers, whoſe landſcape compoſitions form a diſtinct and very beautiful claſs of art. Had theſe lectures been written, a paragraph would, no doubt, have been devoted to this delightful painter.

† A windmill on an eminence overlooking a ſtream.

oſcuro; the laſt ray of light juſt gleams on the upper ſail of the mill, and all other details are loſt in large and ſimple maſſes of ſhade. Chiaroſcuro is the great feature that characterizes his art, and was carried farther by him than by any other painter, not excepting Correggio. But if its effects are ſomewhat exaggerated by Rembrandt, he is always ſo impreſſive, that we can no more find fault with his ſtyle than we can with the giant forms of Michael Angelo. Succeeding painters have ſometimes, in their admiration of 'The Mill,' forgotten that Rembrandt choſe the twilight to ſecond his wiſhes, and have fancied that to obtain equal breadth, they muſt leave out the details of nature in broad daylight; this is the danger of miſtaken imitation.

" Chiaroſcuro is by no means confined to dark pictures; the works of Cuyp, though generally light, are full of it. It may be defined as that power which creates ſpace; we find it everywhere and at all times in nature; oppoſition, union, light, ſhade, reflection, and refraction, all contribute to it.* By this power, the moment we come into a room, we ſee

* All effects of light and dark are but modifications of reflection and refraction, with the exception of the appearances of things ſelf-luminous, as fire, the ſun, &c. which occaſion what we call lights on other objects by being reflected from or refracted through their ſurfaces; leaving, where ſuch reflections or refractions are interrupted by intervening bodies, the reflections of inferior lights from other objects, which being leſs powerful appear as ſhadows.

It has been ſaid that water receives no ſhadow; but this is either equally true of all other bodies, or not true of water, which is undoubtedly ſubject to effects that we can no otherwiſe deſcribe than by the word ſhadow.—When, for inſtance, the ſun is ſhining on the ſea, were it poſſible that the water could be as ſmooth as a mirror, we ſhould ſee his diſc exactly reflected and once only, the ſurface of the water in other places giving an inverted image of the ſky; but as ſuch perfect ſtillneſs never occurs, the light of the ſun is ſpread on the ſurface by innumerable reflections of his diſc from the waves and refractions through them,—the ſpaces between each of theſe *lights* (as we call them) reflecting the ſky,—where again the upper parts of the clouds reflect the ſun, and other portions the blue ſky, or the ſea. The blue of the ſky is occaſioned by ſtill more minute reflections and refractions of the ſun from particles of vapour that the chairs are not ſtanding on the tables, but a glance ſhows us the relative diſtances of all the objects from the eye, though the darkeſt or the lighteſt may be the fartheſt off—It has been ſaid no man has enough of certain qualities that has them not in exceſs, ſo Rembrandt, of whoſe art chiaroſcuro is the eſſence, certainly carried it to an extreme. The other great painters of the Dutch ſchool were more artleſs; ſo apparently unſtudied, indeed, are the works of many of them, for inſtance, Jan Steen and De Hooge, that they ſeem put together almoſt without thought; yet it would be impoſſible to alter or leave out the ſmalleſt object, or to change any part of their light, ſhade, or colour, without injury to their pictures,—a proof that their art is conſummate.

"The landſcapes of Ruyſdael preſent the greateſt poſſible contraſt to thoſe of Claude, ſhowing how powerfully, from

more ſubtle than thoſe that compoſe the clouds, and but for which in place of the azure there would be a void of utter darkneſs. Where clouds or other objects intercept the reflections of the ſun from the waves, the reflection of the ſky remains, cauſing thoſe patches of ſhadow which, ſeen from a low point, ſtripe the ſea with long lines of blue.—The effects are exactly ſimilar on a meadow; the light of the ſun being reflected from or refracted through every blade of graſs, and where intercepted leaving the reflection of the ſky; and on a road, the light is ſpread by reflection from every particle of ſand, gravel, or clay.—Again, if we look cloſe at a poliſhed ball of metal we find a picture of every ſurrounding object, and this at a diſtance forms that appearance of light and ſhade that gives it rotundity to the eye. Let the ball be dimmed or roughened and the ſame general appearance of light and dark is left,—equally, though not ſo palpably, cauſed by reflection, the forms and colours of the objects pictured on the ball being more or leſs blended as its ſurface is more or leſs dimmed.

Of what conſequence, it may be ſaid, is it that the artiſt ſhould know this if he copy faithfully what he ſees? To which the reply is, that it may enable him to ſee better what he copies.—All good colouriſts have, no doubt, recognized the reſults I have ſpoken of in nature whether or not they inveſtigated the principle,—and the purity and evaneſcence of their colouring has been in proportion to their perception of theſe reſults. Paul Veroneſe ſaw nature thus with a truer eye than did Rubens, and a perfect ſenſe of the influence of reflections conſtitutes that extraordinary charm in the works of De Hooge which we ſcarcely the moſt oppoſite directions, genius may command our homage. In Claude's pictures, with ſcarcely an exception, the ſun ever ſhines. Ruyſdael, on the contrary, delighted in, and has made delightful to our eyes, thoſe ſolemn days, peculiar to his country and to ours, when without ſtorm, large rolling clouds ſcarcely permit a ray of ſunlight to break the ſhades of the foreſt. By theſe effects he enveloped the moſt ordinary ſcenes in grandeur, and whenever he has attempted marine ſubjects, he is far beyond Vandervelde."

Conſtable ſhowed a copy of a picture of this claſs by Ruyſdael. "The ſubject," he continued, "is the mouth of a Dutch river, without a ſingle feature of grandeur in the ſcenery; but the ſtormy ſky, the grouping of the veſſels, and the breaking of the ſea, make the picture one of the moſt impreſſive ever painted.

find elſewhere, on canvaſs, excepting in the beſt pictures of Claude.—An inveſtigation of theſe principles will protect the young artiſt from the danger of many unfounded aphoriſms that he is likely to hear from his elders, and meet with in books, as that *ſhadow is colourleſs*—that *lights ſhould be warm and ſhadows cool*, or *ſhadows warm and lights cool*, &c. A knowledge of theſe laws will explain, what his eye will ſoon perceive, that the tones both of lights and ſhades are infinitely varied according to circumſtances;—that as perſpective alters every line to the eye, ſo reflection and refraction change more or leſs every colour,—harmonizing the crude and giving variety to the monotonous;—and that ſhadow, as far as regards painting, can never be colourleſs, for it is never ſolely the reſult of the abſence of light excepting in ſituations with which the painter can have nothing to do, the interior, for inſtance, of a cave to which every opening is cloſed.

I am glad to be able, in ſupport of theſe concluſions, to quote ſo high an authority as that of my friend Mr. George Field, whoſe valuable works on the philoſophy of colour are known to moſt artiſts, and ſhould be to all. In his "Chromatography" Mr. Field ſays, "Colour, and what in painting is called tranſparency, belong principally to ſhade; and the judgment of great authorities by which they have been attached to light as its properties merely, has led to error in an art to which colour is pre-eminently appropriate; hence the painter has conſidered colour in his practice as belonging to light only, and hence many have employed a uniform ſhade tint, regarding ſhadows only as darkneſs, blackneſs, or the mere abſence of light, when in truth ſhadows are infinitely varied by colour."

'It is the Soul that ſees; the outward eyes
Preſent the object, but the Mind deſcries.'

We ſee nothing truly till we underſtand it. An ordinary ſpectator at the mouth of the river which Ruyſdael has here painted, would ſcarcely be conſcious of the exiſtence of many of the objects that conduce to the effect of the picture; certainly not of their fitneſs for pictorial effect.

Conſtable pointed to a copy of a ſmall evening winter-piece by Ruyſdael. "This picture," he ſaid, "repreſents an approaching thaw. The ground is covered with ſnow, and the trees are ſtill white; but there are two windmills near the centre; the one has the ſails furled, and is turned in the poſition from which the wind blew when the mill left off work; the other has the canvaſs on the poles, and is turned another way, which indicates a change in the wind; the clouds are opening in that direction, which appears by the glow in the ſky to be the ſouth, (the ſun's winter habitation in our hemiſphere,) and this change will produce a thaw before the morning. The concurrence of theſe circumſtances ſhows that Ruyſdael *underſtood* what he was painting. He has here told a ſtory; but in another inſtance he failed, becauſe he attempted to tell that which is out of the reach of the art. In a picture which was known, while he was living, to be called 'An Allegory of the Life of Man' (and it may therefore be ſuppoſed he ſo intended it)—there are ruins to indicate old age, a ſtream to ſignify the courſe of life, and rocks and precipices to ſhadow forth its dangers;—but how are we to diſcover all this?

"The Dutch painters were a *ſtay-at-home people*,—hence their originality. They were not, however, ignorant of Italian art. Rembrant had a large collection of Italian pictures and engravings, and Fuſeli calls the ſchool of the Baſſans the 'Venetian prelude to the Dutch ſchool.' We derive the pleaſure of ſurpriſe from the works of the beſt Dutch painters in finding how much intereſt the art, when in perfection, can give to the moſt ordinary ſubjects. Thoſe are cold critics who turn from their works, and wiſh the ſame ſkill had been rendered a vehicle for more elevated ſtories. *They* do not in reality feel how much the Dutch painters have given to the world, who wiſh for more; and it may always be doubted whether thoſe who do not reliſh the works of the Dutch and Flemiſh ſchools, whatever raptures they may affect in ſpeaking of the ſchools of Italy, are capable of fully appreciating the latter; for *a true taſte is never a half taſte*. Whatever ſtory the beſt painters of Holland and Flanders undertook to tell, is told with an unaffected truth of expreſſion that may afford uſeful leſſons in the treatment of the moſt ſublime ſubjects; and thoſe who would deny them poetic feeling, forget that chiaroſcuro, colour, and compoſition, are all poetic qualities. Poetry is not denied to Rembrandt, or to Rubens, becauſe their effects are ſtriking. It does not, however, the leſs exiſt in the works of many other painters of the Dutch and Flemiſh ſchools who were leſs daring in their ſtyle."

LECTURE IV.

June 16th.

OF Conſtable's fourth lecture, I regret to find that even leſs is preſerved than of the preceding ones. He recapitulated the hiſtory of landſcape ſince the revival of the arts, compriſing a ſpace of about ſix hundred years, Titian's "Peter Martyr" forming a central epoch.

He ſhowed engravings from Patel of imitations of Claude, and from Vernet of imitations of Salvator Roſa, and pointed out the inferiority.

" The abſurdity of imitation," he remarked, " is nowhere ſo ſtriking as in the landſcapes of the Engliſh Wooton, who painted country gentlemen in their wigs and jockey caps, and top boots, with packs of hounds, and placed them in Italian landſcapes reſembling thoſe of Gaſpar Pouſſin, except in truth and force. Lambert, another Engliſh imitator of Italian art, but even below Wooton, is now remembered only as the founder of the ' Beef Steak Club.'

" The art of painting was in all its branches in the moſt degraded ſtate, not only in England but thoughout Europe, when Hogarth and Reynolds appeared, and thought and ſtudied for themſelves. Burke has ſaid that Reynolds ' was the firſt Engliſhman who added the praiſe of the elegant arts to the other glories of his country.' But he forgot that Hogarth was born twenty-ſix years before Sir Joſhua, and had publiſhed his engravings of the ' Harlot's Progreſs' when Reynolds was but eleven years old; or it may be he was influenced by the common opinion of that time which we find echoed by Walpole, that Hogarth was *no painter*. It is, however, to Reynolds that the honour of eſtabliſhing the Engliſh ſchool belongs. Hogarth had no ſchool, nor has he ever been imitated with any tolerable ſucceſs."

Among the engravings Conſtable exhibited at this lecture, he placed Sir Joſhua's lovely group of the three Ladies Waldegrave under the Ugolino, and remarked, " how great muſt be the range of *his* genius, who could fill the ſpace of art included between two ſuch ſubjects; Romney, when ſome of his friends thought to pleaſe him by diſparaging Reynolds, ſaid, ' No, no, he is the greateſt painter that ever lived, for I ſee an exquiſite beauty in his pictures which I ſee in nature, but not in the works of any other painter.'*

* This is true, in a greater or leſs degree, as Conſtable has himſelf remarked in the firſt of this courſe of lectures, of every original painter; indeed it is evident that this is the only teſt of originality.

"To Wilſon, who was ten years the ſenior of Reynolds, may juſtly be given the praiſe of opening the way to the genuine principles of Landſcape in England; he appeared at a time when this art, not only here, but on the Continent, was altogether in the hands of the manneriſts.* It was in Italy that he firſt became acquainted with his own powers; and no doubt the influence of the works of Claude and the Pouſſins enabled him to make the diſcovery. But he looked at nature entirely for himſelf, and remaining free from any tincture of the ſtyles that prevailed among the living artiſts, both abroad and at home, he was almoſt wholly excluded from any ſhare of the patronage which was liberally beſtowed on his cotemporaries. Barrett, and the Smiths of Chicheſter, whoſe names are now nearly forgotten, accumulated wealth while Wilſon might have ſtarved had he not been appointed librarian to the Royal Academy. Stothard uſed to relate an anecdote of Wilſon which ſhowed how much he was diſpoſed to turn to nature even in the midſt of art. Stothard, when a ſtudent, aſked Wilſon in the library, to recommend ſomething for him to copy. Wilſon at the moment was ſtanding at one of the windows, which, as the quadrangle of Somerſet Houſe was then unfiniſhed, commanded a fine view of the river. 'There,' ſaid the librarian pointing to the animated ſcene, 'is ſomething for you to copy.'

* The biographers of Wilſon attribute his leaving portraiture for landſcape, to the ſuggeſtion of one of theſe manneriſts, Zuccherelli; and of his obligations to another, Allan Cunningham gives this account. "One day, while ſitting in Wilſon's painting-room, Vernet was ſo ſtruck with the peculiar beauty of a newly finiſhed landſcape that he deſired to become its proprietor, and offered in exchange one of his beſt pictures. This was much to the gratification of the other; the exchange was made, and, with a liberality equally rare and commendable, Vernet placed his friend's picture in his exhibition room, and when his own productions happened to be praiſed or purchaſed by Engliſh travellers, the generous Frenchman uſed to ſay, 'Don't talk of my landſcapes alone, when your own countryman Wilſon paints ſo beautifully.'"

"The landſcape of Gainſborough is ſoothing, tender, and affecting. The ſtillneſs of noon, the depths of twilight, and the dews and pearls of the morning, are all to be found on the canvaſſes of this moſt benevolent and kind-hearted man. On looking at them, we find tears in our eyes, and know not what brings them. The lonely haunts of the ſolitary ſhepherd,—the return of the ruſtic with his bill and bundle of wood,—the darkſome lane or dell,—the ſweet little cottage girl at the ſpring with her pitcher,—were the things he delighted to paint, and which he painted with exquiſite refinement, yet not a refinement beyond nature. Gainſborough has been compared to Murillo by thoſe who cannot diſtinguiſh between the *ſubject* and the *art*. Like Murillo he painted the peaſantry of his country, but here the reſemblance ceaſes. His taſte was in all reſpects greatly ſuperior to that of the Spaniſh painter."

Conſtable ſpoke of Cozens and Girtin as poſſeſſing genius of the very higheſt order, though their works being comparatively few and in water colours chiefly, they are leſs known than they deſerve to be.

"Weſt ſhowed great ability in the compoſition of landſcape, which he ſometimes practiſed for itſelf, with figures entirely ſubordinate. His picture of the reception of Telemachus and Mentor by Calypſo after their ſhipwreck, is an extremely beautiful combination of landſcape and figures." Conſtable exhibited a fine engraving of this picture, begun by Woollett, and finiſhed by Pye.

"As your kind attention," he ſaid, "has ſo long been given to my deſcription of pictures, it may now be well to conſider in what eſtimation we are to hold them, and in what claſs we are to place the men who have produced them.—It appears to me that pictures have been over-valued; held up by a blind admiration as ideal things, and almoſt as ſtandards by which nature is to be judged rather than the reverſe; and this falſe eſtimate has been ſanctioned by the extravagant epithets that have been applied to painters, as 'the divine,' 'the inſpired,' and ſo forth.* Yet, in reality, what are the moſt ſublime productions of the pencil but ſelections of ſome of the forms of nature, and copies of a few of her evaneſcent effects; and this is the reſult, not of inſpiration, but of long and patient ſtudy, under the direction of much good ſenſe.—It was ſaid by Sir Thomas Lawrence, that 'we can never hope to compete with nature in the beauty and delicacy of her ſeparate forms or colours,—our only chance lies in ſelection and combination.' Nothing can be more true,—and it may be added, that ſelection and combination are learned from nature herſelf, who conſtantly preſents us with compoſitions of her own, far more beautiful than the happieſt arranged by human ſkill. I have endeavoured to draw a line between genuine art and manneriſm, but even the greateſt painters have never been wholly untainted by manner.—Painting is a ſcience, and ſhould be purſued as an inquiry into the laws of nature. Why, then may not landſcape painting be conſidered as a branch of natural philoſophy, of which pictures are but the experiments?"†

* "To ſay the truth, men do not appear to know their own ſtock and abilities, but fancy their poſſeſſions greater, and their faculties leſs, than they are; whence either valuing the received arts above meaſure, they look out no farther; or elſe deſpiſing themſelves too much, they exerciſe their talents upon lighter matters, without attempting the capital things of all. And hence the ſciences come to be conſidered as Hercules' Pillars, which are to bound the deſires and hopes of mankind. But as a falſe imagination of plenty comes among the principal cauſes of want, and as too great a confidence in things preſent leads to a neglect of future aſſiſtance, it is neceſſary that we here admoniſh mankind that they do not too highly value or extol either the number or uſefulneſs of the things hitherto diſcovered."—LORD BACON.

† Turnbull, whoſe folio on ancient painting Hogarth ſent to the trunkmaker with leſs juſtice than the 9999th volume of Politics, which he placed in the ſame hamper with it, conſiders landſcape painting as belonging to natural philoſophy, and hiſtorical painting to moral philoſophy. But Conſtable was not

Conſtable thanked his audience for the attention with which they had liſtened to him, and ſaid, "I cannot better take my leave of you than in the words of my friend, Archdeacon Fiſher, who, in an addreſs to the clergy, on one of his viſitations ſaid, 'In my preſent perplexity, the recollection comes to my relief that when any man has given an undivided attention to any one ſubject, his audience willingly yield him for his hour the chair of inſtruction; he diſcharges his mind of its conceptions, and deſcends from his temporary elevation to be inſtructed in his turn by other men.'"

LAST LECTURE DELIVERED BY CONSTABLE.

ON the 25th July, 1836, Conſtable delivered a lecture before the Literary and Scientific Inſtitution at Hampſtead, on the ſubject of Landſcape generally.

In adding the notes I took on this occaſion to the remaining memoranda preſerved among his papers, I ſhall omit paſſages in which he repeated parts of his previous lectures.

He began by ſaying, "The difference between the judgments pronounced by men who have given their lives to a particular ſtudy, and by thoſe who have attended to that ſtudy as the amuſement only of a few leiſure hours, may be thus illuſtrated. I will imagine two diſhes, the one of gold, the other of wood. The golden diſh is filled with diamonds, rubies, and emeralds,—and chains, rings, and brooches of gold; while the other contains ſhell-fiſh, ſtones, and earths. Theſe diſhes are offered to the world, who chooſe the firſt; but it is afterwards diſcovered that the diſh itſelf is but copper gilt,

acquainted with Turnbull's work when this lecture was delivered. He firſt ſaw it at my houſe in January, 1837.

the diamonds are paſte, the rubies and emeralds painted glaſs, and the chains, rings, &c. counterfeit. In the mean time, the naturaliſt has taken the wooden diſh, for he knows that the ſhell-fiſh are pearl oyſters, and he ſees that among the ſtones are gems, and mixed with the earths are the ores of the precious metals.

"The decline of painting, in every age and country, after arriving at excellence, has been attributed by writers who have not been artiſts to every cauſe but the true one. The firſt impreſſion and a natural one is, that the fine arts have riſen or declined in proportion as patronage has been given to them or withdrawn, but it will be found that there has often been more money laviſhed on them in their worſt periods than in their beſt, and that the higheſt honours have frequently been beſtowed on artiſts whoſe names are ſcarcely now known. Whenever the arts have not been upheld by the good ſenſe of their profeſſors, patronage and honours ſo far from checking their downward courſe, muſt inevitably accelerate it.

"The attempt to revive ſtyles that have exiſted in former ages, may for a time appear to be ſucceſsful, but experience may now ſurely teach us its impoſſibility. I might put on a ſuit of Claude Lorraine's clothes and walk into the ſtreet, and the many who know Claude but ſlightly would pull off their hats to me, but I ſhould at laſt meet with ſome one, more intimately acquainted with him, who would expoſe me to the contempt I merited.*

"It is thus in all the fine arts. A new Gothic building, or a new miſſal, is in reality little leſs abſurd than a *new ruin.*

* Archdeacon Fiſher, in one of his letters, that has not been printed, ſays, "I have juſt met with the following obſervation in Lionardo da Vinci, 'One painter ought never to imitate the manner of any other, becauſe in that caſe he cannot be called the child of nature, but the grand-child.'"—Conſtable ſometimes called imitators "Poachers on other men's grounds."

The Gothic architecture, sculpture, and painting, belong to peculiar ages. The feelings that guided their inventors are unknown to us, we contemplate them with associations, many of which, however vague and dim, have a strong hold on our imaginations, and we feel indignant at the attempt to cheat us by any modern mimicry of their peculiarities.*

"It is to be lamented that the tendency of taste is at present too much towards this kind of imitation, which, as long as it lasts, can only act as a blight on art, by engaging talents that might have stamped the Age with a character of its own, in the vain endeavour to reanimate deceased Art, in which the utmost that can be accomplished will be to reproduce a body without a soul.†

"Attempts at the union of uncongenial qualities in different styles of Art have also contributed to its decline." In illustration of this, Constable showed a print from Vernet, the trees of which were in a mannered imitation of Salvator Rosa, without his nature and wildness, while the rocks were in the artificial style of Berghem. "In the foreground," he said, "you will perceive an emaciated French dancing master, in a dress something like one of Salvator's banditti, but intended by Vernet for a fisherman. It is thus the art is deteriorated by the mannerists who employ themselves in sweeping up the painting rooms of preceding ages. Imitators always render the defects of their model more conspicuous. Sir George Beaumont, on seeing a large picture by a modern artist, intended to be in the style of Claude, said, 'I never could have believed that Claude Lorraine had so many

* See Fisher's letter on the death of Mrs. Constable, page 184.

† Nine years have elapsed since these observations were made, and the tendency of taste is still more confirmed in the direction of which Constable speaks. The present Age, distinguished as it is by the advance of the other Sciences, has become, in all that relates to Painting, Sculpture, and Architecture, little else than an Antiquarian Age.—It is well, in all things, as we go on, to look behind

faults, if I had not ſeen them all collected together on this canvaſs.' It is uſeful, therefore, to a painter to have imitators, as they will teach him to avoid every thing they do.

"The young painter, who regardleſs of preſent popularity, would leave a name behind him, muſt become the patient pupil of nature. If we refer to the lives of all who have diſtinguiſhed themſelves in art or ſcience, we ſhall find they have always been laborious. The landſcape painter muſt walk in the fields with an humble mind. No arrogant man was ever permitted to ſee nature in all her beauty. If I may be allowed to uſe a very ſolemn quotation, I would ſay moſt emphatically to the ſtudent, 'Remember now thy Creator in the days of thy youth.' The friends of a young artiſt ſhould not look or hope for precocity. It is often diſeaſe only. Quintilian makes uſe of a beautiful ſimile in ſpeaking of precocious talent. He compares it to the forward ear of corn that turns yellow and dies before the harveſt. Precocity often leads to criticiſm,—ſharp, and ſevere as the feelings are morbid from ill health. Lord Bacon ſays, 'when a young man becomes a critic, he will find much for his amuſement, little for his inſtruction.' The young artiſt muſt receive with deference the advice of his elders, not haſtily queſtioning what he does not yet underſtand, otherwiſe his maturity will bear no fruit. The art of ſeeing nature is a thing almoſt as much to be acquired as the art of reading the Egyptian hieroglyphics. The Chineſe have painted for two thouſand years, and have not diſcovered that there is ſuch a thing as chiaroſcuro.*

us,—but what advance can we hope to make with our faces conſtantly turned backwards?

* Some of the Chineſe painters have lately produced pictures with powerful effects of light and ſhade, in imitation of European art. Specimens of this kind may be ſeen in the ſplendid Chineſe Muſeum, lately opened. Still they are but imitations of art, and are black, heavy, and cold; and deſtitute of the real charm

Conſtable then gave ſome practical rules for drawing from nature, and ſhowed ſome beautiful ſtudies of trees. One, a tall and elegant aſh, of which he ſaid "many of my Hampſtead friends may remember this *young lady* at the entrance to the village. Her fate was diſtreſſing, for it is ſcarcely too much to ſay that ſhe died of a broken heart. I made this drawing when ſhe was in full health and beauty; on paſſing ſome time afterwards, I ſaw, to my grief, that a wretched board had been nailed to her ſide, on which was written in large letters '*All vagrants and beggars will be dealt with according to law.*' The tree ſeemed to have felt the diſgrace, for even then ſome of the top branches had withered. Two long ſpike nails had been driven far into her ſide. In another year one half became paralyzed, and not long after the other ſhared the ſame fate, and this beautiful creature was cut down to a ſtump, juſt high enough to hold the board."

Conſtable exhibited an outline of the principal figure in Fuſeli's "Lazar houſe," and ſhowed that the ſwellings and depreſſions in the outline of a figure in fine action never occur exactly on the oppoſite ſides, and the ſame he ſaid would be found true of trees when healthy.

He quoted from Thomſon's "Seaſons" the ſixteen introductory lines to the "Winter" as a beautiful inſtance of the poet identifying his own feelings with external nature. He noticed alſo Milton's love of landſcape, and how often in his poems the moſt ſimple imagery is mingled with the moſt ſublime. "Thus he has compared the army of the Cherubim attendant on the Archangel, while conducting our firſt parents from Paradiſe, to an evening miſt.

'The Archangel ſtood, and from the other hill
To their fix'd ſtation, all in bright array

---

of chiaroſcuro. Indeed the earlier works of the Chineſe, in which light and ſhade are not thought of, are more agreeable.

The Cherubim defcended ; on the ground,
Gliding meteorous, as evening mift
Rif'n from a river o'er the marifh glides,
And gathers ground faft at the lab'rer's heel,
Homeward returning.'

Introducing the homely incident of the labourer's return, and calling up all the ruftic firefide affociations connected with it in the midft of a defcription of the hoft of Heaven.

"There has," faid Conftable, "never been an age, however rude or uncultivated, in which the love of landfcape has not in fome way been manifefted. And how could it be otherwife? for man is the fole intellectual inhabitant of one vaft natural landfcape. His nature is congenial with the elements of the planet itfelf, and he cannot but fympathize with its features, its various afpects, and its phenomena in all fituations. How beautifully has Milton defcribed the emotions of Adam in the full maturity of mind and perception, his eyes opening for the firft time on the wonders of the animate and inanimate world:

'Straight toward Heav'n my wond'ring eyes I turn'd
And gaz'd awhile the ample Sky, * * *
* * * * * About me round I faw
Hill, Dale, and fhady Woods, and funny Plains,
And liquid lapfe of murm'ring ftreams ; by thefe
Creatures that liv'd and mov'd, and walk'd, or flew,
Birds on the branches warbling ; all things fmil'd
With fragrance, and with joy my heart o'erflow'd ;
* * * * Thou Sun, faid I, fair light,
And thou enlighten'd Earth, fo frefh and gay,
Ye Hills and Dales, ye Rivers, Woods, and Plains,
And ye that live and move, fair Creatures, tell,
Tell if ye faw, how came I thus, how here?'

"'When I behold,' fays Martin Luther, 'the beautiful azure vault of Heaven, befprinkled with conftellations of fhining orbs, the profpect fills my mind, and I feel the higheft gratification at fuch a glorious difplay of Omnipotence. Melancthon wishes to know where are the pillars that support this magnificent arch.'

"At a time when Europe was agitated in an unusual manner; when all was diplomacy, all was politics, Machiavellian and perfidious; Cardinal Bembo wrote thus to the Pope, who had been crowning the Emperor Charles V. at Bologna. 'While your Holiness has been these last days on the theatre of the world, among so many lords and great men, whom none now alive have ever seen together before, and has placed on the head of Charles V. the rich, splendid, and honoured crown of the Empire, I have been residing in my little village, where I have thought on you in a quiet, and, to me, dear and delicious solitude. I have found the country above the usage of any former years, from the long serenity of these gliding months, and by the sudden mildness of the air, already quite verdant, and the trees in full leaf. Even the vines have deceived the peasantry by their luxuriance, which they were obliged to prune. I do not remember to have seen at this time so beautiful a season. Not only the swallows, but all other birds that do not remain with us in the winter, but return to us in the spring, have made this new, and soft, and joyous sky resound with their charming melodies.—I could not therefore regret your festivities at Bologna. Padua, April 7th, 1530.'

"Of the good Bishop Andrews it is related by Fuller, 'that he would often profess that to observe the trees—earth—corn—grass—water,—hearing any of the creatures,—and to contemplate their qualities—natures—and uses—was ever to him the greatest recreation—content—and mirth—that could be.'

"Paley observed of himself, that 'the happiest hours of a sufficiently happy life were passed by the side of a stream;' and I am greatly mistaken if every landscape painter will not acknowledge that his most serene hours have been spent in the open air, with his palette on his hand. 'It is a great happineſs,' ſays Bacon, 'when men's profeſſions and their inclinations accord.' "

From theſe outlines but a faint impreſſion can be formed of Conſtable's lectures, as he delivered them, and in rooms of which one ſide was covered with pictures and prints to which he conſtantly referred. Many of his happieſt turns of expreſſion were not to be found in his own notes; they aroſe at the moment, and were not to be recalled by a reporter unſkilled in ſhort-hand;—neither can the charm of a moſt agreeable voice, (though pitched ſomewhat too low,) the beautiful manner in which he read the quotations, whether of proſe or poetry, or the play of his very expreſſive countenance, be conveyed to the reader by words.

THE END.